PAISANOS

PAISANOS

The Forgotten Irish who Changed the Face of Latin America

TIM FANNING

Gill Books

Gill Books
Hume Avenue
Park West
Dublin 12
www.gillbooks.ie

Gill Books is an imprint of M.H. Gill & Co.

© Tim Fanning 2016

978 07171 7181 1

Print origination by O'K Graphic Design, Dublin
Maps illustrated by Derry Dillon
Indexed by Adam Pozner
Printed and bound by T J International, Cornwall

This book is typeset in 11/15 pt Minion.

The paper used in this book comes from the wood pulp of managed forests. For every tree felled, at least one tree is planted, thereby renewing natural resources.

All rights reserved.

No part of this publication may be copied, reproduced or transmitted in any form or by any means, without written permission of the publishers.

A CIP catalogue record for this book is available from the British Library.

5 4 3 2 1

For Mark and Caroline

CONTENTS

ACKNOWLEDGEMENTS		IX
NOTE		XI
MAPS		XIII
FOREWORD by President Michael D. Higgins		XXI
INTRODUCTION		1

PART ONE: EXILE

1	Wild Geese	9
2	Remaking the New World	23
3	A New Model Army	32
4	The King of Peru	39
5	Spain Under Siege	54
6	The Propagandist Priest	62
7	Merchants, Sailors, Soldiers, Spies	72

PART TWO: REVOLUTION

8	The Battle for the River Plate	91
9	General O'Higgins	104
10	Bolívar's Irish Volunteers	120
11	The Hibernian Regiment and the Irish Legion	141
12	Death in the Andes	162
13	The San Patricios	174
14	The Kingdom of God	185

PART THREE: HOME

15	After the Revolution	195
16	The 'New Erin'	209
17	Making History	216
18	The 'Spiritual Empire'	224

BIBLIOGRAPHICAL NOTE	230
ABBREVIATIONS	232
SOURCES	233
NOTES	244
INDEX	264

ACKNOWLEDGEMENTS

This book would not have been written without the support of Conor McEnroy and the Abbeyfield Group in Paraguay. Not only did Conor, an Irishman living in South America, suggest the idea – born out of his continuing interest in the shared history of Ireland and Latin America – but his generosity allowed me to undertake archival research on both sides of the Atlantic.

Michael Lillis is another Irishman with a deep interest in the historical links between Ireland and Latin America. His continuous support and advice were invaluable during the writing and researching of this book.

I wish to thank the Irish ambassador to Argentina, Justin Harman, who also supported this project from its inception, and the staff of the Irish Embassy in Buenos Aires.

I was treated with unfailing courtesy, kindness and professionalism during my research trips to archives in South America. In Bogotá, I am grateful to the staff at the Archivo General de la Nación Colombia, especially Mauricio Tovar González, and the Biblioteca Luis Ángel Arango. In Santiago, I gratefully acknowledge the help of the staff of the Archivo Nacional de Chile, especially Pedro González Cancino, and the kind help and advice of Julio César Retamal Ávila. In Buenos Aires, I would like to thank all the staff of the Archivo General de la Nación, who did their utmost to help further my inquiries.

While studying for a master's degree in Spanish and Latin American studies at Maynooth University, I had the good fortune to be able to call on the expertise of Dr David Barnwell, who shared with me his interest in the history of the Irish in Spain and Latin America. He gave me several leads and suggestions that have ended up appearing in the present volume. I also wish to thank Susan Leyden of St Patrick's College, Maynooth, for her help in finding material in the Salamanca Archive in the college's Russell Library.

Roddy Hegarty of the Cardinal Tomás Ó Fiaich Memorial Library and Archive in Armagh made many useful suggestions regarding the library's Overseas Archive, which was assembled by Dr Micheline Kerney Walsh and contains copies of thousands of documents from archives in Spain. While many of these documents are now available to view on the Spanish state's archival web site, PARES, the Overseas Archive remains a useful finding guide. I am also grateful to Kate Manning and the staff of University College Dublin (UCD) Archives.

My considerable debt to the many researchers and writers on both sides of the Atlantic who have written about the Irish in Spain and Latin America is more fully acknowledged in the Bibliographical Note and Bibliography at the end of the book, but I must make special mention of Dr Matthew Brown of the University of Bristol. Dr Brown has carried out invaluable research in archives throughout South America into the foreign volunteers who fought for Bolívar and has compiled a database giving details of their origins. He was always quick to respond to my requests for help.

Thanks to Conor Nagle, Ruth Mahony and all at Gill Books, and to Jonathan Williams.

I must also mention Ruth Fanning for giving me a place in which to write at short notice and my father, Ronan, for his help, advice and support, as always. Lastly, thank you, Annalisa, for your endless love, patience and good humour, without which, again, this book would not have been written, and, of course, Chiara.

NOTE

Irish and English forenames and surnames tended to be hispanicised in the Spanish Empire in the eighteenth and nineteenth centuries: Richard became Ricardo, John became Juan, Fitzgerald became Geraldino and O'Donoghue became O'Donojú. Throughout the text I have used the English spelling of the name for those born in Ireland, but for those who were born in Spain or Latin America I prefer the Spanish version, so that the Chilean patriot Juan Mackenna, who was born in County Monaghan, is referred to throughout the text as John Mackenna, while his friend and ally, who was born in Chile, remains Bernardo O'Higgins. Where the birthplace is not clear, I have chosen the Spanish version.

I have used the authentic version of place-names in Spain and Latin America except where there is a well-known alternative English spelling: for example, Seville is preferred to Sevilla.

I have taken the decision to concentrate on the independence struggle in Spain's former colonies on the South American continent during the first decades of the nineteenth century, as well as examining the historical context in Spain and its American colonies. This is because the Irish played a significant role in the independence movement in the southern part of the continent – through the actions of individuals such as James Florence Bourke, William Brown, Peter Campbell, Bernardo O'Higgins and John Thomond O'Brien – and in the northern part through the Irish volunteers in Bolívar's armies. This approach precludes looking at Cuba, which remained a Spanish possession until 1898.

The independence struggle in the Viceroyalty of New Spain – the Spanish administrative territory that covered Mexico, much of the modern United States of America and most of Central America – followed a different course from that of South America. It was at first a popular rising, as opposed to the middle-class-led revolutions. I have included a chapter on Mexico, in addition to those about South America, for two reasons. The first is that the Spanish general who signed the treaty that brought about Mexican independence in an extraordinary act of pragmatism was an Irish-Spaniard by the name of Juan O'Donojú. The second reason is that Mexico honours to this day a battalion of Irishmen known as the San Patricios who fought to preserve Mexican independence from the aggressive designs of the United States.

Brazil is a vast country, which covers almost half the South American continent. It requires its own separate study. However, that is not to say that the course of events in Brazil, especially the machinations of the Portuguese royal family during their exile in Rio de Janeiro and their decision to invade what is now Uruguay, remains completely outside the scope of this book.

The story of the Irish in Latin America is a huge subject. I have tried to give an idea of their broader involvement in the independence struggle while interspersing the narrative with the histories of the most important leaders.

Finally, this is a history not only of the Irish soldiers who helped achieve independence for the republics that came into existence at the beginning of the nineteenth century by force of arms but also of their compatriots in the service of Spain who created the conditions in which independence became possible.

MAPS

1. SPANISH AMERICA, 1800

2. SOUTHERN CHILE, 1820

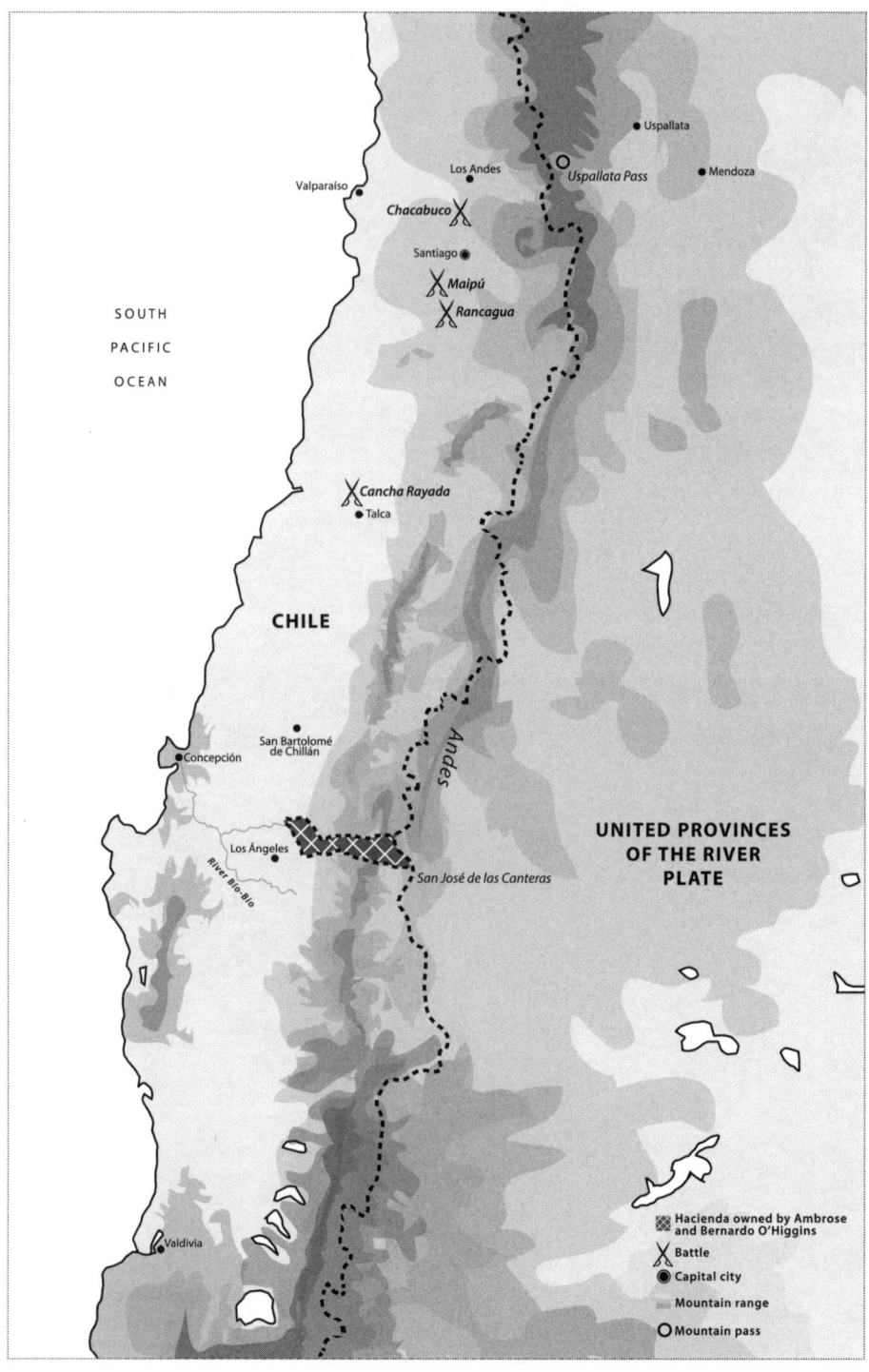

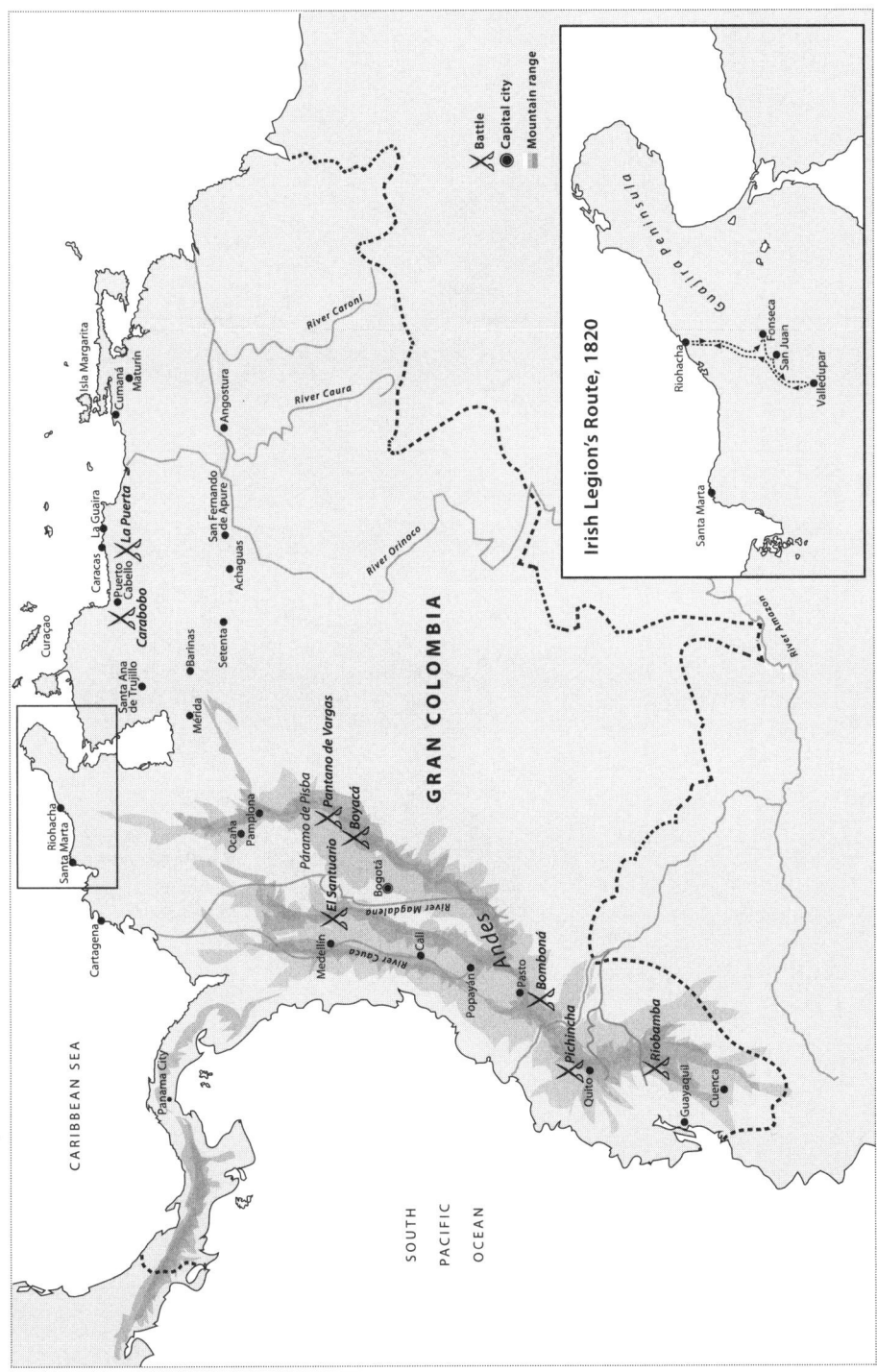

4. PERU, BOLIVIA AND CHILE, 1825

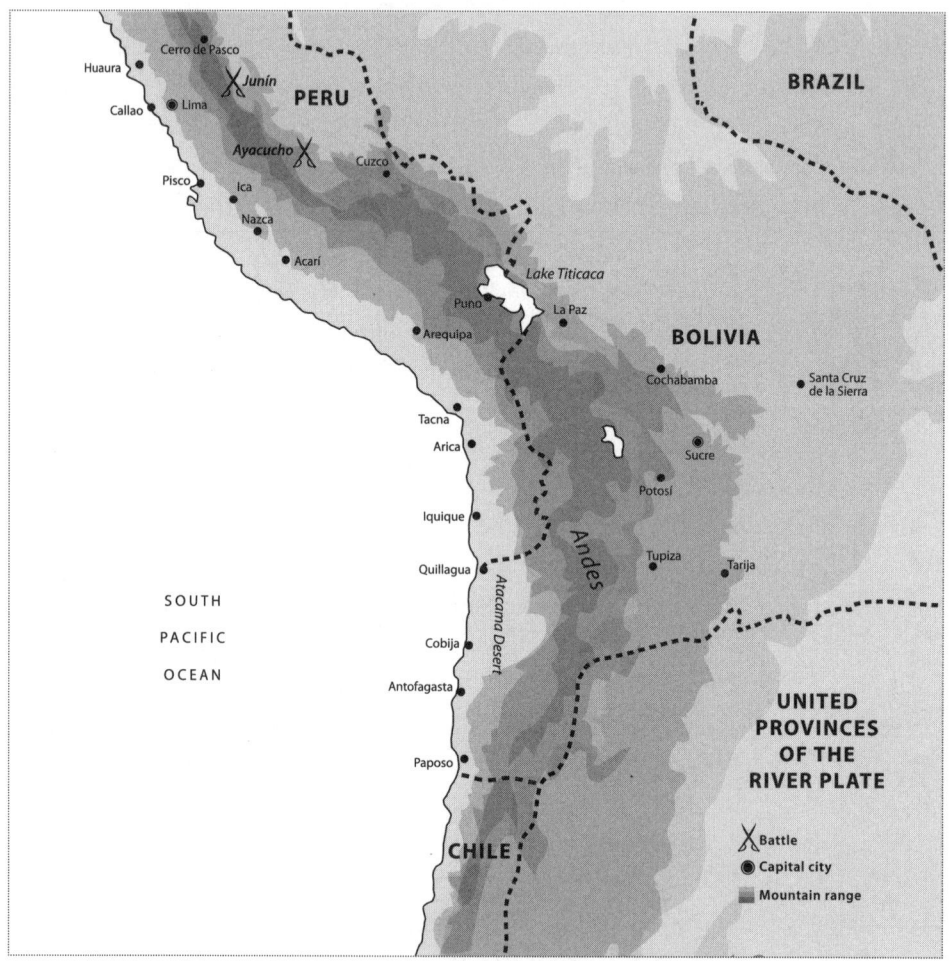

5. THE RIVER PLATE, 1829

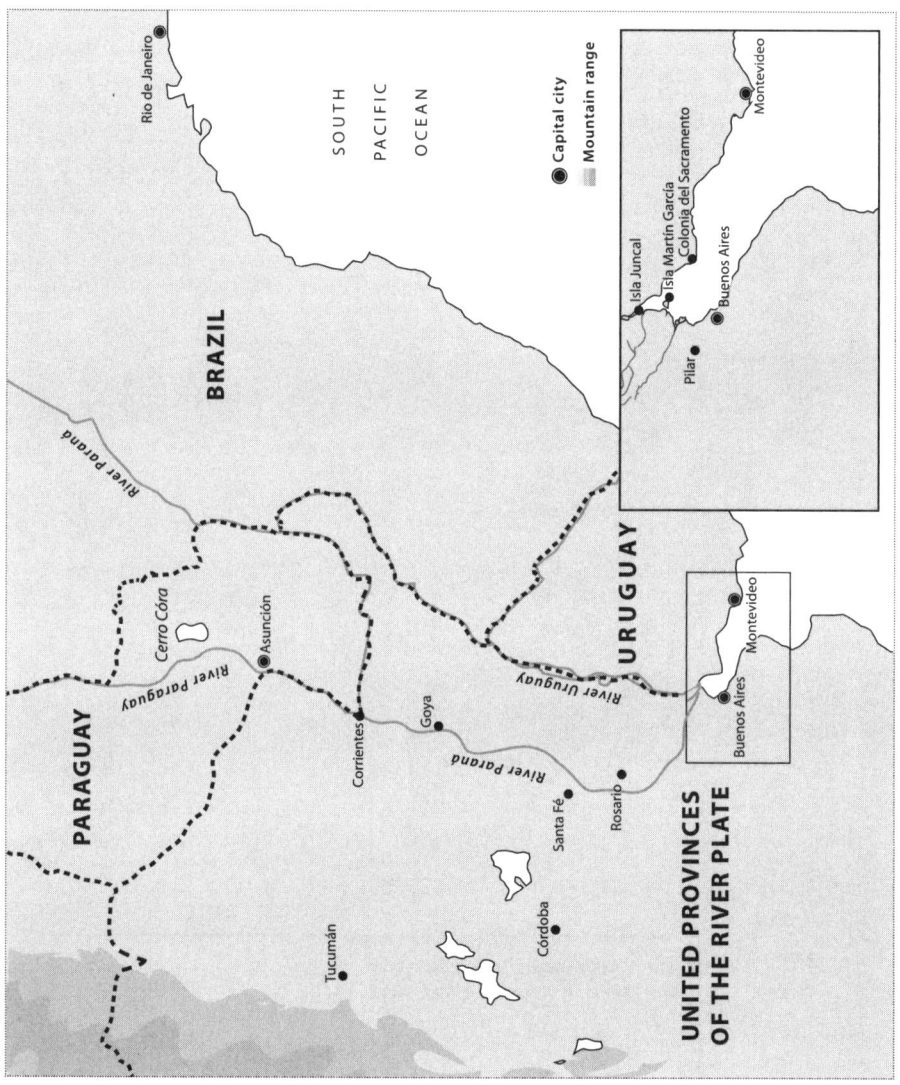

6. THE MEXICAN-AMERICAN WAR, 1846–1848

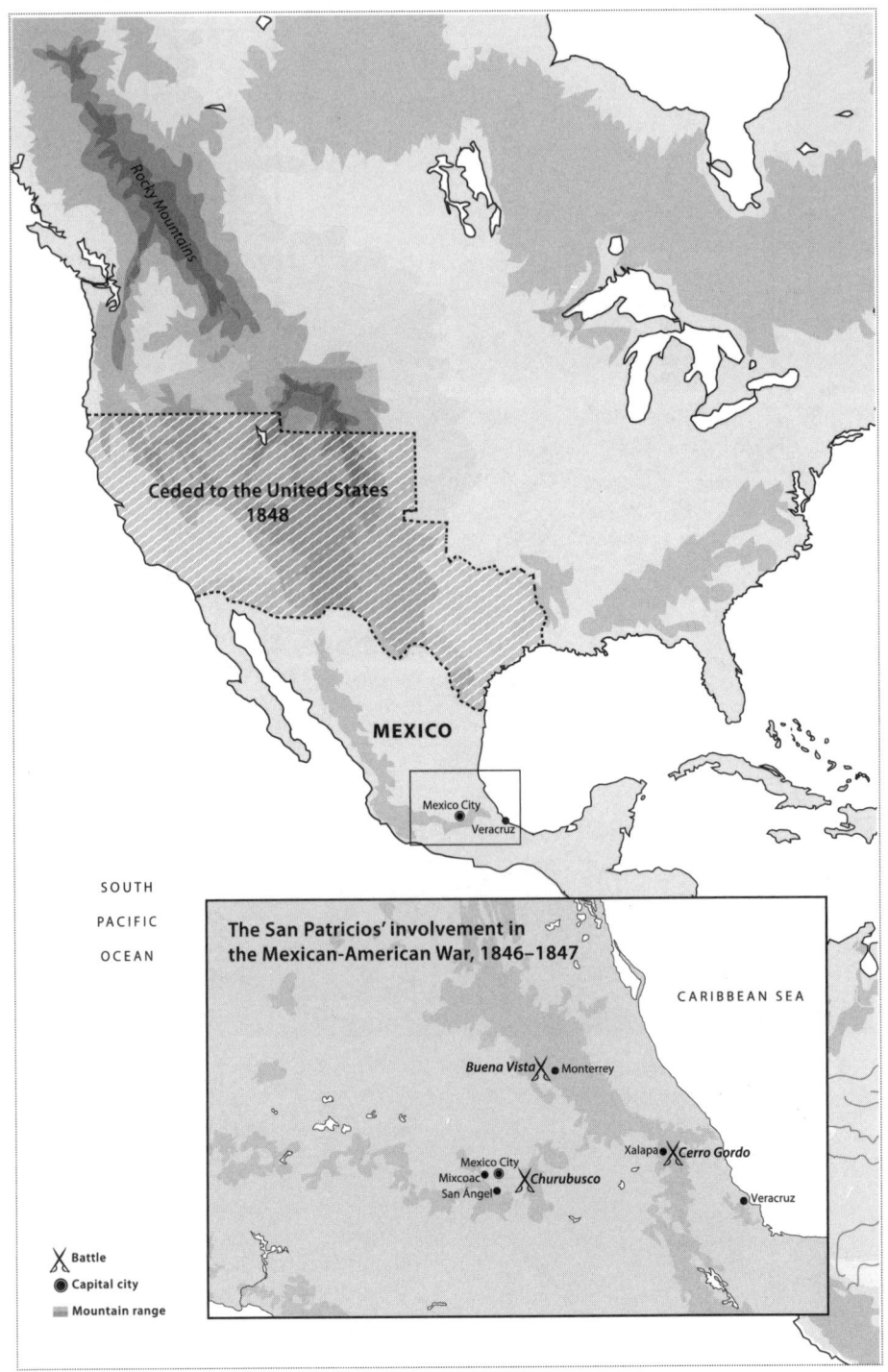

7. THE AMERICAS, TODAY

FOREWORD

I was delighted to be asked to provide a foreword for *Paisanos*, this attractive, important and, I believe, necessary volume on the role played by Irish men and women in the emergence of the new, modern and independent republics of Latin America. The story of historic Irish migrations to Latin America – of Irish service, military and administrative – is known by most only in its broad lines. This valuable piece of scholarship will do much to help redress the balance by introducing to an Irish audience lives that are revered all over Latin America. It will help to bring out the texture, colour and personality of the Irish and those of Irish descent in Spanish-speaking America and the part they played in the establishment of republics throughout the continent.

I would like to pay tribute to the author of *Paisanos*, Tim Fanning, for the depth and breadth of his research, and to Conor McEnroy, who encouraged and assisted him in this endeavour. Conor, along with Michael Lillis and Justin Harman, the Irish ambassador in Buenos Aires, are Irishmen who today are seeking to bridge the Atlantic, bringing Ireland and Latin America closer together, by encouraging work such as this.

Latin America and the course of its political and economic development have occupied a special place in my own heart for over fifty years. During the course of my political and academic career, I have been privileged to witness the conflicts, struggles for human rights and, above all, the generous heart of this continent. It is a region I have journeyed to twice as president of Ireland, visiting, at their invitation, six countries, from Chile at its southern tip, through Argentina, Brazil, El Salvador and Costa Rica, up to Mexico at the northern frontier where English and Spanish-speaking America meet.

This book starts with exile and those exiled, the Wild Geese. In a year dedicated to recalling the founding moments of our Irish independence, when we are asked to fine-tune in an ethical and inclusive way our use of memory, to encounter complexity afresh, it is so appropriate that we pause to discover the contribution made to world history by those exiled Irish men and women, who, after the Treaty of Limerick in 1691 and the punitive laws of the eighteenth century against their religion, settled in Spain and France and moved to the centre of the international conflicts of the day. Their children would go on to deliver the ideas of the Enlightenment under royal patronage as engineers, administrators, cartographers and geographers in Spanish colonies across the world. And their children's children in turn would see the prospects, sow the seeds and deliver the reality of independence from the Spanish Empire, engaging in all the essential conflicts and adjustments that resulted.

I had the great honour, during an official visit to Chile in 2012, of laying a wreath at the monument to Chile's great liberator, Bernardo O'Higgins. Bernardo's father, Ambrose O'Higgins, was born in County Sligo to a modest farming family and went on to become mayor of Concepción, governor of Chile and later viceroy of Peru, the highest office in South America in colonial times. Among the many interesting historical asides in the book, I was intrigued to learn that he introduced the prefix 'O' to his surname later in life in order to strengthen his claim to a Spanish noble title. Ambrose is remembered in Chile for his great achievement in abolishing the *encomienda*, the system of forced labour and dependency for indigenous people that was imposed by the Spanish crown during the colonial period.

However, as the book notes, Ambrose was, fundamentally, an unflinching royalist and an austere and conservative administrator for the Spanish Empire. How remarkable, then, that Bernardo O'Higgins, the son of this loyal servant of the Spanish crown, went on to become one of the greatest exponents of pan-American revolution and liberal republicanism.

Beyond the great historical figures like Bernardo O'Higgins and Admiral William Brown, whose names are remembered in the streetscapes of the great cities of Buenos Aires and Santiago, Tim Fanning has succeeded in bringing to light the stories of lesser-known figures, such as Francis Burdett O'Connor and Daniel Florence O'Leary, both Corkmen, who served as senior officers in the armies of Simón Bolívar.

This book is valuable in bringing the story of Ricardo Wall to a wide audience. How a French-born man of Irish descent became, at the age of 60, chief minister of the Spanish government until he resigned in 1763 is one of the great stories of intrigue of the eighteenth century. How he employed other goslings of the Wild Geese in the administration of European relations with America is recalled today in South America while it gets insufficient attention perhaps in Ireland.

Paisanos also explores the famous Irish battalion, the San Patricios. On my official visit to Mexico in 2013, I had the opportunity to pay tribute to the Irish soldiers of the Batallón de San Patricio, who gave their lives for Mexican independence during the Mexican-American War of 1846–1848. These Irishmen were fleeing poverty and famine in their homeland for a better life in the New World but they had no hesitation in showing their solidarity with the Mexican people in their hour of need, creating what I described at the time as 'an unbreakable link' between the two countries, which happily still exists today.

The relationship between Ireland and Latin America draws on our shared history of struggle against colonialism. At the same time that Irish patriots were challenging the colonial relationship between Ireland and Britain in the late eighteenth century, an emerging sense of nationhood was taking shape in Spain's American colonies. That the modern-day Latin American republics came into being in the early part of the nineteenth century was in no small part thanks to the contribution, in their different ways, of Irish men and women, many of whom were driven by their forefathers' experience of oppression and dreams of liberty for their homeland. In a coincidence of timing, 2016 is not only the centenary of the 1916 Rising in Ireland but also the bicentenary of the Declaration of Independence in Argentina at the Congress of Tucumán. It is a fitting occasion to examine the role played by Irish men and women in the fight for independence at home and abroad.

In this well-researched volume, Tim Fanning highlights the many ways in which the Irish left their stamp on the history of the modern Latin American republics and, conversely, how Irish advocates of home rule such as Daniel O'Connell were inspired by the heroes of Latin American independence, such as Simón Bolívar, José de San Martín and Bernardo O'Higgins. And indeed it was an Irish-Argentine born in Buenos Aires, Éamon Bulfin, who raised the tricolour above the General Post Office during Easter Week 1916, which goes to show that history is no respecter of borders.

They are all here, those who allied themselves with, differed from, reconciled, shared love and dreams: the Paisanos.

In this year of commemorations, it is appropriate, finally, that the author has reminded us of how the Irish were, and continue to be, remembered in

Latin America. It is vital that we cherish the 'unbreakable link' between the peoples of Ireland and Latin America, and what better way to do this than to further explore our common history. As the author points out, while a good literature serves this history in the Spanish language, there is not a comparable literature available in English. This fine book is a welcome contribution to that literature on the history of our exiles and their descendants to which, without hesitation, I suggest we need to pay so much more attention. Tim Fanning gives us a great help in that regard with an exciting and accessible book that is a pleasure to read.

MICHAEL D. HIGGINS
UACHTARÁN NA hÉIREANN
PRESIDENT OF IRELAND

26 APRIL 2016

INTRODUCTION

The contribution of the Irish to the development of the English-speaking part of the Americas has been well documented; less well known is the role Irish men and women played in the modern history of Spanish-speaking America. While the names of William Brown and Bernardo O'Higgins are not unknown in Ireland, and are indeed celebrated, these tend to be thought of as exceptions rather than as the most famous names in a long list of characters, both Irish-born and of Irish heritage, who were pivotal in the transformation of the Spanish colonies in the Americas into modern republics.

The principal reason why the Irish contribution to the achievement of independence in Latin America is not better known is the language barrier. Countless books in Spanish have been published in Buenos Aires, Santiago de Chile, Caracas, Montevideo, Asunción and Bogotá about the Irish heroes of national independence. There are only a few notable exceptions in English.

The second reason is cultural. We know from the cinema and television about the Old West, the gold rushes, the American Civil War, tenement life in nineteenth-century New York and the Kennedys; our knowledge of modern Latin American history is hazier, often translated for us by the Anglo-American eyes of Hollywood.

However, the story of those Irish who came to Latin America in the eighteenth and early nineteenth centuries is no less interesting than that of their cousins in the United States and Canada. Many of them did not go directly to Spanish America from Ireland or England but through Spain. By the middle of the eighteenth century, Irishmen occupied key positions in the Spanish military and political administration. They were emigrants who had escaped political and religious persecution in Ireland for a new life on the continent. Most of them began their careers as soldiers or merchants, using their talents to secure enviable and lucrative jobs in Spain and its American colonies. Born in France to Irish Jacobite exiles, Richard Wall became Spain's prime minister in 1754. Ambrose O'Higgins was the son of small farmers from County Sligo who emigrated to Cádiz in southern Spain and rose to become the viceroy of Peru, the highest-ranking colonial official in the whole of the Spanish Empire. Wall and O'Higgins were among the Irishmen (for they were nearly all men, women then being excluded from high office by legal and social barriers) who helped govern the enormous Spanish Empire.

The children and grandchildren of Irish emigrants to Spain in the eighteenth century also feature on the list of illustrious names in the history of Latin American independence. The most famous is Ambrose O'Higgins's son, Bernardo O'Higgins, who led the fight against the Spanish in Chile and became one of the first leaders of the independent republic.

Though not born in Ireland, these soldiers, merchants and diplomats of Irish ancestry, born in Spain or Latin America, retained a strong feeling for the homeland of their ancestors. The title of this book, *Paisanos,* is a Spanish word that roughly translates as 'fellow-countrymen' or 'compatriots'. Members of the Irish community in Spain and Latin America used this word to describe themselves and their Irish-born family and friends. It encapsulates that feeling of Irishness that was shared by those of common ancestry in Spain and its American colonies before, during and after the wars of independence.

Ramón Power y Giralt is a good example of how Irish communities could retain a sense of shared ancestry while adopting new identities. Power was the son of a Basque of Irish ancestry who emigrated to Puerto Rico in the eighteenth century. The Powers were part of an Irish community of rich planters. Like the children of many rich *criollos* – those of Spanish descent born in the Americas – Ramón was sent to Spain to be educated. He served as an officer in the Spanish navy before returning to Puerto Rico. In 1810 he was elected Puerto Rico's delegate to the Cádiz Cortes, the national assembly that sprang up in response to Napoleon's invasion of Spain. Not only did he win important economic concessions for Puerto Rico, he played a central role in redefining the wider relationship between Spain and its American colonies. In the process he helped forge a Puerto Rican national identity and is today regarded as one of the nation's founding fathers.

The story of the Irish in the eighteenth-century Spanish Atlantic world – the first part of this book – provides the context for the revolutionary period – the second part – during which Irish-born volunteers travelled to Latin America from Irish and English ports to fight in the patriot armies under the command of Simón Bolívar. Irishmen such as William Brown, Peter Campbell, John Thomond O'Brien, Francis Burdett O'Connor,

Daniel Florence O'Leary, James Rooke, Arthur Sandes and Thomas Charles Wright are still remembered in South America for the part they played in the liberation of Argentina, Bolivia, Chile, Colombia, Ecuador, Panama, Peru, Uruguay and Venezuela from Spanish rule. All of them served as senior officers, and two of them, O'Connor and O'Leary, wrote memoirs that became important sources for historians researching the revolutionary period. While they are justly celebrated, there were thousands of other Irishmen who fought for independence in Spanish America who are all but forgotten, not least because some of them have gone down in the annals of history as English. Not only were there a self-styled Hibernian Regiment and Irish Legion but also the majority of the officers and enlisted men who fought in what became known as the British Legions were Irish.

The Irish were present at all the major battles that were fought by Simón Bolívar, the leader of the independence movement in the northern part of South America, during the campaigns that transformed Colombia, Venezuela, Panama, Ecuador, Peru and Bolivia from Spanish colonies into independent republics. But because the whole island of Ireland was then part of the United Kingdom of Great Britain and Ireland, and neither the sources nor the histories discriminated between the nationalities of that state, the Irishmen who fought for the independence of the South American republics were often referred to as *ingleses*.

They fought for different reasons. Some had no money and needed to make a living; others felt the call of adventure. And then there were those, such as Francis Burdett O'Connor, who travelled to Venezuela as a member of the ill-fated Irish Legion and later played a prominent role as a senior staff officer in Bolívar's campaigns in Peru and Bolivia, who drew parallels between the colonial experience of Latin America and Ireland.

The great hero of Catholic Emancipation and advocate of Irish home rule, Daniel O'Connell, drew inspiration from Bolívar. He raised money for the Irish Legion and sent his 14-year-old son, Morgan, to Venezuela to serve as an aide-de-camp to its commanding officer, the roguish County Wexford man John Devereux. Bolívar had already become known as the Liberator before O'Connell was honoured with that title in Ireland.

Irishmen fought on both sides during the wars of independence; so that, while many Irish volunteers were recruited by Bolívar in Irish and English cities or, for economic reasons, joined the patriot armies after emigrating to

South American cities, there were also Irish officers serving in the royalist forces who believed they owed everything to the Spanish king, such as Diego O'Reilly, who committed suicide after being captured by the patriot forces in Peru. There were also those who changed sides, like John Mackenna of County Monaghan, a soldier in the Spanish army, who was appointed governor of Osorno by Ambrose O'Higgins in Chile before he joined the independence struggle alongside Ambrose's son, Bernardo.

The Irish contribution to independence is recalled in Latin American public memory by the names of streets, towns and schools. There are four football teams in the Argentine league named after William Brown, the mariner from County Mayo who is credited with founding the country's navy. The *Pedro Campbell* is a frigate in the Uruguayan navy named after the guerrilla-cum-*gaucho* from County Tipperary who helped win that country's independence.

The role played in the achievement of South American independence by a coterie of Irishmen working for the British government is less well known. In the eighteenth century, Britain was desperate for a share of Spain's colonial markets. The two countries were at each other's throats throughout the period over the Atlantic trade; yet, just at the moment when the first calls for independence were heard on the streets of Buenos Aires, Caracas and Quito, Britain and Spain ceased hostilities and became allies against a common foe, Napoleon Bonaparte. The British now found themselves in the position of having to remain openly neutral regarding independence for the colonies, so as to placate their Spanish allies, while secretly negotiating with the revolutionary juntas that were forming throughout the South American continent. A couple of Anglo-Irish politicians, George Canning and Lord Castlereagh, were central to the formulation of British policy in South America, while the Anglo-Irish diplomat Lord Strangford played a crucial role in implementing it. They were aided in their efforts by an Irish-born Buenos Aires merchant, Thomas O'Gorman, and a colourful French-born Irish spy, James Florence Bourke.

The final part of the book examines the later careers of some of the most notable Irish volunteers to serve in the war who settled in Latin America, many of whom suffered in the civil wars and political intrigues that followed independence. The volunteers for Bolívar's army who braved the Atlantic on overcrowded ships sailing from Irish ports were soldiers – and emigrants.

They included William Owens Ferguson, who was shot dead in a dark alley in Bogotá, a victim of a failed assassination attempt on Simón Bolívar. He was buried with full honours in Bogotá's cathedral and was among those Irish soldiers who were accorded a place in the patriotic pantheon of the new, independent Latin American republics.

In the wake of independence, many foreigners began flooding into Latin America to take advantage of the new economic opportunities afforded by the introduction of free trade. Bernardo O'Higgins, John Thomond O'Brien and Francis Burdett O'Connor were among the revolutionary leaders who sought to introduce Irish settlers to work the depopulated lands of the continent's interior. Some of these schemes proved unsuccessful, but one in particular endured and saw tens of thousands of Irish families emigrate en masse from towns and villages in counties Offaly, Longford and Westmeath in the middle of the nineteenth century. The children of these Irish families who struck out from Irish and English ports for a new life in Argentina and Uruguay were to make substantial contributions to the economic, cultural and social life of their new countries. While these Irish families integrated into their new communities within a few generations, many of their progeny remained proud of their link to their distant homeland across the Atlantic Ocean, exemplifying the ability of Irish communities throughout the world to retain a sense of identity while fully integrating into the host culture.

The Spanish-speaking Irish community has been less visible in Ireland than Irish emigrants in the English-speaking world. It is the purpose of this book to redress that imbalance and recall the Irish soldiers and sailors, entrepreneurs and merchants, diplomats and politicians, priests and pamphleteers, who, just like their cousins who played such a significant role in the creation of the United States, helped forge modern Latin America.

PART ONE

EXILE

Chapter 1

WILD GEESE

In 1754, to the surprise of courtiers and diplomats around Europe, the king of Spain appointed a 60-year-old Irishman as his new secretary of state, or prime minister. There was no doubting the Irishman's talent and experience, nor his loyalty to his adopted homeland: he had, after all, served the Spanish crown ably as a soldier and diplomat for the best part of four decades. However, interested observers could have been forgiven for thinking that Richard Wall's foreign birth and ancestry precluded him from the highest political office in the land. The fact that Wall, an Irishman born in France, could become Spain's most powerful politician showed not only the new secretary of state's well-disguised ambition and skill at political manoeuvring but also the unique position that Irish Catholics enjoyed in the eighteenth-century Spanish Empire.

Wall represented a generation of Irish Catholics who had been denied political and economic opportunities in their homeland because of their religion and who were now hungry for success abroad. While none of his compatriots matched Wall's achievements in the realm of Spanish politics, many of the Irish soldiers with whom he served on the battlefields of Europe, and to whom he later extended patronage, forged equally impressive careers in commerce, the military and the administration of Spain's far-reaching colonies.

Wall became prime minister of Spain at a time when the country's Bourbon monarchs were introducing reforms across the board in a vain attempt to control more closely the governance of their American colonies. They turned to the new scientific, rational processes that were becoming popular in Enlightenment Europe and the expertise of talented, far-sighted men. Irish-born economists and scientists, administrators and soldiers, naturalists and lexicographers – men such as John Garland, Ambrose O'Higgins, Alexander O'Reilly, John Mackenna and Bernard Ward – were at the forefront of the Bourbons' attempts to modernise the Spanish Empire.

Writing in the 1790s, the British politician Lord Holland noted that Spain had taken advantage of Britain's loss:

> Any one conversant with the modern military history of Spain, or with good society in that country, must be struck with the large proportion of their eminent officers who were either born or descended from those who were born in Ireland. The comment, which that circumstance furnishes upon our exclusive and intolerant laws, is obvious enough.[1]

Throughout the eighteenth century these talented emigrants took advantage of an extensive network of patronage in Spain, which saw the Irish favour their families and friends. At the heart of this network was Richard Wall.

Born in the cosmopolitan Atlantic port of Nantes in 1694, Richard was the son of Matthew and Kathleen Wall. Like tens of thousands of other Irish Catholics, the Walls had fled to France after the Treaty of Limerick in 1691, which had brought an end to the war between the victorious William III and the deposed monarch James II. Most of the fighting had taken place on the sodden battlefields of Ireland. At stake had been not only the thrones of England, Scotland and Ireland but also the future of the Irish Catholic nobility. The soldiers and their families who left Ireland for the European continent became known as the Wild Geese. More came in the next decades, realising that there was no future for them in Ireland when the Protestant-dominated Irish Parliament began passing punitive anti-Catholic laws.

Communities of Irish Jacobite exiles formed throughout Europe. Once the Irish were established in a city, their relations followed, lured by the promise of a job and disillusioned by the diminishing opportunities available to them at home. Many of the merchants and artisans who thronged the narrow medieval streets outside the Church of Saint-Nicolas in Nantes on the day of Richard Wall's baptism in 1694 were Irish exiles. Nantes was an attractive place for the Irish, offering rich commercial possibilities, being an important port on the triangular trade route that linked western Europe with Africa and the Americas. Textiles and weapons were loaded on ships at the docks for west Africa; in Africa these goods were bartered for slaves. After crossing the Atlantic the slaves were sold in the American markets and the empty ships were loaded with exotic commodities such as sugar and tobacco for sale in Europe. It was this booming trade in slaves that made Nantes' elite rich.

It was not just economic considerations that drew the Irish to France. The Irish soldiers who had fought for James II at Athlone, Aughrim and Limerick believed that King Louis XIV of France, the powerful Sun King who had supported James II by sending French troops to Ireland, would support a new attempt to restore the exiled Stuart monarch to the throne. Ensconced in the luxurious atmosphere of the Château de Saint-Germain-en-Laye, James was surrounded by conspiring Irish courtiers, dreaming up invasion plans.

Richard's father, Matthew Wall, a native of Kilmallock, County Limerick, was in the service of Henry FitzJames, one of James II's illegitimate children. Matthew's wife, Kathleen, was a Devereux from County Waterford.[2] And so their son was among those Irish men and women who passed through the gilded halls and courtyards of Saint-Germain-en-Laye. Through the patronage that bound the fortunes of prominent Irish families to the exiled Stuart court and the French aristocracy, Wall became a page to the Duchess of Vendôme, Marie-Anne de Bourbon.[3] It was the beginning of a long and fruitful association with the Bourbons. The young Irish boy not only received a superior education but also learnt how to negotiate his way through courtly intrigues.

In 1697 Louis XIV signed the Treaty of Ryswick, briefly putting an end to hostilities in Europe. It meant disappointment for Irish Catholics: the dream of a Jacobite invasion of Ireland was ever more distant. Four years later, however, war returned to the continent over the question of who would succeed to the throne of Spain.

For almost two centuries the Habsburgs had ruled Spain and its colonies. The Spanish Empire at its peak, under Charles V, the greatest of all the Habsburg monarchs, had rivalled any seen in history. It was the first truly global empire, encompassing territory comprising much of southern and western Europe, continent-sized swathes of the Americas, and archipelagos in the Pacific. During the sixteenth century, because of the ambition of the early Spanish Habsburgs and the limitless supply of precious metals arriving in Seville from the American colonies, the disjointed medieval feudal society of peninsular Spain – brought together in 1492 by the Catholic monarchs, Isabel and Ferdinand – was transformed into the glittering metropolis of the Counter-Reformation.

This was the *siglo de oro*, Spain's Golden Age, when writers, poets and artists, such as Cervantes, Lope de Vega and Velásquez, revolutionised European culture and when the most powerful monarchs in the world proclaimed their earthly triumphs with the construction of vast palaces, such as the Escorial, built by Philip II outside Madrid, and gloried in their role as the foremost defenders of the Catholic faith by raising ornate cathedrals and churches, crammed full of American silver and gold. The mighty armadas that set sail twice yearly from Seville to retrieve the loot from the mines of Mexico and Peru were the symbol of Spanish power. Spain's great European rivals, the English, the French and the Dutch, watched hungrily on the fringes of the Spanish Atlantic, waiting to carve for themselves a slice of its enormous markets and to plunder its colonies' resources.

Yet, for all the pomp and majesty of Spanish churches, the splendour of Spanish palaces and the brilliance of Spanish artists, by the beginning of the seventeenth century Spanish power was already an illusion. The veins of gold and silver in Mexico and Peru, which had once seemed inexhaustible, were diminishing. Furthermore, Spain had failed to invest in domestic manufacturing; the gold and silver that did arrive in the port of Seville quickly found its way north, to England, France and the Netherlands, to pay for imported luxury goods. Spain's aristocrats believed that wealth and honour were inextricably linked to landownership and the purity of one's blood – *limpieza de sangre* – not trade and commerce. It was this obsession with a pure bloodline that led the Spanish Habsburgs to interbreed relentlessly, resulting in the last of their line, the enfeebled Charles II – unable to talk until he was four, barely able to eat and incapable of producing an heir because of his physical deformities, including a grotesquely exaggerated version of the famous Habsburg jaw – presiding over the decay of the Spanish Empire in the final years of the seventeenth century.

It was Charles II's death that prompted a new crisis in Europe. The late Spanish monarch had named as his heir Philip, Duke of Anjou, a grandson of France's Louis XIV. The rest of the European powers were fearful that Philip's ascension to the throne of Spain and the possible unification of the Spanish and French thrones under the Bourbons threatened the continent's balance of power. Britain, the Dutch Republic, Austria and the Holy Roman Emperor supported the Habsburg candidate, Leopold, to counter French hegemony. Four years after the Treaty of Ryswick the European powers –

and the Irishmen serving in their armies – were once again at war. The War of the Spanish Succession lasted for 13 years. At its end, Philip was confirmed as king of Spain, the Spanish Empire was stripped of most of its European possessions, and Louis XIV agreed to the removal of Philip from the line of succession to the French throne.

The conclusion of the war and the death of Louis XIV in 1715 brought a new era for the Irish soldiers in the employ of the continental armies. France was becalmed under its new monarch, Louis XV. In contrast, the Bourbon dynasty in Spain was anxious to prevent the further decline of the Spanish Empire and set about modernising the army and navy. The new Spanish king, Philip V, introduced a series of administrative and military reforms in an effort to reinvigorate the government of Spain and its American colonies, and he was hungry for talented and experienced officials and soldiers.

José Patiño was a Bourbon loyalist who had demonstrated his abilities during the war. In 1717 Philip gave him the responsibility of reorganising the navy. One of Patiño's earliest measures was to found a naval school in Cádiz. Richard Wall was among the first cadets. Given the fact that he had to prove he was of noble blood to become a cadet, Wall's admittance may be seen as the 'first step on the long road to assimilation' in Spain.[4] It was also recognition on the part of Wall and, presumably, his benefactors that on the death of the Duchess of Vendôme in 1718, his best career prospects lay in Spain, not France.

The young Irishman entered an exhilarating phase of his life. Cádiz was founded by the Phoenicians about 1100 BC and is one of the oldest settlements on the Iberian Peninsula. Its inhabitants, known as *gaditanos*, have traditionally looked outwards, towards the sea, first the Mediterranean and then, with Columbus's discovery of the Americas, the Atlantic. By the time Wall arrived in the city, Cádiz was the most important port trading with the Americas. Historically Seville had monopolised the Atlantic trade, but by the middle of the eighteenth century, with the River Guadalquivir silting up and with ships of greater draft incapable of forcing their way upriver, it had ceded its position to Cádiz. Into the narrow spit of land upon which Cádiz was built were packed the merchant houses that financed the ships that sailed across the Atlantic. It was from Cádiz that troops, royal administrators, merchants and priests set sail for the New World, and often a new life. It was also in Cádiz that bullion and exotic luxuries, such as tobacco, dyes, cacao and sugar, were unloaded from the ships returning from America before being moved on to northern Europe. To travel legally to Spain's American colonies, one had first to make one's way to Cádiz. In the eighteenth century this was the crossroads of the Spanish Atlantic.

Travellers found the city captivating. After a visit in 1809 Lord Byron wrote that 'sweet Cadiz' was 'the first spot in the creation' and added:

> The beauty of its streets and mansions is only excelled by the loveliness of its inhabitants. For, with all national prejudice, I must confess the women of Cadiz are as far superior to the English women in beauty as the Spaniards are inferior to the English in every quality that dignifies the name of man ... Certainly they are fascinating; but their minds have only one idea, and the business of their lives is intrigue.[5]

It is no wonder that intrigue was in the air. Commercial rivalries flourished between the city's merchants, and Cádiz was an important military garrison and embarkation point for soldiers going to the colonies. With sailors, soldiers and traders constantly passing through the city on their way to and from Spanish America, government spies from rival European powers were everywhere. Foreign agents could learn more about Spain's commercial and military strength by spending a few days in Cádiz than several weeks at court.

The *gaditanos* moved in unison with the tides of the sea, which lapped against the foundations of the city's whitewashed houses. Those families that had made a fortune from trade with the Indies lived in grand mansions furnished with lofty towers from which the tense merchants, awaiting the arrival of their precious goods, peered out to sea. In the poorer quarters of the city, innkeepers, prostitutes and thieves robbed the drunken sailors and bored soldiers awaiting embarkation. Periodic epidemics of yellow fever, transmitted by the mosquitoes that bred in the marshes surrounding the Bay of Cádiz, frequently devastated the population.

This bustling mass of humanity was home to merchants from all over Europe, including a thriving Irish community who got fat from trade with the Americas and northern Europe. Irish merchants had been trading beef, fish and butter for Spanish wine and wool for hundreds of years. Daniel O'Connell's uncle Maurice 'Hunting Cap' O'Connell had made a fortune from smuggling goods between the secluded beaches of the Iveragh peninsula in County Kerry and the ports of northern Spain. In the aftermath of the Williamite wars, Irish families had settled permanently in the south of Spain. The Aylwards, Butlers, O'Dwyers, Lynches, Whites, Powers, Terrys and Walshes were among the Irish families that made a living from commerce in eighteenth-century Cádiz.[6]

The Irish enjoyed a privileged position relative to other nationalities. Since the sixteenth century, when the Spanish monarchs had first assumed the mantle of leaders of the Counter-Reformation and had extended protection to Catholics fleeing religious persecution from other parts of Europe, the Irish had sought shelter in Spain. The Spanish court had given refuge to Irish nobles and had subsidised the Irish Colleges that were founded in Spain in the late sixteenth and early seventeenth centuries for training Irish priests.

The authorities treated the newcomers sympathetically, welcoming the military experience and skill that the Irish soldiers could bring to the Spanish army. By the late seventeenth century Irish Catholics were allowed to apply for royal jobs. In 1701 Philip V decreed that Irish and English Catholics who had been living in Spain for more than 10 years were to be treated as naturalised Spaniards. In 1718 another royal decree gave protection to Irish merchants from embargo in the event of a war with Britain. This favoured status meant it was much easier for the Irish to trade with the Americas than their competitors from such countries as Britain, France and the Dutch Republic. Those sons who did not follow their father and uncles into commerce found a career in the Spanish army, navy or royal administration.

Richard Wall was not in Cádiz for long, because his career in the Spanish navy ended rather abruptly. At the age of 23 he was taken prisoner by the British during the Spanish fleet's attempt to regain Sicily. On his release, and with the Spanish navy routed, he realised that his career would be better served on land, and he petitioned Patiño for a transfer to the army, citing poor health.

The Bourbons had replaced the old Spanish military formations of the seventeenth century, known as the *tercios*, with modern infantry regiments, including the Irlanda, Hibernia and Ultonia, so named in recognition of the fact that they were officered predominantly by Irishmen. Wall was commissioned with the junior rank of *alférez*, approximating to second lieutenant (the lowest commissioned rank), in the Hibernia Regiment, taking part in two more expeditions to Sicily and Ceuta. In 1721 he transferred from the infantry to the dragoons and the Regiment of Batavia. He was a brave, capable officer, but promotion for any officer without funds with which to buy a commission was largely dependent on the vagaries of politics and length of service, and his career stalled.

Wall was not a man to forgo pleasure for the humdrum life of the parade ground; his service record shows that he was prone to spending a lot of time outside camp. But these absences also had a practical purpose. An ambitious young officer in the eighteenth-century Spanish army without powerful relatives or wealth had to be assiduous in cultivating connections at court. Wall's Jacobite friends, most notably James FitzJames Stuart, Duke of Liria, helped him build relations with powerful members of the Spanish court. Liria was a son of the Duke of Berwick, one of James II's illegitimate sons, and Honora Burke, the widow of the Irish Jacobite commander Patrick Sarsfield. Wall's father, Matthew, had served Liria's uncle, Henry FitzJames, in France.

In March 1727 Wall accompanied Liria on an arduous journey across Europe with the aim of convincing the Russian tsar to support Spain and Austria against the alliance of Britain, France and Prussia. Wall was well acquainted with life at court; but it was during this mission to Russia that he learnt the essence of statecraft. Noting that the Irish officer had impressed the king of Prussia, Frederick William I, Liria wrote: 'Wall is a young man of great judgement, ability and skill.'[7] However, Wall evidently found the journey exhausting and suffered from homesickness. In Moscow he refused to leave his room. Liria took pity on the Irishman and in December 1728 granted him permission to return to Spain. In this respect Wall was not unique: many of the Irish felt a visceral attachment to their adopted country, given the sense of dislocation they felt in exile and the warm reception and plentiful opportunities afforded them in Spain.[8]

Wall spent much of the next decade campaigning in Italy. In 1733 he acted as a messenger between the Duke of Parma, the future Charles III, and his parents, the king and queen of Spain. In 1737, in recognition of his services, Wall was admitted to the Order of Santiago.

The Spanish military-religious orders of Alcántara, Calatrava and Santiago date from the twelfth century and the Christian reconquest of Moorish Spain. The Order of Santiago was founded to protect pilgrims on their way to the holy shrine at Santiago de Compostela in Galicia. By the seventeenth century, when the court painter Diego Velázquez was admitted

– the red Cross of St James is displayed on his breast in his masterpiece, *Las Meninas* – the order had ceased to have a military function.

In the eighteenth century, however, membership of the military orders conferred significant social status and was important for those seeking advancement. Only those of noble birth were admitted, and Irishmen had to prove their noble ancestry to the royal authorities with detailed submissions containing witness statements from their fellow-countrymen.

In 1746, at the age of 52, Richard Wall took a bullet wound to one of his kidneys at Plaisance in south-west France and was moved to a hospital in Montpellier to recuperate. His military career was over, though he was promoted to field-marshal the following year. A month later Philip v died and was succeeded by Ferdinand vi, Philip's fourth son from his first marriage. The new king was keen to weaken the influence of his late father's second wife, the Italian-born Elisabeth Farnese. As queen of Spain she had exercised a powerful influence over her husband, governed as she was by her ambitions for her own children. To this end she had insisted that Philip reclaim for her children the Italian territories lost by Spain at the end of the War of the Spanish Succession. However, on his accession to the throne Ferdinand instigated a relatively temperate foreign policy. The Marquis of Ensenada, the Duke of Huéscar and José Carvajal y Lancáster were the three men given the responsibility of implementing this policy, which depended on a rapprochement with Spain's old enemy, Britain.

The powerful Ensenada was one of Ferdinand's most industrious and able ministers. He had worked his way up from humble beginnings in La Rioja to exercise the levers of government in his early forties. Ferdinand was so impressed by the energy and zeal with which Ensenada had reformed the Spanish navy that he gave him responsibility for the ministries of war, the navy, finance and the Indies.

In contrast to the self-made Ensenada, Huéscar was from one of Spain's oldest and most storied aristocratic families: among his other titles was the great Dukedom of Alba. Huéscar was the Spanish ambassador in Paris and a friend of Enlightenment thinkers such as d'Alembert and Rousseau.

Carvajal y Lancáster was Ferdinand's first prime minister, who worked closely with Ensenada to carry out the king's wishes regarding the new foreign policy.

It was through his friendship with influential members of the exiled Jacobite aristocracy that Richard Wall came to the notice of this privileged and powerful group. Huéscar was a brother-in-law of the third Duke of Berwick, son of the aristocrat with whom Wall had travelled to Russia in the 1720s. Wall knew the 27-year-old Berwick from the army.

Skilled in the arts of courtly politics and with a reputation of having been a brave officer on the battlefield, Wall was a good-humoured and gregarious man who was apt to indulge in the sensual pleasures of the eighteenth-century libertine. He felt equally at home in the company of queens and prostitutes. Huéscar, Berwick and Wall were confidants. When Berwick contracted syphilis in 1746, it was Wall, a consummate womaniser who had himself contracted the disease in his mid-forties, who ministered to him, possessing as he did the old soldier's remedy, which in the eighteenth century was mercury.[9]

This was an era in which it was impossible to rise through the ranks without the help of powerful patrons. These wealthy aristocrats were attracted to Wall's easy-going, amiable manner. The English traveller Henry Swinburne, who met Wall shortly before the latter's death, when he was in his eighties, wrote that he was 'fond of talking, but acquits himself so well of the talk, that the most loquacious must listen with patience and pleasure to his discourse, always heightened with mirth and good-humour.'[10] These were the traits that Wall brought to his new career as a diplomat.

The cabal headed by the king's prime minister, Carvajal, came to realise that Wall could be useful to them in pursuing their placatory policy with Britain. It was with this aim in mind that Huéscar sent Wall to London on a secret diplomatic mission. Spain's fears of British commercial encroachment in its American colonies, and British resentment at Spain's interference with its merchant fleet, had resulted in periodic hostilities between the two countries throughout the quarter of a century after the ending of the War of the Spanish Succession in 1715. Under the terms of the Treaty of Utrecht, which ended the war, Britain had been awarded the *asiento* or contract to supply Spain's colonies with African slaves. Britain was also allowed to send a ship of 500 tons once a year to sell manufactured goods into the American markets. It was a concession that undermined Spain's commercial monopoly with its colonies, not least because it enabled the British – already engaged in illegal trading with Spain's American colonies through Jamaica – more easily to smuggle contraband.

Agents of the company established offices in ports throughout Spanish America. Under the terms of the *asiento* a proportion of the profits accrued to the Spanish crown. To ensure that the crown was getting its fair share, and to prevent illegal trading by the British, the Spanish king appointed his own representatives to the company as monitors. Two members of the Irish merchant community in Cádiz, Tomás Geraldino (Fitzgerald) and Pedro Tyrry (Terry), were among the king's representatives in the 1730s. According to Ernest G. Hildner Jr,

> … while the selection of Geraldino was agreeable to the English, that of Tyrry to the company, signed the same day, was far from being so. Tyrry was of Irish parentage and was suspected of ill will toward the British government and of having spied on the fleet at Portsmouth several years before.[11]

In 1739, two years after Tyrry arrived in England, following a breakdown in negotiations over the *asiento* between the two countries, both Tyrry and Geraldino, now the ambassador in London, were recalled to Spain. The same year the War of Jenkins' Ear – known in Spanish as the War of the Asiento – broke out between Britain and Spain after continuing hostilities between the countries' vessels on the Atlantic.

Wall was sent to London to mend fences at the end of the war. With the excuse that he was still suffering the effects of the wound he had received the previous year, he was withdrawn from Geneva, his first posting. In September 1747 he arrived in London, having travelled undercover as a horse-dealer by the name of Lemán to avert the suspicions of the French authorities. Wall's mission was to bring about a peace agreement between Spain and Britain, without marginalising the French. His task was complicated by the fact that he was from a Jacobite family, which, barely a year after Prince Charles Edward Stuart's rebellion had ended in failure at the Battle of Culloden, raised suspicions about his loyalties. The Marquis of Tabuérniga, a duplicitous Spanish aristocrat who was operating as a spy for Britain's powerful Duke of Newcastle and who resented Wall's privileged position at the Spanish court, encouraged these doubts in London.

The diplomat Jaime Masones de Lima was a member of Carvajal's party and a good friend of Wall's. He wrote to Huéscar in 1747 from London warning him that Wall 'was not the most agreeable to that nation because, as well as the fact that being Irish is no recommendation to the English, he has the quality of being in his heart truly French and so any negotiation embarked upon is suspicious.'[12] Wall himself recognised that 'the fact that I am Irish in itself creates suspicion';[13] and after eight fruitless months in London he suggested that he be replaced. 'Whoever it is will be accepted with the greatest satisfaction as long as he is not Irish because it is natural for these people [the English] always to distrust us,' he wrote in a letter to Huéscar.[14] However, Wall's political masters, Carvajal and Huéscar, were not disposed to replace him, despite his increasing entreaties to be allowed return to Spain. They were not impressed by Tabuérniga's intrigues, realising that he wished to sully Wall's reputation at court, and remained convinced of Wall's worth as a diplomat. Wall was to reward their confidence.

In 1748 the Treaty of Aix-la-Chapelle put an end to the war. Though again suffering from homesickness during his prolonged absence from Spain and writing a petition to be allowed home, Wall began to make headway with the British, helped in no small part by his ally, Benjamin Keene, the ambassador to Spain. In 1749 Wall was named ambassador to London, and Tabuérniga was recalled to Spain. Wall now began to earn the trust of the British prime minister, Henry Pelham, and his elder brother, the Duke of Newcastle. In December of that year Wall wrote to Carvajal, informing him of this change in attitude:

> Such is the confidence the two brothers show in me that they have spoken about points of the greatest delicacy for them, and the Duke confessed to me a few days ago that my origins caused their suspicions and distrust. For a long period of time they had me spied upon, during all my conversations and wherever I went, and they even wished to discover if, during dinner, a little more wine than customary would reveal my thinking.[15]

Wall's own awareness of his importance in the diplomatic firmament was reflected in his choice of residence, a grand mansion in fashionable Soho Square with space for an oratory, and in the commissioning of a portrait by the French painter Louis Michel van Loo, in which the subject is depicted regally with ceremonial sword and billowing red sash (see Plate 1).[16]

Wall was now in his late fifties. He was a well-built man with just the beginnings of a paunch. His eyes and his slightly ruddy complexion betrayed a humorous streak and a well-enjoyed life, though one that did not descend into dissipation. He had become more religious as old age approached. However, he continued to indulge in occasional debauches – his growing celebrity presented lots of opportunities for dalliances with London's most attractive women – which would lead to periodic bouts of self-reproach. Though his time in London had brought a turnaround in his fortunes, he remained anxious to return to Spain.

The death of Carvajal in 1754 presented the opportunity. The group that had formed around the late prime minister had fractured in the intervening years, and a struggle developed to replace him as secretary of state. On one side was the faction led by the increasingly powerful Ensenada and the king's confessor, Father Francisco Rábago y Noriega; on the other, the faction led by Huéscar, who, having been promoted to the position of *mayordomo mayor*, or head of the king's household, now had the ear of the credulous Spanish monarch.

Huéscar played on the king's and queen's fears that Carvajal's sudden death would lead to an unravelling of their policy, and he proposed Wall as a suitable replacement. Ferdinand had first wanted the Count of Valdeparaíso to become the new prime minister, but the count, who was a close ally of Huéscar's and Wall's, refused, citing his inexperience, and suggested Wall in his stead. Keene was also eager that Wall, whom he regarded as sympathetic to British interests, should be the next secretary of state.

At the age of 60, the French-born son of Irish Jacobite refugees had become the head of King Ferdinand VI's government. Wall served as prime minister of the Spanish government until his resignation in 1763. Having himself benefited from the patronage of powerful benefactors, he was now in a position to help the careers of his compatriots. Some of them were the children of Jacobite exiles like himself who had arrived in Spain in the early part of the century; others were more recent arrivals who took advantage of the Irish networks that now existed in commerce and the military.

Wall's period of office was contemporaneous with the Seven Years' War and the accession of Ferdinand's more capable half-brother, Charles III, to the throne. It was an era of crisis and change in which Spain and Britain came to blows over the latter's persistent attempts to open up Spanish America to British trade. In response to these threats to its colonies, Charles was determined to increase the pace of reform in the Spanish Empire, with a view to centralising authority in Madrid. Over the next four years Charles and his Irish prime minister were responsible for introducing profound change to Spain and its colonies in the Americas.

Chapter 2

REMAKING THE NEW WORLD

Charles III acceded to the throne in 1759. The new king was a man of simple tastes. He was pious, chaste and hard-working, most unlike the majority of his Bourbon ancestors. His main entertainment was hunting. In a famous portrait by Goya, dating from 1788 (see Plate 2), Charles is depicted in simple hunting costume, a blue sash the only symbol of his royal authority. With his bulbous nose, slightly hunched back and ruddy cheeks, he looks more like an English country parson than the sovereign of a global empire. There is something of Charles's pragmatism in Goya's portrait, a recognition that the concept of kingly authority is changing, albeit very slowly.

Charles was among the most capable of Spain's monarchs, a diligent, thoughtful ruler who interested himself in the business of royal government and employed the talents of his ministers wisely. He had a unified vision for the Spanish Empire and, on acceding to the throne, reformed its government and economy. A new administrative system of intendancies, already in place in Bourbon France, was introduced in an attempt to strengthen royal control over the American colonies, which inevitably led to discontent among the *criollo* elite.

Though personally religious, Charles curbed the power of the Inquisition and attacked the privileges of the Church. Yet first and foremost he was anxious to bolster his own authority. Like his father and half-brother before him, Charles believed in his divine right to rule. In this respect he was very much in the mould of the 'enlightened despot' who believed that scientific progress and rational thought were not incompatible with a medieval, absolutist form of government.

During the seventeenth century the Spanish Habsburgs had been content to let Spain's American possessions govern themselves, having neither the inclination nor the ability to do otherwise. The Bourbons reversed this policy.

Charles wished to turn the old self-governing kingdoms into productive colonies. The quickening pace of Bourbon reform brought many positive changes to Spanish America. New roads and towns were built, and the Enlightenment spirit of inquiry brought scientific advances. The problem was that all this progress was designed for the benefit of peninsular Spain, not for the inhabitants of the colonies.

The reserved, deliberate Charles and the gregarious, buccaneering Wall were starkly contrasting characters. They had first met in Italy in the early 1730s, when Wall's regiment had been sent to support Charles's claim to the Duchy of Parma. Charles had been a callow 16-year-old, who had grown up at court in the shadow of his domineering mother, Elisabeth Farnese. Wall was then in his late thirties, a hardened *teniente coronel* (lieutenant colonel) in the Batavia Regiment of Dragoons. The Irish officer and the young Spanish heir to the throne had gone hunting together, and Wall had delivered messages between the duke and his parents, the king and queen of Spain. In 1734 Wall had served under Charles during the Spanish campaign to conquer Naples and Sicily. However, Charles's accession to the Spanish throne had created problems for Wall. While Charles was personally well disposed to Wall, his favoured courtiers from Italy were less well inclined towards a man they regarded as little more than an interloper.

The new king needed a new way of running the vast empire that he had inherited from his half-brother. He wished to reform government and stimulate the economy to make it more productive; and to do this he required information. And so naturalists, economists, political scientists and geographers were encouraged to produce detailed descriptions of the Spanish Empire's geography, economy, society and administration.

The great German geographer and naturalist Alexander von Humboldt's description of a five-year journey through Spanish America gave European readers a new understanding of a part of the world that had previously been obscure and the subject of wild conjecture. However, his multi-volume account did not begin to appear until 1807. Before Humboldt, however, several Irish writers helped give Charles an idea of how his empire worked and how it might be fixed.

William Bowles was a chemist and metallurgist from County Cork who settled in Spain in 1752 on accepting the position of intendant of the state mines. He travelled extensively throughout the Iberian Peninsula, surveying the country's mineral deposits, inspecting mines and producing studies. In 1775 he published *Introducción a la historia natural y á la geografía física de España,* the first comprehensive account of its kind. In the book Bowles compared parts of Spain with Ireland, noting the similarities between the folk culture of Galicia, the Basque Country and Ireland.[1]

Another influential author was Pedro Alonso O'Crouley, a member of the Irish merchant community in Cádiz who was infused with the intellectual energy of the Enlightenment. O'Crouley was born in 1740, his Irish parents having arrived in the city in the 1720s. He was educated first by the Jesuits in Cádiz and then by the Augustinians in Senlis, north-east of Paris. While studying at Senlis the young O'Crouley developed a curiosity about how the world worked that was to stay with him for the rest of his life. Upon completing his education, he entered one of the city's merchant houses. In 1765 he travelled for the first time to New Spain (present-day Mexico). Ten merchant ships sailed in the flotilla, carrying 8,000 tons of cargo and escorted by two men-of-war to protect against privateers.

O'Crouley travelled back and forth across the Atlantic, immersing himself in the exotic natural surroundings of the New World, constantly taking notes and making sketches. In 1784 his precarious financial situation was eased by his marriage to María Power y Gil, the daughter of one of the wealthiest Irish merchants in Cádiz, which left him free to concentrate on his scientific interests. The fruit of his studies was published in 1774 as *Idea compendiosa del reyno de Nueva España* (edited and translated into English in 1972 by Seán Galvin as *A Description of the Kingdom of New Spain*). O'Crouley crammed information about the geography, natural history, religious organisation and urban development of Mexico into the book, conforming to the Enlightenment idea that every piece of useful knowledge could and should be compiled and stored away for future use. The book included illustrations and tables relating to the landscape and cities of different regions of New Spain, information about their populations, and pictures of indigenous animals and plants.[2]

Antonio O'Brien was the son of an Irish merchant who had settled in Seville. Antonio had served in the Ultonia Regiment before travelling to Peru in 1762, where he worked as an agent for various Cádiz merchants. He also taught in a military school in Lima, which brought him to the attention of the viceroy. In the mid-1760s, at the viceroy's behest, O'Brien drew up detailed plans and maps of the port and fort at Callao. His most notable achievement, however, was the *Explicación de los metales de Huantajaya*, the report he compiled about the silver mines in the north of present-day Chile and the maps he drew to complement his findings. They are not only important sources for the history of this part of colonial Chile, and beautiful examples of eighteenth-century cartography – the viceroy of Peru ordered O'Brien to report on every aspect of the geography, politics, economy and society of this remote region – but may also be seen as the beginning of modern mineralogy and metallurgy in that country.

In a similar vein, King Charles IV – Charles III's son and successor – gave two Irish priests the responsibility for compiling the first Spanish-English dictionary to be printed in Spain. The four-volume *Diccionario nuevo y completo de las lenguas española é inglesa*, published in 1797, was a groundbreaking work in the history of Spanish lexicography. It was compiled by the Dominican friar Thomas Connelly, who was also confessor to the royal family, and the Carmelite Thomas Higgins. Connelly worked on the project for 14 years, borrowing heavily from Samuel Johnson's English dictionary and the Spanish Academy's authoritative Spanish dictionary.

The Bourbons were determined to strengthen their political control of the Americas for the benefit of the peninsular economy. One of Charles III's principal economic advisers was an Irishman named Bernard Ward, a native of the townland of Lisirril in the lake district of County Monaghan, who wrote an influential treatise about all aspects of royal policy in the Spanish Empire.

The Spanish monarchy had been good to the Ward family. Bernard was a director of the royal mint; his wife, Maria O'More, from Ballina, County Kildare, was a lady-in-waiting to the strong-willed Elisabeth Farnese, the Italian-born queen dowager of Spain. The Wards lived in a comfortable house in the Calle de Hortaleza in the centre of Madrid. Their son Felipe was born in May 1758.

Felipe studied at the Seminario de Nobles de Madrid, the elite military school for the sons of the Spanish nobility.[3] To gain entry to the school, candidates had to provide evidence of their unblemished Catholicism, their noble birth, and the identity of their parents and grandparents. In his statement the chaplain of the Flemish company of the Royal Guards, Edmundo O'Ryan, testified that there was 'no more illustrious house in Ireland' than that of the Wards, who, 'as princes of that land, defended and maintained with their houses, lives and goods the Catholic Religion against the English, which turned them into their greatest enemies, and therefore they suffered for more than a century infinite persecution.'[4] Alexander O'Reilly, a kinsman of Ward, and Patrick O'Shea, a lieutenant in the Royal Guards, also testified to the depredations suffered by the Ward family at the hands of the English.[5]

This type of testimony produced by Irish witnesses to prove the noble birth of candidates for admittance to institutions, military orders or higher office in the armed forces and government demonstrated loyalty to the Spanish state. Of course the Irish were tempted to offer glowing references and to wax lyrical about the noble ancestry of the candidate, in case they needed the favour returned, and they did not always have the documentary evidence to support their claims.

Felipe Ward served as a cadet in the Asturias Regiment before transferring to the Irlanda Regiment as a *subteniente* (roughly equivalent to second lieutenant). Later he was transferred to the military academy in Puerto de Santa María, near Cádiz, where he taught mathematics and military strategy to officers and cadets. He also served in New Spain in the Regimiento de Nueva España.[6]

His father, Bernard Ward, was an enthusiastic proponent of state intervention in the economy. In 1750 he recommended a welfare system, alongside the development of agriculture, industry and commerce, to alleviate Spain's chronic poverty. During the next four years he travelled through Europe compiling information for what became the *Proyecto económico*,[7] a comprehensive study of Spain's economic problems and recommendations on how to solve them. On Ward's return to Spain, the king appointed him to the royal economic council and made him a director of the royal glass factory at San Ildefonso, one of the enterprises that Charles III had founded to develop the domestic economy. Two years later Ward was named a member of the royal tax authority.[8]

Ward finished the *Proyecto económico* in 1762, though it was not until 1779 that his widow posthumously published it.[9] The book was in two parts. The first part dealt with peninsular Spain. It recommended the construction of six arterial highways connecting Madrid with the provinces. Other recommendations included a comprehensive geographical survey; the development of canals, such as those Ward had seen during his travels through the Netherlands; a publicly financed credit system; the introduction of modern agricultural methods; and the development of the textile industry. Ward also proposed the setting up of a council devoted to improvements in every sphere of economic activity in Spain and the Americas, comprising 'first-class subjects in terms of intelligence, talent, erudition, zeal and experience.'[10] As his model for this council he cited the Dublin Society (later the Royal Dublin Society), which, 'basing itself on the infallible rule of experience,' had 'managed to shine a light on matters relating to agriculture, industry and other matters under its inspection.'[11] According to Ward,

> ... as the members of that Society are the principal people in the Kingdom [of Ireland], the care of which they all embrace, and their measures have produced such admirable results, a spirit of improvement has diffused throughout the entire body of the Nation; in such a way that what was before the work of a single Society has now become the general concern of almost all the individuals of the Kingdom ...[12]

In the *Proyecto económico* Ward proposed Ireland as a blueprint for how a body of enlightened men, working with the king's ministers, might contribute to the development of agriculture and industry in the Spanish Empire.

> The [Irish] Parliament complies with all that the Society proposes; and the Scientists, the Scholars and other Sages contribute with their observations; and so it is revealed how to discover the quality of the soil, the influence of the weather on its fertility, the best time to sow every seed, while, on the other hand the experts occupy themselves with finding inventions to make work easier, developing knowledge, and perfecting the most common skills ...[13]

In 1775, three years after Ward proposed what he called a council of improvements modelled on the Dublin Society, the first of the 'Sociedades económicas de amigos del país' was founded in the Basque Country. The societies soon spread throughout Spain and its American colonies. These private associations of gentlemen were committed to stimulating the economic and intellectual development of the Spanish Empire, promoted scientific and technological advances, and had the support of Enlightenment thinkers such as Pedro Rodríguez de Campomanes, a future Spanish prime minister.

The second part of Ward's *Proyecto económico* dealt with the Americas. In the opening chapter he levelled some harsh criticisms, questioning why it was that two great civilisations – those of the Aztecs and the Incas – had become, under the Spanish, 'uncivilised, depopulated and almost destroyed.' According to Ward, Spain's American colonies could have become 'the richest in the world' but had remained chronically underdeveloped, because of the corrupt form of government in Spanish America.[14]

Given that his patron was the Spanish monarch, Ward had to make this point delicately, insisting that all those who had gone before had done their best with the primitive scientific and economic tools at their disposal. He balanced his criticisms with laudatory imperial rhetoric, praising the first Spanish explorers and governors for the 'prodigious courage and perseverance of their voyages; the bravery of their conquests; the wisdom of the laws and constitutions for the government of the Indies; and the prodigious prudence and judiciousness of their other institutions.'[15] But now, he insisted, the king could take advantage of scientific and technological innovation, as well as modern economic theory, to introduce a series of reforms in the Americas that would contribute to the development of the economy.

The problem for the Spanish crown was that, despite the inflow of wealth in the form of primary goods and precious metals from the Americas, the peninsular economy was stagnant. Much of the wealth accumulated during the early phase of colonisation had been spent by the Habsburg monarchs on wars, and the flow of silver into Spain had pushed up prices, making Spanish goods more expensive than those of competing powers. In the 1620s the silver that had flowed from the mines of Mexico and Peru began to dry up. By the eighteenth century most of the primary goods that entered Spain through Cádiz were immediately re-exported to northern Europe. What was worse, only a small fraction of the goods consumed in the American colonies were manufactured on the peninsula.

Ward believed that the American question had to be looked at from two points of view: as a market for Spanish goods and as an integral part of the empire which needed to be restructured politically and economically. Just as he had recommended for the peninsula in the first part of the book, Ward proposed an extensive royal survey of Spain's American possessions.

The seeds of a modern state may be seen in the proposals included in *Proyecto económico*, based as they were on the rule of law and the introduction of a modern police force:

> It will be said that I speak of America as if it was a well-populated country in all parts, in which a regular police force can operate, and the institutions that I propose can be easily set up, and as if the Indians were similar to the European Nations.
>
> I realise that half the country is made up of desert, full of plateaux and mountains, without roads through the Provinces, or any comforts: the rivers without bridges, and the inhabitants in many parts little more than irrational; but that does not mean that one should not start with some form of police: so that the defects of the country may be corrected, improvements may be carried out in a determined and willing fashion, and, in order to achieve all this, there will be fixed rules.[16]

As in Spain, for a new centralised police force to be effective a modern communications network was required. Under the Incas the present-day countries of Peru, Chile, Argentina, Bolivia, Ecuador and Colombia had been linked by an extensive communication system. Couriers, called *chasquis*, ran in relays along paths, trails and roads carrying messages from one part of the empire to another. They were stationed in posts called *tambos*, where they could avail of shelter and supplies. In *Proyecto económico* Ward proposed something similar to the *tambos* to facilitate communication and commerce in the Americas.

Ward was also a strong advocate of ecclesiastical reform in the Americas, calling for tighter royal control of clerical appointments and for scrutiny of financial abuses, and questioning why it was that the American missions, 'despite the fact that the Spanish church is the richest in the world,'[17] were being financed by the monarch. He thought the Catholic Church in America should found seminaries to educate the 'sons of Indians' who 'would in time become good parish priests and missionaries to their compatriots.'[18] Indeed Ward wrote that the indigenous people of the Spanish colonies were 'the true treasure of Spain,' who 'carried the heaviest burden on the earth.'[19]

Many of the ideas in the *Proyecto económico* impressed Ward's patrons in government. But there were significant obstacles to be overcome, in the form of financial resources, corruption, and opposition from the *criollo* elite and the indigenous tribes that still held sway in parts of Spanish America. If Charles III and his prime minister were to bring into effect Ward's ideas, they would have to find men capable of introducing efficient methods for taxing, rebuilding and policing the American colonies. Because Wall was at the centre of government, at least in the first years of Charles's reign, and because of their military experience, Irish administrators, engineers and soldiers were centrally involved in this project of remaking Spanish America.

Chapter 3

A NEW MODEL ARMY

In the light of the threat from militarily superior hostile powers, and the humiliating losses that resulted from defeat in the Seven Years' War, the Spanish crown's priority in the second half of the eighteenth century was the modernisation of its armed forces and defensive fortifications. Though many Irish engineers and soldiers took part in this project, it was an army officer from County Meath, Alexander O'Reilly, who made the greatest contribution to transforming Spain's army into a modern, well-disciplined fighting force. Richard Wall may have been at the centre of the Irish community's political network, but it was his compatriot O'Reilly who was respected as one of the shrewdest military brains in Spain.

From solid soldiering stock – his grandfather, John O'Reilly, was a colonel in the army of James II and had fought at the Siege of Derry in 1689[1] – Alexander O'Reilly was born in the townland of Moylagh, near Oldcastle, County Meath, in 1723.[2] His father, Thomas O'Reilly, sent him to Spain to join the army, along with his brothers, Dominic and Nicholas. Thomas's eldest son, James, inherited the family farm.[3]

Alexander was only a child when he was commissioned in the Hibernia Regiment in the 1730s as a cadet – his two brothers also joined the regiment – and 19 when, on 8 February 1743, he and 13,000 Spanish and Neapolitan troops faced the 11,000-strong Austrian and Sardinian army at the village of Camposanto in the north of Italy during the War of the Austrian Succession. When night fell, both sides were forced to withdraw from the field. However, amid the smoke from the guns and the encroaching darkness, many units lost their way and headed towards enemy lines. Unable to move because of a badly wounded foot, O'Reilly spent an agonising night on the field of battle and was bleeding profusely. As dawn broke, an Austrian soldier came across the wounded Irishman and prepared to kill him. Unable to move, O'Reilly made a decision that saved his life. Pretending that he was the son of a Spanish grandee, the Duke of Arcos, he pleaded for his life with the soldier, claiming that his father would pay a substantial ransom for him. Instead of being consigned to history at the end of an Austrian bayonet, he was taken prisoner and brought before an Irish officer serving in the Austrian army. In a display of sympathy towards a fellow-Irishman, and perhaps impressed – if not convinced – by O'Reilly's ingenuity in saving his skin, the officer released him.[4]

O'Reilly was lucky to be alive; the Hibernia had lost 297 men during the battle. On his return to Spain he was the toast of Madrid; the Duke of Arcos found the story of his escape particularly amusing. The well-polished anecdote, and the limp that was to remain with O'Reilly for the rest of his life, helped create an aura of mystique around the young Irish officer.

In 1753, having attained the senior rank of *sargento mayor*, O'Reilly was seconded to the Austrian army as a military observer. Europe was at war once again, and O'Reilly was given the mission of examining the capabilities of one of the best fighting forces on the Continent, the Prussian army. What he saw on the battlefields of Germany left a lasting impression, most of all the discipline with which the Prussians both attacked the enemy and withdrew from engagements.[5] He was especially taken by the figure of Frederick II. In a report written from Prague in December 1758 he wrote of the Prussians:

> Their Brandenburgers and Pomeranians are the best soldiers in Germany. These men are tall, solid, hardened by work, properly trained as soldiers from the cradle, with a discipline in every sphere that is superior to that of every other army; the skill, fearlessness and perseverance of their monarch, and the impression he makes on their morale, are advantages that are difficult to overcome.[6]

O'Reilly's reports demonstrated his keen military mind, and in 1761 the king gave him the opportunity to put his recommendations into practice by creating a special post for him: assistant-general of the infantry.[7] O'Reilly overhauled antiquated military practices, from manoeuvres on the battlefield to the system of pay, and relentlessly imposed the type of discipline he had seen practised in the Prussian army.

O'Reilly's stature in the Spanish army was growing, prompting veneration and jealousy in equal measure. Luis de las Casas was a 17-year-old junior officer from the Basque Country when he served under O'Reilly in Portugal. He wrote of O'Reilly that he was 'able to inspire in me love for the King, zeal for his royal service, an inclination for a military career, much respect for the fulfilment of my duties, integrity and some knowledge of commanding and disciplining units.'[8] But there were also those within the court who were increasingly resentful of the king's closeness to a foreigner.

In the 1760s, O'Reilly was part of a military commission sent to the Caribbean to strengthen Spain's defensive capabilities. The British had captured Cuba from Spain during the Seven Years' War, but the island had been returned during the peace negotiations that ended the hostilities. O'Reilly rebuilt Cuba's defensive fortifications and made extensive recommendations about improving the local economy, including a suggestion that Irish settlers be introduced. He argued that Cuba needed a permanent garrison comprising Spanish officers and troops, regularly relieved and supplied from Europe and reinforced at times of war. Until this point the island had been defended by a handful of veteran soldiers, who often deserted. The commission also recommended the establishment of well-trained militias to supplement the professional soldiers.

The plan was approved, becoming the basis on which Charles III reorganised the army and militias throughout Spanish America. O'Reilly's efforts in Cuba and Puerto Rico, of which he was appointed governor in 1765, resulted in royal decrees on the organisation of Spain's armed forces in Panama (1772), Peru (1793) and New Granada (1794). O'Reilly was given the responsibility for implementing these reforms throughout the Caribbean. In 1765 the king awarded him membership of the prestigious Order of Alcántara,[9] and in 1766 he was named inspector-general of infantry, a post he would hold for 20 years.[10]

O'Reilly had proved himself a brave soldier in northern Italy, had shown his understanding of military theory in Germany and had demonstrated his ample organisational capacity in Spain's colonies in the Caribbean, but it was in Louisiana that he earned his reputation for ruthlessness. France had ceded Louisiana to Spain at the end of the Seven Years' War, but its mostly French settlers were not keen on their new masters and in 1768 ejected the first Spanish governor, Antonio de Ulloa. It was with the mission of reasserting control on behalf of the Spanish crown that, in 1769, O'Reilly, now in his forties and a lieutenant-colonel, sailed from Spain with about 3,000 infantry and cavalry and 50 cannons in a fleet of more than 25 ships.

O'Reilly's flagship, the *Volante*, arrived at the mouth of the Mississippi in July. Weighing anchor near the fort of La Balize to await the fleet's stragglers, O'Reilly despatched one of his officers to deliver a message to the French governor of New Orleans, informing him that he had come to take possession of the city and province of Louisiana on behalf of the king of Spain, and that any opposition would be punished. The arrival of the Spanish fleet threw New Orleans into turmoil, and three of the city's prominent citizens returned with the Spanish officer to plead for clemency. Determined to set an example, O'Reilly ignored their protestations.

The Spanish force sailed upriver to New Orleans, disembarking in the city with great ceremony. The French flag was lowered and the Spanish flag raised. After a solemn mass at which a *Te Deum* was sung, O'Reilly watched his soldiers parading through the city in a deliberate show of strength. The following day he summoned nine of the principal citizens of New Orleans to a banquet and after the meal had them thrown into jail. He also ordered the arrest of another three men. Five of them were sentenced to death by hanging, and scaffolds were erected in the city. However, a hangman could not be found, so they were shot by firing squad. Another five men were sentenced to life in prison in Havana, while the remaining two were acquitted.

The French settlers began calling the new Spanish governor 'Bloody O'Reilly' – a nickname that endures in New Orleans to this day. A French historian of Louisiana, François de Barbé-Marbois, described O'Reilly as a barbarian, who 'indulged in acts of violence and ferocity, which he mistook for prudence and firmness,' and claimed that there were those in the Spanish court who were secretly outraged by the killings but had not thought it wise to disagree publicly with their governor for fear of looking weak.[11] Yet O'Reilly had achieved his aim of restoring order to Louisiana; and if there were those in the Spanish court who disapproved of his actions, the king did not. In 1770 Charles appointed him inspector-general of the colonial army and militias, and in 1771 he was created Count and Viscount of Cavan.[12] The young Irish soldier who had spent the night shivering on the battlefield of Camposanto and wondering if his last hour had arrived was now Count O'Reilly. It was the pinnacle of his career.

O'Reilly did not possess Wall's social graces and was more blunt-speaking than his compatriot. He had a mordant sense of humour, which he used to deflate his more pompous officers and courtiers. In an era and a society in which honour was prized above all else, this did not always endear him to his contemporaries. However, O'Reilly possessed two highly prized qualities: loyalty and amiability. Charles III himself praised O'Reilly for this talent for friendship.[13] In his *Foreign Reminiscences*, Lord Holland remarked of O'Reilly:

> He was quick, coarse, and shrewd, thoroughly acquainted with the Court and people with whom he had to deal, and of parts and courage to avail himself of his knowledge; but he was not exempt from those failings in taste and judgment which are so often objected to in his countrymen, and which not unfrequently mar the fortunes of men, otherwise best qualified to succeed in the race for power and distinction.[14]

Notwithstanding this judgement, it was military failure that marred O'Reilly's career, rather than any inherent vice of his race.

In 1775 the king chose O'Reilly to lead an expedition to occupy Algiers. Pirates operating from along the Barbary coast had been attacking Spanish ships for centuries; the Irishman's mission was to put an end to the menace. O'Reilly set sail from Cartagena in south-eastern Spain that summer with a force of more than 20,000 men in 500 ships. However, spies had forewarned the Algerians, who were lying in wait for the Spanish force. When the soldiers disembarked, the Algerians withdrew in a series of feints before ambushing the Spanish attackers. Some 2,000 Spanish soldiers were killed in the ensuing bloodshed, including five generals.[15] It was a bitter blow to Spanish martial pride, and the blame fell squarely on O'Reilly's shoulders. Now in his early fifties, O'Reilly found his glittering reputation in tatters. Caricatures of him appeared in handbills lampooning the disaster in Algiers, satirical poems mocked his ineptitude and he was given a new nickname, General Disaster. One rhyme ran:

> *Oyendo de los moros el tiroteo,*
> *dijo O'Reilly temblando,*
> *'¡Ay, que me meo!'*
> [Hearing the shots of the Moors,
> said O'Reilly trembling,
> 'Oh, I've pissed myself!'][16]

He served a brief period of isolation before Charles III, a loyal friend who loathed change, brought him back from exile and appointed him captain-general of Andalusia and governor of Cádiz.

The English writer Henry Swinburne spent three days with O'Reilly shortly after the disastrous expedition to Algiers. In Swinburne's account of his travels in Spain, he produced a warm depiction of the Irishman.

> He has much ready wit at his command, especially when he has a mind to turn the laugh against any particular person, in which case he is accused of often carrying the joke too far; and I don't know but he may owe some of his many enemies to the ridicule he has sometimes thrown upon them. Some think him rather too fond of talking, and of making himself the subject of his discourse, but they must acknowledge he speaks with great eloquence in a variety of languages.
>
>   His countenance and figure are rather comely; but a wound in his knee causes him to limp, an imperfection which has afforded his enemies great scope for raillery: the king's fondness for him bears him up against all their efforts to ruin him …[17]

O'Reilly vainly tried to restore his reputation, applying himself energetically to his new job in Cádiz. Travellers to the city praised him for building new houses and streets, introducing improved standards of public hygiene and a municipal police force, supporting the arts and sciences, and helping the poor.

The king continued to rely on his advice. In 1786 the Spanish government wished to create fixed regiments in the Americas, beginning with Cuba, to reduce the expense of shipping troops across the Atlantic. Responding to a request for his help, O'Reilly wrote that 'because he had been dismissed from his position as Inspector-General of the Infantry, he was not able to comply as he would like,'[18] a not-so-subtle dig at the way he had been treated.

There was to be one last act in the Irishman's military career. In 1794, with French forces on the border, the king recalled O'Reilly, now in his early seventies, to action. Ever loyal, he saddled his horse to make the journey from Madrid to Alicante, where he was to join his regiment before travelling to the Pyrenees. However, he died en route of a heart attack – there were rumours that he had been poisoned[19] – and was buried in the village of Bonete.[20]

The name O'Reilly continued to feature prominently in the Spanish army's officer corps after Alexander's death. His eldest son, Pedro, who inherited the title of Count O'Reilly from his father, served in Cuba and married a local woman, María Francisca Calvo de la Puerta. She was descended from the O'Farrell family, who had made their fortune on the island from sugar and slaves, and inherited the title of Duchess of Buenavista from her father in 1797. Pedro was promoted to colonel in the Navarra Regiment in 1796.[21]

Another son, Manuel O'Reilly, also served in Cuba. In 1790 Luis de las Casas, who had fought with O'Reilly in Portugal in the 1760s during the Seven Years' War, was appointed governor of Cuba, and he requested permission for Manuel, then a *subteniente* in the Regiment of the Prince's Infantry, to travel with him and further his military education in the Caribbean. According to de las Casas, Manuel was a sharp, talented young man who would become 'a good servant of the king, as well as an honourable son to his father.'[22] De las Casas argued that a promotion should be given to Manuel O'Reilly because his father, through his 'zeal, skill and perseverance,' had established Cuba's modern military fortifications more than 27 years previously.[23]

Not all were so generous about Alexander O'Reilly's merits. 'His death on the way to the command of an army seemed to complete the fatality attending the attainment of all his objects of ambition,' Lord Holland wrote.[24] This somewhat dismissive appraisal was unfair. The English politician might have regarded O'Reilly as an anachronism by the time he published his reminiscences in 1850, an Irish Jacobite in the service of a power traditionally hostile to Britain. O'Reilly was too loud, too fond of talking, and perhaps not privy to the strict social codes that distinguished the insider from the outsider in polite English society. His career had ended in military failure, and the royalist cause for which he had fought was out of date.

O'Reilly may have had regrets as he lay dying in some inn in Bonete, but the old royalist also had the satisfaction of having achieved great things. He had reformed the Spanish army, he had worked tirelessly to rebuild crumbling, centuries-old forts so as to defend them against attack from British and Dutch pirates, and he had re-established Spanish authority in Louisiana. These accomplishments did not impress an English Whig like Holland, but they earned him the everlasting gratitude of the Spanish crown.

Chapter 4

THE KING OF PERU

In 1751 one of the many Irish merchant families of Cádiz, the Butlers, gave a job to a recently arrived Irishman in the city. The new employee, Ambrose O'Higgins,[1] was rather old to be starting work as a clerk – he was already in his early thirties – but he knuckled down and did what he was told. When he was not busy entering numbers in the long, narrow columns of one of his employer's ledgers, the new clerk would stroll up and down the docks, watching the heavy sacks and chests full of exotic-smelling goods from the Indies being unloaded from the cavernous holds of the wooden merchant ships, pondering the wonders that lay on the other side of the glittering expanse of water.

Ambrose was born about 1721 in the townland of Ballynary on the eastern shore of Lough Arrow in County Sligo to Charles and Margaret Higgins, small farmers. He later founded and named the city of San Ambrosio de Ballenary (present-day Vallenar) in Chile in honour of his birthplace. Though there is little documentary evidence concerning O'Higgins's early life in Ireland, it is likely that he grew up in a modest house, his family struggling to make ends meet in the impoverished Ireland of the 1720s. In any event, the Higgins family's circumstances led them to change their fortunes by moving to Summerhill, County Meath, when Ambrose was still a boy. It may have been that he could not afford to travel to Spain until the middle of the century, when he was already 30 years old. By the time he arrived in Cádiz in 1751 his achievements had not matched his ambition, but he was determined to remedy that fact by his unstinting application to whatever task was at hand. He spent five years working in the city, building important contacts in Irish political and mercantile circles until, in 1756, he had an opportunity to see the New World for himself.

O'Higgins travelled to South America to sell goods on behalf of a group of Cádiz merchants. It is also possible that he visited a younger brother, William, who was living in Asunción.[2] His first port of call was Buenos Aires, from where he set off on the long overland trek towards Chile. The first part of the trip across the pampas – the flat, grassy plains that surrounded Buenos Aires to the north, west and south as far as the eye could see – was not too arduous. It was enlivened by encounters with groups of dusty-looking *gauchos* rounding up the wild cattle that grazed on the pampas, or sitting around at night, expertly carving pieces of beef from a bloody carcass to roast on the camp-fire. Things became more difficult as he rode farther west; for between the pampas and wine country of present-day Argentina and the narrow strip of land that hugs the Pacific coastline – present day Chile – lie the Andes.

If O'Higgins's career had so far been unspectacular, there were signs that he possessed an inner drive, mental resilience and the capacity to endure physical hardship that surpassed that of ordinary men. Summoning all his reserves of energy, he began to climb into the frozen *cordillera* – the part of the Andean mountain range separating the modern republics of Argentina and Chile. The memory of that first punishing climb across the Andes – he was to traverse the mountain range many times – was to remain with him for the rest of his life.

O'Higgins spent two to three years in South America. When he returned to Spain in 1760, he sought to become a naturalised Spaniard so that he could trade in the Americas using his own capital. He also looked for a government job. He was now almost 40 and still had not found his calling.

It was an encounter with John Garland, an Irish-born military engineer in the service of the Spanish crown, that gave his career the push it needed. Garland was highly esteemed by his superiors. Having entered the Spanish army as a cadet in the Hibernia Regiment in 1738, he had risen to the rank of captain when he began his career as a military engineer in the Royal Engineer Corps in 1751. When he met O'Higgins in 1761 he was preparing to travel to South America to work on upgrading the Spanish crown's defensive fortifications in Chile. Garland was impressed by his fellow-Irishman's drive and ambition and employed O'Higgins as a draughtsman. Before leaving Cádiz, O'Higgins took out various loans to invest in goods for sale in the South American market. He also entered into a business arrangement with the wealthy Irish merchant Juan Bautista Power.

Garland and O'Higgins set sail on board the frigate *La Venus* in January 1763, arriving in Montevideo that May. In Buenos Aires, O'Higgins visited some of the contacts he had made during his previous stay in South

America and tried to dispose of the goods he had brought with him from Spain. At the same time he prepared to make the arduous journey overland to Santiago. It was the beginning of winter when he set off; Garland had chosen to remain in Buenos Aires until the spring, but O'Higgins was eager to get to Chile.

O'Higgins arrived in Mendoza in the west of present-day Argentina in late June, having covered 600 miles across the pampas. The distance remaining to Santiago was just over a hundred miles as the crow flies, but once again the cordillera stood in his way. Conditions were even worse than the first time he had made the crossing, because it was the height of winter. O'Higgins trudged up the lower slopes of the Andes but was forced to return to Mendoza during a violent storm. He was unperturbed and tried again a few weeks later. This time he succeeded in making it across the icy passage to the other side of the Andes and down to Santiago. Garland arrived in the city at the end of the year.

In the middle of the eighteenth century the territory roughly corresponding to present-day Chile was administered as a captaincy-general. This meant that, although Chile was under the jurisdiction of the viceroy of Peru, the capital of which was Lima, it enjoyed a considerable amount of autonomy. This reflected Chile's unique geographical position, sandwiched as it was between the Pacific Ocean and the Andes. Its political and military independence was encapsulated in the figure of the governor and captain-general, who in 1763 was Antonio Guill y Gonzaga. Guill was responsible for implementing the Spanish crown's reforms in Chile, the most pressing of which, in the aftermath of the Seven Years' War, was the modernisation of the dilapidated fortifications along the Pacific coastline and the subjugation of the indigenous Mapuche people in the south. To this end, Guill ordered the experienced soldier and engineer Garland and his draughtsman, O'Higgins, to map and rebuild southern Chile.

The region of Chile between Santiago and Cape Horn is one of the most beautiful parts of South America. Hundreds of azure-blue rivers trickle down the snow-capped peaks of the Andes through lush green valleys into glassy lakes. In the 1760s this was a wild and dangerous place, the site of the ever-shifting frontier between Spanish-controlled territory and those lands still under the sway of the Mapuche, who had resisted Spanish rule since the arrival of the first *conquistadores* in the 1540s.

Mapuche is both the name of a specific tribe who lived in the Araucanía region of Chile and a broader term given to the different indigenous peoples who shared linguistic and cultural characteristics and who lived in a region covering the lowlands of southern Chile between the Rivers Biobío and Toltén, a part of the Argentine pampas and the section of the cordillera in between. In the latter half of the eighteenth century unstable truces were punctuated by short, sharp wars between the Spanish and the Mapuche.

The Spanish were acutely concerned about their inability to subjugate the indigenous people in the south and made concerted efforts throughout the eighteenth century to tackle the problem.[3] The frontier between the Spanish Empire in America and Mapuche territory was the River Biobío. This political and cultural border was to shape O'Higgins's future career. Like many a self-made man in the Americas, he was to prove his worth in the harsh, dangerous frontierlands. As if acknowledging the fact, this was where he later established his great *hacienda,* or cattle ranch, Las Canteras, in an area known as the Isla de la Laja, a triangular wedge of lush, grassy land, the bottom corner of which was sandwiched between the Biobío and the Andes.

O'Higgins participated in an assembly of Mapuche chiefs convened by Guill in December 1764. These gatherings, called *parlamentos* in Spanish, took place periodically during the Bourbon era. The 1764 *parlamento* was held near the fort of Nacimiento in the heartland of Mapuche territory. On the banks of the River Biobío – in recognition of the frontier between royalist-controlled lands and Mapuche territory – O'Higgins witnessed the governor, Guill, the Bishop of Concepción, Pedro Ángel Espiñeira, the *oidor* (judge) Domingo Martínez de Aldunate, and Field-Marshal Salvador Cabrito sit down with 200 Mapuche leaders. Thousands of royalist troops and Mapuche warriors hovered in the background in case of trouble. After several days of discussion, the *caciques,* or tribal chiefs, agreed to the Spanish proposal that they settle in towns and allow Christian missionaries among them. In practice the agreement was meaningless and the Mapuche returned to their traditional form of living.

The isolated ports of southern Chile, such as Valdivia, were vulnerable to attack from the fleets of hostile states plying the Pacific, including the British and Dutch. Guill had ordered Garland and O'Higgins to oversee the construction of new fortifications at Valdivia, the most strategically important port in southern Chile, lying at the confluence of the Rivers

Cruces and Calle-Calle. Valdivia was the main access point by sea to the south of Chile and supplied ships making the hazardous journey between Spain and Lima, the viceregal capital which enjoyed a monopoly of trade with the metropolis for most of the colonial period. In the seventeenth century the Dutch had occupied Valdivia briefly. In response, the Spanish had built around Corral Bay an extensive system of forts, one of the biggest in the Americas.

After scouting the terrain in Valdivia, Garland and O'Higgins travelled to the Chilean city of Concepción in the spring of 1764. A devastating earthquake and tsunami had reduced the city to ruins in 1751. It was Garland and O'Higgins who decided where the new city would be built.

Garland threw himself wholeheartedly into the task of rebuilding Valdivia's defences, perhaps to forget the heartbreak of losing his fiancée to another man. In Santiago he had become engaged to María Alcalde y Ribera, the 21-year-old daughter of a wealthy Santiago noble. As a foreigner, he required a licence to marry; but by the time this was granted the young woman had fallen for another. Garland worked side by side with O'Higgins to carry on the work begun by the talented Catalan engineer José Antonio Birt, who had to resign following a horse-riding accident.

The Irishmen's plans for the new system of fortifications at Valdivia were ambitious and expensive. The budget for the construction of four forts was 357,000 pesos, and they estimated that they would need 500 labourers. To supply the bricks required for the construction of the new fortifications, Garland built two factories on an island opposite Valdivia. The factory workers worked day and night to keep the furnaces going, and by the beginning of 1767 Garland had 220,000 bricks with which to start building. He drew elaborate maps and plans of the project, many of which survive in the Spanish archives. He himself bore the cost of the drawing materials, the paper, brushes and inks, which left him frequently without money.

In 1768 Guill appointed Garland as political and military governor of Valdivia, noting that he had 'proved to me on several occasions his love of royal service, his disinterest and his Christian conduct.'[4] Despite this 'love of royal service' Garland was unhappy in Valdivia. It was a remote place, with few luxuries and constantly under threat from the Mapuche. His sense of isolation must have increased when O'Higgins returned to Spain in 1766. Garland was finally relieved in March 1775, but he was not to see Spain again.

Having sailed up the Pacific coast to present-day Panama, he contracted typhus in Portobello and died on board the schooner *Doña Marina* a few days out to sea. In his will he bequeathed 9,000 pesos to the poor widows and orphans of Valdivia.[5] He also left a rich architectural and engineering legacy in southern Chile.

O'Higgins had cited ill health in his petition to be allowed return to Europe in 1766, but it is likely that he wished to lever his achievements in Chile into a new position. To do so, while idling at court he had written the *Descripción del Reyno de Chile* in 1767, in which he outlined his ideas on how best to pacify the Mapuche and to maximise revenue for the Spanish crown. His thoughts on the former were based on his experience of having attended the *parlamento* of Mapuche *caciques* at Nacimiento in 1764.

O'Higgins presented a map of Chile to complement his report (see Plate 5), which he had drawn himself, based on earlier maps. The map, extending from Copiapó to the archipelago of Chiloé, was primitive, but he knew exactly the type of information that would interest the officials at court: the rivers and the position of mercury, gold and copper mines. Splashes of red ink marked volcanoes. Realising that the crown wished to establish the whereabouts of Jesuit property in South America – as the king was in the middle of expropriating the order's possessions throughout the Spanish Empire – O'Higgins wrote in the top left-hand corner of his map: 'Nota bene, the letter "R" marks the missions and possessions which belong to the regulars of the Company [of Jesus] in Chile.'[6] In the region directly south of Santiago, between the Rivers Maipo and Rapel, he wrote: 'All of this territory is very well populated by very industrious and hard-working Spaniards and Mestizos.'[7] He differentiated the indigenous tribes and the areas of southern Chile in which they lived.

O'Higgins turned to Richard Wall to get a hearing at court. Though no longer serving as secretary of state, Wall still had influence, which he used to help his fellow-Irishman. Wall and O'Higgins had very different temperaments. It would be unfair to say that Wall had arrived at the pinnacle of government by accident; but, enjoying the benefit of powerful connections in the Jacobite aristocracy, he had not the steely determination of the self-made O'Higgins. Unlike the austere, unbending O'Higgins, Wall relished the social, sensual and intellectual opportunities afforded him by his position, first as an esteemed diplomat and then as the king's prime minister.

O'Higgins wore his ambition less lightly than Wall, and the obstacles he faced were far greater. Whereas Wall's post-army career suffered only brief setbacks as he glided effortlessly through Europe's courts and salons, opera houses and casinos, O'Higgins grimly crisscrossed the Atlantic and the Andes, gambling everything but always firmly convinced of his own merits. Wall was the ultimate insider – as far as that was possible for a foreigner – gracious and debonair; O'Higgins was the ruthless outsider forcing his way in. But Wall and O'Higgins shared a bond: their Irish origins. It was through Wall that O'Higgins was able to get a petition to the minister for the Indies, Julián de Arriaga, asking for a position as an administrative official in the frontier country of southern Chile. O'Higgins's gamble did not pay off: Arriaga turned down his request.

O'Higgins was undaunted and returned to Santiago in 1769, offering his services to the interim governor, Juan de Balmaseda. Hostilities had recommenced between royalist forces and the indigenous tribes in the south of Chile, and Balmaseda needed tough men to lead the campaign. Now close to 50, but with undimmed energy, O'Higgins embarked on a new career, that of a soldier. Commissioned as captain in a regiment of dragoons, he was ordered south to help lead the campaign against the Mapuche.

O'Higgins owed his subsequent starry rise through the royal administration to his exploits as a soldier in southern Chile. During one engagement he received a serious head injury. Within four short years he had been promoted a *maestro de campo*, or field-marshal, a rank in the Spanish army just below that of the powerful captain-general. The continuing unrest in the south of Chile was a blessing for his career.

The fact that a foreigner was rising so rapidly through the ranks caused fierce resentment among O'Higgins's peers. The extent of this frustration at the fact that countless Irish soldiers and engineers, such as Garland, O'Higgins and the Irish-Spaniard Antonio O'Brien, were being employed in influential positions is captured in a document in the national archives in Santiago that sums up O'Higgins's career between 1769 and 1777: 'It was believed then in Chile that every foreigner was a distinguished mathematician or an excellent engineer and this requirement was what facilitated O'Higgins's entry into the militia.'[8] The author of the document mentions that O'Higgins had been ordered to construct a fort at Antuco but had instead sought a confrontation with the Mapuche and laments the fact that the Irishman was promoted to lead a cavalry company on the Chilean frontier despite the fact that it was prohibited to give this highly sensitive position to a foreigner.[9]

When not putting down rebellions on the frontier, O'Higgins was working on a project that had long been close to his heart. In 1765 he had drawn on his own experiences – he had twice crossed the cordillera in the harshest conditions – to write a report about the viability of building refuges, called *casuchos*, in the Andes between Santiago and Mendoza, crucial for communications between Santiago and Buenos Aires during the winter months. His recommendations had been accepted and the work had been carried out. However, by 1771 these *casuchos* had fallen into disrepair. O'Higgins was given the task of repairing the existing *casuchos* and building new ones. His actions on the frontier – he was regarded as an expert on the Mapuche – had earned him the esteem of his superiors, not least the governor of Chile, Francisco Javier Morales, who granted him a six-month leave to travel to Lima.

Peru had been the jewel in the Spanish imperial crown since the time of Pizarro; and Lima, the seat of the viceroy of Peru, the highest royal official in South America, was known as the *Ciudad de los Reyes*, the City of the Kings. It was the centre of the crown's governmental machinery on the continent. There were about 40,000 *limeños* (residents of Lima) when O'Higgins arrived, making it one of the most populated cities on the continent. The tiny Spanish elite at the top of the social pyramid included the viceroy, the judges or members of the Lima *audiencia*, the highest court on the continent, and the treasury officials who oversaw the collection of revenue. Beneath this small group, which relied upon the favour of the Spanish crown, were the *criollo* aristocracy, who made their living from land ownership and trade. Through Lima's port of Callao went the silver from the mines in Bolivia on its way to Spain and, passing the other way, the luxury goods from Europe.

By the 1770s, however, Lima's importance had diminished and economic power was moving north and west across the continent. The Viceroyalty of New Granada, encompassing present-day Colombia, Ecuador, Venezuela and Panama, had been created in 1717, and ports such as Caracas, Buenos Aires and Montevideo were benefiting from the introduction of less restrictive trade rules. In recognition of the growing economic power of the south-western regions of the continent, the Viceroyalty of the River Plate, roughly comprising the present-day countries of Argentina, Uruguay, Paraguay and Bolivia, was created in 1776, with its capital at Buenos Aires.

Despite Lima's decline, the *limeños* carried on as if they lived at the centre of the universe. The streets were full of rich traders doing business, imperious royal officials riding through the streets in gilded carriages, and hungry pedlars, hustlers and beggars who scraped and scrabbled as best they could for a couple of pesos. Andean villagers flocked to the city, escaping famine and drought and trying to get by from the sale of textiles and foodstuffs. The population was made up of the *peninsulares,* the Spanish-born high officials; the American-born *criollos* of Spanish descent; the indigenous peoples, known to the Spanish as *indios*; the descendants of African slaves; and those of mixed race, such as *mestizos, mulattos* and *zambos.*

In 1773 O'Higgins arrived at the glittering court of the viceroy of Peru, Manuel de Amat, a native of Barcelona, bringing with him a warm recommendation from the Chilean governor, Morales. Amat had become a wealthy man and lived in opulence in Lima's viceregal palace, to which society came bowing and shuffling. His lover was a young actor named Micaela Villegas, who was known to the wider populace as La Perricholi. The nickname derived from her frequent rows with Amat, who, in fits of rage, would call her, in his Catalan accent, a *perra chola,* or Peruvian bitch, which to Peruvian ears sounded like Perricholi. In their more understanding moments Amat would address her as Miquita and promise to erect sumptuous buildings in her honour.

O'Higgins spent three months in Peru, apprising the viceroy of his work in Chile during long conversations, visiting the theatre and the opera, and attending bullfights at the Plaza de Acho, the most famous bullring in Lima. By the time he returned to Chile he had been promoted lieutenant-colonel (second in command) of the corps of dragoons on the Mapuche frontier. He was now a powerful man with connections at the viceregal court in Lima.

O'Higgins was a shrewd and intelligent politician. He worked to establish himself as a go-between with the royal authorities and the Mapuche, putting himself forward as an authority on all matters relating to the indigenous peoples of the south. He was the viceroy's most useful source of information when it came to learning more about the southern part of Chile. He convinced the Mapuche that they should send ambassadors to Santiago to treat with the new governor, Agustín de Jáuregui. He also prepared a report on the defensive installations in the south of Chile that was the basis for improvements in the 1770s.[10]

During his expeditions through the south of Chile, O'Higgins would stay at the home of Simón Riquelme, a local landowner, and his wife, María Mercedes de la Meza, in the town of San Bartolomé de Chillán. Their daughter Isabel was only 12 or 13 when Higgins first met her. The stout, red-faced Irish officer was in his mid-fifties, and his career was finally taking off. Over the next five years, as he passed through the town on his frequent journeys south to the frontierlands, Isabel began to fall in love. O'Higgins seems to have made some form of marriage proposal, and Isabel agreed to go to bed with him. When the 18-year-old Isabel gave birth to a son in August 1778 the Irishman reneged on his promise. There was a 40-year gap between the lovers' ages, and O'Higgins was desperate to prevent any scandal that might damage his career. He also ordered that the baby be taken immediately from the young mother and raised by foster-parents. This cold, calculating act was to have important repercussions for Chile's future.

In 1786 the new viceroy of Peru, Teodoro de Croix, appointed O'Higgins governor of Concepción, one of two new administrative provinces in Chile, the other being Santiago. O'Higgins had found his place in society. 'He was of medium height and fat, had a narrow and coarse face and brown eyes of a harsh and penetrating expression, to which were added a stubborn expression and very thick eyebrows,' according to one of his biographers, Jaime Eyzaguirre.[11] Because of his red face and his bushy eyebrows the local people gave him the nickname of *'el camarón'*, 'the shrimp'.[12] More respectfully, the Spanish crown had awarded him the title of Baron of Ballenar. In 1788, in further recognition of his service, the king appointed O'Higgins the new governor of Chile. Firework displays and a great ball were held in his honour in Santiago.

Owing to the frequent destructive earthquakes that reduced its buildings to rubble, Santiago was a city in a state of constant transformation. Low, lime-washed adobe houses lined the streets, which ran perfectly from north to south and from east to west. In the western part of the city the small hill of Santa Lucía – known in pre-Columbian times as Huelén – protected the *santiaguinos* from the freezing winds that blew down from the sentinel-like Andes, visible in the distance to the east. The River Mapocho flowed through the south-western corner of the city. The centre of Santiago was the Plaza

Mayor or Great Square. The governor's palace, the *audiencia*, the treasury, the town hall and the prison ran along the northern side; the cathedral dominated the western side.

The plump, no-nonsense Irish governor plunged enthusiastically into his new role. He introduced important measures in Santiago relating to public health, infrastructure and crime. There were new rules governing the keeping of animals in the city. Pigs were no longer allowed to roam free but had to be kept indoors or in corrals, and dogs had to be tied up. Citizens were no longer allowed to wash their clothes in the local water sources and were ordered not to throw their rubbish or dead animals into the rivers. Clothes that belonged to those who had died of infectious diseases had to be destroyed. There were new building regulations. Construction had to be licensed by the authorities to ensure the safety and well-ordered development of the city. To prevent street crime it was forbidden to loiter near corners, doors, walls or the entrances to alleys. The new governor forbade the carrying of arms, including pistols, daggers, knives and swords or any other type of sharp instrument; privileged citizens were exempt. The penalty for contravening this law was four months in prison; there was a year-long sentence for those convicted of a second offence; and those convicted a third time faced two years' exile and 200 lashes, to be administered in the street or at the foot of a gallows with the offending instrument tied to their neck.

Tramps and 'bad-living people' were ordered to leave the city, and the unemployed were ordered to work on public schemes or sign up for the militia for six years. Those who sheltered the idle and the lazy faced fines of 30 pesos and six months in jail. Beggars were licensed by the Church and the municipal authority; those found without the requisite documents were treated as vagabonds and given 50 lashes. O'Higgins was committed to rooting out dissent and promised harsh penalties for those found 'plotting or gossiping' in public or in secret against the king or his royal officials.[13]

One of O'Higgins's most significant accomplishments was his abolition in 1789 of the *encomienda*, the system of forced labour for the Mapuche introduced by the Spanish in the early days of the conquest.[14] But the Bourbon reforms were as much about power and control as they were about modernising the colonies. Santiago was a deeply conservative, class-divided society, and the Catholic Church was the supreme arbiter in questions of public morality. O'Higgins was a cold, humourless man, with a strong puritanical streak, who was more than happy to implement draconian punishments for moral transgressors.

Singing or reciting 'indecent, satirical or bad-rhyming verse' in public places was forbidden, as were 'provocative dances'. A curfew banned citizens from walking in the streets and prohibited bars and taverns from opening after 9 o'clock in the winter and 10 in the summer; anyone found to be indulging in 'dances, singing or other noisy activities' after these hours could find themselves in prison for eight days. Wearing outfits that 'did not correspond to one's status, sex or position' could also result in harsh penalties. Nobles could face a fine of 50 pesos; for 'plebeians' the punishment was six months in jail. Gambling and drunkenness were also punished. Men found with women in public places after the curfew could look forward to 30 days in prison; the women were sent to the Casa de Recogidas, a type of prison for fallen women (not unlike the Magdalene asylums of a later era in Ireland). Guards patrolled the streets at night to enforce this strict moral code.

There was a different rule for the elite. The authorities were not to interfere with 'honourable persons, well known and in no way suspicious,' or those who had gone out with 'rational and prudent, or diligent, honest or necessary motives.' There were punitive measures for adulterers. Married men 'found in places other than their residences, must return to live at the home of their respective wives, with the warning that if, after thirty days, they have not done so, they will be arrested and remanded in custody, or escorted to the coast,' from where they would be deported.[15]

During his period of office O'Higgins wrote detailed reports on how to improve the Chilean economy, recommending the cultivation of rice and cotton and the development of mining. In relation to the cotton industry, he suggested using the expertise of Irish women immigrants to teach Chilean children how to work the material properly.[16]

As governor of Chile, O'Higgins helped the careers of several Irish soldiers. At the outbreak of the conflict with revolutionary France in 1793 he not only donated part of his salary to the war effort[17] but paid for the maintenance of four nephews for the duration of the war. Patrick O'Higgins, a *subteniente*, and Peter O'Higgins, a cadet, were serving in the Hibernia Regiment, while Charles and Thomas O'Higgins, both cadets, were serving in the Irlanda.[18] O'Higgins later requested that Thomas be transferred from the Irlanda to the Regiment of Dragoons of the Frontier in Chile. Ambrose

O'Higgins had created this unit especially for the defence of the southern part of the country and wished to see his name carried forward in the unit's officer list.[19]

In 1794 O'Higgins successfully petitioned the Spanish court to give his close confidant Thomas Delphin, who was a colonel in a cavalry regiment in the militia in the south of Chile, the rank of lieutenant-colonel in the Spanish army.

There was perhaps a less severe side to the bullish Irishman. According to friends, including Delphin and the lawyer Juan Martínez de Rozas, who was to become an important figure in Chile's independence struggle, O'Higgins would talk animatedly about his son, Bernardo, and explain his reasoning for sending him to Europe.[20] Delphin later testified that O'Higgins had felt deeply the injury he had done to Isabel Riquelme.[21]

In 1796 O'Higgins was created Marquis of Osorno. The award of a title by the Spanish crown was dependent on proof of noble blood, and this was the reason why he began calling himself O'Higgins instead of Higgins. Of even more significance, on 16 September 1795, the king appointed O'Higgins viceroy of Peru, the highest royal office in Spanish America. The young Irish clerk who had left the family farm in County Meath for a job in a Cádiz counting-house now held the most powerful position in the Spanish colonial administration. He also became an extremely wealthy man, drawing an annual salary of 70,500 pesos.

For the next five years, until his resignation in 1800, O'Higgins worked to strengthen the position of the Spanish crown in South America, rebuilding coastal defences and collaborating with the Inquisition in suppressing the circulation of seditious newspapers.[22]

O'Higgins gave important jobs to members of his family, trusting them to carry on the important work of maintaining the viceroyalty's defensive strength. In 1796 he entrusted his nephew Thomas O'Higgins with the task of inspecting the garrison on the archipelago of Chiloé in the south of Chile and establishing the best route for a new road between the main island and the newly settled city of Osorno. He ordered his nephew to visit Valdivia and the 'principal Chiefs of the Indians and confirm them in the ideas of peace and fidelity which the Viceroy himself desires from them' and to offer the Mapuche 'special protection if they continued in a good disposition.'[23]

Thomas O'Higgins embarked from Callao on board the brig *Limeño* on 12 September 1796, bound for Valparaíso and Santiago. He then travelled south by sea towards Valdivia and Osorno. He spent eight months in the south of Chile, inspecting militias, examining the defensive and infrastructural requirements of the region and meeting the *caciques*. During his mission O'Higgins received word that Spain was at war with Britain. In Valdivia he ordered an increase in the number of artillerymen.

Thomas O'Higgins presented his report to his uncle in Lima on his return eight months later. It contained important observations on the political, economic and military situation in southern Chile for the prosecution of the war with England. He also wrote to the king's prime minister, Manuel Godoy, informing him of the peaceful relations between the settlers and the Mapuche.[24] The viceroy was extremely pleased with his nephew's work and sent him to Spain to report in person to the court, given that 'one could not trust pen or paper in the present circumstances of war.'[25] O'Higgins also recommended his nephew's promotion to lieutenant-colonel. However, the promotion was refused, on the grounds that O'Higgins had served only 11 years in the army.[26]

John Mackenna was another Irishman who benefited from O'Higgins's largesse. Born in 1771 in Castleshane, County Monaghan, to William Mackenna and Leonora O'Reilly, Mackenna was the nephew of Count Alexander O'Reilly, into whose care he had been placed as a boy. In 1791, while serving in Spain under the orders of his uncle, Mackenna had conceived a plan to create an elite Irish-Spanish Legion within the Spanish army to fight revolutionary France. Mackenna's idea was to amalgamate the three existing Irish regiments, the Irlanda, Hibernia and Ultonia, with three of the best remaining regiments in the Spanish army. The resulting force of some 50,000 men would have been led exclusively by veteran Irish officers. The septuagenarian O'Reilly had looked with favour on Mackenna's proposal but had turned it down on the grounds that the Spanish government would not accept it.[27]

Having served his apprenticeship in the Spanish army, Mackenna travelled to South America in 1797, arriving in Lima with a recommendation for the Irish viceroy. O'Higgins was impressed with the young man from County Monaghan and appointed him governor of Osorno. Over the next decade Mackenna laboured to improve southern Chile's defensive fortifications, continuing the work of his compatriots Ambrose O'Higgins, Thomas O'Higgins and John Garland.

Those Irishmen who had benefited from Ambrose O'Higgins's help were eternally grateful. In 1811, on the eve of war between the Chilean patriots and Spain, John Mackenna, then the patriot governor of Valparaíso, wrote that Ambrose O'Higgins 'had a clarity of intelligence that simplified the most complicated and difficult problems.' He added that his life, 'faithfully related, would present one of the most beautiful moral lessons in the history of humanity. I know of none better to imprint upon the spirits of the young the inestimable value of inflexible honour, untiring work and unshakeable strength.'[28]

Why did Mackenna, a patriot who was preparing to break Chile's connection with Spain, hold the late viceroy in such esteem? After all, as viceroy of Peru, O'Higgins was a symbol of Spanish tyranny. It was perhaps because Mackenna could see that the stern, unyielding viceroy of Peru had turned his ambitions into reality, that it was possible for an Irishman from a humble background to succeed in the New World against the odds. In a letter to Bernardo O'Higgins, Mackenna wrote:

> Hannibal, Caesar, Maurice [of Nassau] and Frederick [the Great] had great advantages at the start of their lives in relation to their social situation, fortune and education. Your father, though descended from a noble family, the lords of Ballinary, found himself launched into a strange country at the start of his career, without money, without family and without friends. He died at 80 years of age in the office of Viceroy of Peru, having passed through every rank over the course of seventy years, from a humble employee of a Cádiz merchant house to the highest position that can be granted to a commoner, having achieved this not through corruption or favouritism but despite them and because of his outstanding talent as a soldier and a statesman.[29]

Ambrose O'Higgins had been an unflinching royalist but he was a source of inspiration to Mackenna because he represented what it was possible for an Irishman to achieve in the Spanish Empire. The most renowned names of the next generation of Irish emigrants to Spain and its colonies would earn their fame by destroying the very foundations of that empire.

Chapter 5

SPAIN UNDER SIEGE

In the months straddling the end of 1807 and the beginning of 1808, tens of thousands of battle-hardened French soldiers began flooding through the icy passes of the Pyrenees onto the plains of northern Spain. To enforce the continental blockade of British trade, the French emperor, Napoleon Bonaparte, had sent General Jean-Andoche Junot to invade Portugal, Britain's oldest ally. The Spanish government had agreed to allow French troops cross its territory on their way to Portugal, having negotiated a treaty with Napoleon under which Spain would receive a third of Portuguese territory.

In the spring of 1808, however, as the frost receded on the Castilian plain and the snows melted on the ridges, the French troops who had been fanning out across northern Spain seized Pamplona, Figueras, Barcelona and San Sebastián. Napoleon had shown his hand; the French invasion of Spain had begun.

The Spanish court was in panic. Though Charles IV shared his late father's passion for hunting, the comparisons stopped there. Charles III had been a reforming, energetic monarch; his son was an ineffectual leader, widely regarded as feeble-minded and more interested in leisurely pursuits than in the business of government. The real powers behind the throne were Queen María Luisa and her lover, Manuel Godoy, the former royal bodyguard who had risen to become the prime minister.

Lord Holland summed up the dysfunctional family dynamic of the Spanish Bourbons in his *Foreign Reminiscences*, recalling that Charles IV had often remarked to his father, the then king, Charles III, about how lucky princes were to be 'exempt from the lot to which too many husbands were exposed; first, because their wives were more strictly educated than private women; and, secondly, because if viciously inclined, they could seldom find any royal personages with whom they could indulge such evil propensities.' To which the old man would reproach his son for his stupidity: 'Carlos,

Carlos, what a fool you are!' or employ one of his favourite maxims: 'Yes, all of them are whores.'[1]

To make matters worse for the family, Charles IV and María Luisa's son Ferdinand, the present heir to the throne, was an impetuous, cruel young man who was fiercely resentful of his mother's lover, Godoy, whom he believed was scheming to seize the crown for himself.

In March 1808, with French troops occupying the northern part of the country, the royal household fled south from Madrid. On 17 March Ferdinand's supporters organised an uprising against the king and queen and the unpopular Godoy, which became known as the *motín,* or mutiny, of Aranjuez, the site of the winter palace where the king and queen were staying. In a panic, Charles abdicated in favour of his son.

The arrival of Ferdinand VII on the throne was greeted with celebration. He was known to the people as *el deseado,* the desired one, because it was hoped that he would be able to tackle the problems that had afflicted Spain during the previous 20 years of misrule.

However, Charles immediately realised that he had made a mistake in abdicating and he desperately tried to reverse his decision. It was too late. In May 1808 Charles, María Luisa and Godoy were brought under French guard to the Château de Marracq in Bayonne. Napoleon also summoned Ferdinand to Bayonne. In a farcical encounter, the French emperor forced Ferdinand to return the Spanish crown to his father. He then ordered Charles to hand it over to himself. Now believing the Spanish crown to be in his gift, Napoleon bestowed it upon his own brother, Joseph Bonaparte.

Napoleon had taken advantage of the internecine conflict at the heart of the Madrid court to further his own dynastic ambitions in Europe, yet he had underestimated Spanish popular opposition to French rule. While there were those among the Spanish elite – the so-called *afrancesados* – who accepted their new masters, the wider population rose up against the French in the name of the dethroned Ferdinand VII. Throughout Spain, local councils, or juntas, operating independently of one another, organised resistance to the French. The people's rebellion and the terrible French reprisals that followed are hauntingly depicted in Goya's companion pieces *The Second of May, 1808* and *The Third of May, 1808* (see Plates 6 and 7), which are on display in the Prado in Madrid.

For most of the previous century Britain and Spain had been sworn enemies, but in July 1808, in the face of French aggression, they ceased hostilities and became allies. While the British landed an invasion force in Portugal under the command of the Dublin-born lieutenant-general Arthur Wellesley, the future Duke of Wellington, the regional juntas in Spain formed themselves into one council, which became known as the Supreme Central Junta, and succeeded in driving Joseph Bonaparte from Madrid.

In response, Napoleon invaded Spain at the end of 1808 and quickly re-established control of most of the country, including Madrid. The junta fled to Seville. Spain was now under French occupation, except for Andalusia. In January 1810, as the French drove into Andalusia, the Supreme Central Junta ordered the convocation of a *cortes* or representative assembly. The junta promptly dissolved itself, handing authority to a five-man regency council, which governed in the name of the imprisoned Ferdinand VII.

The convocation of the Cádiz Cortes, as it became known, was a revolutionary moment in the history of Spain and its empire, not least because it was the first time the metropolis had granted the right of representation to the colonies. The *cortes* were an institution that dated from the Middle Ages. Historically they had played an important role in safeguarding the rights of the citizens against arbitrary royal power, but by the eighteenth century they acted in a purely advisory capacity to the monarch and were rarely summoned. The assembly that met in Cádiz, which had become the last stronghold of opposition to the French, may be regarded as a forerunner of the modern representative institutions that are prevalent today in western democracies. Cádiz was the birthplace of Spanish liberal democracy.

On the morning of 24 September 1810 elected representatives from throughout the Spanish Empire met in the town hall – it had been turned into the Royal Palace of the Regency – on the Isla de León, the island connected to Cádiz by a sandbar and separated from the mainland by salt marshes. The deputies then walked down to the parish church for a special mass, celebrated by the Cardinal Archbishop of Toledo. After the reading of the gospel the Bishop of Ourense, Pedro de Quevedo y Quintano, who was also president of the five-man regency council, said a prayer exhorting God to look with favour on the efforts of the Cortes. He was followed by the secretary of state, Nicolás María de Sierra, who requested the deputies to swear a number of oaths.

> Do you swear loyalty to the holy, catholic, apostolic, Roman religion, without acknowledging any other in this realm? Do you swear to

maintain the integrity of the Spanish Nation, and do everything to free her from her wrongful oppressors? Do you swear to maintain our beloved Sovereign, Don Ferdinand VII, in his realms, and, failing this, his legitimate successors, and do all that is possible to rescue him from captivity and restore him to the throne? Do you swear to carry out faithfully and legitimately the responsibility that the Nation has placed on you, keeping the laws of Spain, except those that must be modified, altered or changed for the good of the nation?[2]

Having affirmed the oaths in unison, the representatives walked in pairs up the nave of the church to the altar, where they placed their hands on the gospel. Quevedo concluded the oath-taking ceremony by intoning: 'If you do this, God will reward you; if not, he will demand it of you.' The mass ended with the hymn *Veni Sancti Spiritus* and a *Te Deum*.

Far from being a revolutionary body, the regency council saw its role as preserving the status quo until the return of Ferdinand VII. The Cortes had other ideas.

The deputies then walked over to the Teatro Cómico, a recently built theatre that served as the Cortes's first meeting-place. On the stage was an empty throne, which represented Ferdinand's captivity, in front of which sat the members of the regency council. The diplomatic corps, senior army officers and 'ladies of first distinction' were placed around the sides of the auditorium. The higher floors were taken up by an 'immense', 'distinguished throng'. On the entrance of the deputies the crowd proclaimed repeatedly, 'Long live the Nation!'[3]

More than 70,000 French troops were besieging the Isla de León and Cádiz while the Cortes was deliberating. The big guns of the French artillery rained shells down upon the city for almost two years while the deputies wrestled with revolutionary legal and political concepts. The steady flow of British soldiers coursing through the city, both those awaiting deployment to the mainland or those recovering from their wounds, focused the deputies' minds. Out at sea, Britain's Royal Navy maintained a blockade of French-controlled ports along the adjacent coast. Almost all the deputies from the colonies had been unable to reach Spain in time for the opening session of the Cortes and were represented by substitutes. The only exception was the deputy representing Puerto Rico, a young man from an Irish family named Ramón Power y Giralt.

Ramón was the son of Joaquín Ramón Power, a Bilbao-born member of a wealthy Irish merchant family originally from County Waterford based in Cádiz. An agent for a slave-trading company, Joaquín Power had emigrated to Puerto Rico in his mid-forties, marrying a Puerto Rican woman, María Josefa Giralt. He had established a plantation on land granted to him by the Spanish crown – taking advantage of the crown's efforts to modernise agriculture in Puerto Rico – on which he grew cacao, sugar, tobacco, cotton, peppers and indigo, among other crops.[4]

There was a strong Irish planter community in Puerto Rico. With their contacts in Europe, their commercial and technological expertise, and the fact that new immigrants to Puerto Rico had to be white and Catholic, men like Joaquín Power and Thomas O'Daly – a military engineer from County Galway who had served in the Ultonia Regiment and later under the command of Alexander O'Reilly – had become extremely wealthy. But an attempted invasion of Puerto Rico by the British in 1797 had brought the Irish community to its knees. The invasion force had numbered 10,000 troops, carried on board a convoy of more than 60 ships, yet they had been unable to penetrate the island's superb defensive fortifications, which had been designed and built by the Irishmen Alexander O'Reilly and Thomas O'Daly, and had been repelled by the efforts of the Puerto Rican defenders.[5]

The successful defence of the island had given the *criollo* elite a new sense of themselves as Puerto Ricans. However, in the aftermath of the attempted invasion the Spanish governor, Ramón de Castro, had ordered the surveillance of foreigners and issued expulsion orders, directed for the most part against the Irish planter community, accusing them of treachery and being in communication with the British. Among those who were given eight days to leave the island were Jaime Quinlan, Jaime O'Daly, Miguel Conway, Juan Nagle, Miguel Kirwan, Patricio Kirwan, Felipe Doran, Patricio Fitzpatrick and Antonio Skerret. The Irish had eventually proved their innocence, but not before suffering losses and significant hardship in prison.[6]

Ramón Power was the second of six children. Like many boys born into Irish merchant families in the Spanish Atlantic world, he was destined from an early age for service in the armed forces, entering the naval school in El Ferrol in 1792. He served as a naval officer for the next two decades, rising to the rank of captain. On his return to Puerto Rico in 1801 to attend to family business after his father's death, he was given command of a ship carrying post between the island and the Venezuelan mainland. Upon the convocation of the Cádiz Cortes, the island's pre-eminent families elected him as their representative.

On 25 September 1810, the second day of the opening session, Power was elected first vice-president of the Cortes. Along with the fact that he was the only elected representative from the colonies who had reached Spain for the opening session (the other colonies were represented by substitutes), his position meant that he was the unofficial spokesman of the American deputies. He used his role not only to advance the interests of his native island, and especially the Puerto Rican merchant class, but also to redefine the relationship between Spain and its colonies.

The deputies who attended the Cádiz Cortes were split between liberals, influenced by Enlightenment ideas, who wished to introduce reforms abolishing privilege and despotism, and conservatives, who regarded the assembly as an interim solution until Ferdinand could be restored to the throne. The Catholic priests Santiago Key Muñoz,[7] representing Tenerife, and Juan Bernardo O'Gavan, representing Cuba, were among the notable conservative deputies who attended the Cortes. Both were of Irish ancestry. Key's paternal grandfather, Diego Key, or James Key, was from County Kilkenny. The surname Key may have derived from Kelly or Keogh.

Like Power, Key was a vociferous defender of the interests of the people who had elected him, the islanders of Tenerife, who showered him with honours in thanks for his efforts.[8] He demanded an episcopal see for Tenerife, clashed with his fellow-deputies from the Canary Islands over the fruits of government largesse and was a vigorous defender of Church privilege in the face of state encroachment. In November 1812 he reminded the Cortes that the new constitution was based on the 'profession, defence and conservation of the Catholic religion; anyone who offended the religion, its rites, its priests or its practices ... was in violation of the Constitution and its enemy, and was a bad citizen and a bad Spaniard ... did not deserve public confidence nor a public position.'[9] In January 1813 he voted against the abolition of the Inquisition. He was less inflexible when it came to pardoning those accused of having collaborated with the French.[10] O'Gavan represented the province of Santiago in Cuba and argued for greater investment in the island and freedom of trade.

The Cortes was further divided between the peninsular and American deputies. The American deputies themselves were split between liberals and conservatives, with individual regions and socio-economic groups having different interests. Power represented the wealthy plantation owners in Puerto Rico, many of them Irish or of Irish extraction, who wished to see Spain's monopolistic practices in the colonies reformed. He demanded investment for the island, including the foundation of universities and hospitals, the right to free trade, the appointment of *criollos* to government posts, freedom of the press, and the abolition of sales taxes, customs duties, tithes and state monopolies. All these demands were contained in specific instructions given to Power by the five Puerto Rico *cabildos,* or municipal councils, that he was representing in Cádiz.

The Cortes granted Power's proposal to separate the posts of military governor and *intendente,* or chief tax collector, in Puerto Rico. Previously the governor, Salvador Meléndez, exercised both functions. The Cortes also approved measures for improving port facilities on the island, an important concession for Puerto Rico's commercial interests, and gave permission for the creation of an economic society of friends, similar to those that had been proposed by Bernard Ward and that had emerged in peninsular Spain in the eighteenth century. These reforms became known as the *ley Power* (Power's law).

Power not only won economic reforms for his region but in his speeches to the Cortes, he also articulated a growing sense of nationhood among the American *criollos*. He envisaged a Puerto Rico free to develop and expand commercially but within the Two Spains (as Peninsular and American Spain were then known). He and his fellow-American deputies, as Marie-Laure Rieu-Millan has written, 'represented the white *criollo* society from which they came, eager for reform, but also anxious about immediate political independence.'[11]

These anxieties arose from the emergence in 1810 of independence movements in Caracas, Buenos Aires and Mexico. Unlike the more radical *criollos* who were to challenge the very authority of the crown, Power and the other liberal deputies from America wished to achieve economic and political freedoms for their regions while professing loyalty to the Spanish crown. 'The inhabitants of Puerto Rico are also Spanish,' Power wrote in August 1810, 'they have the same rights as the rest, and finding themselves separated from Caracas by a sea of 200 leagues [700 miles], they are equal to anyone in terms of their loyalty and patriotism.'[12] In February 1811, in a speech to the Cortes, he attacked a crackdown on political undesirables in Puerto Rico, which had been authorised by the regency council in response to the growing unrest in Caracas, where a recently formed junta had proclaimed its independence.

> The Regency Council, in issuing this order, degrades the majesty of sovereignty, confusing it with the most oppressive despotism; and the circumstances in which it has taken this measure are the least opportune in respect of Puerto Rico, and the least politic to calm the troubled emotions of the American peoples, which must have been the end desired ... The island of Puerto Rico has sworn to adhere herself eternally to our cause; she has sworn subordination and respect to the authorities; but she does not wish nor should she wish to be a slave.[13]

Power's dogged efforts at Cádiz on behalf of his homeland and the American colonies in general ensured his legacy. However, he was not able to enjoy the approbation of the Puerto Ricans in his lifetime, dying in Cádiz, aged 37, during an outbreak of yellow fever in June 1813.

The culmination of the Cortes's work was the 1812 constitution, which influenced political thought throughout Latin America. While never fully enacted in Spain, it contained many of the liberal precepts that were to inform the political ideas and future written constitutions in the Americas, including the 1824 constitution of Mexico. The 1812 constitution established national sovereignty, universal male suffrage and freedom of the press. These new ideas were disseminated in the pages of a thriving newspaper industry in Spain and beyond, including one published in London by a Spaniard of Irish extraction.

Chapter 6

THE PROPAGANDIST PRIEST

Political journalism in Spain was born out of the decision by the members of the Cádiz Cortes to abolish restrictions on the press. Consequently the debates between liberals and conservatives in the Cortes were reported with great interest not only in Spain but also abroad.

One of the most perceptive and interested observers of the Cortes was the Irish-Spaniard José María Blanco White. The White family had adopted the surname Blanco (*blanco* means white in Spanish) when they settled in Spain; José María adopted the double surname Blanco White when he was in England. From his exile in London this rather severe, impassioned, intolerant young man became not only one of the foremost propagandists for Spanish liberalism but also a fierce critic of Spanish rule in the American colonies. His fiery polemics in favour of American independence were to earn him the opprobrium of both Spanish conservatives and liberals. His biographer, Manuel Moreno Alonso, goes so far as to describe him as 'the "inventor" of Liberalism in Spain'[1] and says that 'one can say that until the Generation of '98, nobody raised in such a continual and obsessive manner what, afterwards, has been called "the subject of Spain".'[2]

Blanco White possessed the zeal of the convert. He was born in Seville on 11 July 1775 into an exaggeratedly pious Irish family in deeply Catholic southern Spain whose estates in Ireland had been expropriated in the Cromwellian era. His great-grandfather was living in County Waterford when he sent four of his five children abroad 'to escape the oppression of the penal laws.'[3] Blanco White's grandfather settled in Seville, where he inherited the substantial business of his merchant uncle, Philip Nangle. The connection with Ireland remained strong when Blanco White was growing up. His grandfather's 'love of his native land could not be impaired by his foreign residence,'[4] and English was spoken at home with 'an Irish pronunciation.'[5] Blanco White's own father had been sent back to Ireland as a child so that 'he might also cling to that country by early feelings of kindness.'[6]

When Blanco White was a child, the family business began to fail and the money that remained was 'just enough to save the family from such poverty as might have entirely changed their condition in the world.'[7] Blanco White's aunt married an Irishman named Thomas Cahill, who took over the running of the business. Their daughter, Blanco White's cousin, married another Irishman, by the name of Beck, one of the many Irish clerks employed by the Whites, who then took over the business in partnership with Blanco White's brother. The White family in Seville thus preserved their links to the ancestral homeland. Blanco White wrote that his family was 'a small Irish colony, whose members preserve the language and many of the habits and affections which its founder brought to Spain.'[8]

Blanco White was introduced to the family business at an early age, learning reading and writing from one of the Irish clerks. As a 12-year-old he was employed in the office copying correspondence, invoices, bills of exchange and bills of lading. When he declared to his parents that he wished to become a priest, they greeted the news with enthusiasm. Blanco White's father was a devout man who would spend hours in church. His son attributed his religiosity to his having spent his childhood in Ireland and wrote of his father that he 'combined in his person the two most powerful and genuine elements of a religionist – the unhesitating faith of persecuting Spain: the impassioned belief of persecuted Ireland.' On his father's death 'multitudes of people thronged the house to indulge a last view of the body,' such was his 'purity', ' benevolence', and 'angelic piety'.[9] Blanco White's mother, a member of the impoverished Spanish gentry, was equally religious.

His parents sent Blanco White to the Dominican College in Seville at the age of 14, but he was soon in trouble. Demonstrating the type of intellectual independence that would later lead him to fall out with his superiors in the Catholic Church, he got into an argument about Aristotelian logic with one of the Dominican friars. His exasperated mother removed him from the college and sent him instead to the University of Seville. Though he had already begun to show doubts about his chosen path, he did not stop studying for the priesthood. After his ordination in 1800 he continued to question Catholic doctrine and struggled to reconcile his beliefs. He later wrote:

> At length the moment arrived when, by the deliberate admission of the fact that the *Church had erred,* I came at once to the conclusion at which every sincere Roman Catholic, in similar circumstances, must arrive. I

concluded that Christianity could not be true. This inference was not properly my own. The Church of Rome had most assiduously prepared me to draw it.[10]

His conversion to liberalism – and English Protestantism – far from being Damascene, as he might have wished to paint it in later life, was gradual, founded upon a logical dismantling of the tenets that formed the basis of his education as a priest. Even before he was ordained, he had begun to think about how he might best escape the predicament of choosing to be a priest when he no longer believed in the Church.

In September 1808, in the middle of the tumultuous events that were shaking the political foundations of the country, a group of Madrid liberals published the first edition of a new journal, the *Semanario Patriótico* (Patriotic Weekly). According to Moreno Alonso, 'the *Semanario* was nothing less than the first Spanish publication in which political questions were debated continually and systematically in public.'[11] The Madrid lawyer and poet Manuel José Quintana was the driving force behind the journal. Quintana held a famous *tertulia* or salon at his residence in the city, which Blanco White, now an ordained Catholic priest, regularly attended. In December 1808 Quintana gave up the editorship to work exclusively for the Supreme Central Junta, and he appointed Blanco White and Isidore de Antillón the new editors. Blanco White and Antillón demanded in the pages of their weekly that the junta instigate reforms, and they defended those Enlightenment ideas, such as liberty and equality, that the conservative members of the Supreme Central Junta considered dangerous.

The government-in-exile in Seville was divided between the liberals, who wished to see the introduction of Enlightenment ideas, the replacement of royal absolutism with constitutional monarchy and the abolition of the Inquisition, and the absolutists, who wished to protect the Church's and landed aristocracy's traditional privileges. Blanco White found himself torn between competing ideas. He was opposed to revolutionary Bonapartism but unable to identify with the new sense of 'patriotism' that was coursing through the country.

> I am indeed ready to acknowledge that I never felt that kind of *patriotism*, which makes men blind to the faults of their own country, as well as to their own. Spain, as a political body, miserably depressed by its

government and Church, ceased to be an object of admiration to me at a very early period of my life ... But I had that in my breast which would have made me readily sacrifice myself for THE PEOPLE among whom I grew up to manhood ...[12]

In his autobiography, written from both a political and a temporal distance, Blanco White summed up how he had responded to the French invasion.

> I never for a moment doubted the *justice* of the Spanish cause, or justified the manner in which Napoleon endeavoured to bring about the change of the Spanish dynasty. I only questioned the *expediency* of a popular rising. But since that rising had actually taken place I would have defended the cause of Spain against France at all risks.[13]

Blanco White and Antillón were forced to publish the *Semanario* under the watchful eye of the Supreme Central Junta; in an instance of poacher-turned-gamekeeper, Quintana had now become the government censor. The Supreme Central Junta's opposition to the editors' liberal ideas forced it to cease publication in the summer of 1809.

Gaspar Melchor de Jovellanos then offered Blanco White a position on the commission to organise the convocation of the Cortes. Jovellanos was a member of the Supreme Central Junta and one of the pre-eminent thinkers and statesmen in Enlightenment Spain. Despite his admiration for Jovellanos, Blanco White refused, not wishing to associate himself with the conservatism of the Supreme Central Junta. He did agree, however, to prepare a report on behalf of the University of Seville, which had been asked to give its opinion on the best way of convoking the Cortes.

To carry out his task, Blanco White requested that he be allowed access to books prohibited by the Tribunal of the Holy Office of the Inquisition. 'It is true that we had very little occasion for such books as we were likely to take out of their possession; but there was a kind of triumph in this recovery of books that were completely lost to the world,' he wrote.[14] The forbidden books were stored in one of the rooms of the Inquisitor's Palace in Seville. Blanco White sifted through the worm-eaten, dust-covered volumes that had been left to crumble into insignificance, emerging with some treasures, including two copies of Diderot's *Encyclopédie*, of which he wrote:

That work must have been frequently seized by the Tribunal: the floor was covered with volumes of its various dictionaries tumbled in distracting confusion. I now forget what other works I was able to save from the worms, which, with a devouring power, of which people who have not seen their ravages in hot climates can form no conception, had reduced a great number of volumes to fragments.[15]

In 1810, depressed at the course of events in his homeland, Blanco White finally left Spain – and the Catholic priesthood. 'The name of *Priest* irritated and depressed me; and yet I could not wash off that odious mark, even if I had tried to do it with my blood.'[16] He was determined never to return.

His departure was a relief to his parents, who were convinced that he would fall under the sway of the Bonapartist party were he to remain in Spain. In fact he was a firm opponent of the French Revolution and statist terror in all its guises. However, such was the political chasm between parents and child that, before his departure for England, Blanco White's mother had begun avoiding him in case he dropped some heresy into the conversation that would require her to denounce him to the Inquisition. About his self-imposed exile he wrote:

> The desire to leave [Spain] had, for many years, been working in my inmost soul, and so identified had it become with my whole being that there hardly was a thought, a feeling, into which the wish of expatriation had not insinuated itself: but before this moment, it acted in the character of despondency, and like a poisonous root, its multiplied fibres conveyed a sickening breath to every perception and thought.[17]

This inner turmoil was hidden behind an ascetic exterior. Those who met the recently arrived Blanco White in London might have been surprised to hear of his origins in southern Spain, perhaps less so if they discovered that he was of Irish extraction. He bore a pinched expression on a face that was long, narrow and pale, colouring pinkish at the nose. His demeanour was quietly fervent.

Blanco White embraced England, converted to Anglicanism and began studying the country's institutions, of which he became an ardent admirer. He began publishing a Spanish-language newspaper, *El Español*. For five years, between 1810 and 1814, he worked day and night, writing fiery denunciations of the political and religious situation in Spain, translating English newspaper articles and parliamentary debates in the House of Commons, a body for which he had much love, and poring over proofs in his flea-bitten lodgings in Duke Street, not far from Downing Street. 'My health was ruined to such a degree that life has ever since to me been a source of nearly unmixed suffering,' he wrote of that period.[18] Within the pages of *El Español* he criticised the twin tyrannies of the *ancien régime* and Bonapartism while also casting a cold eye on the formation of the Supreme Central Junta and the regency council, the proceedings of the Cortes and the drafting of the 1812 constitution. He also attacked the Inquisition, describing its abolition in 1813 as 'one of the most noble and glorious measures' adopted by the Cortes.[19]

The British government had an abiding interest in separating Spain from its colonies, and it used Blanco White and his newspaper to further this policy. On the recommendation of the British ambassador in Cádiz, Henry Wellesley (younger brother of the foreign secretary, Richard Wellesley, and of the commander-in-chief of the British army on the peninsula, Arthur Wellesley), the government made Blanco White a half-yearly payment of £125. Copies of *El Español* espousing the Anglo-Spanish alliance and Britain's liberal institutions were carried by British ships from England to besieged Cádiz. 'The [British] Government at home had received (I have reason to believe) frequent information of the good effects of the *Español* in directing public opinion,' he wrote in his memoirs, 'and removing the suspicions and prejudices which a numerous and active Anti-Anglican party was constantly endeavouring to keep up.'[20]

Blanco White was now a paid propagandist for the British government, though he denied any editorial interference: 'I formed and stated my views to the best of my knowledge, honestly intending to serve the cause of liberty and humanity, without giving way to any influence except that of superior knowledge and experience in politics.'[21]

In line with British interests, *El Español* was a firm supporter of independence for the American colonies, which earned Blanco White the enmity of the conservative members of the regency council and the Cortes. In 1810, in the pages of *El Español,* he welcomed the news that Caracas had proclaimed independence from Spain. Defending himself later from accusations that he was doing the bidding of the British government, he wrote:

> The honest joy which this event raised in me was greater than my readers can imagine: *honest*, indeed, it was; for my exultation proceeded from the most benevolent and disinterested sources, and my approbation of the step which the Hispano-Americans had taken, was grounded on principles of the truth of which I had no doubt. I had for many years lived in an habitual detestation of political despotism, and of its main prop, the Church ... My desire that mental freedom should spread over the world was neither limited nor qualified by political considerations. I knew that the Spanish Colonies had been cruelly wronged by the mother country, and ardently wished to see them legislating for themselves.[22]

There is no reason to doubt that Blanco White genuinely believed in Latin American independence, both for the reasons quoted above and because of his commitment to English liberalism. In Cádiz, however, both the regency council and members of the Cortes roundly attacked him as a traitor. They accused him of being in the pay of the British government and being fervidly anti-Catholic. Both accusations, of course, were true. 'The conviction that I had been engaged by the English Government for the purpose, as they imagined of taking possession of Cádiz and the Spanish Colonies, was almost universal in that town,' he wrote.[23]

South American independence meant open markets for British manufactures and cheap raw materials, at a time when Napoleon's continental blockade was hurting British industry. At the same time the British government was fearful of French influence over the new regimes, of the possible repercussions for Britain's own colonies, and of damage to the alliance with Spain. British policy was conducted through hidden channels. Encouraged by the Wellesleys, Blanco White disseminated pro-British propaganda both in Spain and among Spanish circles in London. The fact that he later received a pension of £250 from the British government tends to discredit his protestations that he was an independent operator.

When *El Español* ceased publication in 1814, Blanco White found himself at the forefront of the campaign to block Catholic Emancipation, which not only earned him the disdain of his Irish relations but also embarrassed his Whig friends, such as Lord Holland, whose son he tutored. His intense anti-clericalism meant that he was incapable of recognising the injustice of anti-Catholicism in Ireland.

On 3 June 1832 he travelled to Ireland for the first time, in the midst of a cholera epidemic. He had been invited to tutor the son of the newly appointed Anglican archbishop of Dublin, Richard Whately, a friend from Oxford, at his residence, Redesdale House, in Kilmacud, County Dublin. He was exceptionally nervous about his trip to Ireland – dreading 'the effects of my coming so near the *Cholera* and the *Priests*'[24] – and fell ill shortly before departing. He later wrote:

> Since the moment indeed when I accepted the kind invitation of the Whatelys, I have not ceased to consider Ireland as a place of danger to me. The idea that a mass of hatred is actually collected against me in this country of my forefathers is exceedingly painful to my mind. The contrast, therefore, between the love of my friends in England, and the virulence of my unknown enemies in Ireland, is always present to my feelings. *Tantum Religio potuit suadere malorum!** No sacrifices on my part can procure even a slight allowance of candour among people maddened by the mixed feelings of religious party, and political ambition! This conviction cuts me to the heart.[25]

Nevertheless Blanco White was impressed by the first sight of the Irish coast 'as it rose out of the waves brightened by the early sun of an unclouded morning.'[26] His welcome in Ireland was much warmer than he expected. Archbishop Whately and his wife greeted him affectionately. Redesdale House was a comfortable home with fine views of Dublin Bay and the Wicklow Mountains, and Blanco White would spend hours walking in the well-kept gardens.

His host was an eccentric figure. During his time as principal of St Alban's Hall, Oxford, Whately was known as the 'White Bear'. It was alleged that he trained his dogs to climb trees in order that they would jump down from the branches at his command to frighten undergraduates who were so bold as to walk with their female companions along the banks of the River Cherwell. He was a loner who preferred solitary walks in nature to the intrigues and politics of the city. He was passionate about mathematics, philosophy and education, writing several school textbooks and founding the chair of political economy at Trinity College, Dublin.[27]

---

* 'So much evil could religion induce' (a quotation from the Roman poet Lucretius, *De Rerum Natura*).

Blanco White arrived in Ireland at an interesting time. The Whigs had appointed Whately to Dublin in an effort to reform the Church of Ireland and support the introduction of the government's education plan, which proposed the establishment of a system of government-funded non-denominational national schools. Whately's arrival caused waves in Ireland's Anglican hierarchy. His fellow-bishops regarded him with contempt for his uncouth manners – he was prone to contorting his legs at the dinner table in such a way that guests might find his foot in their lap[28] – and for his brusque way of dealing with people, but more especially for the fact that he was the creature of the Whig government.

Despite his grave misgivings before leaving England, Blanco White was also taken with the Irish people. After dinner with a Mrs Latouche and her niece, Miss Boyle, he expressed himself 'very much pleased with this first specimen of Irish ladies in their own country. It would be difficult indeed to meet with more superior persons in any country.'[29]

But he was shocked by the virulence of the debate about religion in Ireland and the efforts of the Church of Ireland to prevent the government financing education for Catholics. He became depressed after hearing a preacher denounce the government for attempting to bring in a non-denominational form of primary education.

> Were it not for my attachment to the Whatelys, and for the hope that I may be of essential service in the education of their boy, who is growing very much attached to me, and requires a tutor who will teach him *for love*, not for money – I would quit this country – I would fly a second time from the Popery of Protestants, as I did from that of the Spanish Romanist.[30]

He added:

> Nothing can be more preposterous than the determination to compel the Government of Great Britain and Ireland, not to assist the poorer classes of Roman Catholics with *national* funds, unless they receive education according to the religious principles of the Established Clergy – unless they submit to learn reading and writing under (what they believe to be) a constant danger of seduction from their own religious principles.[31]

As far as Blanco White was concerned, this attitude on the part of Ireland's Protestant bishops was just another form of religious tyranny.

When he was not tutoring the Whatelys' son, he spent his time working on a book about the Spanish Inquisition. Despite his distress at what he regarded as the bigotry of the Church of Ireland, he came to enjoy his time in Ireland, believing that his arrival in the country had brought 'a probable improvement in my religious notions and feelings.'[32]

He moved into the Archbishop's Palace at St Stephen's Green for a period to better concentrate on his studies, and began to question his commitment to the Church of England. But after a while he was unable to reconcile his growing criticisms of the Established Church with the hospitality he was being shown by the archbishop.[33] After three years in Ireland, having rejected Trinitarianism, he returned to England in 1835, embracing Unitarianism. He died in Liverpool in 1841.

Blanco White's life had been full of paradoxes, perhaps arising from his complex sense of identity, not least the fact that he was a fierce defender of religious liberty in Spain while denying toleration to his Catholic relatives in Ireland. His very surname suggests, despite his self-imposed exile, an unwillingness to leave behind his Spanish roots while desperately trying to integrate himself in the culture of his adopted country.[34] He was one of the great liberal Spanish thinkers, who pungently criticised the Catholic Church's abuses and royal misgovernance. Towards the end of his life, during his three-year stay in Ireland, he came to see that by denying political and civil rights to Irish Catholics, the Established Church was engaging in the same tyranny from which he had escaped.

> A *national* religion which is not professed by the whole nation is a contradiction. A *national* religion which gives maintenance and precedence to the professor of certain dogmas, may be defended on the ground of *expediency* arising from peculiar circumstances. But a *national* religion which renders any number of members of the nation of a worse condition than others, if they do not profess it, is *established persecution*.[35]

Chapter 7

MERCHANTS, SAILORS, SOLDIERS, SPIES

When the Spanish first arrived in the Americas they created two administrative regions, the Viceroyalties of Peru and New Spain. The latter covered Mexico, central America and the present-day south and western United States; the former covered those parts of the South American continent that were not under the jurisdiction of the Portuguese.

The Viceroyalty of Peru was a vast territory, stretching from the Caribbean to Cape Horn, encompassing deserts, glaciers, freezing-cold mountain ranges, tropical jungles and desolate plains. On the Pacific coast, Lima was the capital of the Viceroyalty of Peru, whose rich merchants and royal officials had made their fortunes from the city's trade monopoly with Spain. On the other hand, the region around the River Plate estuary on the Atlantic coast was a backwater for much of the colonial period. This was perhaps a little surprising, given the relative proximity of Buenos Aires to the metropolis, compared with Lima. However, during the first couple of centuries after the conquest, the Spanish were interested only in the silver that flowed out of the Andean mines, especially the famous *cerro rico*, or rich mountain, at Potosí.[1] Indentured indigenous labourers and African slaves worked day and night, year after year, in the infernal depths, pulling ton after ton of the precious metal from the mountain's bowels. Mules then painstakingly hauled the great chests of silver through the rocky Andean passes to Lima's port, Callao, from where the bullion was shipped north along the Pacific coast to Panama City, where it was unloaded, brought overland in mule-driven carts across the narrow isthmus that connects North and Central America with South America, and loaded once more onto ships at Portobello, bound for Seville.

By the 1770s, however, the idea of wealth had changed. Whereas previously the Spanish monarchs had estimated the value of the colonies in pieces of eight, they now began to appreciate the economic and strategic importance of other parts of the empire, including Buenos Aires. It made much more sense to ship goods to and from the Atlantic coast of South America than to navigate around the treacherous southern seas off Cape Horn. At the same time the residents of Buenos Aires, known as *porteños*, had begun to exploit the natural resources of the hinterland.

The Argentine writer and historian Félix Luna described the city's early inhabitants as living 'like sailors shipwrecked between two great seas, the Pampas and the River Plate'.[2] They relied on smuggling goods through the port and cattle-hunting expeditions to the pampas, the never-ending grasslands that stretched out to the north, west and south of the city. During these expeditions, known as *vaquerías,* between 10 and 15 hardy souls – the first *gauchos,* much celebrated in Argentine culture – would spend weeks on the pampas gathering the wild herds of cattle that roamed the plains. Luna colourfully depicted their way of life and the primitive use to which they put the wild animals they had rounded up.

> When they found the unclaimed cattle, they would nick their shanks with the tip of a sickle-shaped rod and the beast would fall to the ground immobilised. The second step was to slit the throats of the hundreds of struggling beasts and skin them.
>
> The only part they took was the animals' hides, which were loaded onto huge wagons, taken to be tanned and then shipped abroad. That was the sum total of *Porteño* exports. The rest was all thrown away: the meat, the horns, the tallow ... One can picture the Pampas strewn with carcasses scavenged by wild dogs and rats, the plague of the countryside.[3]

By the eighteenth century, with the wild herds all but disappearing, the *porteños* had begun domesticating cattle, and the first ranches, or *estancias,* were born. It was the beginning of Argentina's meat-exporting industry.

In recognition of the region's new-found prosperity, the Spanish crown created the Viceroyalty of the River Plate in 1776, out of territory formerly belonging to the Viceroyalty of Peru, with Buenos Aires as its capital. The new administrative region comprised the present-day countries of Argentina, Uruguay, Paraguay and Bolivia. Two years later the crown allowed Buenos Aires to trade with Spanish and colonial ports. This inevitably led to resentment in Lima, which had previously enjoyed a monopoly.

Foreign-born merchants and agents flocked to Buenos Aires, taking advantage of these new commercial and professional opportunities. By the beginning of the nineteenth century there was already a small Irish community living in the city, including missionaries, soldiers in the pay of the Spanish crown, and merchants. In 1807 a census of foreigners was held. Among the Irish residents was James Egan, a 58-year-old blacksmith from Dublin, living in the house of Isidore Peña in the Calle San Juan. He had been in the city for six years, having arrived from the United States.[4]

Michael Gorman, a doctor born in Ennis, County Clare, was the viceroyalty's first chief medical inspector and among the city's most eminent residents. He had studied in France before arriving in Spain in the middle of the eighteenth century. He had worked in hospitals in Galicia and also participated in a diplomatic mission to London, where he had studied a new method of vaccination. He had later served as an army surgeon with the Hibernia Regiment of the Spanish army in north Africa. In 1776 he travelled to Buenos Aires as a surgeon with the first viceroy of the River Plate, Pedro Antonio de Cevallos.[5] Gorman helped modernise the practice of medicine in the Viceroyalty of the River Plate, supervising hospitals and assessing the fitness to practise of doctors and surgeons.

Cevallos's successor, Juan José de Vértiz, petitioned the Spanish court to have Gorman appointed *protomédico,* or chief medical inspector. But the tough-minded minister for the Indies, José de Gálvez, suspected that Gorman was a spy and refused to confirm his appointment. He cited the fact that Gorman was a British subject and also the confession of a former Jesuit priest by the name of Francisco Josef Marcano y Arismendi. According to Marcano, who was being held prisoner in Madrid on suspicion of being involved in the 1780 rebellion in Peru led by Tupac Amaru, Gorman was carrying out a secret correspondence with the British government.[6] The Spanish government later changed its mind and awarded him the chair of medicine in Buenos Aires.

Michael Gorman realised the commercial opportunities that were available to energetic young men in the River Plate and wrote to a relation, Thomas O'Gorman, urging him to come to Buenos Aires. The younger O'Gorman was born in Ennis in the 1760s. He had left Ireland for France as a young man because of religious persecution, according to the naturalisation papers he later submitted to the Spanish authorities.[7] He served as an officer in one of the French army's Irish units, Walsh's Regiment, before it was disbanded in the aftermath of the French Revolution. In 1792 he was living in

Mauritius, in the Indian Ocean, where he had married Marie-Anne Périchon de Vandeuil, the daughter of a French colonial official.

On receiving his relative's letter, and full of the possibilities that life in the Americas could offer, O'Gorman decided to make the long journey halfway across the world. He arrived in Montevideo with his wife, two small children and his in-laws in July 1797. He first decided to try his luck in Paraguay, where he hoped to establish a sugar and indigo plantation, using machinery and tools that he had brought with him from Mauritius.

O'Gorman had ambitious plans. He intended to import 600 African slaves to work the land and dreamt of persuading artisans and farmers from Ireland and east India to come to Paraguay. The Irish would introduce their methods of salting meat and making cheese and butter; meanwhile tanners, spinners, weavers and dyers from the Coromandel coast would work with 'the unique cotton from Paraguay, whose soil is exactly the same as that of eastern India.' All this economic activity, O'Gorman assured the Spanish authorities, 'would tip the balance of trade in favour of the Spanish crown in the European markets.'[8] He concluded:

> Aware of your worthy ideas regarding the development of His Majesty's domains, the petitioner dares to hope that you will not remain indifferent to the suggestions of an individual who offers to give of his experience, industry and fortune, with no greater cost to the State than the incorporation of his honourable family into the association of the King's vassals and the concession of some lands that until now have produced nothing more than thistles and brambles and fed wild beasts and vermin ...[9]

O'Gorman's enthusiasm was not enough, and he failed to convince the authorities of the benefits of his scheme. So he turned to commerce. It is likely that he began his new career smuggling goods in and out of Buenos Aires before gradually becoming a legitimate member of the *porteño* business community. The vagaries of war were to help Thomas O'Gorman make his fortune.

Britain and Spain had been engaged in hostilities for most of the period between 1796 and 1808. The underlying issue was Britain's determination to open up Spain's American colonies to British manufactures; Bourbon Spain was equally determined to pull the colonies closer to the metropolis.

Incapable of defending its colonies, and with its colonial revenue slowing to a dribble, Spain was forced to liberalise its trading regime with South America, which inevitably resulted in rival powers, chiefly Britain, gaining increased access to the continent's markets. The constant wars were also taking a heavy toll on the customs and merchant houses in Buenos Aires. To make matters worse, merchant ships were being pressed into service against Britain's Royal Navy, bankrupting commercial houses in Spain and South America. Out of necessity, the Spanish crown loosened trade restrictions, allowing neutral ships access to Spain's colonial ports.

Thomas O'Gorman took full advantage, proposing to the authorities that he arrange for ships registered in the United States to import and export goods between Buenos Aires, Philadelphia and Hamburg.[10] It was at this moment that the *criollo* merchant classes, who had seen their ambition thwarted by the monopolistic practices of the Spanish and who were fired by revolutionary political concepts of liberty emerging from North America and Europe, found common cause with British commercial interests. During the next couple of years the already hazy borders between commerce, diplomacy and espionage disappeared in Buenos Aires.

As the debt-ridden O'Gorman was trying to enter the ranks of the wealthy foreign merchant community on the strength of the Spanish crown's decision to liberalise colonial trade, his French wife was causing a stir among the upper echelons of Buenos Aires society. Marie-Anne (or Ana, as she was known in Spanish) O'Gorman was a social butterfly, determined that her luxurious house would be the most fashionable salon in the city. She entertained dashing aristocrats and officers, foreign merchants and businessmen, and professional revolutionaries. Her soirées were an occasion for the wealthy elite to show off and served as a meeting-place for the leaders of the independence movement, foreign diplomats and spies.

By 1803 the O'Gormans' marriage was disintegrating. Thomas was spending more and more time away on business, and Ana was provoking the scorn – and perhaps jealousy – of *porteño* society with her scandalous love affairs. One of her lovers aroused particular interest. In 1804 this mysterious stranger, recently arrived in Buenos Aires from Europe, began to appear at the best parties in the city, including those of the viceroy, Rafael de Sobremonte. Some believed the new arrival to be a Prussian officer; others swore he was a wealthy French émigré. In fact he was a French-born Irishman by the name of James Florence Bourke, and he was a British spy, his fluency in several languages allowing him to adopt different guises according to the occasion.

Not only was Bourke having a love affair with Ana O'Gorman, a married woman, he was also an old comrade-in-arms of her husband. Bourke and Thomas O'Gorman most probably knew each other from their time in the Irish regiments of the French army. If not, they certainly knew the same people, because it was with Thomas O'Gorman that Bourke sailed to Buenos Aires from London in 1804 on an espionage mission entrusted to him by the British government.

It has often been assumed that Bourke was born in Ireland. In fact he was born in Lorient in Brittany on 5 May 1771.[11] His father, Richard Bourke, was an Irish Jacobite from Lacken, County Mayo, who had emigrated to France in the middle of the eighteenth century and had served as a captain in Lally's Regiment of the French army. Bourke had married Marie-Jacquette Saint-Jean, a 15-year-old local girl, in 1765.[12] Like his father, James Florence Bourke was destined for a soldier's life, enlisting in another Irish unit of the French army, Dillon's Regiment. His younger brother, Jean-Raymond-Charles Bourke, enlisted in Walsh's Regiment, rising to become a hero of the Revolution and the First Empire and a general under Napoleon.[13] However, James was destined to serve a different master.

In 1792 he was garrisoned in the West Indies, in present-day Haiti. The following year, after being defeated by a British force under Lieutenant-Colonel John Whitelocke, the men of Dillon's Regiment deserted to the British army en masse.[14] It was shortly afterwards that Bourke began his career as a spy, reporting directly to the British commander-in-chief, the Duke of York. Bourke spent several years in Germany, picking up fluent German, which allowed him to pass as a Prussian officer when he arrived in Buenos Aires in 1804. His mission in South America was to gauge the appetite for British intervention in the River Plate region, and with the help of Ana O'Gorman he made contact with the underground leaders of the city's independence movement.

Bourke travelled overland into Chile, ascertaining the political mood and taking note of the colony's military strengths and weaknesses.[15] So far, he had managed to avoid detection by the authorities, but on his way back to Buenos Aires he was arrested in Upper Peru (present-day Bolivia) and condemned as a spy. He managed to extricate himself from his perilous situation only by pleading that he was a French subject and an ally of Spain. On his release, after a spell in Brazil, he sailed for Lisbon.

The British Foreign Office used Bourke's intelligence reports to consider an expedition to the River Plate. The government had been weighing a plan for an invasion of South America for several years. With the French enforcing a blockade of British goods on the Continent, the government was coming under increasing pressure from manufacturers to open new markets. In the summer of 1806 Britain had given some limited support to the Venezuelan revolutionary Francisco de Miranda, who had led a small expedition to his homeland with 200 men recruited in New York. Miranda's plan was hopelessly ill-conceived, and the Spanish army easily routed the invading force. However, Miranda returned to London a hero, and there were those in the highest political and military circles, including the foreign secretary, George Canning, and the secretary of state for war and the colonies, Lord Castlereagh,[16] who continued to listen with interest to his ideas.

While Miranda had been preparing his expedition to Venezuela, Rear-Admiral Home Riggs Popham of the Royal Navy had been mulling over his own plans. In early 1806 Popham was off the coast of South Africa, supporting the British occupation of the Cape of Good Hope under the command of Lieutenant-General David Baird, when he conceived the idea of attempting an invasion of the River Plate, an idea that had been floated by the British government as early as 1790. In 1804 Popham had presented a memorandum about a proposed invasion to the First Lord of the Admiralty, Viscount Melville. Unaware that a new government – the 'ministry of all the talents', headed by Grenville – had taken office, he took matters into his own hands and launched an invasion.[17]

Popham gave command of the expedition for invading Buenos Aires to Brigadier-General William Carr Beresford, the illegitimate son of the Marquis of Waterford, George de la Poer Beresford, and a nephew of John Beresford, who had been one of the most powerful men in the Irish House of Commons before its dissolution in 1801 under the terms of the Act of Union. Beresford was an experienced soldier. He had fought in Britain's colonial wars around the globe, including campaigns in France, the Caribbean, India and Egypt, losing the sight in one eye during a shooting accident in Nova Scotia. For the expedition to the River Plate, Baird assigned the Light

Company of the 71st Regiment of Foot under the command of another Irish officer, Lieutenant-Colonel Denis Pack, a native of County Kilkenny.

The troops sailed for South America in April 1806, arriving in the River Plate at the end of June. On 25 June a force of about 1,500 men landed at Quilmes, about eight miles south of the poorly defended city of Buenos Aires. Beresford realised that if he were to take and hold Buenos Aires, he would have to pretend that he had more troops than the meagre number at his disposal, and so sailors, orderlies and servants were hurriedly disguised as soldiers.[169] The ruse worked. After a brief skirmish with a hastily assembled force of Spanish and *criollo* defenders, Beresford marched into Buenos Aires, and thus began the brief British occupation. The viceroy, Sobremonte, fled the city with the treasury.

The British immediately opened up the port to foreign trade and reduced import and export duties. Indicative of the commercial objectives of the invasion was the realisation by one member of Beresford's expedition that there existed in Buenos Aires a market for British manufactures, including

> ... household furniture, musical instruments, and compositions, hardware of all sorts, long knives in sheaths always worn by the Peons, hammers, wedges, pickaxes, steam-engines, mechanical manufactures of shew and genius, fowling-pieces, with all their ammunition in mahogany boxes, lead in every form, black and blue cloths, stout woolen-cloths, printed cottons for gowns and pantaloons, calicoes, nankeens, boots, shoes, kerseymeres, mostly sky-blue, low cottons-cloths, blankets, ladies' dresses the most modern, their shoes and silk stockings ornamented, cheese, butter, flower [*sic*], and garden seeds.[19]

The response in Buenos Aires to the arrival of the foreign troops was mixed. Many well-to-do *porteños* were disinclined to oppose the British, and it was left to Spanish monopolists and the middle classes to organise resistance. These militias would later give the *criollos* the political power that the Spanish crown had denied them.

It was a French officer in the service of the Spanish crown, Santiago de Liniers,[20] who led the expedition to retake Buenos Aires from the British. Liniers had been a frequent attender at Ana O'Gorman's salon, and had become her lover. Meanwhile, Thomas O'Gorman cosied up to the British occupying force, gaining commercial contracts from Beresford.

At the beginning of August 1806 Spaniards and *porteños* joined forces to form militias in order to expel the British occupiers. They were based on the regional origins of the unit's volunteers: Andalusians served together, as did Basques and Catalans. There were many Irish names in the militias, including those of Spanish-born merchants, Irish-born merchants and British army deserters. They included the Irish-born Robert Dunne, who was appointed a sergeant in a company of grenadiers in 1807.[21] Carlos Fitzgeld, or Fitzgerald, enlisted as a private in the Tercio de Andaluces, an Andalusian unit, which signified his membership of that region's thriving Irish merchant community. His commanding officer remarked on his 'spirit and bravery' during the fighting.[22] He was subsequently commissioned a second lieutenant.

Another noted veteran of the militias during the English invasions was the Buenos Aires-born *criollo* Domingo French. His ancestors, Frenches and Joyces from County Galway, had left Ireland for Spain in the seventeenth century. French was an enthusiastic supporter of Argentine independence and later became a leader of the May Revolution in 1810.

After fierce fighting in the streets of the city, Beresford surrendered to Liniers. The disgraced viceroy, Sobremonte, was overthrown and Liniers appointed in his place. It was an unprecedented event: the appointee of the Spanish crown had been displaced by the choice of the people. Most of the Irish soldiers who had participated in Beresford's expedition were taken prisoner, including 17-year-old Edward Neil.[23] Many deserted to the other side. Patrick Island, a relative of Beresford's, had been injured by an African slave during the fighting in Buenos Aires and had been taken in by a *criollo* family who had seen him fall in the street outside their house. During his convalescence he fell in love with the householder's daughter, Bartola Gómez, and proposed marriage. Once recovered, he joined the patriot troops to fight against the British.

The British government made a second attempt to establish a foothold in the River Plate in February 1807 when another expeditionary force successfully invaded Montevideo. Under the command of General Sir Samuel Auchmuty and comprising 4,000 men, the British force included an Irish unit, the 1st Battalion of the 87th Regiment of Foot, led by Sir Edward Butler. The regiment suffered heavy losses during the battle to take Montevideo, with an estimated 146 casualties.[24] From Montevideo the British launched a second assault on Buenos Aires in July 1807 under the command of Lieutenant-General Sir John Whitelocke. This assault failed, thanks to the bravery of the city's militias. These militiamen instilled a growing sense of national pride in the Buenos Aires *criollos* and showed them that Spain was incapable of protecting them from external threats. Instead, after the first invasion, Liniers drafted all males capable of serving into the militias, creating a martial climate in the city.

Meanwhile, on the eve of the French invasion of Spain, James Florence Bourke was spying on the Spanish court at El Escorial – the monumental monastery and royal palace built by Philip II outside Madrid at the end of the sixteenth century – gathering intelligence about French troop movements on the Iberian peninsula and promoting the British interest to the royal family and the queen's powerful favourite, Godoy, to the exclusion of the French. He was also trying to win to the British interest Juan Martín de Pueyrredón, who the Buenos Aires *cabildo* had sent to Spain to ask for military assistance.

Bourke employed all the arts of a modern agent in eliciting information for his masters in London. He used lemon juice to write invisible letters, concealed papers in false compartments, adopted different nationalities and disguises, and exercised considerable powers of seduction. His adaptability and talent for shifting identities, which he shared with many other Irish exiles in continental Europe, served him well as a spy. In the poisonous atmosphere of the Spanish court he used these skills to flatter, threaten and cajole.

As his cover, Bourke claimed to be seeking the restitution of a title that had long been held by his family, having secured an introduction to the French ambassador to Spain, François de Beauharnais. When Beauharnais indiscreetly advised Bourke that a change of regime in Spain was imminent, the Irish spy went to work on the queen and Godoy. He first seduced María Luisa behind the back of her husband, Charles IV, and her lover, Godoy. He had fostered a reputation as a wealthy 'man of sciences' and would deliberately drive past the queen in his elegant carriage to gain her attention.[25] According to Bourke, the queen

> ... sent one of her equerries, who had been her lover, to know who I was, my answers did not satisfy her curiosity – but on the contrary gave her greater desires of knowing me – I was acquainted with the character of women in general, but particularly with hers – consequently very soon was honoured with her personal society in the most private manner ...

During these conversations in María Luisa's boudoir Bourke realised that he would have to gain the confidence of Godoy. He induced one of Godoy's lovers to introduce him as a 'man of the greatest ability in medicine, and who had travelled much in South America, in search of botany and mineralogy.'[26] Once he was alone with Godoy, Bourke produced a snuff box with a secret compartment, from which he produced a note from Beauharnais. When Godoy refused to take the note, evidence of Napoleon's plan to invade Spain, Bourke produced a pistol and 'told him with some vehemence' that he was a British officer and a friend, and that it would be in Godoy's interest to read it. To prove his identity, he also produced the pass that he had been given by the Admiralty, which he had secreted in the handle of a knife.

> From that moment I directed all the operations of the Court. I was presented to the Queen and King as the Savior [sic] of the Crown – orders were immediately dispatched to the Spanish troops already on the frontiers of Portugal to retrograde, the French were delayed in their march by the want of many things which might have been supplied them – and by that sure source of information, I was made acquainted with every thing in Europe ...[27]

Bourke returned to London at the end of 1807. Since he was anxious to keep his identity a secret from the rest of the court, he posed as a German sailor from Trieste. On his departure from Spain he carried with him a letter from María Luisa to her daughter, Carlota Joaquina, sister of the heir to the Spanish throne, the future Ferdinand VII, and wife of the Portuguese prince regent, John VI.

Bourke briefed Castlereagh back in London. The cabinet gave him *carte blanche* to manipulate the Spanish court to further British interests. In the meantime, however, Charles IV had abdicated and Napoleon had begun the invasion of Spain. With royal authority in Spain crumbling, and powerless to resist the mighty French armies pouring into the country, Charles and Ferdinand agreed to travel to Bayonne to meet the French emperor.

Bourke attempted to prevent Ferdinand falling into Napoleon's hands and set off after the young king. 'The dangers of the undertaking were ... eminent,' Bourke recalled, 'however the desire of serving my King and rise myself in the estimation of my Country, raised my imagination to be blind to any thing like danger. With money, disguise, determination, goodwill and presence of mind, I completed my undertaking.'[28] But he was still unable to intercept Ferdinand.

Instead, Bourke worked to build Spanish opposition to the French while reporting on their troop movements. Back in London, he urged the British cabinet to aid the patriot forces in the north of the country. He offered to return to Spain, believing he was ideally suited to lead the fight against the French.

> I certainly <u>knew</u> more than those who spoke good Spanish only. I know nations. I have learnt them in the true book. I was perfectly acquainted with the politick of Spain – character, resources, and topographical <u>advantages</u>. I likewise knew the French, better, perhaps than their General, their secrets and resources.[29]

In his narrative of events, written in 1809, Bourke boasted that 'with 200,000 pounds and 40 men' he would have been able 'to bring off Bonaparte from Bayonne.'[30] Instead, the British government proposed that Bourke go to Mexico with an expeditionary force that was then being prepared by Arthur Wellesley at Cork. It was later suggested that he would travel to Boulogne to prepare the ground for a possible British expedition. Finally, it was decided that he would be sent to Buenos Aires to gauge political opinion, manipulate the leaders of the independence movement and stymie French designs in the River Plate region.

The tense political situation in Buenos Aires had been exacerbated since the British invasions by the intrigues of the Spanish princess Carlota Joaquina, who had fled with the rest of the Portuguese court to Brazil during the French invasion of Portugal in November 1807. Carlota was the eldest daughter of King Charles IV of Spain. Upon Napoleon's dethronement and the imprisonment of her brother, Ferdinand VI, Carlota, now resident with the Portuguese royal family in Rio de Janeiro, began harbouring ambitions of ruling over Spain's American possessions.

Bourke travelled to Rio to establish with the British representatives to the Portuguese royal court a secure means of communication through which he could pass secret messages from Buenos Aires to London. Among the most important figures at the royal court in Rio was the Anglo-Irish diplomat Percy Clinton Sydney Smythe, Lord Strangford. He was the eldest son of Viscount Strangford, a County Meath clergyman who had fought in the American War of Independence, and his American-born wife, Marie Elizabeth Philipse. The young Smythe had had literary ambitions and after graduating from Trinity College in Dublin had shared lodgings with the poet Thomas Moore in London. On the death of his father in 1801 he had succeeded to the title of Viscount Strangford and shortly afterwards had entered the diplomatic service.

Strangford had been appointed *chargé d'affaires* in Lisbon in 1804. It had been through him that Bourke had sent his secret communications from the Spanish court to the British cabinet. In 1807 Strangford, then ambassador to Lisbon, had advised the royal family to flee to Brazil.

Between 1808 and 1815, as Britain's representative to the court in Rio, Strangford played a crucial role in aligning Portuguese royal policy towards Spain's American colonies with British interests.[31] Primary among these interests was preserving the British alliance with Spain, and so Strangford deflected Portugal's imperial ambitions in South America. He found himself hindered, however, by the machinations of Rear-Admiral Sidney Smith, the renowned veteran of the American and French revolutionary wars, who had been ordered to Brazil to guard against a French invasion. Smith was an ally of the *carlotistas,* Carlota's followers, who wished for an aggressive policy towards the Spanish colonies, and was determined to lead an invasion of the River Plate on behalf of the Portuguese crown. According to the historian John Street, 'Smith, with his rather far-fetched scheme for opening that area to British trade by means of establishing Carlota there, might represent what the British commercial interest wanted, but Strangford, equally alive to the need for markets, would not prejudice his country's good relations with Spain for their sake.'[32] Strangford eventually had Smith replaced by the Irish-born vice-admiral Michael de Courcy, son of Lord Kingsale of County Cork.

Yet before his departure Smith had pressured Bourke into staying in Rio, despite the latter's wish to remain incognito and to travel immediately to Buenos Aires. Learning that he was in Rio, the prince and princess requested Bourke's presence at court. Carlota was immediately taken with the Irish spy. 'I gave her the letter from her mother,' Bourke wrote, 'and from that moment to the day of my departure from the country, I have been her only confidant and her secret friend, and she has at all times in public made it a point to mark me with every distinction in her power.'[33]

Carlota informed Bourke of the intrigues at court and gave him sight of her correspondence. She was determined to get rid of Liniers, who was now viceroy in Buenos Aires and whom Bourke had met regularly in Buenos Aires in 1805. The British suspected the French-born Liniers of Bonapartist sympathies; the rumours about him were not helped by the fact that it was well known that he was having a love affair with the French-born Ana O'Gorman, who had since earned the nickname La Perichona, after La Perricholi, the viceroy of Peru's nefarious lover, and her own maiden name, Périchon.

Bourke had also been one of Ana O'Gorman's lovers, and he assuaged Princess Carlota's fears about La Perichona's supposed influence on the Buenos Aires government.

> The Princess gave me an <u>authentic</u> document to act in her name for the mutual interest of England and Spain, but expressed her fears that, though she was certain Liniers would be superseded, he would resist the power of the Junta, particularly as long as a well known French woman had that great influence over him. I acquainted her with what I knew of said woman and that I would endeavour to remove <u>her</u>.[34]

Bourke and Liniers had a testy meeting when the former landed in Buenos Aires, with Liniers accusing the Irishman of being a provocateur and of having deceived the leaders of the independence movement when he had last been in the River Plate. Bourke dismissed Liniers and his court to his superiors as Bonapartists who were putting on a show of their patriotism.

> Every thing was French about Liniers. The dresses, the French hairdressers, tailors, shoemakers etc., etc., whom I had known formerly as such, were his aides du camp, colonels, majors etc., etc., etc. By pressing so much my departure, I found that he was afraid I might see his mistress, or that she would know I was there.[35]

Bourke returned to Rio, where he discovered that Sidney had been recalled and that Strangford was plotting to have him removed. Realising that Strangford had poisoned the mind of the Portugese prince regent against him, Bourke voluntarily returned to London. In his memorandum to the British government he put forward what he believed was the best policy regarding South America:

I therefore conclude that to obviate any difficulties, disputes or revolutions among the Spanish Americans, and consolidate more forcibly the dislocated interests of Old Spain, and more forcibly forward His Majesty's Government's views in South America by an unrivalled commercial link with those people, it becomes urgently necessary to use the influence that Govt must naturally have over the Junta of Seville to name without loss of time <u>Dona Carlota Joaquina de Bourbon, Infanta of Spain, Regent of Spain and its Americas</u> and Her Royal Highness would enter in a secret treaty with this country by which she would engage as much as possible and to her utmost power (when once established with the reins of Govt) to forward the interest of Great Britain on the greatest scale etc., etc., the object of the Power she has vested in me being perfectly secret, and tending to that sole object.

I will likewise observe that no man will ever obtain the influence I have over the Princess and I am confident that no man living could serve his country more effectually near that eminent lady than,

[signed] J. Burke.[36]

The British government could not openly pressure the authorities in Buenos Aires to allow foreign trade, but private interests could. Both the large *estancia* owners and foreign manufacturers were anxious to open up trade.

In July 1809 Baltasar Hidalgo de Cisneros arrived in Buenos Aires to become the new viceroy, replacing Liniers, who voluntarily relinquished power. The financial situation was dire. The cost of the war against the British and the disruption to trade from the wars in Europe, and the concomitant reduction in duties and taxes, had emptied the treasury. A financial stimulus was desperately required. In August a Dublin merchant, John Dillon, petitioned Cisneros to be allowed to land goods in Buenos Aires. The goods had been loaded in Cork for Brazil, but, finding that the market there was saturated, Dillon had taken the decision to try his luck farther down the Atlantic coast in Buenos Aires. While foreign merchants and their agents were in favour of free trade, as were the *estancieros,* there were also those who had an interest in preserving the monopoly of trade with Spain. Nevertheless Cisneros granted permission to Dillon to land his goods. The city was in too much need of the duties; and a new era of free trade had begun.

In May 1810, responding to events in Spain, where the Supreme Central Junta had been dissolved and the regency council had taken its place, the citizens of Buenos Aires overthrew Cisneros. On 25 May an elected junta took power, ostensibly governing in the name of the deposed King Ferdinand VI. The actions of the new government were to bring it into conflict with the regency council in Spain, which considered the behaviour of the independent-minded citizens of Buenos Aires a direct challenge to its authority. It ordered the navy stationed in Montevideo to blockade the rebellious *porteños*. The leaders of the Buenos Aires junta realised that if the new independent government of the former Viceroyalty of the River Plate was to survive, it would have to run the Spanish blockade and build its own navy to protect its commerce. The problem was that there were no experienced naval officers among their ranks; and so they turned to a little-known Irish merchant mariner. His name was William Brown.

PART TWO
REVOLUTION

Chapter 8

THE BATTLE FOR THE RIVER PLATE

The May Revolution in Buenos Aires raised fundamental questions for the future of the territories that comprised the Viceroyalty of the River Plate. Since the foundation of the viceroyalty in 1776, the capital city, Buenos Aires, had gained in importance as the Bourbons centralised power in their American colonies. This caused resentment in the provinces. The fact that the new junta in Buenos Aires saw itself as inheriting the authority and functions of the viceroy, and attempted to exercise them throughout the territories that made up the former viceroyalty, led to increased bitterness on the part of provincial towns, which wished to follow the example of the recently established United States of America and create a federal system.

The first problem for the junta, however, was continuing royalist opposition. In Córdoba, Liniers and the local bishop led a counter-revolution against the junta, which was swiftly put down by troops from Buenos Aires. More sustained royalist opposition came from the north, in Paraguay and Upper Peru, and to the east, across the River Plate in Montevideo.

In Paraguay, local militias under the command of the Spanish governor, Bernardo de Velasco, repelled an expeditionary force sent by the Buenos Aires junta under the command of General Manuel Belgrano. These same militias then overthrew Velasco, leading to an independent Paraguay. Unlike the other leaders of the independent South American states that were to emerge from the revolutionary period, the Paraguayan dictator José Gaspar Rodríguez de Francia built his regime on economic self-sufficiency rather than free trade.

The Buenos Aires junta sent another force to Upper Peru, which was also defeated. Upper Peru was a rich province, full of precious metals; it was also a royalist heartland, which rejected the authority of Buenos Aires. Though it had been absorbed into the Viceroyalty of the River Plate in 1776, economically and politically the region had always looked west, towards

Lima, the capital city of the Viceroyalty of Peru. It was not until 1825 that Upper Peru proclaimed independence from Spain.

The most dangerous royalist threat to Buenos Aires came from Montevideo. In the aftermath of the May Revolution, Montevideo became the new viceregal capital and centre of royalist power in the River Plate region. From Montevideo the royalist navy was able to control the entrance to the River Plate estuary, disrupting trade and bombarding Buenos Aires. Despite fierce opposition from some patriot leaders, the Buenos Aires government began putting together a navy to counteract the royalists' sea power and to blockade Montevideo. The man chosen to lead this navy into battle against the royalists was William Brown, a 36-year-old sailor from Foxford, County Mayo.

Brown was a steely, driven individual, who had arrived in Buenos Aires determined to make his fortune. The royalist navy was preventing him from trading fruit and hides across the River Plate estuary, and so he offered his services to the patriots. His Irish biographer, John de Courcy Ireland, has written that the 'essential' Brown was not 'the Admiral, nor the leader of men, the nation-builder, the merchant, the shipowner, or even the strict but affectionate family man, but William Brown the Master Mariner.'[1] It was his tenacity, his stubbornness in overcoming formidable challenges – whether it was the might of the Spanish fleet or the treacherous currents of the River Plate – that separated him from his peers; but he still expected those around him to live up to his own exacting standards. He had a fierce temper and was not averse to meting out severe punishment to those he felt were not pulling their weight. Lashings were common on board his ships, and there were instances of him forcing men to run the gauntlet. He was energetic, brutal and a fine sailor.

Doubt surrounds Brown's ancestry, with de Courcy Ireland suggesting that he was the illegitimate son of George Browne, collector of revenue for the Foxford district.[2] The traditional narrative, discounted by de Courcy Ireland, has it that he arrived in Philadelphia as a boy with his father, who died shortly afterwards, leaving William to cope on his own. The story goes that a merchant captain spotted William wandering alone by the docks and took pity on him, offering him work as a cabin boy and thus giving him his first start as a sailor.

What we know for certain is that by the time Brown arrived in Buenos Aires, lured by commercial opportunities, he was an experienced merchant mariner. In 1810 he was trading arms and munitions across the River Plate estuary, even managing to capture a royalist ship. In 1811 he travelled overland from Buenos Aires to Chile on a commercial trip, crossing the Andes at the Uspallata Pass. On his return to Buenos Aires he was caught burying money outside the city. He was charged with planning to export money illegally and imprisoned, but was released after he contacted the head of the British naval station in Buenos Aires, who pleaded for clemency.[3]

In 1812 Brown moved with his family permanently to Buenos Aires. He bought a piece of land and built the Casa Amarilla – the Yellow House – close to the city's famous Boca district. The original house was later demolished, but in 1975 the commission to mark the bicentenary of Brown's birth launched a project for rebuilding it. The new Casa Amarilla is a short distance from the famous Bombonera football stadium, home to the passionately supported Boca Juniors, and houses a museum and permanent exhibition of artefacts related to Brown's life.

Brown was a tall, well-built man with a heavy brow, a shock of red hair and piercing blue eyes. His strong, rough-hewn physical characteristics are still evident in the photographs that were taken of him dressed in his admiral's uniform towards the end of his life (see Plate 12).

In 1814 Brown's formidable naval skills brought him to the notice of the Buenos Aires government, which was desperate to break the Spanish blockade. In March he was offered command of a small fleet of ships and the rank of lieutenant-colonel, with the responsibility for blockading Montevideo and protecting Buenos Aires from attack. The Buenos Aires government had few ships: the frigate *Hércules*, the corvettes *Céfiro*, *Belfast* and *Agreable*, the brig *Nancy*, a couple of small fishing smacks called sumacas, the *Itatí* and *Trinidad*, the schooners *Esperanza*, *Juliet* and *Fortuna*, the sloop *Carmen*, the gunboat *Americana*, and the feluccas *San Martín* and *San Luis*. They were merchantmen that had been hastily transformed into warships. The patriots had few qualified naval officers. Many of those who were recruited by the Buenos Aires government were foreigners – Irishmen, Englishmen and North Americans – including James King, the Irish captain of the 18-gun *Céfiro*.[4]

Brown sailed from Buenos Aires on 8 March on board the *Hércules*, along with the *Céfiro* and the *Nancy*. He soon spotted a Spanish squadron, under the command of Jacinto de Romerate, on its way to the island of Martín

García. At the entrance to the River Uruguay, some 30 miles north of Buenos Aires, the island was a crucial strategic point on the River Plate estuary. Because of the superior numbers of the Spanish squadron, Brown decided to await reinforcements. The *Juliet, Fortuna, San Luis* and *Carmen* arrived from Buenos Aires the following day, and Brown's combined fleet sailed for Martín García. The Spanish fleet was anchored on the south-east side of the island, protected by a gun battery. Nevertheless, Brown ordered an attack.

The *Hércules* sustained heavy fire and ran aground. It lay bows-on to the Spanish positions, making it a sitting duck for the enemy guns. Its sails were in ribbons, the hull had been breached in more than 80 places and, because of the position of the ship, Brown was unable to direct more than three guns towards the enemy. Still, he ordered his men to keep firing throughout the night while he tried desperately to make running repairs, using leather hides to patch up the holes in the hull. At high tide the *Hércules* freed itself. Despite the damage to the ship and the casualties his crew had suffered, Brown was determined to attempt a landing at Martín García. According to the naval historian Miguel Ángel de Marco, 'Brown was conscious that if he did not achieve a victory, the [Buenos Aires] government and public opinion, so unenthusiastic about the navy, would lack confidence in his future actions.'[5] Having repaired the *Hércules* as best he could, Brown managed a landing on Martín García, seizing the battery and directing fire on the Spanish. Romerate managed to escape up the River Uruguay.

Brown had achieved the impossible, humbling the superior Spanish fleet with a handful of patched-together merchantmen. In April, with the reputation of the infant Argentine navy at a high point, Brown sailed for Montevideo, blockading the city and taking Brazilian and Spanish ships as prizes. On 14 May the commander-in-chief of the naval station at Montevideo, Miguel de la Sierra, sailed out to do battle. Brown drew him out to deep water in order to prevent him making a retreat. There was a ferocious exchange of fire, which ended inconclusively. Brown attempted another attack two days later and suffered an injury to his foot when a cannon escaped its breech ropes. However, he was still able to command the attack from a chair lashed to the deck of the *Hércules*. On 17 May most of the Spanish ships had been captured or destroyed. The royalist governor of Montevideo, Gaspar de Vigodet, surrendered the city shortly afterwards, and Brown returned to Buenos Aires a hero.

The adulation with which the *porteños* greeted him was short-lived. The war with Spain continued, and as long as the royalist fleet, based in Callao in Peru, was able to harry the Pacific coastline, it remained a threat. In October 1814, royalist forces supported from Callao routed Chilean patriots at the Battle of Rancagua, forcing the leaders of the independence movement into exile across the Andes. The Buenos Aires government now declared open season on Spanish shipping, and Brown rejoined the war as a privateer.[6]

In October 1815 he set sail from Buenos Aires on board the *Hércules*. His brother-in-law, William Chitty, was captain of the ship, while his brother, Michael Brown, commanded a second ship, the *Trinidad*. Brown arranged to rendezvous with Hippolyte Bouchard, the French commander of another privateering mission to the Pacific, at an island off the Chilean coast, south of Santiago.

Before Brown left for the Pacific, however, he received countermanding orders from the authorities in Buenos Aires, which he chose to ignore. His decision to press on was to have grave consequences.

The journey around Cape Horn was in itself a hazardous undertaking. The seabed surrounding the Horn is a ships' graveyard, the last resting-place of vessels that have been wrecked by terrific storms, treacherous currents and the jagged coastline. The *Hércules* and *Trinidad* were battered by waves that crashed over their topmasts as they fought their way around Tierra del Fuego before they found shelter in the western approaches to the Magellan Straits. Having made contact with Bouchard off the coast of Chile, Brown and his men began the hunt for Spanish prizes. After taking a couple of Spanish ships in open waters, Brown made straight for Callao, attacking royalist gunboats within sight of the shore and capturing the frigate *Consecuencia*.

Brown next headed north along the coast of Peru towards Guayaquil, an important royalist port in present-day Ecuador. The squadron sailed up the River Guayas, opening fire on the forts defending the city downriver. Brown was hoping to surprise the garrison at Guayaquil, but news of the patriot force travelled overland, and the royalists were prepared when the enemy appeared. The *Trinidad* was grounded when the tide ebbed, allowing the garrison of one of the royalist forts to concentrate their fire on the deck. Despite Brown having surrendered, the royalists boarded the ship and began executing the surviving crew. They stopped only when Brown threatened to blow up the ship's magazine.

Brown was taken prisoner but was released in a negotiated exchange. He sailed west to the Galápagos to make repairs before making for Buenaventura in Peru, then in the control of local insurgents, to refit and prepare for the journey back to Buenos Aires. After another hazardous trip around Cape Horn, Brown and his starving, weary crew limped up the Atlantic coast of Argentina towards the River Plate estuary; but, perhaps wary of the consequences of his decision to ignore the countermanding orders from Buenos Aires, he took the unusual decision to resupply in the Brazilian port of Pernambuco before sailing north to British-controlled Bridgetown in Barbados, where he hoped to sell his cargo. He arrived in September 1816.

Brown clearly believed that the British would adopt a sympathetic attitude to his activities. Instead, the captain of a British sloop took the *Hércules* and its rich cargo as a prize and brought Brown as a prisoner to Antigua, the British headquarters in the Lower Antilles. Brown was in effect charged with being a pirate, operating outside the law – a rich piece of hypocrisy, given the long history of British piracy against the Spanish fleet in the Caribbean.

To make matters worse, both Brown and his brother were severely ill. Michael Brown was suffering from scurvy, while William had contracted malaria. For seven long months, in the deadening tropical climate of the Caribbean, Brown suffered physically and mentally. His ship, the *Hércules*, and his cargo were sold, he was away from his family for over a year and he was in disgrace in Buenos Aires, accused of being a traitor. In April 1817 he sailed for London to appeal the decision of the vice-admiral's court in Antigua. Though the appeals court ruled partly in his favour and he received some of the money raised from the sale of the *Hércules*, he now found himself at the centre of a new action taken by the Spanish ambassador in London. Eventually, having settled both cases, Brown set sail for Buenos Aires, arriving in October 1818, only to be arrested again and brought before a court-martial.

Brown was at his lowest ebb. He had suffered constant physical and mental tortures for three years. He had been battered during two journeys around Cape Horn. He had been taken prisoner twice. He had fallen sick, almost dying of malaria, and endured constant pain from rheumatism. He had been called a pirate by the British government and a low traitor by the government of the United Provinces of the River Plate – later renamed the Argentine Republic – for which he had risked his life on numerous occasions. To cap it all, in September 1819 he contracted typhoid.

These torments were enough to have broken another man, and they almost killed William Brown. On 23 September he threw himself from the roof of a three-storey building. But something deep within him refused to give way, and he survived the fall. Having broken his thigh bone, he was confined to bed for six months.

A court-martial in Buenos Aires found Brown guilty of disobeying orders, stripping him of his rank and depriving him of the remainder of the money he had made during his Pacific campaigns. The civil government took a more lenient view and restored him to the rank of retired colonel. With his military career seemingly over, Brown settled down to a civilian's life and to finding a way to restore his fortune.[7]

While Brown was playing a crucial role in solidifying the regime in Buenos Aires, another Irishman was among the leaders of a group rebelling against it. In the Banda Oriental – the territories north of the River Plate estuary and east of the River Uruguay, which roughly approximates to the present-day state of Uruguay – a local chieftan, or *caudillo*, named José Gervasio Artigas and his band of *gaucho* guerrillas had been challenging the authority of royalist Montevideo. Artigas had been born in Montevideo in 1764 to a wealthy family but as a young man had spent a lot of time on his family's farms and had fallen in love with the *gaucho* lifestyle. Giving up his studies, he began cattle-smuggling, which put him at odds with the wealthy *estancia* owners. Despite his brushes with the law, and to obtain a pardon from the authorities, Artigas had joined the royalist army in the 1790s and had helped drive the British out of Buenos Aires in 1806.

The following year the British took Artigas prisoner when they occupied Montevideo. He escaped and began a guerrilla campaign against the British, helping restore Montevideo to Spanish control. After the May Revolution of 1810, Artigas threw in his lot with the Buenos Aires junta in an effort to expel the Spanish from Montevideo, leading a band of about 200 men which harassed Spanish troops throughout the Banda Oriental. In 1811 he and his men joined troops sent from Buenos Aires to besiege Montevideo. However, the recently appointed Spanish viceroy, Francisco Javier de Elío, had appealed for help from the Portuguese court in Rio, and an army of 5,000 Brazilian soldiers helped relieve the siege. Fearing for its own survival, the Buenos Aires junta signed a truce with Elío. A disillusioned Artigas and his men retreated west across the River Uruguay. Buenos Aires now considered Artigas a threat and sent troops into the region of Entre Ríos to find and kill him.

Among Artigas's most trusted lieutenants was Peter Campbell, one of the most romantic figures of all those Irish men and women who swam in the revolutionary currents that were flowing through South America. His story seems to leap from the pages of a picaresque novel. He was a soldier, a deserter, an adventurer, an outlaw, a cowboy, a revolutionary, a military innovator, a naval strategist, a hero and a villain. In his memoirs, the Scottish businessman John Parish Robertson depicted Campbell as a stage Irishman.

> 'Por Dios!' said he; 'don't you know Peter Campbell?' – 'Camp-*béll*,' he continued, laying a strong accent on the last syllable. 'Pedro Camp-*béll*,' (Paythro he pronounced it,) 'as the Gauchers call me? Troth, now, an' don't ye know me; Paythro Camp-*béll*? An' ye never heerd of that name, then you're the only gentleman in the who'al of the country as has not.'[8]

The footnote attached to this passage in Robertson's memoir – 'I will not repeat the profane adjuration by which Mr. Campbell enforced his argument'[9] – simply adds to the author's condescension. Yet from Robertson's depiction of Campbell, and the story of how he became a *gaucho*, one gets a sense again of the adaptability of the early nineteenth-century Irishman and of how reputation depends on context. To the Buenos Aires junta, Campbell was a bandit and secessionist, fit to be hunted down and shot; to the later historians of the Uruguayan state, Campbell was a hero and the founder of its navy. Such is the esteem in which he is held by the Uruguayan government that the navy continues to name ships after him, the latest being the frigate *Pedro Campbell*, commissioned in 2008.

Born in County Tipperary about 1780, Campbell had been apprenticed as a tanner before enlisting in the 1st Battalion of the British army's 71st Regiment of Foot. In 1806 he had participated in Beresford's invasion of Buenos Aires and was wounded. During Whitelocke's failed expedition to occupy Montevideo in 1807 he was captured by royalist forces and held in present-day northern Argentina. Once he gained his freedom, he deserted and travelled into the pampas in the Argentine province of Corrientes.[10] This was frontier territory, where hard-living *gauchos* and enterprising traders made their money from cattle, sheep, sugar and timber.

Campbell found work as a tanner and was drawn to the *gaucho* life, adopting their distinctive dress and way of living. Some of the skills that the *gaucho* required when living on the pampas were not dissimilar to those

Campbell might have learnt as a child in Tipperary. He was an accomplished horseman and was proficient with a blade. During the frequent brawls that erupted in the frontier towns of the pampas, he used a large carving-knife together with a poncho as a shield in order to defend himself. John Robertson described first meeting Campbell in Corrientes:

> Sitting one evening under the corridor of my house, there came up to my very chair, on horseback, a tall, raw boned, ferocious looking man, in Gaucho attire, with two cavalry pistols stuck in his girdle, a sabre in a rusty steel scabbard pending from a besmeared belt of half-tanned leather, red whiskers and mustachios, – hair uncombed of the same colour, matted with perspiration, and powdered with dust. His face was not only burnt almost to blackness by the sun, but it was blistered to the eyes; while large pieces of shrivelled skin stood ready to fall from his parched lips. He wore a pair of plain ear-rings, a foraging cap, a tattered poncho, blue jacket, with tarnished red facings; a large knife in a leathern sheath; a pair of potro boots, and rusty iron spurs, with rowels an inch and a half in diameter ... The Hibernian brogue; the mangled Spanish; the countenance when closely scanned; the carroty locks, and bright grey eyes, all revealed to me a son of the Sister Isle, transformed into a more fearful looking Gaucho than any native one I had ever beheld.[11]

Campbell enjoyed a legendary reputation in Corrientes – 'being in the confidence of Artigas, he brought, in aid of his personal claims to deference, the acknowledged favour and patronage of that lawless but omnipotent chieftain'[12] – and offered his services to John Robertson and his brother, William. For the first decade after 1810 the region to the west of the River Uruguay was full of Artigas's *gaucho* and indigenous fighters. Many inhabitants of this wild country believed Artigas and his men to be heroes, fighting both Spanish and *porteño* tyranny; Artigas's enemies regarded them as nothing short of bandits and cattle-rustlers. From Campbell's point of view, cattle-rustling was a legitimate act of war: 'By troth, Don Pépe's [Artigas] an honest gentleman; and if so be he's compelled to take the cattle now and then, sure, where's the harm, when it's for the good of the counthrey?'[13] Campbell's sympathies may have derived from the fact that he was born in Ireland in the late eighteenth century, at the height of the enclosures of common land. Once employed by the Robertsons, he changed his attitude.

John Robertson's depiction of Corrientes in 1815 is that of unbridled anarchy, not dissimilar to Hollywood portrayals of the Old West.

> The estancias became depopulated, the herdsmen were seized upon for soldiers; all the natural ties of society were broken or relaxed; the country was overspread with fierce and lawless banditti; rapine and lust stalked over the length and breadth of the land; agriculture was abandoned; the inroads of the Indians from the Great Chaco were frequent; such herds of horses and cattle, as were too numerous and too much dispersed to be systematically driven from the territory, sought shelter in the woods, and there became *alzado* or wild; the forests teemed with untamed colts; large flocks of vultures were to be seen hanging over the newly dropped calves and foals, ready to devour them; wild dogs, called *cimarrones*, like evening wolves, ranged the country in droves; the houses were abandoned, and rare was the mounted gaucho to be met with who was not a robber or assassin, often both.[14]

What Robertson was depicting was the death throes of an itinerant *gaucho* culture that was already being replaced by the large-scale cattle ranches. Ironically, the '*gaucho*' Campbell did much to bring an end to the old ways. Despite their disdain for the *gaucho* way of life, the Robertsons were businessmen, and if they were to do business in Artigas's territory they needed the help of one of his trusted allies. Campbell acted as an intermediary for the Robertsons. He traversed the countryside with a group of loyal followers – including his second-in-command, a fellow Tipperary-man who went by the name of Eduardo – persuading *estancieros* by means of money and luxury goods to gather and sell him hides, wool, horsehair and skins. Acting on behalf of the Robertsons, Campbell persuaded local landowners to modernise their businesses, in order that they would be in a position to better supply the Robertsons with the agricultural produce they required. The Scots then sold the produce down the river in Buenos Aires.

Over the next half-century many Irishmen would make spectacular fortunes on the Argentine pampas, trading not only in hides, skins and wool but also in meat, facilitated by innovations in the technology of preservation. John Robertson wrote that Campbell

> ... aroused the small towns and villages, as well as the estancias, from their dormant position into an active pursuit of business. He knew all

the inhabitants personally, and he picked out, with much sagacity, those who were likely to serve him best. He made contracts with them, or he drove them into Corrientes or Goya, to replenish their shops from our warehouses, or with the money we advanced to lend increased activity to their *esquinas* or pulperias; the pulpero being the combined 'grocer and spirit dealer' of South America.[15]

Campbell was as much an enforcer as a businessman, leaning on those *peons* or *gauchos* who were not disposed to see things his way. 'His physical strength, – his undaunted, if not ferocious, courage when roused, – his dexterity with his knife, and his ever ready appeal to that, or to his gleaming sabre,' John Robertson recalled, 'cowed all spirits less daring than his own and left him undisputed master of the field.'[16]

The Robertsons employed wagon trains to carry the huge quantities of hides that were being gathered by Campbell across the north-east territories of present-day Argentina. These wagon trains transported the hides from the *estanciero* to Goya on the River Paraná, from where they were brought more than 400 miles downriver to Buenos Aires and shipped to England.

Perhaps Campbell's greatest attribute was loyalty. He was not an ideologue, or personally ambitious. After deserting the British army he became a frontiersman, hitching his fortunes to Artigas and putting all his talents at the *caudillo*'s disposal, like a faithful sheriff's deputy.

In 1815 Artigas wrested control of Montevideo from the Buenos Aires government and founded the Federal League, comprising representatives of the Banda Oriental, parts of the south of present-day Brazil and the provinces of Misiones, Corrientes, Entre Ríos and Córdoba in present-day north-east Argentina. Artigas was now a real threat to the hegemony of Buenos Aires over the region. In 1816 Portugal invaded the Banda Oriental, capturing Montevideo from Artigas at the beginning of the following year. For the next three years Artigas fought a guerrilla campaign against Portugal and Buenos Aires.

Artigas had great faith in Peter Campbell's fighting capabilities. Campbell harried royalist, Paraguayan, Portuguese and *porteño* forces on land and sea. He formed a mounted regiment of indigenous Guaraní soldiers, armed with rifles and bayonets. They were a fearsome sight to the enemy as they charged across the plains at a gallop. In 1818 Artigas appointed Campbell commander-in-chief of his naval forces, an appointment that earned him the accolade of 'founding father of the Uruguayan navy.' He led expeditions up and down the Rivers Paraguay and Paraná from his base at Corrientes, a few miles downstream from the confluence of the rivers, using shallow-draft boats, known as *piraguas*, to board enemy vessels. Their knowledge of the strong currents at the point where the two rivers meet – after which Corrientes, or San Juan de las Siete Corrientes (St John of the Seven Currents), situated on a bend in the Paraná, takes it name – allowed Campbell and his fellow-guerrillas to surprise any approaching enemies sighted up- or downriver.

When their former allies in the Federal League turned on them in 1820, Artigas and Campbell had to accept defeat. Campbell was captured and exiled to Paraguay. The dictator, Francia, allowed him to settle in the province of Ñeembucú. The one-time revolutionary leader from County Tipperary took up his former trade of tanning in the city of Pilar in the south-western corner of present-day Paraguay, where he died in 1832.

In 1961 Peter Campbell's remains were discovered in the city cemetery and were transferred to Uruguay, where they were buried in the Naval Academy in Montevideo.[17]

After Artigas and Campbell's defeat at the Battle of Tacuarembó, the Portuguese annexed the Banda Oriental, and it became a province of Brazil. In 1822 the province formed part of the Brazilian Empire, whose sovereign, King Pedro I – the former prince regent of Brazil and son of the Portuguese king, John VI – declared independence from Portugal. While the government in Buenos Aires had allied itself with the Brazilians to defeat Artigas, it regarded the annexation of the eastern bank of the River Uruguay by the Brazilians as a threat to its interests and urged the local populace to rebel. The Brazilians responded by sending a squadron to the River Plate, which anchored off Buenos Aires. The economic blockade threatened the foundations of the infant state, and at the end of 1825 the Buenos Aires government turned in desperation to William Brown.

The Irish admiral could have rejected their advances in a fit of pique – after all, he had felt humiliated and scorned by his treatment at the hands of the government – but he had a strong commitment to service and realised that the Brazilian blockade threatened all the residents of Buenos Aires. He was again obliged to create a navy from scratch. Brown also had to face a far superior Brazilian navy, which could count on experienced Portuguese naval officers. He had 12 warships and 10 gunboats and fewer than 1,000 men; the

Brazilians had 129 ships and 10 gunboats in the River Plate alone. Brown had 150 cannon; the Brazilians had 1,600.

Brown's primary objective was to keep the sea lanes open in order to prevent the Buenos Aires economy from collapsing. He could not hope to win a major naval battle against such an overwhelmingly superior force. Brown's naval officers included John King from County Mayo, captain of the *Congreso*, James Kearney, one of the gunboat captains, and Francisco Lynch, born in Buenos Aires, the harbourmaster.[18]

In June 1826 Brown's small squadron repelled a larger Brazilian force at Los Pozos, ensuring control of the River Plate's sea lanes. He was once again a hero in Buenos Aires. But the Brazilians continued blockading shipping entering the River Plate estuary. In February 1827, at the Battle of Juncal, Brown routed a Brazilian squadron. It was a significant victory and kept open the lines of communication to the United Provinces' expeditionary force in the Banda Oriental.

At the end of 1827 the British government mediated a peace treaty between Brazil and the United Provinces, and in 1828 the Republic of Uruguay came into existence. William Brown returned home, having played his part in the creation of the continent's newest state, entering politics and becoming governor of Buenos Aires. He was in his early fifties and once again a respected naval hero; but this was not to be his last campaign.

In 1841 he once again took charge of the Argentine navy when war broke out with Uruguay. After a trip to his homeland in 1847, during which he witnessed the devastating effects of the Great Famine, he retired to his home in Buenos Aires. The great hero of Argentine independence died in 1857.

Chapter 9

GENERAL O'HIGGINS

In 1800 a Chilean merchant named Nicolás de la Cruz travelled with his family to the Andalusian port of Sanlúcar de Barrameda at the entrance to the River Guadalquivir. The de la Cruz household were fleeing a particularly virulent outbreak of yellow fever in Cádiz. Sanlúcar had once been an important port in its own right, its inhabitants living off the returning American galleons, their holds packed tight with gold and silver. These were the ships that were too large to navigate their way up the river to the docks at Seville. The town was also home to many religious orders. Generations of missionaries touched Spanish soil for the last time in Sanlúcar before setting off for the New World.

De la Cruz was a wealthy man and, unlike some of the poorer inhabitants of Cádiz, had been able to escape the disease-ridden city. However, the yellow fever followed him and his family and soon it had entered the house in which they were staying, striking down de la Cruz's ward, a 22-year-old Chilean by the name of Bernardo Riquelme. As the patient writhed with the fever and vomited up black bile, the doctors who had been summoned declared that there was nothing more they could do, and the local priest was called to administer the last rites. The rest of the household withdrew to await the inevitable news while the dying man was anointed with the holy oils.

Through those dark days and nights the young Bernardo suffered alone, thousands of miles from home, with no friends or family to keep him company. His guardian, de la Cruz, was a cold, uncaring man who showed little interest in his charge. But, summoning inner reserves of strength, the patient demanded that the doctors treat him with quinine. The treatment shifted the fever, and gradually he recovered. Bernardo Riquelme had proved that he was a survivor, an attribute he had inherited from his father, Ambrose O'Higgins, the viceroy of Peru.

Ambrose O'Higgins had abandoned Bernardo's mother, Isabel, after their brief dalliance in 1777 and was a distant, unfriendly figure throughout his son's youth. Nevertheless the father controlled his destiny for the first two decades of his life. Bernardo was born in Chillán, formerly San Bartolomé de Chillán, in southern Chile, on 20 August 1778. His mother and her family looked after him for the first years of his life; but one day in 1783 three soldiers – a lieutenant, a sergeant and a corporal – arrived at the Riquelme house demanding that the four-year-old Bernardo be handed over to them. The order had come from Colonel Ambrose O'Higgins.

The soldiers tore the child from his mother's arms and rode north to Talca, a town some 85 miles from Chillán, where he was placed in the household of the Portuguese merchant Juan Albano Pereira.[1] Shortly after his arrival in Talca, Bernardo was baptised in the Church of San Agustín, four-and-a-half years after his birth. Albano and his wife acted as godparents. The baptism was performed *sub conditione* – a conditional baptism performed in the Catholic Church when a priest was not sure whether or not a previous baptism had taken place. The priest who performed the baptism, Don Pedro Pablo de la Carrera, wrote that he was unable to establish whether the child had already been baptised, or the identities of the priest and godparents who might have taken part in any such ceremony – an indication of the furtive behaviour of all who were charged with looking after the young Bernardo.[2] It seems that there were in fact two baptisms, both of which Ambrose O'Higgins had ordered to take place.[3]

To quell the mounting rumours in Talca surrounding Bernardo's paternity, and conscious of the fact that his son's guardian, Albano, was elderly and ill, O'Higgins sent Bernardo back to Chillán to be educated by two Franciscans, Francisco Javier Ramírez and Blas Alonso, who were in charge of the Colegio de Naturales. The Jesuits had originally founded the college to provide education for the sons of the indigenous chiefs, or *caciques*. The Franciscans had taken it over when the Jesuits were expelled from South America in 1767.

O'Higgins then resolved to remove his son from Chile, sending him thousands of miles away to Peru. He gave the mission of removing the boy from the school in Chillán to his old comrade-in-arms and compatriot Thomas Delphin. The Franciscans handed the boy over to Delphin in the middle of the night, so as to avoid the Riquelme family trying to prevent Bernardo from being taken from his home. Delphin then rode with Bernardo to Valparaíso, where they boarded a ship bound for Lima. In the viceregal capital Delphin handed the boy over to another Irishman, a merchant by the name of John Ignatius Blake. It was Blake who now took responsibility for Bernardo's upbringing and education.

Bernardo spent four years at a college in Lima, under the supervision of Blake, before Ambrose O'Higgins, now approaching the zenith of his career, and perhaps fearing that a whiff of scandal could hamper his ambitions, ordered Bernardo to Europe. For the next six years the young man who had suffered the pain of being removed from his mother at an early age was to encounter privations and indignities. In 1796 he arrived in Cádiz, where he met de la Cruz – Albano's brother-in-law – who had been employed as a tutor by his father.

De la Cruz made it known that he was ill-disposed to help or show kindness to his new charge, sending Bernardo to London, where he arranged for him to be looked after by the eminent watchmakers Emanuel Spencer and John Perkins. Once again little concern was shown to the young guest from South America, and Bernardo was left penniless, relying on the kindness of strangers. In 1799 he wrote to De la Cruz, wondering why he had received no response to his letters: 'I do not know what to attribute it to; whether my parents have deserted me, or what must have occurred, since on the other hand I cannot believe that you have forgotten and abandoned me.'[4] Without money or the means to further his education, Bernardo resolved to return home to South America.

It was in Richmond in Surrey, at the house of a Mr Eels, that Bernardo was finally shown some kindness. He enjoyed walks along the Thames with his host's charming young daughter, Carlota, and began mixing with other South American émigrés living in London, among the most famous of whom was the Venezuelan revolutionary Francisco de Miranda.

Born into a wealthy Caracas family in 1750, Miranda had left home for Spain at the age of 21. Enlisting in the Spanish army, he fought under the Irish general Alexander O'Reilly in the disastrous Algerian campaign of 1775, and came to his attention for having allegedly embezzled funds from his regiment. He had also fought in the American War of Independence on the side of the British before becoming disillusioned with his fellow-officers.

Despite his privileged upbringing, Miranda felt himself something of an outsider. In Venezuela the *criollo* elite of Caracas had never accepted Miranda's father, who was from the Canary Islands, because he was a Spaniard, while in Spain Miranda was looked down on as an American. His experience of prejudice in the Spanish army radicalised him, and in the late 1780s he embarked on a peregrination across Europe. It was as much a sexual as an intellectual odyssey, from the evidence contained in the diary he kept of his adventures. Travelling through central Europe, Italy and Greece, he never seems to have passed up a sexual opportunity. Even Catherine the Great of Russia seemed powerless when faced with his techniques of seduction. But while Miranda was clearly enjoying himself, he was also busy watching and listening, formulating the political and military ideas with which he hoped to achieve Venezuelan independence.

In 1791 Miranda enlisted in France's revolutionary army, becoming friendly with various Girondin leaders and fighting in the campaigns against the Prussians the following year. During the Terror he was arrested and brought before the Revolutionary Tribunal. Through luck he escaped the guillotine twice, but when accused a third time of plotting against the government in 1797 he decided to make his escape, landing in England in January 1798. When Bernardo met him, Miranda was trying to convince the British government that it was in its interest to support his schemes for independence.

The Miranda whom the impressionable Bernardo Riquelme met in London was by this time a professional revolutionary. He was the picture of the eighteenth-century libertine, and middle age had not dulled his appetites, political, intellectual or sexual. To the 20-year-old Chilean, very much an *ingénue*, he must have seemed a most exotic creature. However, unlike the other male figures in his life, who had treated Bernardo with disdain – including his father, who refused to reply to his letters – Miranda, then in his late forties, showed kindness to Bernardo, dispensing words of friendly advice. 'Never let misery or despair take possession of your soul,' wrote the teacher to his student when Bernardo was readying himself to return to South America, 'since once you give yourself over to these feelings, you will be incapable of serving your country.' Miranda recommended distrusting 'any man that has passed the age of forty, unless you are sure that he enjoys reading, and especially those books that have been forbidden by the Inquisition.'[5] He also warned:

> Youth is the age of ardent and generous feelings. Among those youths of your age you will find many ready to listen and easy to convince. But, on the other side, youth is also the age of indiscretion and of reckless acts.

So that one must fear these defects in the young, as much as you would timidity and worry in the old.[6]

These few words of counsel governed the future actions of Bernardo Riquelme. Not a man to doubt his own worth, Miranda advised Bernardo to retain the letter and reread it on the crossing to South America, destroying it once he had arrived.

Bernardo returned to Cádiz in 1799, hoping for a recommendation from Nicolás de la Cruz so that he could enlist as an officer in the Spanish navy. Once again de la Cruz showed himself unwilling to help, and Bernardo decided to return to Chile. The voyage across the Atlantic was perilous – not least, as he wrote to his mother, because 'the seas were full of English corsairs and men-of-war.'[7] He set sail on 3 April 1800 on board the frigate *Confianza*, bound for Buenos Aires. The *Confianza* was travelling in convoy to guard against an attack from the British. Four days into the journey Bernardo was woken up in the middle of the night with the news that some sails had been spotted on the horizon. He hurriedly dressed and had just arrived on deck when a cannonball fizzed through the top of the mainsail. The captain of the *Confianza* tried to flee, but the Spanish ship proved too slow for the British 46-gun frigate and two 74-gun ships of the line in pursuit. Bernardo was taken prisoner and brought to Gibraltar, where he spent three days without food.

On his release, the penniless Bernardo made his way to Algeciras on foot, where he had the good fortune to meet his cousin Thomas O'Higgins, a captain in the Spanish army who had been travelling in the same convoy and had also been taken prisoner by the British. Thomas gave him some money and paid for his passage to Cádiz.

Once again the British attempted to capture their ship, but this time the cousins made it safely to port. Forced to fall on the mercy of de la Cruz one more time, Bernardo wrote of his despair in a letter to his father: 'At present I do not know what to do. I have abandoned all hope of seeing my father, my mother and my homeland, frustrated by the greatest dangers.' He added: 'Goodbye, most-loved father, until heaven concedes me the pleasure of giving you a hug: until then I will be neither content nor happy.'[8]

Worse was to come. Penniless, homesick and forced to rely on the charity of the begrudging de la Cruz, Bernardo was now stricken down with yellow fever. Once he had recovered, De la Cruz threw him into the street, at the instigation of his father. Ambrose O'Higgins had been relieved of his position as viceroy of Peru, in part because it had been discovered that Bernardo had been consorting with Miranda, a known enemy of the Spanish crown, in London. In a fury, O'Higgins had written to de la Cruz, telling him to throw his son out of his house. It was the most miserable moment of Bernardo's young life. He wrote to his father seeking an explanation:

> I, sir, do not know what offence I have committed to deserve such a punishment, nor do I know how I have been ungrateful (one of the offences that I most detest), since all my life I have tried with the utmost determination to give pleasure, and seeing frustrated this my sole ambition, irritating my father and protector, I remain confused.[9]

Bernardo's fortunes turned on the death of his father in March 1801. Despite his lack of paternal love, and the role that his son had played in his downfall as viceroy of Peru, Ambrose O'Higgins named Bernardo as the principal beneficiary of his will. He inherited his father's vast estate in the south of Chile, which included more than 4,000 head of cattle, transforming him into one of the richest landowners in the country. The once poverty-stricken exile was suddenly a man of substance and had no trouble finding the money to pay for his passage back to South America.

In September 1802 Bernardo Riquelme disembarked at Valparaíso in Chile after a five-month voyage at sea. Against the express wishes of his father's will, he now began using his surname. The illegitimate son, Bernardo Riquelme, had become Bernardo O'Higgins Riquelme, proud heir of the late Irish-born viceroy of Peru.

The *estancia* known as Las Canteras de San José, close to the Chilean town of Los Ángeles, covered more than 750 square miles. It was in a region known as the Isla de la Laja, the boundaries of which were the River Laja to the north, the Andes to the west and the River Biobío to the south-east. This was the wild frontier country that Ambrose O'Higgins had known so well. He had spent much of his adult life here, fighting or negotiating with the Mapuche, and had bought Las Canteras in 1785, naming as administrator one of his fellow-officers, Pedro Nolasco del Río. Upon finally taking possession of the *estancia* in 1804, having had to make the long journey to Lima to conclude the execution of his father's will, Bernardo O'Higgins began life as a modernising *estanciero* or ranch-owner. He ordered a round-up of the *estancia*'s livestock, planted 85,000 vines and fruit trees, and dug irrigation ditches.

For the first time in his life O'Higgins was able to spend time with his family. He was devoted to his mother, Isabel, and his half-sister, Rosa. The young man who returned to the Riquelme household was, according to his biographer, Eugenio Orrego Vicuña, 'handsome, strong, in good physical condition and with an erudition that outdid that of most young men of the era.' Orrego Vicuña wrote that O'Higgins was

> ... of medium height, a sturdy build, a robust walk, the face full with most regular features that could without difficulty pass for beautiful; the skin tanned, clear eyes, an open forehead, the hair slightly wavy and somewhat reddish, the mouth well-drawn and the gloss of youth on the cheeks, evidence of his Irish origins.[10]

For the next five years O'Higgins lived the life of a gentleman-farmer. In 1811, during the early years of the independence movement, he wrote to the Irishman John Mackenna: 'I could have become a good campesino and a useful citizen, and if I had been lucky enough to have been born in Great Britain or Ireland, I would have lived and died in the fields. But I first drew breath in Chile and I cannot forget what I owe to my homeland.'[11]

In 1810, reacting to events in Buenos Aires, the royal governor of Chile, Francisco Antonio García Carrasco, began arresting and deporting to Lima *criollos* suspected of sedition. Fearful of the consequences if Carrasco was to remain as governor, the Santiago *audiencia*, or royal court, replaced him with an 82-year-old Chilean aristocrat by the name of Mateo de Toro Zambrano. Under the guidance of his secretary, Juan Martínez de Rozas, the lawyer from Mendoza who was quietly directing events behind the scenes, Zambrano called a meeting of the city's open council. At the meeting, held on 18 September 1810, a ruling junta was formed, with Zambrano as president. The junta organised a national militia, opened Chile's ports to foreign trade and called a national congress, while still proclaiming its loyalty to King Ferdinand VII.

O'Higgins offered his services to Rozas. He formed two cavalry regiments, hoping that he would be appointed a colonel and be given command of one of them. Instead, Rozas appointed him *teniente-colonel*, a lower rank, and gave his own brother-in-law the rank of colonel and command of O'Higgins's regiment. An intensely disappointed O'Higgins considered leaving Chile and enlisting in the ranks of the patriot army in Buenos Aires. However, he changed his mind, demonstrating not for the last time his willingness to sacrifice his own ambitions for the good of the cause. 'Instead of accusing my friend Rozas of bias and injustice, which at first I had been inclined to do,' he wrote to Mackenna, 'I resolved to reserve my indignation for the declared enemies of our cause and convince Rozas of his error by my actions and not my words.'[12]

Mackenna warned O'Higgins about what to expect during the inevitable war with Spain:

> I have known the character of the Spanish for a long time; I know their pride, their ignorance, their stubbornness and their complete intolerance. They are the same men who fought against the Dutch under Philip II: two and a half centuries have changed nothing in them, at least to improve them.[13]

He predicted that the Spanish officers would employ brutal tactics to crush the young independence movement in Chile and advocated responding in kind. Mackenna's reflections on the qualities of a good soldier were based on his experience of fighting in Spain's wars in North Africa and against the First French Republic during the War of the Pyrenees between 1793 and 1795. Mackenna was dismissive of the Spanish officers with whom he had served. 'Very often I have been left perplexed at the thought of how the poor conduct of the Spanish army and navy officers is more often than not rewarded rather than punished,' he wrote, 'while good conduct is almost always disregarded.'[14]

Mackenna told O'Higgins that to learn the best way to organise a cavalry regiment he should seek out one of the sergeants who had served in his father's dragoon regiment, learn all he could from this man and then begin raising his own regiment, 'because there is no better way to learn yourself than to teach others.'[15] He also congratulated O'Higgins on how he had overcome his disappointment at not being named a *coronel*.

> ... I cannot finish [this letter] without expressing my most fervent approval of your conduct in not harbouring rancour at what, as an Irishman, I have the privilege of calling the 'nepotism' of our old friend Rozas. From the number of coronels that he has rustled up for

the brothers of his wife, I fear that skirt has influenced, more than was necessary, these appointments.[16]

In April 1811 an army colonel named Tomás de Figueroa attempted to crush the independent junta in Santiago and prevent elections to the new National Congress. The 1st Regiment of Grenadiers, under Mackenna's command, easily extinguished the rebellion after skirmishing with royalist troops in the Plaza de Armas in the centre of Santiago. Figueroa was shot and the royal *audiencia* was abolished.

When the National Congress met in June 1811 it was the moderate reformers who dominated. Representing Los Ángeles, O'Higgins became the voice of the radical minority. When the Congress elected a new, more moderate junta, Rozas was sidelined and withdrew to the city of Concepción in the south of the country. O'Higgins also briefly withdrew from public life to recover from a bout of pneumonia. In their absence a new political and military force emerged on the scene: José Miguel Carrera.

Born in Santiago, Carrera was a dashing 25-year-old, a former *sargento mayor* in the Spanish army who had fought against Napoleon. On hearing of events in Chile, and governed by fierce personal ambition, he had returned to his homeland in July 1811. For the next decade Carrera and his brothers, Juan José and Luis, who were also officers, vied with O'Higgins for control of independent Chile. It was a vicious, bloody struggle that ended in the premature deaths of both José Miguel Carrera and John Mackenna.

José Miguel Carrera was at the militant end of the political spectrum, desiring the complete separation of Chile from Spain. His first act upon his return to Chile was to overthrow the governing junta. The moderates were swept aside and a new junta, which included Mackenna, took its place in September 1811. Two months later, Carrera once again overthrew the government and assumed dictatorial powers. A new junta was established under Carrera's presidency, which O'Higgins reluctantly joined.

Carrera and O'Higgins had much in common. Both had been sent to Spain as boys to receive an education and had fallen under the influence of Enlightenment ideas. Both believed in full independence for Chile at a time when the majority of their class, the wealthy landowning *criollos*, preferred to hold on to the reforms won so far within the Spanish Empire. Yet there were significant differences of temperament and politics. O'Higgins had suffered the anxieties attendant upon his status as an illegitimate child and an outsider; Carrera was from one of the oldest, most respected *criollo* families in Chile and was supremely confident.

O'Higgins was a resolute general on the battlefield but believed in seeking compromise as a politician. He was convinced that the revolution must be based on representative institutions, advocated a National Congress and had made his support for Rozas dependent on the convening of such an assembly. This was despite his awareness that such institutions might weaken the revolution, which he made known in a letter to Mackenna: 'For my part, I have no doubt that the first Congress of Chile will demonstrate the most puerile ignorance and be guilty of all sorts of madness.'[17]

Carrera was an authoritarian. He believed that the weak, divided Congress was harmful to the survival of an independent Chile. O'Higgins resigned when Carrera abolished the Congress and arrested his rivals, including Mackenna. In the south of Chile, Rozas organised resistance to Carrera's government in Santiago, forming a militia and establishing a junta in Concepción.

O'Higgins worked feverishly to prevent civil war. In February 1812 representatives of Carrera and the Concepción junta signed a peace treaty. In July an insurrection in Concepción toppled Rozas, leaving Carrera the undisputed leader. O'Higgins retired to his *estancia*.

O'Higgins returned to public life in 1813 when the viceroy of Peru, José Fernando de Abascal, sent a military expedition to re-establish his authority and that of the metropolis over Chile. The government was ill prepared. In May 1814 O'Higgins signed a treaty with the Spanish commander that recognised the provisional government of Chile; but Abascal refused to accept the terms and appointed a new commander, Mariano Osorio, who marched on Santiago.

It was in the town of Rancagua, 50 miles south of Santiago, that O'Higgins and Chile's patriot army made their famous last stand. For two days O'Higgins and his men held out against the Spanish forces, but by the evening of 2 October Rancagua was ablaze. After cutting off the town's water supply, the Spanish had resorted to burning out the patriots. O'Higgins ordered the remains of the army to force their way through the Spanish cordon towards Santiago.

Following what became known as the Disaster of Rancagua, the patriot army and their families – men, women and children, their belongings borne by mules and llamas – trudged east across Chile's central valley. They were heading into exile, fearful of the retribution that would be meted out by the royalists, who were now in complete control of their country. Their destination was Mendoza, in the heart of present-day Argentina's most important wine-growing region.

Mendoza had originally formed part of the Captaincy-General of Chile under the ultimate authority of the viceroy of Peru in Lima, but in 1776 it became part of the new Viceroyalty of the River Plate, the capital of which was Buenos Aires. The city was an important way station. It was here that travellers making the overland journey from Buenos Aires to Santiago would rest before beginning the painful ascent of the cordillera.

Bernardo O'Higgins, his mother, Isabel, and his half-sister, Rosa, were among the refugees. The weary travellers found shelter from the elements in the refuges that Bernardo's father had built half a century earlier, but they were low on provisions and had to slaughter their horses and mules for meat.

On the other side of the Andes, in the town of Uspallata, General José de San Martín was waiting to welcome the Chilean exiles. San Martín was a liberal army officer and veteran of the Peninsular War from the Argentine province of Corrientes who, in 1811, had been initiated into the Lautaro Lodge, the masonic-like organisation dedicated to the overthrow of the Spanish government of South America. San Martín had arrived in Buenos Aires in 1812 and helped organise a new lodge to disseminate the revolutionary message. He had become convinced that the best way to protect the revolution in Argentina and drive the Spanish from South America was to attack the royalist heartland of Peru from Chile. To do this he had asked the government in Buenos Aires to name him governor of Cuyo province, whose capital was Mendoza. However, his plans were upset by the defeat at Rancagua and the fierce political rivalries that existed among the Chileans.

Hungry and ill-disciplined Chilean soldiers, exhausted by their journey across the Andes, were flooding into Uspallata, causing chaos. San Martín asked O'Higgins to take command of them and restore order. This infuriated José Miguel Carrera when he arrived in Uspallata shortly afterwards. Relations between O'Higgins and Carrera, which were already strained after Rancagua, were now at breaking-point, and the Chilean community in Cuyo divided between *o'higginistas* and *carreristas*.

In a memorial to the Buenos Aires government signed by O'Higgins and Mackenna the *o'higginistas* condemned the Carrera brothers.

> When that beautiful country has had the misfortune of falling under the painful and shameful yoke of a cruel tyrant, we find ourselves obliged, for the honour of the cause of America, to reveal to the eyes of the entire world, the authors of such an ill-fated event.
>
> Chile has seen itself suffocated by the audacity of these conspirators, who for a long time have carried with them the execration of its people … From the dark moment when the Carreras took control of the Government, even the most innocent knew that the day would come when the leader of the Lima troops would make all Chileans cry tears of blood …[18]

The *o'higginistas* blamed the Carreras and their cowardice in not coming to the aid of the besieged patriot troops for the defeat at Rancagua.

San Martín was afraid that Carrera and his supporters might challenge his authority and ordered troops stationed on the border with Chile back to Mendoza. Meanwhile, Mackenna travelled to Buenos Aires to report to the government. Carrera also sent emissaries, including his brother Luis. On 30 October, San Martín ordered the arrest of José Miguel and Juan José Carrera and sent them under escort to Buenos Aires.

The enmity between O'Higgins and the Carreras deepened the following month when news reached Mendoza of Mackenna's death at the hands of Luis Carrera in Buenos Aires. Carrera had challenged Mackenna to a duel and shot him in the neck, severing an artery. Carrera was arrested but was freed when Carlos María de Alvear, an old friend of José Miguel Carrera, became supreme director of the United Provinces.

This was a bleak period for O'Higgins. Forced into exile, he had lost Mackenna, his closest political ally and friend, and seen the man responsible for his death set free. The Carreras were once again in the ascendancy, and the prospects for an invasion of Chile were poor. Ferdinand VII had returned to the throne of Spain – after the French defeat in the Peninsular War – and had begun dismantling the liberal reforms introduced by the Cádiz Cortes and ratified in the constitution. The king was determined to restore his authority in the Americas and prepared to send an expedition of 10,000 royalist troops from Cádiz to the River Plate. In Chile the royalist authorities were instigating punitive measures and imprisoning those patriots who had failed to escape across the Andes. O'Higgins had lost all his material possessions, had no income and was forced to rely on the charity of friends.

The resignation of San Martín's adversary Carlos María Alvear as supreme director of the United Provinces brought fresh hope. Preparations for an invasion of Chile began, and at the beginning of 1817 San Martín's Army of the Andes, with Brigadier O'Higgins in command of the second division, began the march across the cordillera. San Martín's plan was for the army to enter Chile at various points along the western slopes of the Andes. O'Higgins marched north from Mendoza, crossing the Andes at Los Patos, and then swung south into the Putaendo valley and the town of Los Andes. The men battled freezing temperatures, drifts of snow and the thin air as they climbed to almost 10,000 feet above sea level. The officers struggled to keep the soldiers provisioned along the narrow paths that cut through the mountains. Spies warned the Spanish authorities of the imminent invasion but were unable to specify from where exactly the attack would come.

The decisive battle came at a ranch called Chacabuco on 12 February. The patriots triumphed and marched into Santiago unopposed. On 15 February the interim governor of Chile, Francisco Ruiz Tagle, called an assembly of notable citizens to appoint the new political leader. San Martín was the man chosen, by overwhelming acclamation; however, San Martín was determined to press on with his mission to rid the continent of the Spanish, and politely declined. The following day the Santiago aristocracy chose Bernardo O'Higgins as supreme director of Chile, a position he was to hold for the next six years.

O'Higgins was faced with a range of problems, not least the continuing royalist resistance in the south of the country, which remained a threat until the Battle of Maipú in April 1818. He also had tough political decisions to make. He owed his position as supreme director to the goodwill of the Buenos Aires government and his fellow-members of the secretive Lautaro Lodge, whose principal concern was the independence of the rest of the continent and the introduction of genuinely liberal government. O'Higgins, San Martín and Juan Martín de Pueyrredón were all members of the Buenos Aires lodge, and upon taking control of Chile they founded a lodge in Santiago. O'Higgins had to consult his fellow-members before making civil and military appointments, resulting in resentment from the Chilean aristocracy, who believed that Argentines were directing their government. The *criollo* elite were also wary of assaults on their privileges and resented what they perceived to be the anti-clericalism of the new regime, such as O'Higgins's decision to exile the royalist Bishop of Santiago, José Rodríguez Zorilla.

But though the royalist threat gradually receded, many difficulties remained, not least challenges to O'Higgins's authority from the Carrera brothers and the guerrilla leader Manuel Rodríguez. The latter had been a close friend of José Miguel Carrera, under whom he had served in the governing junta. In exile in Mendoza after the Battle of Rancagua, San Martín had selected Rodríguez for intelligence work in Chile. He had slipped across the frontier to report on royalist troop movements and had passed through the countryside disguised as a peasant, monk or servant. In March 1818, after the patriots suffered a setback against royalist forces at the Battle of Cancha Rayada, Rodríguez had taken control of the government, handing out weapons to the people of Santiago and founding a militia known as the Hussars of Death. Members wore black uniforms with a white skull and crossbones on the collar. His cry of 'We still have a homeland, citizens!' rallied spirits in Santiago and prepared the inhabitants to defend the city from the royalists. But after the Battle of Maipú, Rodríguez was imprisoned and put to death; his body was thrown into a ditch. Though it is unlikely that O'Higgins gave the order to kill him, some Chileans regarded him as the unseen author of Rodríguez's death.

The Carrera brothers were another threat to O'Higgins. Juan José and Luis Carrera had been arrested in Mendoza in 1817. The news that they had been shot reached Santiago days after the Battle of Maipú, and the blame was squarely attached to their arch-enemies, San Martín and O'Higgins.

O'Higgins was regarded by some – not least the supporters of the Carreras – as a ruthless tyrant. He had adopted conciliatory positions towards his political enemies for the sake of national unity in the early years of the revolution. Now convinced by bitter experience that the revolution would collapse into anarchy without firm government, he alienated powerful sections of Chilean society. His commitment to pan-American revolution and liberal republicanism was not consistent with their interests. O'Higgins was first and foremost a revolutionary. He wished to end privilege in Chile and introduce republican institutions, but having seen how representative assemblies had contributed to the fall of the *patria vieja* (old fatherland) – the period of independence between the first junta in 1810 and the Disaster of Rancagua – he came to believe that force was sometimes a necessary evil.

O'Higgins's greatest achievements in government were the founding of the Chilean navy and the organising and financing of San Martín's liberation expedition to Peru. O'Higgins was acutely aware that Chile was vulnerable to royalist attack as long as the country's thousands of miles of coastline were left unprotected and the Spanish remained in control of neighbouring Peru. With the help of the roguish Scottish naval officer Thomas Cochrane, who had fled financial scandal in Britain, and with limited resources, O'Higgins built the navy from scratch, helping to curb Spanish sea power in the Pacific.

Away from affairs of state, O'Higgins took solace in his family. He lived with Isabel and Rosa in the former governor's palace in the Plaza de Armas in Santiago. He never married, though he did have a son, Demetrio, from a brief love affair. The English author Maria Graham, who visited the palace in 1822, described the supreme director as 'short and fat, yet very active: his blue eyes, light hair, and ruddy and rather coarse complexion, do not bely his Irish extraction; while his small and short hands and feet belong to his Araucanian pedigree.'[19] Of his character Graham wrote: 'He is modest and simple, and plain in his manners, arrogating nothing to himself; or, if he has done much, ascribing it to the influence of that love of country which, as he says, may inspire great feelings into an ordinary man.'[20] Now in her early sixties, Isabel was a small, pretty woman, deeply devoted to her son. Several Mapuche children, whom O'Higgins had adopted while campaigning in the south, also lived in the palace. Maria Graham presented a picture of domestic happiness in her journal after a visit.

> The Director was kind enough to talk to them in the Araucanian tongue, that I might hear the language, which is soft and sweet; perhaps it owed something to the young voices of the children. One of them pleased me especially: she is a little Maria, the daughter of a Cacique, who, with his wife and all the elder part of his family, was killed in a late battle. Doña Rosa takes a particular charge of the little female prisoners, and acts the part of a kind mother to them. I was charmed with the humane and generous manner in which she spoke of them. As to Doña Isabella, she appears to live on her son's fame and greatness, and looks at him with

the eyes of maternal love, and gathers every compliment to him with eagerness.[21]

Surrounded by his loving family but also scheming advisers, such as the unpopular Spanish-born minister Antonio Rodríguez Aldea, who insulated him from public opinion, O'Higgins failed to realise that both conservatives and liberals were conspiring against him. The continuing war in Peru, which the Chilean government was financing, had at first added to his reputation as one of the great liberators of the continent, but the crippling cost to the treasury and O'Higgins's authoritarian style had made him unpopular. The fact that he was an enemy of privilege and corruption meant little to those who believed that they should enjoy the fruits of independence. By the time O'Higgins realised that his situation was precarious and had rid himself of Aldea, it was too late, and opposition to his rule had coalesced around Ramón Freire, a former comrade-in-arms. On 28 January 1823 O'Higgins resigned; six months later he went into exile in Peru, accompanied by Isabel, Rosa, Demetrio and an adopted Mapuche girl named Petronila. He was never to set foot in Chile again.

Chapter 10

BOLÍVAR'S IRISH VOLUNTEERS

The Irish contribution to the patriot war effort was not confined to the exploits of illustrious army and naval officers such as Bernardo O'Higgins and William Brown. Thousands of Irishmen enlisted in the patriot armies between 1817 and 1824, most of them fighting in the northern part of South America. Some had seen service in the Napoleonic Wars; others had had no military experience before embarking on the voyage across the Atlantic. Hundreds died from tropical diseases, such as yellow fever; others deserted soon after discovering that the riches they had been promised were no more than an illusion. But there were also those who distinguished themselves on the field of battle and earned a place among the heroes of the independence wars.

Their motives varied considerably. Some were driven by financial need, others by a spirit of adventure. Daniel Florence O'Leary was the teenage son of a Cork butter merchant who left home in search of glory, 'since there is nothing to compare to making noise in this world.'[1] Francis Burdett O'Connor was also from County Cork. He claimed to have come to South America to practise the art of war in order that he could use his new-found skills in the liberation of Ireland from British rule. According to O'Connor's memoirs, when he mentioned this on the eve of the invasion of Peru, Bolívar replied: 'Comfort yourself, my dear O'Connor, help me in this campaign, which I hope will be the last, and I will give you a regiment of my *llaneros**to help you liberate your homeland, your Ireland.'[2] John Devereux, who founded the Irish Legion, which fought in Venezuela, wrote that he 'cherished the delightful hope of coupling the glories of the country of my birth, with the new-born liberties of that country of my adoption.'[3]

The majority of the Irishmen who fought in South America were responding to calls for volunteers from Simón Bolívar and Venezuela's

---

* Plainsmen or cowboys, from the Spanish word *llano*, meaning plain.

patriot government. Bolívar was born in Caracas in 1783 to a wealthy *criollo* landowner. He studied in Europe, where, in the aftermath of the American and French Revolutions, he became attracted to the political ideas of Enlightenment thinkers such as Voltaire, Rousseau and Montesquieu. The *criollos* of Caracas had first declared independence in 1810, and Bolívar had travelled to London as part of a delegation that was seeking recognition from the British government. During their stay in London they had persuaded their compatriot Francisco de Miranda to return home and become the figurehead of an independent Venezuela.

When Spain regained control of Venezuela in 1812, Bolívar became the leader of the independence movement, replacing Miranda. The latter had been condemned as a traitor by his fellow-patriots for signing a treaty with the Spanish and he ended his days rotting in a Cádiz jail. Bolívar launched a new, brutal campaign against Spanish rule in his native land, which he described as a 'War to the Death'. The patriots had some initial successes, but the royalists were able to redouble their efforts in 1814. The Peninsular War was over and Napoleon was defeated, leaving the restored Spanish monarch, Ferdinand VII, free to send troops to South America. The arrival of a 10,000-strong royalist force from Spain under General Pablo Morillo forced Bolívar to retreat into the Venezuelan plains at the beginning of 1817. This desperate situation forced the patriots to seek help from abroad.

In 1817, having established a base in Angostura (renamed Ciudad Bolívar in 1846) on the banks of the River Orinoco in what is now south-east Venezuela, Bolívar ordered his agent in London, Luis López Méndez, to recruit volunteers for the patriot army. Méndez was assisted by the American William Walton. The majority of the officers and enlisted men who served in these foreign units were Irish,[4] tempted by promises of adventure and riches in exotic South America. On the streets of Dublin, Belfast and Liverpool, handbills and posters advertised the attractions of joining the fight for South American liberty. One handbill passed around Dublin promised volunteers that they would receive 'Four pence in the Shilling more than the British Army'; a free passage to Venezuela and 60 dollars upon arriving; a daily ration of a pound of beef or pork; a pound of bread; a pound and a half of potatoes, and a noggin of whiskey, oatmeal and butter on the passage; 'a Proportionate share of Land, Captures and Prize Money;' 200 acres of land and 80 dollars with which to purchase agricultural implements; and a full discharge and leave to sell the land with free passage home after five years of service.[5] It sounded too good to be true, and it was: there was no money, no land and a scarce amount of food when they arrived in South America.

A trickle of volunteers began to arrive in early 1817, but it was not until the middle of the year that Bolívar's agent, López Méndez, made systematic efforts in London to raise integrated units for service in Venezuela. The first wave of recruits travelled across the Atlantic in the second half of 1817 in half a dozen ships, under the command of six men whom the patriot government had awarded the rank of colonel in the Venezuelan army. Two of them were Irish: Henry Croasdaile Wilson, the choleric and conniving son of an Anglican family from County Galway, and Joseph Albert Gillmore, a former officer in the Royal Artillery from County Antrim.

The first ship to set sail from Portsmouth at the end of July was the 250-ton corvette *Two Friends,* carrying the Scottish colonel Donald MacDonald and 80 officers and enlisted men belonging to the 1st Venezuelan Lancers, all of whom were promised a daily ration of meat and biscuit, a pint of wine, a half pint of spirits and a bottle of porter, in exchange for the £40 cost of their passage. The volunteers spent several days waiting to embark while the money was found for provisioning the ship. Many were anxious to leave, having run up debts on shore; some had been arrested. When at last the ship departed, at 10 p.m. on 31 July 1817, according to one officer, 'all was hurry and confusion, and the appearance of the cabins presented a second chaos; the floors were strewed with beds, bedding, trunks, and packages of every description; upon these sat, smoking and drinking, those thoughtless adventurers, celebrating in noisy mirth their escape.'[6]

The ship was inadequately provisioned, and it put in at Madeira, where supplies of wine, spirits and fruit were brought on board. According to the sardonic author of *The Narrative of a Voyage to the Spanish Main in the Ship 'Two Friends'*, one party of six officers brought on board 180 gallons of spirits; 'this quantity for their number was enormous, but in order to reduce it, they were daily, nay, hourly drinking.'[7] This constant imbibing and the resentments caused by MacDonald, who, according to the same officer, 'imagined himself our commanding officer, demanding our respect for his authority,'[8] were the cause of frequent squabbles.

The determination of the ship's company to hold the ceremony marking the crossing of the Tropic of Cancer, during which a sailor dressed as King

Neptune would shave the heads of the uninitiated, caused further rows. According to the anonymous officer, some of the men were 'determined to resist every attempt to subject them to its endurance, and armed with pistols, placed themselves at one end of the cabin, threatening with death those who should endeavour to coerce them'.⁹ The *Two Friends* landed at the Danish island colony of Saint Thomas in September 1817. MacDonald was later killed on the banks of the Orinoco by members of an indigenous tribe en route to Bolívar's headquarters in Angostura.

The other five ships which carried the first wave of volunteers recruited en masse encountered horrendous storms before they had even left the English Channel. The corvettes *Britannia* and *Prince* and the frigates *Dowson, Indian* and *Emerald* embarked at the end of November and beginning of December, carrying Colonel Gustavus Hippisley's 1st Venezuelan Hussars, Wilson's 2nd Venezuelan Hussars, or Red Hussars, Colonel Peter Campbell's 1st Venezuelan Rifles, or Black Rifles, Colonel Robert Skeene's 2nd Venezuelan Lancers and Gillmore's artillery brigade. All these units were top-heavy with officers and NCOs, because it was intended to raise most of the troops in Venezuela.

The *Prince*, the *Britannia* and the *Emerald* arrived in the Caribbean in January and February 1818. The *Dowson* and the *Indian* were travelling in convoy. While the former managed to find shelter in the Cornish harbours of Falmouth and Fowey from the severity of the gales blowing across the English Channel, the *Indian* was lost, along with Colonel Skeene. Only five men survived the wreck, one of them an Irish officer by the name of John Johnston. Not to be deterred, Johnston managed to get to Venezuela and served with distinction in Bolívar's armies.

The first wave of volunteers were poorly informed about what to expect in South America. The more self-regarding officers ordered expensive dress uniforms for the sumptuous balls they expected to be held in their honour and practised cavalry charges – of little use where they were going – on the lawns of their town houses. They left unpaid outlandish bills from military outfitters in Dublin and London, which they expected the Venezuelans to honour, and dreamt about the vast country estates in South America they would enjoy in return for their services. According to the anonymous officer who sailed on board the *Two Friends,* 'it was evident they had formed high anticipations of the resources of the republic, and had pictured to themselves Oriental splendour and enjoyment.'¹⁰

An Irishman on board the *Two Friends* who had fought in the 1798 Rising in County Wexford had little time for the officers' pomposity. Colonel MacDonald had outfitted his officers in 'green dragoon jackets, trimmed with silver lace and faced with scarlet; epaulettes, with the rising sun of Venezuela: shackaes [shakos] mounted with silver lace and gold cord, and surmounted with a yellow and blue plume.'[11] From his corner in steerage, the gruff Irishman would pass comment on the officers who strutted up and down the deck in their finery: 'By Jasus, give me a pike, or a half pike, and I'll be a better commander than any of ye! Wasn't I at Vinegar-hill, where ye dars'nt show your noses – 'twas too hot for ye.'[12]

The English colonel Gustavus Hippisley, who had been the first to sign up with Méndez and for this reason insisted on being given command of all the foreign regiments that sailed to Venezuela, is perhaps the best example of the type of swaggering, deluded gentleman-soldier who landed in South America expecting every type of luxury. According to Alfred Hasbrouck, Hippisley had ordered that his officers be uniformed in 'dark green jacket with scarlet collar, lapels and cuffs, figured gold lace around the collar and cuffs, an ornamental Austrian knot on the arm, a lace girdle, and dark green trousers edged with similar gold lace down the sides, crimson sash and Wellington boots [calf-length leather boots].'[13]

The experience of most of the Irishmen who served in northern South America followed a predictable course. The officers spent the journey across the Atlantic drinking claret and madeira; the enlisted men would drink their daily ration of grog, if there was one, and grumble about the officers. The large quantities of alcohol consumed led to fights, especially duels among the officers. These were generally inconclusive: it was difficult to take aim on a pitching deck. An unpopular Irish officer on board the *Two Friends* fought a duel with a master's mate, which, according to one of his fellow-officers, 'created a little interest and variety to our conversation.' The men exchanged fire, but neither hit the mark; the seconds then intervened to end the duel 'without detracting from the courage of either.'[14] During another duel on board the same ship, two Irish officers let off six shots at each other, only to discover, much to the amusement of the spectators, that they were firing corks.

Upon disembarking at a neutral island in the Caribbean, the volunteers were transferred to the patriot-controlled Isla Margarita, or Margarita Island, about 400 square miles in area and less than 20 miles from the royalist-controlled coast, the Spanish Main. Once they realised that the promises of money and honours were hollow, many of those officers who had not already succumbed to tropical fever elected to resign their commission and either seek immediate passage back across the Atlantic or look for a more hospitable environment on one of the other Caribbean islands. Those few who were able and who chose to carry on had to make their way to the patriot capital at Angostura. This involved sailing south-west towards the Orinoco delta and upriver through the tropical jungle of south-east Venezuela.

Many of the Irish, including Daniel Florence O'Leary, who was not yet 20, were young men who had never left their parish before embarking on this great adventure. O'Leary's father, Jeremiah O'Leary, was a prominent Catholic merchant in Cork city and was friendly with Daniel O'Connell. O'Connell was a great admirer of Bolívar and may have influenced the young O'Leary's decision to enlist as a cornet (the lowest rank of cavalry officer) in Wilson's Red Hussars. O'Leary embarked on the *Prince* with the rest of the regiment at Portsmouth in December 1817. Most of his fellow-officers fought boredom by drinking and duelling, but O'Leary was not interested and hid himself away in his quarters, reading Spanish literature and grammar. His fellow-officers were determined to have an adventure; O'Leary was deadly serious about shaking the foundations of an empire.

Getting to the Caribbean was only half the battle. From Isla Margarita the Irish volunteers had to make their way towards the heart of Venezuela. If they were able to find a ship that would take them, they would sail south-east along the coast of the South American mainland towards the River Orinoco. Finding the correct channel was difficult, because the tall trees of the jungle presented a uniform appearance all along the coast. It was also difficult to approach the mainland because of the heavy groundswell and the breaking waves.

The appearance of powerful reddish-brown currents signified that they were close to the *boca grande,* the great mouth of the river. The squawks of eerie-sounding birds, the growls of jaguars from the darkness of the trees on each bank and the evil-looking crocodiles that trailed like assassins through the water beside the shallow-bottomed *flecheras* that carried them deeper into the jungle reminded the Irish volunteers of how far away from home they were.

One volunteer, Richard Longville Vowell, found that the scenery was 'strikingly beautiful' and, 'when viewed from a ship's deck, as she glides slowly along the smooth water, presents a magnificent moving panorama.' He was fascinated by the sheer size of the vegetation.

> The banks, on each side, are covered with impervious forests of majestic trees; chained, as it were, to each other by the *bejuco*, or gigantic creeping plant of South America, which grows to the thickness of an ordinary cable ... Among the branches, monkeys of every description gambol, and follow the vessel, springing from tree to tree by means of the *bejuco*, which has obtained from this circumstance its Indian name of 'monkey's ladder'.[15]

The hot and humid climate made it difficult to breathe – the temperature could climb as high as 40 degrees Celsius during the day – and the volunteers' throats were constantly parched from the lack of fresh water. Desperate for a cooling draught, they would reach into the fetid river, swallowing the dirty water cradled in their cupped hands, only to be clutching their stomachs in agonising pain a little later, having vomited the meagre contents back where they came from.

Depleted by desertion and sickness, Hippisley's and Wilson's units arrived in Angostura in March and April 1818 and joined those who had arrived with MacDonald's lancers. Gillmore's artillery brigade had broken up in confusion in the West Indies, and Campbell had returned home from the Antilles after the death of his son. Campbell's replacement, Colonel Richard Piggott from County Kerry, led the remaining officers and men of the Rifles to Angostura.

About 150 or 200 of the 800 men who had sailed across the Atlantic made it to patriot headquarters deep in the Venezuelan jungle. However, their circumstances had improved little, if at all. Built on a hill on the southern bank of the river, Angostura was a mean-looking place, far from the comforts of home. At the crest of the hill was a small fort and lookout, beneath which was the military hospital, housed in a former convent. The half-built cathedral on one side of the town's main plaza was the only concession to European notions of civilisation. The only decent buildings in town – built of stone, bricks and tiles, as opposed to the wattle-and-daub huts of the townspeople – were home to the patriot congress and the billets of the senior officers. The barracks was little more than a series of vermin-infested huts. If they were lucky, the Irish junior officers would be given a tattered straw mat for a bed.[16]

There was little to eat, especially for those officers who had no money. Alfred Hasbrouck's magisterial book *Foreign Legionaries in the Liberation of Spanish South America* colourfully describes the volunteers' mealtimes in Angostura:

> When a distribution of rations was necessary, a bullock was lassoed and tied to a stake. It was then killed by stabbing in the neck. Very often no attempt was made to bleed the animal properly before it was skinned. The flesh was then torn and scraped off the bones with utter disregard of precautions to keep it clean. The fact that it might be covered with sand and grit as well as flies, when issued to the ultimate consumer, apparently received little consideration by those in charge of the operation. To secure this ration, even the officers must go for it themselves, and each one carried home his chunk of beef in the heat of the day to cook it as best he could without utensils. Then, when the best pieces had been issued out for immediate roasting, stewing or boiling, the remainder, consisting generally of the muscular tissue, was cut into long narrow strips and hung in the sun to dry for several days. When these strips had become as hard and dry as rope they were considered properly cured, and could be kept indefinitely.[17]

There were certain luxuries to be had in Angostura, however, for those who could afford them. In March 1819, according to the newspaper *Correo del Orinoco*, a consignment of goods brought across the Atlantic by the frigate *George Canning* had arrived from London. This included:

> Sadlery, Horsewhips, Dressing Cases, and Ladies' Work – Boxes, Ladies' Dresses; Scented Soap of various kinds; Hair, Tooth, Shaving and Coat-Brushes; ready-made Duck Trousers of the best quality; Razors, Penknives, and Scissors; Shoe-Brushes and Blacking; – also, Pistols and Swords, and good Porter.[18]

The great scourge of the jungle was tropical disease, especially yellow fever. The unfortunate soldier who was bitten by an infected mosquito would start to experience thumping headaches, chills and muscle pains; he would then begin to vomit black bile. The lucky ones would then make a full recovery, but a significant minority would experience internal haemorrhaging and liver failure, which would cause their skin to take on the jaundiced complexion from which the disease takes its name. In April 1818 Sergeant-Major Thomas Higgins had succumbed to fever on the river before even reaching Angostura. Lieutenant Michael Plunkett died shortly afterwards. Each morning those who had died during the night were brought to the cemetery on the outskirts of the town and buried, with little ceremony, sometimes not even a coffin.[19] Richard Longville Vowell wrote in his memoir: 'No place in the world could be more admirably calculated to foster and mature that fatal disease than the sultry city of Angostura, with its stagnant, half putrid lagoon; its *matanzas* [slaughterhouses]; and its thousands of raw-hides drying on the pavement in front of the stores, in preparation for shipment.'[20]

The regimental commanders embarked on scouting missions into the hinterland to find the men they needed to fill their complement of troops. The bulk of the men who served under the Irish officers in the foreign regiments were members of indigenous tribes who had lived on the Capuchin missions in the area, or the descendants of African slaves. Piggott's rifle regiment comprised Irish and English officers and indigenous and *mestizo* troops.[21]

A handful of the English and Irish officers were disgusted by their treatment in Venezuela and attacked the patriot government in the pages of the press when they returned home. They wrote memoirs in which they bemoaned their fate and warned prospective recruits of the dangers that faced them in the tropical jungle. In the preface to his book Colonel Hippisley gives a sense of how the Europeans, who were used to modern logistics, were completely unprepared for the conditions and terrain they found in South America.

> The utter want of a commissariat, and the intolerable heat of the climate, involve a complication of miseries which no European constitution can withstand; and the author has to lament the death of the great majority of his companions, who perished, like infected lepers, without sustenance and without aid from the unfeeling wretches in whose behalf they fell.[22]

The anonymous author of *The Narrative of a Voyage to the Spanish Main in the Ship 'Two Friends'* wrote in the preface that he was 'merely animadverting upon the conduct of the cause, and its probable progress, with the view of explaining his motives, for dissuading his countrymen from giving implicit credit to the specious promises and false representations of interested individuals.'[23]

However, many of the foreign officers adapted to the harsh conditions as best they could without significant complaint and fought bravely in the long, hard campaigns that followed. William Jackson Adam noted in his memoir that the articles and books that appeared in Dublin and London were written by disgruntled officers – 'those heroes,' as he sarcastically described them – and had the purpose of rendering 'plausible and praiseworthy' their 'desertion from the cause of liberty.' They 'not only tended to bring disgrace upon the promulgators of *their disgrace*, but to bring into discredit that noble cause in which, on the first going off, they were so eager; but the difficulties and dangers of which they had not sufficient courage to withstand.'[24]

With the officer corps decimated, the remnants of the 1st Hussars and Red Hussars were amalgamated into one regiment under Hippisley's command and received orders to join Bolívar in San Fernando, about 270 miles west on the River Apure, a tributary of the Orinoco. San Fernando was full of injured soldiers and refugees from the battles that had been fought against the Spanish in the early months of the year.

The officers in their spanking new uniforms arrived in San Fernando to meet their comrades-in-arms, *llanero* and indigenous troops, dressed in little more than rags, who fought for General José Antonio Páez, a bluff, no-nonsense plainsman with no formal education, far removed in class and temperament from Bolívar and the other aristocratic *criollo* officers. However, it was not long before the impoverished foreign officers were forced to sell their beautiful uniforms in exchange for food. For much of the campaign it was the Venezuelan officers and their men who paraded in the scarlet uniforms of the British infantry, while the Irish and English officers were dressed in rags.

In the town of Achaguas, close to San Fernando, Daniel O'Leary witnessed Colonel Wilson attempting to subvert Bolívar's authority after the latter had returned to the patriot capital, Angostura. Wilson began heaping praise on Páez during a banquet, even going so far as to suggest that the Venezuelan should be named captain-general of the patriot armies. With his eye on the main chance, Wilson offered to raise thousands more men in England, which he himself would command on his return. O'Leary was disgusted by what he regarded as an act of treachery towards Bolívar and was distressed at the treatment and execution of royalist prisoners. The earnest, intense young officer from County Cork took his mission in South America very seriously, unlike some of his more bumptious fellow-officers, and requested separation from his unit and a transfer to Angostura.[25] He had a firm early nineteenth-century sense of honour, evidence of which is contained in a letter he wrote much later – when he was married and had a newborn son, whom he named Simón. In the letter to his wife, Soledad, he expressed his hope that his son would be 'virtuous and honourable, and that, at the same time, he would not deceive others, nor let himself be deceived.'[26]

In Angostura, Bolívar learnt of Wilson's dealings with Páez and arrested him. Wilson was thrown out of the army, and out of Venezuela.[27] On his return to Ireland he launched a propaganda campaign against Bolívar and the patriot cause; the patriot newspaper published in Angostura, the *Correo del Orinoco*, responded by accusing him of treachery and suggested that he was lucky that he had escaped Venezuela with his life.

> If the Colonel had picked up his sword on behalf of the insurgents' cause with even half the vigour with which he employed his pen against it, he probably would have had no differences with [Bolívar] who, after all, could not be the terrible person who has been painted by Colonel Wilson.[28]

It was later alleged that Wilson was a spy, who had taken money from the Spanish ambassador in London to foment trouble in the patriot ranks.

In the aftermath of the incident with Wilson, O'Leary asked to be transferred to a Venezuelan unit so that he could improve his Spanish. He was assigned to General José Antonio Anzoátegui's personal guard. It was at this point in 1818 that O'Leary first met Bolívar, who seems to have approved of the Irishman's conduct.[29] It was the beginning of a close relationship, which – while not always quite as harmonious as has sometimes been made out – lasted until Bolívar's death in 1830. According to O'Leary,

> Bolívar had a high forehead, but not very wide and furrowed by lines – the sign of a thinker. His eyebrows were bushy and well-formed. His eyes were black, alive and piercing. His nose was large and perfect; he had on it a small wart that bothered him quite a bit, even though it disappeared in 1820, leaving an almost imperceptible mark. He had prominent

cheekbones; the cheeks hollow since I first met him in 1818. His mouth was ugly and his lips were somewhat thick. The distance between his nose and his mouth was significant. His white teeth were even and most beautiful; he looked after them with care. His ears were large but well-positioned.

His hair was fine and curly; he wore it long in the years 1818 to 1821, when it started to grey, upon which he started to cut it. His sideburns and mustaches were red; he shaved them for the first time in 1825.[30]

Bolívar had dark, coarsened skin – not surprising given the amount of time he spent in the saddle. He was not tall: five feet six inches. Neither was he broad: he had a narrow chest, a slim frame and 'small and well-formed hands and feet, which a woman would have envied.'[31]

O'Leary betrays the fascination Bolívar exerted on his subordinates and perhaps the intimacy engendered by weeks and months in the field together. The Liberator's small vanities sat side by side with a fierce intelligence. It was this keen mind that enabled him to conjure up a daring plan to break the military deadlock between the patriot and royalist forces.

At the end of 1818 a new wave of volunteers began arriving in Angostura, recruited in the cities of Ireland and England by Colonel James Towers English, a Dubliner who had enlisted in Hippisley's 1st Hussars, and Colonel George Elsom. English was the enterprising son of a Dublin merchant. Orphaned at 11, he had found work supplying horses to the British army before joining the army's commissariat as a clerk. In 1817 he was commissioned as a lieutenant-colonel in Hippisley's 1st Hussars. He had ingratiated himself with General Páez by giving him water in the heat of battle when the latter was suffering from an epileptic fit. Páez later presented English with a bloodied lance as a souvenir, which the Irishman was depicted holding in a portrait he had commissioned when he returned to England.[32] In the middle of 1818, realising that the Venezuelan Republic was still in desperate need of men, English had signed a contract with the vice-president, Antonio Zea, worth 300 pesos a man, to raise a further thousand troops in Britain and Ireland.

About 1,200 men recruited by English arrived in Angostura. Though they became known as the British Legion, about half the enlisted men were Irish. Officers compiled a list of the British Legion's NCOs and privates in Achaguas in December 1820.[33] Of the 310 men listed, at least 142, or 46 per cent, were Irish (there may have been more; some of the names are illegible).

The bulk of the remainder were English, Scottish and Welsh, but there were also Germans, Italians and Venezuelans, as well as volunteers born in India and the United States.

The Irish NCOs and privates came from all over Ireland. Only three of the 32 counties are not represented on the Achaguas list: counties Clare, Leitrim and Offaly. Two-thirds of the Irishmen who appear on the list were from Leinster and Ulster. Dublin provided 30 of Leinster's 50 volunteers, including Sergeant John James, a 47-year-old shoemaker, Private John Middleton, a 46-year-old watchmaker, and Private James O'Neill, a 33-year-old bootmaker. On the other hand, only a handful of the volunteers from Ulster were from Belfast. Many of the Ulstermen had been employed in the textile industry and came from its traditional heartland: of the province's 49 volunteers, 39 came from counties Antrim, Armagh, Cavan and Down. Eleven of the Ulstermen gave their occupation as weavers, including 30-year-old Bugler James Rhodes from Armagh and 24-year-old Private James Murray from Ballymena. One, 33-year-old Private James Gilbert from Portaferry, was a cotton-spinner. The high percentage of textile workers perhaps reflected a slowdown in the industry in the aftermath of the Napoleonic Wars.

Of the 43 volunteers who came from Connacht and Munster, 21 were from County Cork, six from County Tipperary, five from County Mayo, and four from County Kerry; there were two each from counties Galway and Sligo and one each from counties Limerick, Roscommon and Waterford. They included Sergeant John Noble, a 33-year-old labourer from Sligo, Corporal John Ryan, a 29-year-old carpenter from Limerick, Private Thomas Ryan, a 44-year-old gardener from Bandon, and Private Martin Hopkins, a 26-year-old weaver from Castlebar.

The Irish volunteers on the Achaguas list ranged in age from 16 to 51 according to the ages they gave the officers, although there may have been younger and older men in the ranks. More than half were in their twenties. There were also 13 volunteers aged 19 and under, 28 were in their thirties, 18 in their forties and four in their fifties.

Sixty-four of the Irish volunteers, 45 per cent of the total, gave their occupation as labourer. But there were also artisans and tradesmen, including bookbinders, tailors, smiths, breeches-makers, carpenters, apothecaries, shoemakers, reed-makers, pipe-makers, watchmakers, gardeners, hairdressers, servants, cutters, furriers, sailors, cabinetmakers, bricklayers, bakers, woollen drapers, musicians, ironfounders, cordwainers [leather workers], painters, glaziers, clerks, butchers, glass-blowers, car men, weavers, cotton-spinners and beaters.

Another regiment of 300 Irish volunteers sailed from Cobh on 17 July 1818 under the command of Major Beamish. All the officers were family or friends of Beamish, and nearly all had seen military service.[34] Ten days into the voyage, however, Beamish collapsed and died from a stroke, prompting the main body of the volunteers to demand that the captain return to Ireland. One of those on board, Captain Cowley, who took command and wrote an anonymous account of his service in the Venezuelan army entitled *Recollections of a Service of Three Years during the War-of-Extermination in the Republics of Venezuela and Colombia,* recalled that he and his fellow-officers were fearful of a mutiny. At one point the men attempted to rush the armed officers and throw them overboard, but they were repelled. Afterwards, according to the author,

> ... my antagonists were, as before, very violent, and still demanded our immediate return to Ireland, pressing me for an answer on the spot, which I purposely avoided giving as long as possible, wishing to gain time to prepare against a desperate attempt, which I had reason to expect they would make to gain possession of the ship. I observed that they were arming themselves with handspikes, spars, and every other means of an offensive nature within their compass, and consequently felt assured of an attack the very first opportunity.[35]

The officers were confident of the seamen's loyalty and ordered two of the eight 12-pound guns in the hold to be brought onto the deck and loaded as a deterrent. A hundred muskets were also brought up and loaded. Believing that one particular junior officer was instigating the unrest, the author took it upon himself to question the men, against the advice of the other officers, who believed he would be thrown overboard.

> ... but I had more confidence in them; I knew that Irishmen, although easily heated, are as easily cooled ... I accordingly went forward, throwing my sword and pistols on the deck, and asked them directly if my suspicions were correct.[36]

The men informed on the mutinous young officer, who tried to strike Cowley with a handspike. He was finally thrown overboard with a rope tied around his waist to cool his temper, the effect of which was that 'on being hoisted on board again he was pale and ill from fright, and did not recover during his stay with us sufficiently to leave his cabin.'[37]

Further ships crossed the Atlantic carrying soldiers under the command of another Irishman, Lieutenant-Colonel John Blossett, English's second-in-command. English himself sailed in February 1819 and arrived in Isla Margarita that April, where he was promoted to brigadier-general in command of the Irish and British volunteers but under the orders of the Venezuelan-born General Rafael Urdaneta. One contemporary wrote of English:

> As an officer, he was destitute of energy, and experience; as a man he was generous and open-hearted. All that can be said of him in reference to his conduct as commander of the British legion is, that he mistook his profession, for which indeed he was physically unfitted.[38]

Ordered to make an assault on the Venezuelan mainland, Urdaneta set sail on July 1819 with an expeditionary force of 1,200 men, about 800 of whom were Irish and British volunteers, under English's command. They took the fortress of El Morro and the town of Barcelona before marching north-east towards the town of Cumaná. But Urdaneta and English argued about their next step. The aim of Urdaneta's campaign was diversionary, to pin down royalist troops who might otherwise be deployed against Bolívar elsewhere, and it was anticipated that any gains made by the patriot armies could not be sustained. Urdaneta favoured bypassing Cumaná, where there was a royalist garrison, and marching inland towards Maturín. However, English thought it vital that an assault be launched on Cumaná, fearing that prolonged inactivity among the troops might well lead to mutiny.

Urdaneta eventually agreed to an attack but warned English that the consequences of the action, which he thought suicidal, would fall on the Irishman's shoulders. Attempting an attack on a defensive battery outside the town, an assault party of volunteers was forced into a ditch. Urdaneta ordered a retreat, during which the volunteers suffered heavy casualties from Spanish gunfire. About 150 of Urdaneta's men were killed or injured. The general was now determined to march towards Maturín in the interior.

Pleading illness, English was allowed to return to Isla Margarita, where he died in September 1819.

The colonel's funeral was carried out with a great deal of ceremony, the Irish officers and men parading behind the coffin with arms reversed, along with Venezuelan soldiers, staff officers, naval officers, sailors and marines. At 4 p.m. on 29 September, to the beat of a muffled drum, the procession began moving slowly out of Juan Griego, the main town on Isla Margarita, towards the grave. Three musket volleys rang out as the coffin was lowered into the ground, answered by artillery from the nearby forts and the vessels in the bay. The death of their compatriot moved the Irish soldiers. According to William Jackson Adam, as the soldiers made their way back to their lodgings in Juan Griego 'the sun was sinking into his watery bed in unusual splendour, and the music playing our national air of "Patrick's Day," reminded us of the land of our nativity, from which we were separated, and to which, like our departed countryman, many were destined never to return.'[39] The Irishman John Blossett replaced English as commander of the British Legion.

While Urdaneta was leading the attack on royalist positions on the Venezuelan coast, Bolívar and Páez were taking the fight to the Spanish on the country's plains. The Dubliner James Rooke, who came from a family steeped in the tradition of service in the British army, was among the most prominent Irish officers during the campaigns on the *llanos* between 1817 and 1819. Rooke's father was a wealthy English soldier and politician who had served as an aide-de-camp to the unpopular Lord Lieutenant of Ireland George Townshend in the late eighteenth century. Rooke senior had obviously enjoyed his time in Dublin, producing three illegitimate children, including James, with his Irish lover. The younger Rooke had enlisted as a second lieutenant in the 49th Regiment of Foot in 1791 and fought in the French Revolutionary Wars.

He seems to have had plenty of money. In 1798, having bought a commission as major in the Queen's Light Dragoons, he married Mary Rigge, a doctor's daughter from Bristol. They settled in the ranger's lodge of Cornbury Park at Charlbury in Oxfordshire, the estate of the Duke of Marlborough, where Rooke took like a duck to water to the life of a country squire. He passed his days hunting, shooting and gambling; his nights were spent carousing in social circles that included the Prince of Wales. However, like many members of the minor gentry, he was getting himself deeper and deeper into debt at the card table and racetrack. In 1801 he abandoned his family, selling his racehorses and hunters and fleeing to France, where, on the resumption of hostilities between Britain and France, he was arrested.[40]

Escaping his captors, he made his way to Cádiz and once again was commissioned in the British army. He fought his way across the continent – he was possibly present at Waterloo – and served as an aide-de-camp to the Prince of Orange. After 1815 and the end of the war in Europe he was a widower without prospects, his wife having died the previous year. Always hungry for adventure, he decided to visit his sister, who was married to the British governor of Saint Christopher Island (popularly called Saint Kitts).

It was a fateful decision. It was in Saint Kitts that Rooke fell in love with a 'very fascinating and elegant' local woman by the name of Anna, who had been educated in England.[41] It was also where he learnt that the Venezuelan government in Angostura was looking for volunteers, and so he wrote to Bolívar proposing that he raise a regiment of hussars in Trinidad. This came to naught, and instead Rooke offered his own services as a soldier. James and Anna Rooke arrived in Angostura on a merchant vessel in 1818. They set up house and lived off the allowance Anna's father sent her, though it was seldom enough to keep them afloat. While Rooke was off recruiting in the depths of the jungle for indigenous troops, Anna began a love affair with one of her husband's comrades, causing scandal and becoming the main source of conversation among the Irish and English volunteers.[42]

Rooke's military experience ensured that he was given the rank of lieutenant-colonel and a command of unit of hussars. However, not everyone was impressed by Rooke. Daniel O'Leary had time to cast a critical eye over his fellow-countryman in Angostura and found him wanting.

> Happy with everyone and with everything, and especially himself, he seemed less than indifferent, pleased with the life he was leading. To him, the climate of Apure was soft and healthy and superior to any other, until he entered the territory of New Granada, the climate of which, according to him, had no rival in the world.[43]

Rooke may have been a faintly ludicrous character, but he was also accustomed to the hardships of campaigning – he was, after all, a more experienced soldier than the callow O'Leary. There was also perhaps the fact that Rooke's roguish, devil-may-care attitude was anathema to the

1. The son of Irish Jacobite exiles to France, the soldier and diplomat Richard Wall rose to become prime minister of Spain and helped the careers of many Irishmen in Latin America. (Portrait of Richard Wall, Spanish Ambassador to Britain (1694–1778), 1753. Artist: Louis Michel van Loo, 1707–1771. Oil on canvas. Photo © National Gallery of Ireland, NGI.4660)

2. *Charles III in Hunting Dress*, by Francisco Goya. The Bourbon king implemented far-reaching reforms in Spanish America. (*GraphicaArtis / Getty Images*)

3. Born in County Meath, Alexander O'Reilly modernised Spain's armed forces and rebuilt the Spanish Empire's military defences. (Alejandro O'Reilly (1722–94) *(oil on canvas)*, Francisco José de Goya y Lucientes (1746–1828) / Museo de San Telmo, San Sebastian, Spain / Bridgeman Images)

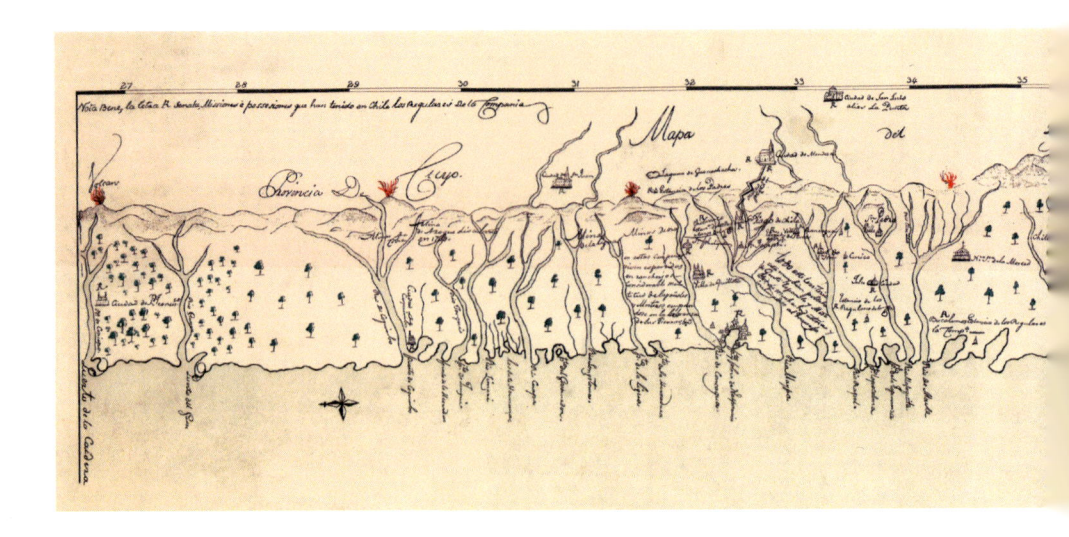

4. The County Sligo-born Ambrose O'Higgins rose through Spain's colonial administration to become the viceroy of Peru, the most powerful and distinguished office in South America. (© *Topfoto / Topham Picturepoint*)

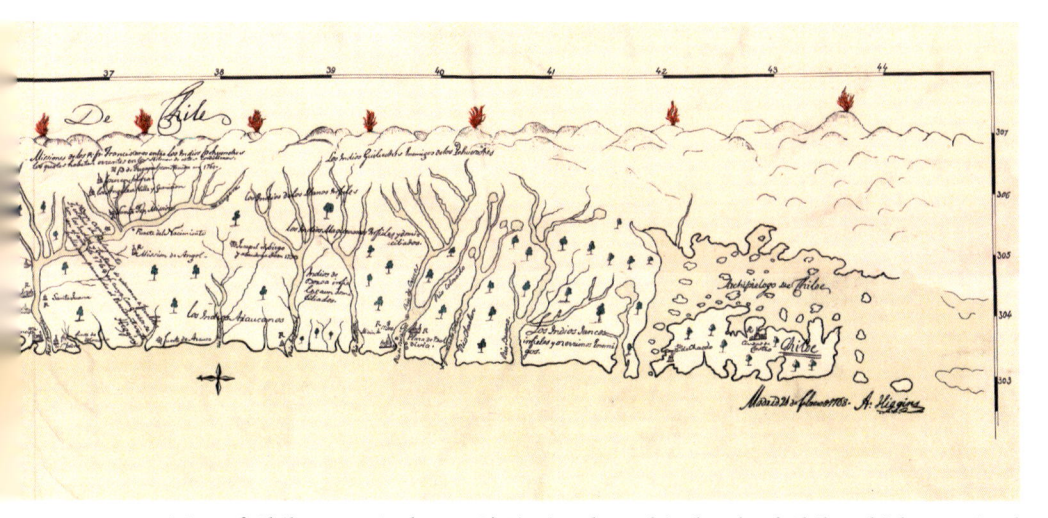

5. Map of Chile, 1768. Ambrose O'Higgins drew this sketch of Chile, which contained valuable topographical information, in a bid to curry favour at the Spanish court. (*Mapoteca Archivo Nacional de Chile, N° 858*)

6. *The Second of May, 1808*. Francisco Goya's portrayal of the popular uprising against the Napoleonic occupation of Spain. (*The Art Archive / Alamy Stock Photos*)

7. *The Third of May 1808*, Francisco Goya's haunting depiction of the reprisals that followed the popular rising against the French occupation of Spain. (Execution of the Defenders of Madrid, 3rd May, 1808, *1814 (oil on canvas), Francisco José de Goya y Lucientes (1746–1828) / Prado, Madrid, Spain / Bridgeman Images*)

8. Born in Puerto Rico into an Irish family, Ramón Power y Giralt was one of the most outspoken critics of Spanish policy in the Americas at the Cádiz Cortes and helped transform the relationship between Spain and her colonies. (*Museo de la Cortes de Cádiz. Agradecimiento al Excmo. Ayuntamiento de la ciudad de Cádiz.*)

9. *The Proclamation of the 1812 Constitution*, by Salvador Viniegra. Spain's liberal constitution was drafted by the Cádiz Cortes and influenced political thought throughout Latin America. (*Lucas Vallecillos / Iberfoto / Mary Evans*)

10. Born into an Irish family in Seville, José María Blanco White renounced the Roman Catholic priesthood and went into exile in England, from where he championed Latin American independence in his newspaper, *El Español*. (*Edward Gooch / Hulton Archive / Getty Images*)

11. *The Inquisition Tribunal*, by Francisco Goya. Blanco White was an ardent critic of the Spanish Inquisition. (© *The Art Archive / Alamy Stock Photo*)

12. William Brown was the County Mayo-born founder of the Argentinian navy and hero of the Argentinian wars of independence. He lived to see the advent of photography in his retirement in Buenos Aires.

13. Bernardo O'Higgins was the illegitimate son of Ambrose O'Higgins. He led the fight for Chilean independence, becoming the country's supreme director. (© *Topfoto / Topham Picturepoint*)

14. The County Monaghan-born John Mackenna was a protégé of Ambrose O'Higgins and fought alongside his son, Bernardo O'Higgins, in Chile. Mackenna was killed in a duel in Buenos Aires. (*Colección fotográfica Museo Benjamín Vicuña Mackenna, N° Sur 9-332*)

15. O'Higgins and the patriot forces made their famous last stand against Spanish forces at the Battle of Rancagua in 1814. They finally defeated the Spanish in 1817 to seal Chilean independence. (*Biblióteca del Congreso Nacional de Chile / BCN*)

16. Bernardo O'Higgins's mother, Isabel Riquelme, was a constant source of consolation to the Chilean leader. (*Biblioteca Nacional de Chile*)

17. The Venezuelan-born leader of the patriot armies in the north of South America Simón Bolívar became known as the Liberator. His call for foreign volunteers led to thousands of Irishmen crossing the Atlantic to fight for Latin American independence. (*DeAgostini / Getty Images*)

18. Daniel Florence O'Leary was the son of a Cork butter merchant who fought with Bolívar in Venezuela, Colombia, Ecuador, Peru and Bolivia, rising to the rank of general. He later served as a diplomat in Europe and South America. (*Museo Nacional de Colombia*)

19. Another Corkman, Francis Burdett O'Connor, fought with the Irish Legion in Colombia before joining campaigns in the Andes. He retired to Tarija in Bolivia, where he wrote his memoirs.

20. Bolívar's Irish troops braved blizzards and hazardous mountain passes during their march across the Andes from present-day Venezuela into Colombia in a successful bid to surprise the Spanish forces. (© *Look and Learn*)

21. Irish troops were present at the Battle of Boyacá, 1819, the decisive engagement in the fight for Colombian independence. (*El Palacio Federal Legislativo de Venezuela*)

22. John Devereux was a colourful veteran of the 1798 Rebellion from County Wexford and the leader of the Irish Legion, which fought a brief, inglorious campaign in northern Colombia. (*National Library of Ireland*)

23. *General Devereux's Patriots of 1817*, a sketch of the officers who served in the Irish Legion by William Sadler, which was later used to advertise confectionery. (*National Library of Ireland*)

24. Born in County Wicklow, John Thomond O'Brien emigrated from Ireland to Buenos Aires, serving with the patriots in Argentina, Uruguay, Chile and Peru. (*National Library of Ireland*)

25. Thomas Charles Wright was born in County Louth. He fought with the patriots before settling in Ecuador, where he founded the country's naval academy. (*Instituto Nacional De Patrimonio Cultural / Colección Estrada Ycaza*)

26. The Irish soldiers of the Mexican army's Battalón de San Patricio (Saint Patrick's Battalion), known as the San Patricios, fought bravely at the Battle of Churubusco in 1847, one of the key battles in the Mexican-American War. (© *World History Archive / Alamy Stock Photo*)

27. The United States army executed members of the San Patricios for desertion after the Battle of Churubusco. (*Herbert Orth / The LIFE Images Collection / Getty Images*)

28. The County Cork-born Eliza Lynch is a national heroine in Paraguay for her brave stand at Cerro Corá during the War of the Triple Alliance in 1870.

29. Born into an Irish family in Argentina, Camila O'Gorman is a tragic figure in the nation's history. She was executed for eloping with a Roman Catholic priest.

30. The Argentinian leader Juan Manuel Rosas ordered the execution of Camila O'Gorman and Fr Uladislao Gutiérrez after the Catholic Church denounced the couple. (*Sacrificio de Camila O'Gorman y del Sacerdorte Gutiérrez, impresa por Gosselin. Complejo Museográfico Provincial Enrique Udaondo, Luján, Buenos Aires*)

sober, level-headed O'Leary. Whatever the truth of the matter, Rooke was to prove that what he lacked in seriousness he made up for in bravery on the battlefield.

Meanwhile, Major Arthur Sandes had replaced Colonel Piggott, who had fallen ill and returned home, as commander of the 1st Rifles. Sandes was a member of the Protestant ascendancy from Glenfield, near Listowel, County Kerry.[44] Under Sandes, the 1st Rifles, or Black Rifles, as they were also known, became one of the crack units in the patriot armies. They were at the centre of nearly all the main actions to liberate the northern part of South America, from their first skirmishes with Spanish troops on the shores of the Orinoco in 1818 to the liberation of Bolivia high in the Andes in 1825.

Throughout 1818 and early 1819 Irish volunteers fought with the patriot armies on the *llanos*. Although the patriots controlled the plains, Isla Margarita and much of the east of the country, their cavalrymen were incapable of making inroads into the highlands and the towns on the northern coast of Venezuela, which were defended by the better-trained royalist infantry.

The Irish soldiers who fought in South America in the early nineteenth century experienced many privations. They endured endless forced marches through humid jungles, strength-sapping climbs over dizzying mountain passes and long days of hunger and boredom in disease-ridden Caribbean islands. How they spent their precious free time depended on their station in life. Because many of the Irish officers who served in the patriot armies left a written record, it is possible to build a more accurate picture of their day-to-day experiences than those of the enlisted men.

Alcohol helped both the enlisted men and the officers relieve the tedium of life in camp. Francis Burdett O'Connor recalled a party held by Irish officers at Huamachuco in the highlands of northern Peru. It was common for Irish officers on campaign in South America to have a drink together when their paths crossed. An Irish sea captain had given O'Connor a couple of bottles of whiskey with which to celebrate St Patrick's Day. Even though the day in question had passed, the Irish officers raised a toast in honour of their patron saint. Among those present were Francis Burdett O'Connor, Arthur Sandes and William Owens Ferguson.[45]

Gambling was another common pastime in the patriot army. According to General William Miller, the English veteran of the Napoleonic Wars who fought in Chile and Peru,

> ... perhaps no other vice, singly, produced so many drawbacks to the patriot cause as the unfortunate propensity to play on the part of ministers, envoys, and officers of all ranks, who too frequently dissipated public property intrusted [sic] to their care. Insubordination, desertion, occasional defeat, and a prolongation of the miseries of war, were some of the natural consequences of the unhappy propensity.[46]

The officers and men played cards and even organised horse races. It was not only money they played for. On the same night that the Irish officers had toasted St Patrick, Francis Burdett O'Connor watched as his fellow-countryman Arthur Sandes and his commanding officer, General Antonio José de Sucre, tossed a coin for the hand in marriage of a wealthy Quito heiress. Sandes was engaged to be married to the daughter of the Marquis of Solando; Sucre also wished to marry her and suggested to Sandes the idea of tossing a coin to decide the matter. O'Connor agreed to witness the bet and threw the coin in the air. Sandes lost.

In the early part of 1819, frustrated at the patriots' lack of progress in Venezuela, Bolívar made an inspired if risky decision: he would march west across the Andes into New Granada (present-day Colombia) and drive south towards Bogotá. The daring plan required tramping across the Venezuelan flood plains towards the province of Casanare, where the patriot forces under General Francisco Paula de Santander were stationed. The joint army would then climb through the Andes by way of a bleak crossing called the Páramo de Pisba before falling upon the more lightly manned royalist garrisons in New Granada. Bolívar was counting on surprise and the fact that the people of New Granada, having suffered the depredations of the Spanish, would be sympathetic to the patriots.

On 26 May 1819 Bolívar's army of some 2,000 men marched west from the town of Setenta. They included a reconstituted British Legion under James Rooke and the Rifles under Arthur Sandes. It was at the height of the rainy season, and the men sometimes had to wade waist-deep through the flooded plains. To make matters worse, many of them were ill from their poor diet. They had eaten nothing but unsalted meat for months, having no access to bread, fresh fruit or vegetables.[47] And the vertiginous, snow-covered peaks of the Andes beckoned on the horizon.

On 11 June 1819 Bolívar's units merged with those under Santander at the town of Tame.[48] On the 22nd, having struggled through the heat and humidity, Bolívar's army began to climb the steep paths into the mountains. Five days later the vanguard dispersed a royalist force of 300 men, an action that proved to be a fillip to the morale of Bolívar's soldiers, who now faced a tortuous climb to the Páramo de Pisba. The freezing cold and altitude sickness were now the enemy. Most of the men, used to the stifling heat and humidity of the tropical plains, did not have adequate clothing or boots; the Irish captain, John Johnston, had managed to salvage a pair but threw them into a river in order to share the same privations as his fellow-officers.[49] As the army limped up the eastern face of the cordillera the horses began dying on the narrow mountain trails, blocking the path of the rearguard, which was already struggling through blizzards and ice storms. The men began to suffer from dysentery. Hundreds died from hypothermia or disease.

On 5 July the vanguard and the first half of General Anzoátegui's division reached Socha, where they were welcomed by local people with bread, tobacco and cups of cloudy chicha, an Andean drink brewed from maize. Nine days later the rearguard, including the British Legion, which had lost a third of its number, limped into Socha. Down the valley the royalist forces were waiting.

On 11 July, Bolívar led a thousand men of Santander's division into the village of Gameza. General Barreiro's royalist forces were positioned outside the town, on the other side of the river. During the ensuing battle Santander was injured; and, faced with royalist reinforcements, the patriots withdrew. The arrival of the British Legion strengthened Bolívar's hand, and on 25 July, at the Pantano de Vargas (Vargas Swamp), Bolívar's army of 2,600 men faced a 3,500-strong royalist force. Bolívar's troops were largely untested and, because of the gruelling conditions of the Andes crossing, his cavalry and infantry regiments were lacking horses and equipment. Barreiro ordered the King's 1st Regiment to attack the left flank of the patriot army, held by Santander's division. Seeing that the patriot troops were offering little opposition, Barreiro urged the centre of his troops forward. Sandes's Rifles and the Barcelona Regiment bore the brunt of the royalist assault and began moving backwards. With things looking desperate, Bolívar ordered Colonel Rooke and the 2nd Rifles to advance. Rooke took two musket balls in his left arm during the battle, but the charge of the 2nd Rifles helped save the day. Though neither side could claim victory, Bolívar's army had survived when it looked as if it would suffer a crushing defeat. The surgeon Thomas Foley from Killarney amputated Rooke's arm, and he was left behind in the monastery of Tunja to recuperate; but he died shortly afterwards. Sandes and O'Leary had also received wounds. Sandes's wound was the more serious, but O'Leary bore the mark of a sabre on his forehead for the rest of his life.

Two days after the battle at the Pantano de Vargas, Bolívar declared martial law. All New Granadans between the ages of 15 and 40 were ordered to report to the army. O'Leary was put in charge of turning them into soldiers. He was not impressed by the appearance of the indigenous recruits who turned up at the headquarters in Corrales de Bonza.

> Nothing could be less military than the outfits they wore: a grey, woollen hat, wide-brimmed with a low crown covered a head that reminded one of Samson, before the fatal scissors would cut off his long, thick hair; an immense, square blanket, of rough wool, with an opening in the middle, through which passed that enormous head, hung from the shoulders to the knees and gave them the appearance of men without arms.[50]

O'Leary stripped them of their ponchos and began to drill them. However, he found it difficult to teach them the rudiments of shooting 'without them closing their eyes and throwing their heads back, putting in danger their own lives and those of their companions, rather than their opponents.'[51] Despite his misgivings, O'Leary boasted that 'inside a few days, 800 of these recruits, divided into companies, presented from a distance an imposing sight, and in the Battle of Boyacá, as in all those that were fought afterwards, the indigenous peasants proved that there were no better infantry soldiers in South America than them.'[52]

On 7 August the decisive battle took place at Boyacá Bridge, resulting in a comprehensive victory for the patriots. Bolívar now marched towards the prize of Bogotá. Receiving news of the spectacular royalist defeat, the viceroy of New Granada, Juan José de Sámano, and many of the other higher royal officials fled the viceregal capital with their families, fearing for their lives.

The Liberator's daring strategy had paid off. The arrival of English's volunteers and the experience and bravery of Irish officers such as Rooke, Sandes and O'Leary had helped Bolívar get his campaign off the ground. In December 1819 the patriot government in Angoshura proclaimed the foundation of Gran Colombia (encompassing the modern-day states of Colombia and Venezuela). But this was only the first step in a long-drawn-out war that would see Irish soldiers fight throughout the northern part of the continent for the next six years.

Chapter 11

THE HIBERNIAN REGIMENT AND THE IRISH LEGION

The regiments that had set sail from Irish and English ports throughout 1817 and 1818 had been thinned by desertion and disease. But, despite the horror stories that were beginning to emerge in the Dublin and London newspapers by courtesy of disgruntled officers such as Henry Croasdaile Wilson and Gustavus Hippisley, Irish volunteers kept arriving in the Caribbean, lured by the promises of unscrupulous recruiters.

Between 1818 and 1820 two Irishmen, Thomas Eyre from County Galway and John Devereux from County Wexford, led recruiting drives for volunteers to serve in Bolívar's armies.

Thomas Eyre was the youngest son of Richard and Anchoretta Eyre of Eyrecourt, County Galway. The family were descendants of Cromwellian planters who had settled near Portumna, and Richard Eyre was a former county high sheriff. Thomas Eyre was suffering from financial troubles when he made the acquaintance of Gregor MacGregor, a Scottish soldier who had fought in the Peninsular War. MacGregor had been one of the first European officers to enter the service of the patriot armies in South America and had fought for four years, between 1812 and 1816. Though he seems to have been a capable soldier, he was over-fond of money and drink and was utterly unprincipled. He was a plump, graceful, well-dressed gentleman-soldier who could charm any company and whose military record, at least in the early days of his American adventures, was exemplary. However, his excessive attention to frivolous details – the cut of a uniform, a desire for titles – so beloved of a certain type of eighteenth-century British officer, gave warning of his superficiality; for he was one of the most daring, incorrigible conmen to emerge in the early nineteenth century, a forerunner of a modern property shark.

After his first stint fighting in South America, MacGregor hit on a scheme for selling land in Florida to investors in Savannah, Georgia. With 150 men raised in the United States and the West Indies, MacGregor had landed at Amelia Island near Jacksonville in north-western Florida. Failing to make progress inland, he had set up a government on the island, with himself at its head. When the treasury ran low, he fled to England. He then managed to inveigle £1,000 out of Bolívar's agent López Méndez in exchange for raising men and equipment for the patriots. When he failed to make good this promise, López Méndez had him arrested.

Having fallen out with the Venezuelans, MacGregor struck a bargain with an agent by the name of José María del Real to provide troops for New Granada. It was under MacGregor's patronage that Eyre began recruiting for what became known as the Regiment of Hibernia or Hibernian Regiment.

Eyre's competitor, John Devereux, was from Taghmon, County Wexford. He had fought, as a 'mere lad', in the 1798 Rising; his conduct during the Battle of New Ross was described by the United Irish leader Thomas Cloney as 'truly heroic'.[1] After the rising, the British government accused Devereux of complicity in the massacre of Protestant prisoners in County Wexford and sentenced him to transportation for life, but he received an amnesty and emigrated to the United States.

In 1806 Devereux had been allowed to return to Ireland, but in 1807 the government denied him permission to travel to his home county, which had been the centre of the insurrection in 1798. Instead he travelled to France, returning to the United States in 1815.[2] It was in Baltimore, home to many Latin American exiles, that Devereux had hit upon the idea of supplying arms to the patriots, and in 1815 he had managed to secure a meeting with Bolívar in Cartagena on the Caribbean coast of present-day Colombia. During this meeting Devereux had proposed raising men in Ireland for service in the patriot armies. He had then travelled to Buenos Aires, where he had tried to raise a loan for the patriot army and where he was appointed envoy of the Buenos Aires government to the United States.

Devereux had been in Haiti in 1818 when he reiterated to Bolívar his proposal to raise units of volunteers in Ireland. Bolívar accepted, and Devereux, who was now calling himself 'General' Devereux, despite holding no such rank in the patriot army, began his recruitment drive for what became known as the Irish Legion.

Ireland was the most fertile recruiting-ground for the British army, and in the aftermath of the Battle of Waterloo and the arrival of peace in Europe there were thousands of unemployed Irish soldiers trying to earn a meagre living in Ireland and Britain. Eyre's and Devereux's recruiters scoured Dublin and Belfast, as well as Liverpool and other English cities, to fill battalions for service in Venezuela. Their efforts to raise men for the Venezuelan army received considerable publicity, and handbills and posters were produced to advertise the lucrative rewards on offer. One of Devereux's handbills, distributed on the streets of Dublin, promised:

> The most flattering encouragement will be given to such young Men, of good Character, as shall be found qualified for GENERAL DEVEREUX'S Irish Legion, about to Sail direct for the Head Quarters of the Supreme Chief, none but effective and spirited Men need apply; well disciplined Soldiers, who have their Discharges, will be preferred, and will find this a most favourable opportunity to improve their Fortunes and acquire a handsome Provision for themselves for Life.[3]

Throughout the recruiting period, service in the patriot armies was linked to emigration and desperate Irish families were tricked into travelling with the false promise of virgin fertile land.

Devereux's most influential backer was Daniel O'Connell, who organised and attended a much-publicised dinner in honour of the founder of the Irish Legion at Morrison's Hotel in Nassau Street, Dublin. O'Connell spoke in glowing terms of Devereux's enterprise and bought commissions for his 14-year-old son, Morgan, who became a member of Devereux's staff, and his nephew, Maurice,[4] who, after the Irish Legion disbanded, became a lieutenant in the Rifles and died in Quito from disease.[5]

Such was the jealousy and backbiting between Eyre and Devereux as they recruited their respective armies for service in South America that the former challenged the latter to a duel. But Devereux declined the challenge.[6] According to Colonel Michael Rafter, who served with Eyre in the Caribbean,

> ... this was a great source of triumph to the Hibernians, whose numbers rapidly increased in consequence; but the temporary success of Eyre was counterbalanced by a most weighty consideration:— the uniform of his regiment was excessively plain, while D'Evereux's lancers strutted about the streets of Dublin blazing in all the splendour of plumed helmets, burnished sabres, and richly laced jackets, and the clicking of their spurs, and the tinkling of their chains, sounded the death knell to the pride

of the mortified Hibernians, who never failed to discover [reveal] their envy when they happened to come in contact with their well-dressed brother Patriots. Quarrels and riots ensued, daily encounters took place, and, if Colonel Eyre had not prudently prohibited his officers from wearing their uniform, the streets of Dublin would have overflowed with that Patriot blood which was to have been shed in the emancipation of the suffering Americans.[7]

In the alehouses of Belfast, Dublin and Cork, recruiters came to blows as they vied with each other to fill the ships leaving for the Caribbean. Given the profits to be made from the sale of commissions in these regiments, it was not uncommon for agents of the same cause to compete for officers. Advertisements promising generous financial rewards and adventure in exotic climes were common throughout Ireland, luring bored, impecunious half-pay officers to stump up the last of their shrinking funds for the chance of fame and fortune in a distant world far from the daily drudge.

Overladen ships left Irish ports throughout 1819 with hundreds of men, women and children on board – many soldiers brought their families with them – excited about the promise of a better life in the New World. Eyre and Devereux had become wealthy men from the sale of commissions in their regiments. Eyre was alleged to have raised £13,000, of which only £7,000 was spent on equipping the expedition to Venezuela, before he set sail for the Caribbean at the head of the Hibernian Regiment to join the rest of MacGregor's legion.[8]

About 600 men had sailed under MacGregor's command, arriving in Haiti in the early part of 1819.[9] Bolívar never authorised MacGregor's actions in the West Indies, and his expedition descended into farce. Having successfully dislodged the Spanish from their garrison in the small town of Portobello in present-day Panama, MacGregor fell idle. His officers got drunk on looted liquor, fraternised with the townspeople and failed to impose the slightest military discipline. When a royalist force, under the orders of the Dublin-born Spanish general Alexander Hore, who had arrived in South America with General Morillo's expedition in 1815, arrived to retake the town, MacGregor slipped away by jumping out of a window into the sea and swimming to one of his ships, abandoning his officers and men.

MacGregor made for Haiti to join Eyre and the 500 men of the Hibernian Regiment. He now decided to restore his reputation by launching an attack on Riohacha on the New Granadan coast. In September 1819 the *Amelia*, the *Alerta* and the *Lovely Ann* set sail from the port of Les Cayes on the southwest coast of Haiti for the South American mainland, some 450 miles away. There were 235 men, 15 women and four children on the ships. Eyre, his wife and children and the rest of the Hibernian Regiment sailed on the *Amelia*.[10] Within a few days at sea three officers, seven enlisted men, three women and two children had died from fever, including one of Eyre's daughters, who, in the words of one of the officers on board, Colonel Michael Rafter, was 'an amiable young creature, whose gentle manners and delicate frame, were but ill calculated to encounter the dangers, fatigues and privations, of such an enterprize [sic], and whose melancholy fate excited a considerable degree of sympathy'.[11]

Rafter was highly critical of MacGregor, and with good reason. MacGregor had deserted Rafter's brother in Portobello; Rafter's brother was subsequently executed by the Spanish. In his memoir of the expedition, Rafter was scathing of MacGregor's behaviour, not least on board the *Amelia*.

> The weather side of the quarter deck was always held sacred for the perambulations of His Excellency, while twenty officers and three ladies, huddled together on the lee side, gazed on the mighty man, whose thoughts were supposed to be pregnant with the destruction of armies and the fate of empires; and in the contemplation of his greatness, they lost all sense of the privations they suffered for his exultation. The cabin of the vessel, which was large enough to give shelter to all the officers, was occupied by General M'Gregor and the ladies; while the rest, forced to 'bide the pelting of the pitiless storm,' upon deck, bore, without a murmur, the constant drenching they received from the torrents of rain, that fell daily, and almost hourly, during the passage.[12]

The landing at Riohacha took place in the early hours of 5 October 1819. Lieutenant-Colonel Norcott led the attack; MacGregor and his staff officers remained on board to finish their night's sleep, as did Eyre, who was ill. About 210 men landed on the beach near Riohacha, including the men of the Hibernia Regiment, led by Major Atkinson. The royalists were forewarned, however, having found in Portobello MacGregor's correspondence with the patriot leaders in Riohacha. Skirmishes took place throughout the night while the patriots awaited the arrival of their commanding officer. After he was attacked by a small royalist force, Norcott ordered an advance through the thick jungle that surrounded the town. Atkinson was killed, but after five hours of fighting the patriots drove the royalists out of Riohacha.

MacGregor and his staff officers had attempted a landing just before dawn but, coming under fire, had retreated to the ship. It was not until MacGregor saw that the town was in the possession of his troops that he made another landing and took command. The patriots had by now broken into the town's stores and liberated every bottle of wine and spirits they could find. As MacGregor and his staff officers marched through the town, his own troops abused him for what they regarded as his cowardice.

The tropical heat, disease, the fear of a Spanish attack and plentiful amounts of alcohol caused madness and confusion to reign in Riohacha. MacGregor was incapable of enforcing discipline and, paranoid that he would be ousted by his own officers, sought to scheme with the *criollo* and indigenous townspeople. He began to call himself the Inca of New Granada and insisted on being referred to as 'His Majesty the Inca'. He attempted to raise a cavalry regiment comprising indigenous troops to protect him from his own men, who were busy looting every household object of value they could find in Riohacha.

The fearful officer corps resorted to desperate measures. One officer hacked off an unfortunate soldier's hand with a sabre; another officer, incensed at the reply he received from an Irish soldier of the Hibernian Regiment, drew his pistol and shot him dead. Adding to the hysteria was the fact that the hostile Riohacha citizenry laid siege to the town. Rafter recalled:

> M'Gregor was entreated frequently to come to some certain resolution, but in vain; he appeared to be in the situation of a man under the operation of the nightmare, who beholds indistinctly the most horrible sights, but is rendered incapable by some invisible power of flying from them.[13]

Some of the officers, now convinced that remaining in Riohacha spelt certain death, decided to flee. MacGregor concocted a plan of escape, summoning the remaining officers in Riohacha to a council of war and informing them that an attack was imminent. Having promoted Eyre to general, he advised him that, for their safety, he should send his wife and children onto one of the ships at anchor off the coast, and volunteered to escort them. Once on board the ship with Eyre's wife and children, MacGregor gave the order to put to sea, once again abandoning his officers and men. The Spanish forces, supplemented by *criollo* and indigenous soldiers, launched an attack, slaughtering what remained of the patriot garrison. Eyre and the remaining officers retreated to Riohacha's fort, but their resistance was ended when a stray bullet hit a box of cartridges. Eyre and his comrades were killed in the explosion. Of the 66 officers, 169 enlisted men, 15 women and four children who had sailed from Haiti to Riohacha, Rafter estimated that only 23 officers, 47 enlisted men, one woman and two children had survived.[14]

MacGregor ended his days in Caracas, dying in 1845, but not until he had swindled yet more unfortunates in a scheme that promised investors good agricultural land in the fictional Central American country of Poyais. When the emigrants arrived, they found that all their money had bought them was a few acres of impenetrable, useless jungle on the Mosquito coast, with no way of returning home.[15]

Six months after the Hibernian Regiment's failed expedition, John Devereux's Irish Legion launched another assault on Riohacha from Isla Margarita. Despite his protestations of zeal for the cause of liberty, Devereux's main interest was money. Not only did he convince hundreds of his desperate compatriots to join the Irish Legion, making handsome profits in the process, he also set up an office in Liverpool to sell land in South America to prospective emigrants, much in the manner of MacGregor's notorious scheme. However, Devereux had to abandon this side of his business once the Venezuelans discovered what he was up to. In the meantime he had taken £15 each from the first shipload of poor emigrants, who arrived at their destination to discover that there was no land or anybody to look after them.

Devereux was too busy selling commissions to worry too much about the practicalities of equipping and transporting more than a thousand men across the Atlantic. That task fell to Lieutenant-Colonel William Aylmer, who led the Irish Legion in Venezuela in Devereux's absence. Aylmer, from Painstown, County Kildare, had been a United Irish leader during the 1798 Rising, in command of 3,000 men at Timahoe, on the Bog of Allen.[16] He was subsequently exiled from Ireland by the British government and joined the Austrian army as a cadet in the light dragoons. He became a captain of cuirassiers and was chosen to tutor army officers belonging to the British prince regent's own regiment of hussars after the peace. There is some dispute about whether Aylmer was relieved of his duties by the prince regent because the role he had played during the 1798 Rising had become an embarrassment or he chose to leave of his own volition.

Aylmer returned to Ireland after Waterloo and was idling his time in Painstown in 1819 when he decided to help Devereux recruit men for the Irish Legion.[17] He raised the 10th Lancers, commissioning a family friend, Francis Burdett O'Connor, as a junior officer.

Born in County Cork in 1791, O'Connor grew up among the Protestant gentry on the Connerville estate outside Bandon. Despite later claims of Gaelic ancestry, the family were descended from a wealthy English merchant named Conner. The Cork branch of the family was originally a bastion of conservatism, dedicated to defending Ireland from attack on behalf of the crown and hunting down Whiteboys, members of the Catholic agrarian secret society that was pledged to fighting excessive rents and tithes and the enclosure of the land. But there seems to have been a radical shift in the politics of two members of the family, Francis's father, Roger, and his uncle, Arthur, who embraced Catholic Emancipation and the revolutionary creed of the United Irishmen and changed their name to O'Connor in a gesture of solidarity with the Catholic Irish. The plight of their sister Anne, who committed suicide after she was refused permission to marry her Catholic lover, may have influenced their attitude.[18]

Roger O'Connor participated in the 1798 Rising and was imprisoned by the British government.[19] His brother, Arthur, a radical MP, journalist and United Irish leader, much influenced by Enlightenment ideas and the example of the French Revolution, was arrested and charged with treason in 1797. On his release from prison in 1802 he entered service in France and was promoted a general by Napoleon.

Francis's brother, Feargus, was a Chartist leader who became influential in British radical politics, while his godfather, Sir Francis Burdett, after whom he was named, was a reforming English MP. Upon Roger's release from prison the family had gone to live at Dangan Castle, near Trim, County Meath, the former home of the Duke of Wellington's family, the Wellesleys.[20] The castle burnt down shortly after Roger had taken out an insurance policy for £5,000.[21] In his memoirs Francis took responsibility for accidentally starting the fire in which his mother died, but there must be a strong suspicion that it was a deliberate act of arson by his father.[22]

Roger O'Connor was a wild, impulsive man. He was accused of organising the 10 highwaymen who robbed the Galway mail coach, carrying the cash from the Ballinasloe horse fair, in 1812.[23] His defence at the trial was that he had held up the coach not for money but to retrieve incriminating letters that were intended for use in a legal case being taken by a peer against O'Connor's friend Sir Francis Burdett. The plaintiff believed that Burdett was conducting a love affair with his wife. Burdett testified at O'Connor's trial, and he was acquitted.

Francis O'Connor was also something of a dreamer. He had tried to run away to France to join Napoleon's forces after hearing about the general's escape from Elba in 1815 but Burdett dissuaded him from doing so.[24] Francis heard of Devereux's expedition to South America from William Aylmer. After his discharge from the Austrian army Aylmer had been enjoying the leisurely pursuits of a country gentleman and was a frequent visitor to Dangan Castle, where, with the O'Connor brothers, he indulged his passion for hunting. According to O'Connor,

> [Aylmer] passed his time visiting all his neighbours in their country houses, remaining days and even whole weeks in some of them, as was the Irish custom, by which the landlords, after having received the best possible education and having left the family home, occupied themselves with nothing else but country pursuits, hunting foxes, deer and hares with hounds; shooting birds and fishing in the summer ...[25]

It was from this class of radicalised, idle young Irishmen that many of Devereux's officers were drawn. O'Connor was certainly receptive to the romance of the South American adventure as described by Aylmer during visits to Dangan Castle. Aylmer encouraged O'Connor to help him raise a regiment in counties Kildare and Meath, arguing that, because he himself had been absent from the country for so long, 'the local people did not know him.'[26] O'Connor's participation, Aylmer argued, would smooth over any difficulties.

O'Connor at first refused to take part, having resolved to emigrate to the United States 'because the British government was persecuting all my family for the reason that my father and my uncle Arthur had been at the head of the 1798 rebellion.'[27] However, the prospect of taking part in the expedition continued to tempt him. He was possessed of an 'independent and indomitable spirit', 'an ardent love of liberty and republicanism' and 'democratic ideals,' according to his grandson, Tomás O'Connor d'Arlach, and was fired up by having witnessed the 'ruin of his family and the oppression of his country.'[28] O'Connor finally changed his mind when a letter arrived telling him that he had been named lieutenant-colonel in Aylmer's Lancers regiment, and he rushed to Dublin to join his unit. His brother gave him money towards the cost of arming, equipping and provisioning the men.

The fare on the ships crossing the Atlantic was meagre. In the early 1800s it was common for the officer in charge of provisioning a ship to skimp on quality and pocket the proceeds; sometimes he ran off with the funds altogether without buying a piece of biscuit. For most of the crossing, the diet consisted of salted meat and hard biscuit – or hardtack, as it was called. Of course wealthy senior officers might enjoy lavish dinners for the first days of the voyage, but then they too were forced to subsist on the mean rations of a pre-refrigerated age, made more palatable by plentiful quantities of claret and madeira. The ships that carried the officers and enlisted men of the Hibernian Regiment and Irish Legion were poorly provisioned. The Irish Legion's 2nd Lancers, who sailed on board the *Hannah* in July 1819, survived on rice, porridge and molasses for breakfast and pork or 'bad' beef and black biscuit for dinner. Each man received an allowance of two ounces of water a day.[29]

The Irish Legion's 1st Rifles sailed for the Caribbean in June and July 1819 under the command of Colonel Robert Meade. While Meade travelled in June with about 200 officers and enlisted men on board the *Charlotte Gambier,* his second-in-command, Lieutenant-Colonel Robert James Young, from Culdaff, County Donegal, set sail from Liverpool on board the *Laforey* on 4 July 1819 with 30 officers, 199 enlisted men, 11 women, six children and a crew of 16. The crossing was far from smooth, typical of that experienced by those who sailed with the Irish Legion.

Shortly after leaving Liverpool some of the officers began to complain that there were not enough provisions on board to last the journey. Excessive drinking exacerbated the problem. One of the men was alleged to have stolen the rum ration of some of his neighbours and got so drunk that he was arrested. As he was about to be tied to the forecastle, he drew a couple of knives and threatened to stab anyone who came near him. He was court-martialled and sentenced to three dozen lashes.

The discontent spread to the point where Young, having consulted the ship's captain, agreed that they would put in at Waterford for further supplies of water and to 'get rid of the troublesome characters.'³⁰ Forty-two men and five officers were put ashore, who 'endeavoured to excite, by false reports, feelings extremely prejudicial to our expedition.'³¹ Young responded by placing a statement in the newspapers to the effect that he had provisioned the ship adequately.

With the threat of mutiny quelled, Young and the rest of the regiment set sail once again. However, the officers and men continued to fight the tedium of the long ocean voyage by getting drunk. Much of the drinking took place during meetings of the Black Lion Club, which had been founded by Young and his fellow-officers after three-and-a-half weeks at sea. The club met on Thursdays and Saturdays at 8 p.m. The lengthy rules stipulated that the meetings on Thursday should end at 10 p.m. and on Saturdays before midnight. Young, the president of the club, wore a cap with the initials of the Black Lion Club marked in green ribbon, while each member had to sing a song or recite a line of verse during meetings. Talk of politics or religion was forbidden, and the penalty for those who infringed the rules was a draught of salt water. The inaugural meeting of the club must have been a raucous affair. According to Young, 'the novelty of the Club, upon our first meeting, induced several of the members somewhat to exceed, the consequence of which was a violent headache to myself next day, which was the first indisposition I had since leaving Liverpool.'³²

Even his hard-drinking fellow-officers were astounded at the quantities imbibed by a Scottish officer on board the ship. Young recounted the officer's daily regimen as follows: 'At five in the morning a glass of sling,* a smoke at 7, Breakfast at 8, a glass of grog after, some Toddy at 11 o'clock, Solomongrundy† at one, dinner at 3 o'clock, two tumblers of grog after, a smoke at 5 o'clock, tea at 7, a nip at 8, and a smoke at 9, and then turn in, except upon the meetings of the Club, which enabled him to take four additional tumblers, and to this rule of living he strictly adhered.'³³

On 12 August the Black Lion Club met to drink the health of the prince regent on his birthday. 'This night the members rather exceeded their quantum,' wrote Young, 'but [it] was considered pardonable in honour of

---

* A type of punch favoured in the navy.
† Also known as *salmagundi*, a salad typically eaten at sea and made up of whatever what was at hand, such as chopped meat and vegetables.

the day.'[34] On 17 August the members resorted to drinking the wine that had been laid in for the sick. Young explained the club's reasoning in his journal: 'Having none on board and drawing near the conclusion of the voyage, we determined to punish a few bottles. The Doctor became rather intoxicated, and fell over the tiller ropes on leaving the Cabin.'[35]

Another vice of the Regency-era Irish officer which was common on the passage across the Atlantic was duelling. William Jackson Adam of the Irish Legion complained of being awakened on the *Hannah* in the early morning by pistol shots.[36] The Irish private Benjamin McMahon, who had set sail from the Custom House in Dublin in the summer of 1818, claimed that he had witnessed 15 duels between officers during the two-month journey.

> But, strange to say, only one person was wounded, and that in the heel – the motion of the vessel, perhaps, prevented them from taking good aim. These duels arose out of the most foolish and childish disputes, generally through gambling transactions. Towards the end of the voyage the captain put a stop to this altogether, because, although they missed one another, yet they constantly hit the rigging and cut it up. We had no quarrels amongst the men.[37]

On board the *Laforey,* Young took a dim view of duelling, arresting two of his officers on their way to a duel and making further arrests when the ship landed at Barbados. From there the regiment sailed to Isla Margarita, which Young described as 'the receptacle of Pirates, Corsairs, and all manner of villainy.'[38]

The Irish Legionaries were dismayed to find scenes of abject misery in the Caribbean. Soldiers who had fought on the Venezuelan mainland and been withdrawn to Isla Margarita were dying in their dozens, either of yellow fever or of their untreated wounds. There was also the danger of attack from the islanders themselves. Two officers were found murdered, stripped naked and with their heads cut off. On their way to their temporary quarters on the night they disembarked, the men passed the skulls of 400 Spanish prisoners, who had been beheaded on the orders of General Juan Bautista Arismendi.[39] According to one officer, Arismendi, a native of the island, was 'the chief, and idol of his countrymen, to whose regard and esteem his great exertions and sacrifices in their defence have deservedly entitled him.'[40] He had driven the Spanish from the island, and Bolívar had rewarded him with the command of Venezuela's Army of the East.

Juan Griego, the principal town on the island, was home to about 500 residents. Most of the single-storey dwellings were made of mud and straw but there were a few tiled houses made of stone. In the local hostelry the Irish officers played billiards and card games with French merchants. The local market sold turtle, fish and fruit. Pork and goat were also available. However, fresh water was in short supply.

The Irish soldiers were soon struck down with heatstroke and disease. Drunkenness was rife. Five days after landing on Isla Margarita, Young had had enough and begged permission to return home, citing fever. He was granted leave of absence. Leaving the rest of the regiment to their fate, he set sail for the British-controlled island of Jamaica with some of his fellow-officers, two of whom died en route. After a period of recuperation, he embarked for England on 26 October, a mere two months after arriving in the Caribbean.

His was not an uncommon experience, for all the Irish officers, accustomed to the temperate climate of Europe and the rarefied customs of the Old World's armies, struggled to adapt to the harsh tropical conditions. The fact that the sick and injured remnants of English's volunteers, who had retreated from the mainland after the defeat at Cumaná, were already on the island when the Irish Legion arrived did little for morale. When confronted with the inhospitable environment and the fact that there was no money to pay them, many officers returned home.

Of the approximately 1,000 officers and men who had sailed from Ireland and Britain with the Irish Legion, about 80 officers and 500 NCOs and privates remained by November 1819. They were quartered in the town of Pampatar, on the westernmost point of Isla Margarita. The Irish units included the 1st Rifles, under William Richard Derinzy; the 1st Lancers, under Francis Burdett O'Connor; a battalion of light infantry, the Cundinamarca, under the command of Lieutenant-Colonel Luke Burke, which had been recruited in Ireland and was officered by decorated Irish veterans of Waterloo; and a company of men from English's British Legion who had returned from Maturín under the command of Major John O'Lawlor.[41] The Irish soldiers, many of them dying of disease in makeshift hospitals, were close to starvation. Duelling again took its toll on the Irish officer corps. 'They would drink too much wine – giving rise to rash and heated quarrels – and the following day one of the rivals would end up dead,' O'Connor wrote.[42]

The senior Irish officers made representations seeking transport to Angostura and stating that they wished to serve under Bolívar's orders.[43] Admiral Pedro Luis Brión refused their request, replying that if the Irish Legion 'is truly desirous of serving under the orders of General Bolívar and the glorious cause of Venezuela it will realise the importance of active service during the present crisis when a simultaneous movement of all the Republic's forces is the best measure for exterminating the enemy.'[44]

As the Irish historian Eric Lambert points out in his detailed account of the foreign participation in Bolívar's campaigns in the north of South America, the Venezuelans had difficulty getting information about the Irish Legion's situation on Isla Margarita, owing to the distances and terrain involved.[45] In November 1819 the patriot government was based in Angostura, while Bolívar was more than 600 miles away in Bogotá. Communication between Angostura and Isla Margarita was not much easier, given the terrain and the fact that the royalist army lay in between. Complicating matters was the fact that the patriot leaders in Angostura were manoeuvring against each other.

Nevertheless, patriot propaganda heralded the arrival of the Irish troops with great fanfare. Bolívar's proclamation of welcome was printed in the *Correo del Orinoco*. Addressed to the 'Brave Soldiers' of the Irish Legion, it read:

> Irishmen! – Separated from your homeland in order to follow your generous sense of feeling, which has always distinguished you among the most illustrious Europeans; I have the glory of counting you as adopted Sons of Venezuela, and as defenders of the Liberty of Colombia.
>
> Irishmen! – Your sacrifices exceed all reward, and Venezuela does not have sufficient means to remunerate what you deserve; but as much as Venezuela possesses, as much as she has at her disposal, she will gladly give up to the distinguished foreigners, who have brought their lives and their services as tribute to the nascent Republic. The promises that the virtuous and brave General Devereux has made to you in recompense for your incorporation to the Liberating Army will be religiously fulfilled on the part of the Government and People of Venezuela. Believe that we would rather prefer the deprival of all our Property than to deprive you of your sacred Rights.

> Irishmen! – History and the blessings of the modern World will give to you your most just and sublime compensation.
>
> SIMÓN BOLIVAR[46]

Respite from the fever-ridden climate of the island came when Bolívar ordered Colonel Mariano Montilla, a native of Caracas, to assume command of the Irish Legion in the absence of Devereux. He arrived in Isla Margarita with his chief-of-staff, the Irish officer Edward Stopford, at the end of December and was shocked by the insubordination of the Irishmen. However, he was determined to carry out his orders. During the next three months the senior officers drilled the men and created new units in an attempt to impose discipline.

The Irish Legion set sail for the mainland in March in warships under the command of Brión. Montilla was commander-in-chief; Stopford was chief-of-staff. The force comprised the Lancers under O'Connor, the Cundinamarca battalion of light infantry under Burke, and a company of riflemen under O'Lawlor. Lieutenant-Colonel William Richard Derinzy and Captain Robert Parsons served as aides-de-camp to Brión.

Born on the Dutch-controlled island of Curaçao into a merchant family from present-day Belgium, Pedro Luis Brión had fought for the Batavian Republic against the British as a young man. He later studied naval science in the United States before returning home and joining the patriot cause. He was both generous and flamboyant: on the quarterdeck he wore a hussar jacket, scarlet pantaloons with gold lace down the side, a field-marshal's hat with 'a very large Prussian plume', and 'an enormous pair of dragoon boots, with heavy gold spurs of a most inconvenient length.' Coming across a Spanish squadron lying at anchor in a bay with most of its crew ashore, Brión, at the head of the patriot fleet, contented himself with 'firing a salute of twenty-one guns, and hoisting a demi-jean [demijohn] of wine, and a living turkey, at each yard-arm of his own vessel.'[42] He was deeply anglophobic, which he did not bother to hide from the British officers, and was attempting to wrest command from Montilla.

Devereux had not arrived from Ireland by the time the Irish Legion embarked for the mainland on 4 March 1820. Because the Legion's officers were unable to speak Spanish and Montilla could not speak English, orders were communicated in French. The expedition, comprising some 800 men, sailed for Riohacha, which a few months previously had been occupied and then deserted by the Hibernian Regiment.

Approaching the mainland, with the white peaks of the Sierra Nevada in the distance, the men could see the Spanish flag flying over a tower guarding the town. But the royalist troops had withdrawn and the residents had fled, and the patriots marched into Riohacha unopposed. The Spanish flag was lowered and that of the Irish Legion, a gold harp on a green field, was raised in its place. A general order was issued forbidding looting; however, two hours later 'a soldier and a black were taken in a house.' Lots were drawn, and the unfortunate black man, having lost, was shot by firing squad.[48]

Aylmer and O'Connor shared lodgings in Riohacha. Aylmer was deeply disillusioned at having been deceived into believing that he would be promoted to general and that he would receive generous pay once he arrived in South America. For a few days the Irish officers drilled and instructed the men, before the patriots began the march south to link up with Urdaneta's forces.

Their route took the troops through the territory of the Guajiro people, who were loyal to the royalist cause, on the Guajira peninsula, straddling the border between north-west Colombia and north-east Venezuela. The first stretch of the journey ran through dense forest, which gave way from time to time to Guajiro villages. At Fonseca the Legion skirmished with the Guajiro. Afterwards it was discovered that the German engineers who were in the vanguard had been killed in an ambush and their bodies hacked to pieces.

At the town of San Juan the Guajiro again attacked the Irish Legion. O'Connor's horse fell beneath him and he was forced to proceed on foot. Water was scarce, and the men frequently collapsed, stricken by heat, thirst and illness. Occasionally a party would be sent back down the path to report on the well-being of stragglers and would find their mutilated bodies.[49] At Valledupar, Montilla received word that a party of officers and soldiers, who had been left behind at Riohacha because of injury, had been attacked by the Guajiro at a town called Moreno while they were trying to catch up with the main body of the Legion. The survivors had managed to retreat to Riohacha.

Three days later Montilla convened a council of war. Unsure of Urdaneta's position, and fearful of being cut off from Riohacha by royalist forces, he asked his officers whether they should still try to link up with Urdaneta or return to Riohacha. All the officers, except O'Connor, favoured returning to Riohacha. O'Connor recalled years later in his memoirs:

> I stated to the commander-in-chief that the troops were happy and very willing to continue marching, and would overcome any obstacle that might present itself; but that if we embarked on a countermarch, I would not be able to answer for the preservation of order and discipline, nor for the subsequent fate of the division; assuring the commander-in-chief that I knew the Irish better than he; and that the result would make him see the truth.[50]

O'Connor was overruled, and the Irish Legion marched back to Riohacha.

O'Connor's prediction came true, and the volunteers, fed up with a lack of basic rations and pay, became mutinous. When a royalist force approached Riohacha, all the units, except O'Connor's 10th Lancers, refused to leave their quarters. The Lancers managed to get the better of the enemy but failed to pursue them. O'Connor recalled that Montilla had been impressed by the bravery of the Irishmen.

> Talking that afternoon with Colonel Montilla, in a meeting with the other officers, he expressed his regret at having returned from Valledupar, and said that he had had no idea of what class of soldiers were the Irish; that he had been left in true admiration when he heard my voice urging such a small column into battle, and carrying a bayonet in the middle of the smoke, towards the enemy lines ...[51]

If this was the case, Montilla was soon to change his opinion.

When the royalists returned to occupy positions around Riohacha, the Irish Legion advanced en masse to join battle and gained a victory, albeit with 37 soldiers left dead on the field of battle. However, after returning to Riohacha, the Legion, apart from the Lancers, refused to fight any longer, complaining that they had not been paid, that they had been forced to march without food or water, and insisting that they be evacuated to a British-controlled island. Several merchant ships were in Riohacha at the time and these were requisitioned for the transport of about 500 soldiers, women and children to Jamaica. The Lancers, who had maintained their discipline despite suffering the same privations as their comrades, covered the rest of the Legion as it embarked. The Legion's commander, William Aylmer, now a colonel, who was suffering from fever, had wished to stay in Riohacha and had asked O'Connor to travel with the Legion to Jamaica to report to the authorities about what had occurred. However, Aylmer was so ill that a decision was made to evacuate him. He died shortly after arriving in Jamaica, where he was buried. About a hundred members of the Lancers remained in Riohacha with Montilla.[52]

The mutiny severely dented the reputation of the Irish volunteers, and Bolívar's recruitment of foreign soldiers came to an end. The patriot newspaper *Correo del Orinoco* claimed in its edition of 5 August 1820 that 'the Irish are brave but insubordinate, their great defect has paralysed the greater part of our most important plans.'[53] An anonymous letter published in the same edition reflected the feelings of the *criollo* officers:

> They [the mutineers] have been unmasked and made a name for themselves as the greatest thieves and rebels in the world, and we have been these last days in a state of war with these villains in order to contain them.[54]

Montilla expressed his disgust in a letter to Bolívar, published the following month in the *Correo del Orinoco*. He described the scenes in Riohacha as the Irish troops awaited embarkation.

> The Irish should have remained in their quarters until they were directed towards the merchant ships that were to take them to Jamaica, as was their wish; but in a few short hours they gave themselves over to the greatest disorder, beginning with looting the few miserable reliquaries that remained in the houses of the residents of Riohacha, getting drunk on the spirits that were in those houses and ending by setting fire to the whole town, which neither the Government nor the senior officers could do anything to prevent.[55]

A few days after the Irish Legion arrived in Jamaica on 5 June 1820, Devereux landed on Isla Margarita. Having made handsome profits from the sale of commissions in the Irish Legion, he had been facing arrest on charges of fraud in Ireland. Disgruntled officers had begun returning to Ireland and demanding satisfaction. Initially fêted by Dublin society, Devereux was now a pariah – though his friend Daniel O'Connell kept faith in him – and sought to remake himself in South America. While hungry Irish privates had roamed Isla Margarita looking for food, Devereux and his staff enjoyed sumptuous hospitality.

O'Connell's son, Morgan, was one of Devereux's staff officers. He was 15 when he arrived in 'the sandy oven of Margarita'.[56] On their arrival O'Connell and the rest of Devereux's Irish staff were entertained lavishly by General Arismendi in his headquarters. Of the occasion on which he was first presented to Arismendi and his officers, the young O'Connell wrote to his father:

> I never saw such a dinner. We began with turtle soup; then fowls, fish, yams, bananas, game, etc., and the largest turkey I ever beheld, as large as a sirloin of beef! all sorts of spiced and forced meats, and a dessert of fruits, half of the names of which I don't recollect.[57]

After the meal, toasts were drunk to Bolívar and the elder O'Connell, who was described by one of the Irish officers present, a Colonel Low, as 'the most enlightened, the most independent, and the most patriotic man, not only in Great Britain, but in all Europe.'[58] Low's seven-year-old son, who had sailed with him to Venezuela and spent his days practising his riding and swordsmanship, made quite an impression on the young O'Connell.

> Several other toasts followed. The last was also from Colonel Low's little son; who quite spontaneously getting up on his chair, gave – 'May the first man that deserts his colours have a sword through his body!' His father assured us that he had not said a word of it to him. The little fellow also said to our general, in Spanish – 'General, there are ten thousand enemies in front; lead on your men, draw your sword, and remember the cause!' He is a little Irishman.[59]

A few days later O'Connell enjoyed lavish quantities of champagne at a dinner given by the governor, Francisco Gómez. Unfortunately, during a fandango after dinner, O'Connell's cousin, Maurice, perhaps having drunk too much, tore a lady's gown with one of his spurs.[60]

It was a far cry from the horrors experienced on Isla Margarita by the main body of the Irish Legion. Of those who reached Jamaica in one piece many were transported to Canada, where they ended their days as settlers; others eventually made it home to Ireland. Some faced financial ruin. Matthew Macnamara, a Dublin merchant, had been named commissary-general of the Legion by Devereux. He was responsible for chartering vessels to carry the officers and troops to South America and was led to believe that he would be able to draw bills on the Venezuelan government. However, he discovered that the patriot Ministry for the Interior was unwilling to honour the bills. In December 1820 he petitioned Bolívar, seeking redress for the money he had invested in fitting out and victualling the ships that carried the Irish Legion across the Atlantic. He claimed to have abandoned his business in order to serve the Venezuelan Republic and that his 'two warehouses, among the biggest in Dublin, were for fourteen months used as barracks, and my own house as a guesthouse for officers.'[61] Macnamara wrote that he had been motivated by the noblest principles, 'always sure of the independence of Colombia,' and had procured money, property and credit from his friends. Macnamara insisted that he had been ruined by the Venezuelan government's refusal to pay. He said that his warehouses had been looted of all the goods required for the passage of 5,000 men across the Atlantic, that his house had been sold and one of the ships seized. To avoid 'further persecutions and arrests,' he had travelled to Venezuela to 'implore that the justice of Your Excellency, so universally admired, extends towards those shipowners, those who risk their ships at times when no insurance can be sought.'[62]

Macnamara cast the blame for Devereux's failures on the machinations of the Spanish government in Ireland and Britain, claiming that

> ... the powerful and effective efforts of the Duke of San Carlos, the Spanish [prime] Minister, and his innumerable spies and informers, all funded with a great quantity of money from Spain, helped by the extraordinary effect of the English decree on foreign enlistment, which is a threat to experienced officers of not only being deprived of half their pay, but also to their liberty, have banished all hopes and impeded the efforts of General d'Evereux to bring together the proposed force for Your Excellency.[63]

Macnamara claimed that these spies were operating in 'every city and town,' and that 'some newspapers in England and Ireland, which before seemed to follow liberal principles, were bought and corrupted: while the Spanish Minister was deliberately establishing newspapers in London to frustrate the efforts of General d'Evereux and his friends.'[64] He defended the behaviour of the officers and men of the Irish Legion, arguing that the treatment they had received had forced them 'from pure necessity to abandon an enterprise upon which they had embarked with the greatest enthusiasm,' adding that 'if the difficulties that had arisen in raising this Legion had come to the notice of Your Excellency, justly, it would not have been possible to attach any blame to General d'Evereux, whose efforts, though unfruitful, were incessant, and whose character no-one exceeded in patriotism, disinterest and generosity.'[65]

It is hard to agree with Macnamara's judgement. Even if Devereux had been motivated by such noble feelings, he had failed his men miserably. Though history has not been kind to him, depicting him as the worst kind of profiteer, who made money out of suffering Irish soldiers, some of his fellow-officers were more charitable, and he subsequently received a pension from the Venezuelan government. Devereux himself refused to take the blame for what became of the Irish Legion. 'To each and all who joined my standard', he wrote in a letter to Daniel O'Connell in 1824, 'I frankly explained the hardships which awaited them, and that our way to success must be fought thro' sickness, perils and fatigue.'[66]

The men, women and children who sailed with the Irish Legion suffered horrendous torments in the Caribbean. Many of those who did not succumb to disease on Isla Margarita sailed for other islands in the Caribbean, hoping to find a permanent home, or a way of returning home to Ireland. But there was a handful of veterans, such as Francis Burdett O'Connor, who remained in South America and fought with distinction for the rest of the war.

Chapter 12

DEATH IN THE ANDES

Thomas Charles Wright led the small scouting party into the dense vegetation, listening for any sound that might alert them to the presence of the enemy – not an easy task amid the strange noises that seemed to echo off the verdant canopy of branches.

Born in Queensborough, County Louth, Wright was a captain in the Rifles Regiment, which had sailed with the first wave of volunteers, and was securing the perimeter of the patriot camp for the night. The dreaded fizzing sound of an arrow reached his ears before he felt a searing pain in his right shoulder. The patriot troops shouted in confusion and began firing into the trees while a sergeant tried to extricate the arrow from Wright's arm. Just as he pulled it from his commanding officer's shoulder, he too was struck with an arrow. Wright survived to report the attack to his superiors, but his sergeant died.

After the Battle of Boyacá, Bolívar had ordered the Rifles to march north from Bogotá towards Pamplona. Wright was injured while the Rifles were marching through royalist-controlled territory. Their orders were to link up with the Irish Legion and march towards the River Magdalena. They faced stiff resistance. Capuchin missionaries, who were fiercely loyal to the Spanish crown, had been organising bands of Guajiro to attack the patriot forces moving through this part of present-day north-west Colombia. Wright recalled that twice a day the Guajiro would attack the Rifles as they desperately searched for the Irish Legion. The Guajiro were skilled in the use of the bow and arrow and would attempt to isolate members of the column trudging through the jungle. Once they spotted a patriot lookout on his own, one of their warriors would crawl along the ground until he was within firing distance. He would let loose an arrow, then run up and grab the stricken guard's firearm before disappearing back into the trees. After one incident, during which an officer and three men of the regiment were ambushed, the Rifles took extra precautions when making camp, sending scouting patrols, like the one Wright was leading when he was injured, into the jungle.[1]

In November 1820 the Rifles took part in the siege of the heavily fortified town of Ciénaga de Santa Marta – aided by the Irish Legion's Lancers, who had remained behind after the events in Riohacha – injuring or killing 700 royalists. Two Irish officers, Major William Peacock and Captain James Phelan, died from injuries received in the battle, and both Arthur Sandes and Peacock were cited for bravery. The patriots marched into Santa Marta a few days later.[2]

Meanwhile the political landscape in Spain had changed. Ferdinand VII was determined to crush the continuing resistance to Spanish rule in the Americas by reinforcing royalist forces. Ten battalions were preparing to embark at Cádiz at the beginning of 1820 when a group of liberal officers, headed by Rafael de Riego, mutinied. They imprisoned the king and demanded the full enactment of the Cádiz constitution, which had been cast aside by Ferdinand on his restoration in 1814.

At the end of November Bolívar and the commander of the Spanish forces, General Pablo Morillo, met and signed a truce at the Venezuelan town of Santa Ana de Trujillo. Afterwards Morillo sailed for Spain, leaving the Spanish army in the hands of General Miguel de la Torre.

The armistice was broken in 1821. Bolívar's divisions assembled in the west of Venezuela for the last push towards Caracas. The battle that decided the future of the country was fought at Carabobo, just west of the Venezuelan capital. The British Legion, under the command of Colonel Thomas Ferriar, fought as part of the 1st Division of Infantry; the Rifles, under Sandes, were part of the 3rd Division.

Following the patriot victory at the Battle of Carabobo, Bolívar was able to concentrate his attention on the south. Meanwhile in Chile, O'Higgins and San Martín were preparing to move north into Peru. The patriot armies were now able to bring to bear a pincer operation, with the goal of removing the last bastion of Spanish power from the continent: the Andean territories belonging to present-day Peru, Ecuador and Bolivia.

O'Higgins and San Martín realised that the security of an independent Chile depended on driving the Spanish from their stronghold in Peru. Chile continued to be vulnerable along its thousands of miles of coastline from Spanish expeditionary forces, which were manned and supplied from Peru. It was vital, therefore, that this continuing threat be destroyed. To do this, O'Higgins had secured the services of the Scottish admiral Thomas

Cochrane to command the patriot fleet and hunt down Spanish warships and transports. In August 1820 a joint Chilean-Argentine expedition of about 5,000 men set sail from Valparaíso for Peru on board 25 ships. The Chilean government bore the cost of the expedition, which put a significant strain on its finances.

Cochrane's chief surgeon was John Oughan. Born in Ireland, Oughan had studied in London and Edinburgh before emigrating to the United States, where he enlisted in the army being raised by the Carrera brothers for the liberation of Chile. He had participated in Belgrano's campaign in Upper Peru before joining Cochrane's expeditionary force. After the war in Peru had ended, he worked in Tucumán in northern Argentina before settling in Buenos Aires, where he became a prominent member of *porteño* society. Not long after his arrival in the city, however, he threatened to shoot the British vice-consul, Woodbine Parish, and was committed to an asylum. In a celebrated and scandalous case, Oughan protested that he was sane. Two medical inquiries found likewise, but Parish was determined to keep Oughan committed and managed to have an English doctor, Henry Bond, examine the patient. In his report Bond concluded that Oughan was suffering from an 'indisposition of his moral faculties,' and Parish convinced the authorities to have Oughan repatriated.[3]

San Martín was commander-in-chief of the Peruvian expedition, and among his aides-de-camp was an Irishman named John Thomond O'Brien. From Baltinglass, County Wicklow, O'Brien had sailed for Buenos Aires in 1811, hoping to make his fortune as a merchant. He had been lucky to make it to South America after his ship struck rocks off the island of Fernando Pó (present-day Bioko) along the coast of west Africa, leaving only a handful of survivors. O'Brien was caught up in the independence movement shortly after arriving in the River Plate, fighting in Uruguay under General Miguel Estanislao Soler. He was injured during the siege of Montevideo and was present for the royalist surrender of the city on 23 June 1814. He later took part in the campaign against Artigas before enlisting as an officer in a cavalry regiment in San Martín's Army of the Andes.

O'Brien was a buccaneering character, whose womanising often got him into trouble. According to one story, after surviving the shipwreck off west Africa in 1811 he had boarded an English ship to complete his voyage to South America. During the passage he had seduced the daughter of an English

Quaker couple. At the father's request, the ship's captain, also a Quaker, had removed O'Brien from the ship.[4]

Preparing for the invasion of Chile in Mendoza, O'Brien had got himself into trouble again, making insinuations about a relative of one of his fellow-officers, the Argentine general Juan Lavalle. O'Brien's remarks had infuriated Lavalle, and the two men fought a duel with sabres in the main thoroughfare of Mendoza, which left O'Brien with a scar on his wrist.[5] O'Brien was also a bullfighting aficionado and had enjoyed showing off to the ladies of Mendoza in the bullring, tying ribbons around his legs to better demonstrate his dexterity in front of the bull.[6]

As one of San Martín's staff officers, O'Brien was present at the Battles of Chacabuco, Cancha Rayada and Maipú, earning promotion to the rank of colonel. After the Battle of Maipú he went home to Ireland; but he returned to South America in time for the expedition to Peru, having been promoted to the rank of *sargento mayor*. During the Peruvian campaign he reached the rank of colonel.

San Martín's Liberating Army of Peru landed near the town of Pisco, about 130 miles south of Lima, in September. At the beginning of October, after the failure of peace talks between San Martín and the viceroy of Peru, Joaquín de la Pezuela, a division of the patriot army under General Juan Antonio Álvarez de Arenales, began moving south, capturing the towns of Ica, Nazca and Acarí, before wheeling north into the sierra. The viceroy, Pezuela, was fearful that Arenales would attack Lima, and he sent a division east to cut off his army.

The commander-in-chief of the royalist division was an Irish-Spaniard named Diego O'Reilly. He led his troops into the Andes, to the Cerro de Pasco, a town built on silver-mining which is 14,000 feet above sea level. With the hollowed-out mountain behind them, the royalists faced Arenales's numerically superior forces. The patriot armies routed O'Reilly's division, taking him prisoner. He was brought to San Martín's camp and allowed return to Spain along with other royalist officials. Facing disgrace and with his career in ruins, O'Reilly committed suicide by drowning, jumping off the ship taking him home.

Meanwhile San Martín's forces had embarked for the north, and on 20 November 1820, from the balcony of a house in the town of Huara, San Martín proclaimed the independence of Peru. The north of Peru declared itself in favour of the patriots, and by the summer of 1821 the bulk of the royalist forces retreated from the viceregal capital of Lima into the Andes. On 12 July, San Martín entered Lima in triumph. Three days later the principal residents of the city signed a solemn act of independence, and on 28 July San Martín once again formally declared the independence of Peru.

Motivated by his dream of a unitary South American state, Bolívar also wished to drive the Spanish from Peru, including the landlocked fastness of Upper Peru – present-day Bolivia. First, however, he directed himself towards the *audiencia* of Quito, the Spanish administrative unit roughly analogous to the territory of modern Ecuador but including parts of southern Colombia, the northern part of Peru and parts of north-west Brazil.

In 1809 the *criollos* of Quito had been among the first in South America to declare themselves independent, overthrowing the *audiencia* and creating their own junta loyal to Ferdinand VII. This short-lived government fell in 1812 and Spanish authority was restored, until in October 1820 a new junta in the Ecuadorean city of Guayaquil declared its independence. The Guayaquil junta was determined to declare itself independent not only of Spain but also of Gran Colombia. While this might have been desirable in principle, in practice the Guayaquil insurgents needed Bolívar's help to drive the Spanish out of Quito. It was in preparation for the invasion of Ecuador that Bolívar, with his headquarters in the north of Gran Colombia, near Lake Maracaibo, sent Daniel O'Leary to Panama to take charge of the Alto Magdalena Battalion.

Panama had declared its independence in November 1821 in a bloodless revolt, the Spanish garrison having left the isthmus to reinforce Ecuador. Fearing a Spanish invasion, the Panamanians had voluntarily agreed to become part of Gran Colombia. The Venezuelan general José María Carreño was sent to Panama to take charge of the patriot troops; Francis Burdett O'Connor was appointed his chief-of-staff. Shortly after arriving, O'Connor was ordered to raise and take command of an infantry battalion and was given the rank of lieutenant-colonel.

In the sleepy town of Panama, thousands of miles from home on the Pacific coast, the two young Irish officers, O'Connor and the recently arrived O'Leary, watched pearl fishermen ply their trade by the rocks that rose out of the bay, 'talking always of our distant homeland, our unforgettable and beloved Ireland.'[7] While O'Leary would shortly set sail for the port city of Guayaquil, O'Connor was left languishing reluctantly in Panama.

Bolívar planned to squeeze the Spanish in a two-pronged attack. While a force of 3,000 men under his command would attack overland from the north, a second force, under the command of General Antonio José de Sucre, which had landed at Guayaquil, would help distract the Spanish forces from the south. O'Leary and the Alto Magdalena Battalion were supposed to reinforce Sucre, but by the time they arrived in Guayaquil, in March 1822, the Venezuelan general, having defeated a royalist force sent from Quito to put down the insurgency, had already departed.

Marching from the north with 3,000 men, including the Rifles under the command of Colonel Arthur Sandes, Bolívar was faced with a hostile local population and exceptionally difficult terrain. Quito is almost 10,000 feet above sea level, and the route through the Andes was over dangerous ravines, fast-flowing rivers and vertiginous mountain paths. The royalist commander, Colonel Basilio García, chose to make his stand at a *hacienda* called Bomboná in the shadow of a volcano named Galeras.

The Spanish were in a commanding position. Between the patriot and royalist lines was a ravine. The royalists entrenched themselves in a heavily wooded area commanding elevated positions from which to fire down upon Bolívar's left flank, while to the patriots' right was the torrential River Guáitara. Nevertheless, on the morning of 7 April 1822 Bolívar ordered an attack. While two battalions, the Bogotá and the Vargas, under the command of General Pedro Torres, attacked the centre, General Valdés and the Rifles, under Sandes's orders, climbed the volcano to fall on the royalists' right flank, using their reversed rifles with fixed bayonets to get grip on the treacherous slopes.

Captain Ramírez and Captain Thomas Charles Wright led two companies in a bayonet charge of the royalist right flank. Meanwhile Torres's battalions were being cut to ribbons by the royalists, losing two-thirds of their men. Despite the heavy losses, they managed to dislodge the royalists from their entrenched positions, in no small part thanks to the actions of the Rifles battalion. The official battle record, written by Bolívar's chief of staff, General Bartolomé Salom, stated: 'The Republic owes this victory to the talents and military virtues of General Valdés, as well as the invincible Rifles battalion and its colonels Barreto and Sandes, and the graduate lieutenant colonels Ramírez and Wright.'[8]

The victory at Bomboná had come at a great cost: hundreds of patriot soldiers had been killed. Bolívar was not able to pursue the fleeing royalist troops, because night had fallen by the time the battle was won. Lacking troops and supplies, he was forced to retreat north. Yet his victory at Bomboná had also forced the governor of Quito, General Melchor Aymerich, to divide his forces. This left Quito vulnerable to attack from Sucre's forces in the south. On 24 May 1822, on the slopes of Mount Pichincha, overlooking Quito, Sucre defeated the royalist army, leaving Bolívar to accept the capitulation of the royalist town of Pasto.

Two months later one of the most celebrated events in the history of South American independence took place in Guayaquil.[9] On 26 July, San Martín and Bolívar met in private to discuss the future of the independence campaign. At stake was the direction of the war in Peru and its future political system – San Martín favoured an independent monarchy with a European prince taking the crown, Bolívar wished for a republic – and whether or not Guayaquil was to become part of Gran Colombia or the new Peruvian state. Bolívar was to get his way. Ecuador became part of Gran Colombia, and Bolívar arrived in Peru shortly afterwards to prosecute the final campaign against the Spanish in the Andes. Having done so much to drive the Spanish out of Chile and Peru, San Martín meekly – or nobly, depending on one's point of view – acceded to Bolívar's wishes, returning to Argentina and shortly afterwards going into exile in France.

Prepared now to drive the Spanish from their mountain strongholds in the Peruvian Andes, Bolívar arrived in Lima in September 1823. On 10 September the Peruvian congress awarded him full military powers.

The Spanish forces were in disarray. The liberal regime had fallen in Spain and Ferdinand VII had once again set about restoring his absolutist view of the monarchy. The Spanish officers were divided between liberals and absolutists. The Basque-born General Pedro Antonio de Olañeta, a convinced absolutist, led a revolt from Potosí in present-day Bolivia against José de la Serna, a liberal who was now the acting viceroy. This forced de la Serna to send troops loyal to Spain, under the command of General Jerónimo Valdés, to Upper Peru to put down Olañeta's insurgency.

Shortly after arriving in Peru, Francis Burdett O'Connor was appointed chief-of-staff to General Sucre. At a council of war in Huamachuco, in Peru's northern highlands, Bolívar asked O'Connor to give his views on the best way to proceed; this was despite the fact that O'Connor was the only colonel present, the rest being generals. O'Connor recalled the scene in his memoirs:

> I stood up immediately, and, concentrating on the map, I indicated our position, from the Cerro de Pasco, from Cuzco, from La Paz, from Potosí and from La Lava, twelve leagues [40 miles] to the south of Potosí, where it was said that General Valdés had marched against Olañeta. I demonstrated the long distance that separated Cuzco, the headquarters of the viceroy, and La Lava, and gave my opinion that, without losing any time, the campaign in the South should begin. I continued establishing my view with reasons and arguments in my favour when General Bolívar rose from his seat, and started to fold up the map, saying: 'This young officer is giving us a true lesson in the art of war. There is nothing left to be said, nor to be heard. Tomorrow the army marches.'[10]

O'Connor admitted the self-serving nature of the story, and that it was possible that Bolívar, 'a man of limited patience', would have behaved the same way if any of the other officers present at the council had said the same thing.

Thousands of patriot troops began moving south through the Andes in June 1824 towards the Cerro de Pasco and the royalist army. The trek through the mountains was hazardous, with cavalrymen being forced to dismount at the end of the day and continue marching in the dark along narrow paths above precipices of hundreds of feet. Battalions became lost, confused about where the right path lay. General William Miller, in his memoirs, recalled the confusion:

> The frequent sound of trumpets along the broken line; the shouting of officers to their men at a distance; the neighing of horses, and the braying of mules, both men and animals being alike anxious to reach a place of rest, produced a strange and fearful concert, echoed, in the darkness of the night, from the horrid solitudes of the Andes.[11]

The misery was compounded by the painfully cold temperatures and frequent snowstorms. To the rear a commissary drove the thousands of head of cattle that had been requisitioned along the way to feed the army.

It took a month to reach the Cerro de Pasco, thousands of feet above sea level. In the freezing conditions Bolívar and his staff reviewed their battalions. At a banquet given for the officers in the house where he was staying, Bolívar asked O'Connor to add a toast to the many that had already been given. O'Connor was momentarily stumped but recovered in time to toast 'the Colombian army, which is ready to liberate Peru from the Spanish yoke.' According to O'Connor, Bolívar then jumped up on the table, threw back his drink and hurled his glass against the wall, saying, 'This is my toast.'[12]

On 6 August, at Junín, close to the Cerro de Pasco, the patriot cavalry defeated the Spanish forces under the command of José de Canterac in an encounter in which not a single shot was fired. Though it was not much more than a skirmish, the victory at Junín raised the morale of the patriots, and they drove south towards Cuzco, the former capital of the Inca Empire, close to the ruins at Machu Picchu. In October Bolívar handed command to Sucre in order to return to Lima, where he hoped to raise funds and troops for the war effort.

The patriot armies were now about 150 miles from Cuzco as the crow flies, but between them and the Spanish lay winding mountain roads and the River Apurimac. The royalists, with their strength recovered following the recall of Valdés's division from Upper Peru, now prepared to attack. On 3 December, Valdés attacked Sucre's rearguard at a place called Matará, which comprised General Lara's division. It was the Rifles Battalion, under the command of Colonel Sandes, that bore the brunt of the attack.

Though more than 200 men had died, and hundreds more were dispersed, the Rifles had managed to fend off Valdés's division, allowing the bulk of the army to escape. Six days later Sucre led his armies into battle against the royalists at Ayacucho, one of the most famous names in the history of South American independence. Almost 1,500 royalist soldiers were killed; the patriot fatalities were less than 400. A handful of Irish officers – Sucre's chief-of-staff, Colonel Francis Burdett O'Connor, the Rifles' commanding officer, Colonel Arthur Sandes, the Rifles' medical officer, Hugo Brown Blair, the Rifles' company commanders, William Owens Ferguson and Thomas Charles Wright – were on the battlefield on that momentous day.

Two days after the famous victory, O'Connor had a row with his immediate superior. Sucre had asked O'Connor to draw up a list of the army's strength. He wished to have included on the list those soldiers belonging to the Rifles Battalion who had dispersed after the attack at Matará. O'Connor presented the list to Sucre without writing down the names of the absent men. Sucre was furious and, plucking a pen from behind his ear, scribbled out a name on a piece of paper in front of him. The royalist general Canterac, who had been invited to dine with Sucre that same day, entered O'Connor's office afterwards and asked him what he had done to provoke the general; O'Connor replied that he had done nothing, to which Canterac replied that he had just come from Sucre's office and had seen a list of proposed promotions to general on his desk. According to Canterac, at the top of the list was O'Connor's name with a fat line through it.

On 25 December 1824 the patriots entered the ancient city of Cuzco. O'Connor was underwhelmed.

> I thought I would find the splendid vestiges of the ancient Peruvians' might and civilisation, but, unfortunately, the Spaniards had destroyed and defaced everything, and the city had been modernised ... How impressive was the architecture of the Peruvian Indians, and how surprising were their buildings! What a shame that the conquistadors, only greedy for gold, did not understand their merit and did not know how to preserve them! There are remains here of a very ancient and very advanced civilisation.[13]

Olañeta had refused to recognise the terms of Canterac's surrender and continued to resist the patriot armies in Upper Peru. In January Sucre marched towards Puno, on the shores of Lake Titicaca. After the patriot victory at Ayacucho, much of Upper Peru now transferred its loyalty, including La Paz and Santa Cruz. It was in the south of the country, in the mining district of Potosí, that Olañeta made his last stand. It is somewhat fitting that this final act of resistance took place close to Potosí's legendary *cerro rico*, the 'rich mountain' that had been discovered by the Spanish *conquistadores* in the sixteenth century and had supplied what had at one time seemed a never-ending river of silver from the colonies to the metropolis. It was the lure of South American silver that had brought the Spanish to the New World in their droves. Having been driven from virtually the rest of South America, it was at Potosí that the last royalists tried desperately to hang on.

Despite his altercation with O'Connor after the Battle of Ayacucho, Sucre gave the Irishman command of two battalions of the Peru Division and the Junín Cavalry Regiment. O'Connor marched towards Puno on the shores of Lake Titicaca, and then on to La Paz. He and his battalions left La Paz in the vanguard of the patriot army to head south towards Potosí. Outside La Paz he was met by a German soldier with a message from Olañeta; the soldier also handed over a small pouch containing poison. Olañeta had hoped to get one of the patriot officers to poison Sucre in exchange for 10,000 pesos. O'Connor took the soldier prisoner and passed him over to Sucre.

In his memoirs O'Connor tells the story of how he came to be ruminating on the future of Upper Peru as he travelled south. Casimiro Olañeta was a nephew of the royalist general who, in opposition to his uncle, had come to espouse liberalism and had joined the patriot cause. He asked O'Connor whether he believed Upper Peru, once freed from the grip of his uncle, should become part of the new independent Peruvian state or the United Provinces of the River Plate, present-day Argentina. Up to the late eighteenth century Upper Peru had been part of the Viceroyalty of Peru and looked towards Lima; then, in 1776, it became part of the Viceroyalty of the River Plate, with its capital in Buenos Aires. As told in his memoirs, O'Connor had been poring over maps of the region and had become well versed in Upper Peru's history and traditions. He replied:

> Doctor Olañeta, if this country of Upper Peru offers as many natural resources further on, towards the south, towards La Quiaca, as we have come across since the Santa Rosa pass, which I understand is the correct boundary to the north, I do not see why there is any reason for it to become part of Lower Peru or of the Argentine Republic.[14]

According to O'Connor, Olañeta immediately galloped off in the direction of General Sucre. When O'Connor arrived at the camp, he entered Sucre's lodgings, where all the officers rose from their seats, embraced the Irishman and proclaimed him in one voice, 'Founder of the New Republic'.[15]

On 29 March 1825 the patriot armies marched unopposed into Potosí. General Olañeta had retreated south. Ten days later, as O'Connor marched towards the south, he received word that Olañeta had been killed in a mutiny at Tumusla. The war in Upper Peru was finished; and – but for a few royalist strongholds, such as Callao – so was Spain's South American empire.

The cost to the Irish officers and men had been considerable. In his memoirs Thomas Charles Wright listed the fatalities among the Rifles' predominantly Irish officer corps. While his account is not definitive, it gives a good indication of the heavy toll exacted. According to Wright, four officers, Captain Fallon and Lieutenants Edward Poole, John Seymour and a man named Reid, had died of yellow fever shortly after arriving in Venezuela. Lieutenants Westbrook and James Byrne died in the Andes and on the campaign in New Granada in 1819. Three of the Rifles' officers died from injuries sustained in combat with indigenous warriors near Lake Maracaibo in 1820: Lieutenant Reynolds was shot through the heart by an arrow, Captain James Phelan died after his leg was amputated, and Major William Peacock similarly never recovered from his injuries.

Yellow fever claimed the lives of Captain François Schwitzgibel, Lieutenants Bunbury, Macnamara and French, and the Rifles' surgeon, Dr O'Reilly. Daniel O'Connell's nephew, Lieutenant Maurice O'Connell, died from fever in 1822, as did Captain George Featherstonhaugh and Lieutenant Charles Church. Major Charles Rudd contracted an illness and died in 1823 in Esmeraldas. Captain Duxbury died from injuries sustained at the Battle of Ayacucho in 1824, as did Lieutenant Timothy Keogh. Finally, the regiment's commanding officer for most of the campaigns, Colonel Arthur Sandes, died from dropsy at the age of 39 in the Carmelite Convent in Cuenca, Ecuador.[16]

Of the 21 officers mentioned above who died, at least 12 were Irish. And that was just the officer corps of the Rifles; hundreds, if not thousands, of Irish sergeants, corporals and privates were buried in unmarked graves in the frozen earth of the Peruvian Andes, the sun-baked sand of Isla Margarita, and the mulch of the Amazon basin. They had come for different reasons: some had died fighting for personal gain, others for honour and glory, while a handful had a genuinely cherished belief in liberty for South America. Whatever their reasons, without their efforts the history of the continent would have been very different.

Chapter 13

THE SAN PATRICIOS

On 8 October 1821 a liberal Spanish army officer by the name of Juan O'Donojú, born in Seville to Irish parents, drew his last breath in Mexico City. The official cause of his death was pleurisy, though some suspected he had been poisoned.

O'Donojú had arrived in Veracruz on the east coast of Mexico in July 1821 after being appointed *jefe político superior*, or supreme political head, of the Viceroyalty of New Spain by the new liberal Spanish government. He was, in all but name, the last viceroy of New Spain, a territory that in 1821 encompassed Mexico, Cuba, the present-day Dominican Republic, most of Central America and much of the modern United States, including California, Arizona, Nevada, Colorado, New Mexico and Texas. Unlike Ambrose O'Higgins, who, during the last years of his life, ruled in splendour from the viceregal palace in Lima over much of the Andean part of South America, O'Donojú was not to enjoy the trappings of the viceregal court; yet his contribution to the modern history of Spanish America was perhaps even more significant than that of O'Higgins. Less than two weeks before his death, many thousands of miles from his masters in Spain, O'Donojú decreed the independence of Mexico from the Spanish Empire.

The declaration of Mexican independence by O'Donojú and the conservative Mexican army officer Agustín de Iturbide took place against a background of continuing violence between rebel factions and Spanish troops. While the leaders of the independence movements in South America were predominantly aristocratic or middle-class, inspired by Enlightenment ideas, the rebellion against Spanish rule in Mexico was more complex, made up of different groups with often competing interests. The initial revolt was led by Miguel de Hidalgo, the parish priest of Dolores, a small town about 170 miles to the north-west of Mexico City. Hidalgo attributed the sufferings of his poor parishioners to Spanish misrule, and from the front of the parish church he issued the famous *Grito de Dolores*, or Cry of Dolores, which is celebrated today in Mexico as the crucial moment in the history of national independence. Hidalgo urged his parishioners to rise up against the authorities and led his indigenous and peasant followers into battle under a flag depicting the Virgin of Guadalupe, the most venerated Marian icon in the world. Despite early successes, however, Hidalgo procrastinated when he had Mexico City at his mercy, giving the viceroy time to organise his troops and crush the rebellion. Hidalgo was tried by the Inquisition and beheaded. Another Catholic priest, José María Morelos, replaced Hidalgo at the head of the independence movement, but in 1815 he was also captured and put to death.

For the next five years guerrilla forces under the leadership of Guadalupe Victoria and Vicente Guerrero continued to attack Spanish outposts. But events in Spain changed attitudes in Mexico. Riego's liberal *coup d'état* in 1820 horrified the conservative elite in Mexico, including Agustín de Iturbide, a monarchist officer who had been fighting the rebel forces since 1810. On hearing of the change of government in Spain he and his fellow-conservative *criollos* changed tack, advocating independence from liberal Spain in order to preserve the privileges of the Church and the powerful landowners. Iturbide persuaded Guerrero to join this new independence movement, which based its programme for government on the Plan of Iguala or Plan of the Three Guarantees. These guarantees were: the maintenance of the monarchy, the preservation of Church privileges, and equal treatment for *peninsulares* and *criollos*. Iturbide and Guerrero formed the Army of the Three Guarantee to consolidate their power. By the time O'Donojú arrived in Mexico, most of the country supported the cause of independence.

Iturbide and O'Donojú made strange bedfellows. The Mexican was of Basque ancestry on his father's side and came from a conservative landowning family. He had fought rebellions against Spanish rule for a decade when the arrival of the liberals to power in Spain turned him into an advocate of independence. He was personally ambitious and was accused of corruption and cruelty, but he was also deeply popular among conservative elements of Mexican society. On the other hand, O'Donojú was a liberal and a freemason.

Born on 30 July 1762 in Seville, Juan O'Donojú was baptised nine days later in the Sagrario, the parish church connected to the city's giant gothic cathedral. His father, Richard Dunphy O'Donoghue, was from Glenflesk,

County Kerry; his mother, Alice Ryan, was from Inch, County Tipperary.[1] Juan enlisted in the Ultonia Regiment at the age of 19. He was a colonel when the French invaded Spain in 1808 and was given command of a regiment of light infantry. In November 1808 he was accused of treachery and ordered to face a court-martial in the aftermath of the disastrous Battle of Tudela in Navarre, in which Napoleon's forces comprehensively defeated a Spanish force outside the town.[2]

But his disgrace did not last long. In May 1809 the Supreme Central Junta recognised the bravery of the troops under O'Donojú's command in an action against the French near the village of Algorfa in Alicante.[3] In 1811 he was captured by the French and imprisoned in Bayonne. He managed to escape and made his way to Cádiz, where he was appointed inspector-general of cavalry and then minister for war. As such he was responsible for the organisation of the Spanish army during and after the war and was in constant communication with Sir Arthur Wellesley, commander-in-chief of the British forces. He was also responsible for the prosecution of the war against the rebels in Spain's American colonies.

Ferdinand VII returned to the Spanish throne in 1814, and O'Donojú was arrested for his liberal sympathies and the fact that he was a freemason and imprisoned in the Castle of San Carlos, on the outskirts of Palma on the Mediterranean island of Mallorca. He spent four years in prison, suffering tortures that left permanent scars and probably hastened his death.

The restoration of the liberal constitution in 1820 brought a change in O'Donojú's fortunes. The new government appointed him to the Viceroyalty of New Spain as *jefe político superior*, with a view to him carrying out a liberal policy. He replaced the outgoing viceroy, Juan Ruiz de Apodaca, who had been overthrown by the Spanish field-marshal Pedro Francisco Novella. O'Donojú was under the impression that he would be welcomed in Veracruz, given his mission to reform the institutions in Mexico on a liberal footing; instead he was faced with a widespread conservative-led insurgency. Without men or resources, he quickly agreed to a meeting with Iturbide. The result was the Treaty of Córdoba, signed by O'Donojú and Iturbide in the town of that name on 24 August 1821. The treaty put into effect the form of government envisaged in the Plan of Iguala and became the basis for a newly independent Mexican empire.

The Spanish government rejected the Treaty of Córdoba, and – not for the first time – O'Donojú was accused of treachery. He himself was convinced that he had acted correctly, inspired by a political view that held the liberty of the people as sacred. He wrote that he was convinced that every society had the right 'to declare its liberty and defend at the same time the life of the individual,' and that any efforts made to 'oppose that sacred torrent, once its majestic and sublime course had begun,' were useless.[4] In September he convinced Novella to lay down his arms and accept the independence of Mexico. On 23 and 24 September 1810 Iturbide's troops marched into Mexico City to acclamation. Three days later the country's independence was officially declared in the city.

O'Donojú now found himself in an invidious position. He was unable to return to his homeland, where he was regarded as a traitor for having, seemingly without a thought, given away most of Spain's remaining American possessions. Though he was popular with the Mexican people, he was wary of accepting a position in the new regency council offered to him by Iturbide. He felt that he could not accept the conservative nature of the new government, which was hostile to liberals and to freemasons. He also realised that Iturbide was anxious to consolidate his own personal power, without a rival for the people's affections. In any event, within days of the declaration of independence O'Donojú was struck down with a debilitating illness. He died on 8 October, at the age of 59, only two months after he had arrived in Veracruz. He left behind his impoverished widow, María Josefa Sánchez, and three children. As befitted the extraordinary role he had played in the achievement of Mexican independence, O'Donojú's body was embalmed and placed in the vault reserved for the Spanish viceroys under the magnificent baroque Altar of the Kings in Mexico City's cathedral.

Exactly 300 years after Cortés had vanquished the Aztecs, Mexico was at last free of Spanish rule. Iturbide took control of the provisional governing junta, and in May 1822 he was proclaimed Emperor Augustine I of Mexico, after Ferdinand VII had rejected an offer to become the first monarch of the independent Mexican Empire. Iturbide was crowned in July 1822 in a lavish coronation ceremony in the cathedral in Mexico City, ruling until March 1823, when growing opposition forced him to abdicate. That same year the Federal Republic of Central America, consisting of present-day Costa Rica, El Salvador, Honduras and Nicaragua, seceded from the Mexican Empire.

A federal republic replaced the monarchy in 1823. Over the next two decades conservatives and liberals, centralists and federalists fought for power in Mexico. Successive governments attempted to revive a faltering economy and stave off secessionist threats from the regions, all the while contending with the threat of invasion from hostile powers, including Spain, France and the United States. In 1835 the Mexican state of Texas rose up against the conservative government of General Antonio López de Santa Anna. The unrest was driven by more than 20,000 Anglo-American ranchers who had settled in Texas and were disturbed by the government's new centralist constitution. Santa Anna led an expedition to quell the uprising, wiping out the defenders of the mission station of El Álamo near San Antonio. The outrage felt by the Anglo-Americans at Santa Anna's bloody actions led to the famous call 'Remember the Alamo!' In April 1836, at the Battle of San Jacinto, the Anglo-Americans defeated Santa Anna's army, and an independent Republic of Texas seceded from Mexico. It was the decision a decade later by the United States government to annex Texas that led to the Mexican-American War.

On 10 September 1847, just as the first rays of the sun began to appear over the horizon, the residents of a small Mexican village were awakened to shouts and the sound of rattling cartwheels. San Ángel has since been swallowed up by Mexico City's urban sprawl, but in the middle of the nineteenth century it was a typical Mexican village. At its heart was the plaza of San Jacinto. On that September morning, however, it was not the church that dominated the square but a large gallows, with 16 nooses hanging from a beam 40 feet long, towards which a ragged group of prisoners, members of the Mexican army, were marched by their blue-uniformed guards, members of the United States army. There was a tense atmosphere in the square as US officers and local villagers waited for the gruesome spectacle to begin.

Sixteen of the prisoners were brought to a halt under the gallows. The remaining 14 were brought to the other side of the square and tied to some of the trees in front of the parish church, under whose branches the villagers would normally take shelter from the midday sun. The guards moved towards the prisoners tied to the trees and stripped them of their uniforms. A United States general then gave the order for the lashings to begin. The men who carried out the punishment were Mexican muleteers. They used knotted rawhide lashes, which, according to an eyewitness, gave the backs of their victims the 'appearance of a pounded piece of raw beef, the blood oozing from every stripe.'[5]

Perhaps the most barbaric part of the morning's proceedings was the branding. The officer in charge of the punishment ordered a brazier to be lit, and when the branding iron was red-hot it was applied to the face of each prisoner, leaving the letter D, for deserter, indelibly scarred in the flesh of their cheek. The screams of the men as the iron seared the skin pierced the early morning air of San Ángel.

The prisoners who had been left to stand underneath the gallows were now hoisted onto eight mule-drawn carts, their heads placed in the nooses. The US officer in charge of the execution beckoned forward the five Catholic priests who had been watching silently from beside the door of the church. They were led onto the back of the carts by a priest carrying a large wooden cross. The priests heard the men's last confession and administered the last rites. The order was then given for the carts to move away, and the bodies of the 16 men dropped. Some of the men died instantly, their necks broken by the fall, their bodies twitching involuntarily, as if participating in a ghastly parody of a village dance; the more unfortunate ones, including Captain Patrick Dalton, slowly choked to death, their feet a matter of inches from the earth and the promise of life. The dead bodies were then cut down and brought to the cemetery in a neighbouring village. Iron collars with long spikes were placed around the necks of the surviving prisoners before they were led off to jail.[6]

Two days later the US army repeated the exercise on a hill close to the Mexican village of Mixcoac. This time there were 30 nooses attached to the gallows. Among the men sentenced to death was Francis O'Connor (not to be confused with Francis Burdett O'Connor). He had at first been reprieved, owing to the fact that he had lost both his legs in battle and was dying from his wounds; but the officer in charge of the execution, an Irish-American by the name of Colonel William Harney, ordered him to be brought up from the prison. Harney refused to carry out the executions until he could see the United States flag flying over the fort at nearby Chapultepec, where the US army was besieging the Mexican garrison. Throughout the morning the prisoners stood sweating on the back of the carts, the nooses around their necks. Finally, at about 9:30 a.m., Harney saw the Stars and Stripes raised over Chapultepec, and he gave the order for the carts to be moved away.

Alongside the 30 men who died that morning, another eight were given 50 lashes and branded.

The men who died at the hands of the US army on those September mornings in 1847 were members of the Mexican army's Batallón de San Patricio, or St Patrick's Battalion. To the officers of the US army who court-martialled and executed them, the prisoners who died – most of them Irish – were traitors, who had deserted their country; in Mexico they are honoured as heroes who fought for the liberty of the Mexican people in the face of US aggression.

There is also a racial and religious aspect to the story of the San Patricios; for, while Catholic and Protestant and Irishman and Englishman fought alongside each other for South American liberty, the men who made up the St Patrick's Battalion were mostly Catholic Irish emigrants, escaping not only poverty but also the religious and racial prejudice that existed among the predominantly Protestant officer corps of the United States army.

Captain John Riley from Clifden, County Galway, was among the Irish prisoners who would bear the physical and emotional scars for the rest of their lives. He was one of the tens of thousands of Irish immigrants who were flooding into North American cities in the 1840s. Their arrival coincided with the rise of the nativist movement, whose anti-Catholicism extended into the upper echelons of the United States army. Desperate to make a living, Riley had joined the US army as a private. The Irish Catholics who enlisted in the army were treated as little more than cannon fodder. Realising the extent of anti-Catholic prejudice in the US army, and the large number of foreign soldiers within its ranks, the Mexican government launched a propaganda campaign to entice them to desert.

Riley was among hundreds of Irishmen who deserted the United States army to fight for the Mexicans. Writers and historians have ascribed religious and cultural motives to the Irish deserters, believing that they saw parallels in the Mexican-American War with their experience in Ireland. And there is much to suggest that this is true. Riley is believed to have given the battalion its name and its flag. The flag had a green background, with an image of St Patrick embroidered on one side and a harp and shamrock on the other.[7] However, as in all wars, there must also have been more prosaic factors at work. The Irish deserters may have expected better treatment from the Mexicans; some of them may have been coerced into joining after being taken prisoner; others may have been seduced by a way of life that seemed to offer more than they would find back in the tenements of the North American cities from which they had come. In his book *The Irish Soldiers of Mexico*, Michael Hogan questions various hypotheses about the San Patricios. He writes:

> Some American historians claim the concept of the 'Irish Catholic Battalion' was simply Mexican propaganda. Others claim that it was a concept originated by nativists to cast aspersions on the loyalty of Irish troops serving the American Army and thus minimize their contributions. Another revisionist viewpoint, denying or minimizing the Irish/Catholic connection, may have been inspired by the Irish-Americans themselves who were anxious to be assimilated in American society. Thus, they were eager to insist that the San Patricio Battalion was simply a mixture of races and that religion was not an issue. The majority of Irishmen and Catholics did, in fact, remain loyal to their adopted flag during the Mexican War despite provocation and abuse.[8]

The St Patrick's Battalion has earned an honoured place in the history of modern Mexico, not just for its willingness to fight but for the skill and bravery with which it undertook the fight. Riley was a talented soldier who by April 1846 had organised himself and 47 other Irishmen into a small artillery unit. By the summer there were more than 200 soldiers in the battalion, organised in two companies. Most were Irish, but there were also Mexicans of recent European descent, as well as other European-born volunteers, many of them German.

In August 1846, determined to reverse a series of defeats at the hands of the US army during the summer, the Mexican government recalled Santa Anna from self-imposed exile. Santa Anna now became the pre-eminent military commander, replacing General Pedro de Ampudia, whose capitulation to General Zachary Taylor's besieging troops at Monterrey had weakened his reputation.

In February Santa Anna led the 20,000-strong Army of the North towards a mountain pass called Buena Vista in the Mexican state of Coahuila. On the morning of 23 February the San Patricios directed their fire along the American line. From the crest of a ridge they manned three 16-pound guns, training their sights on the enemy positions. Despite superior numbers,

Santa Anna's army was tired from the long march north; the Americans were better trained and had superior artillery. By the end of the day, however, Taylor's army had sustained heavy casualties, and more than a thousand men had deserted.[9] Nevertheless, Taylor claimed victory at Buena Vista, citing the battle as part of his campaign for the presidency of the United States the following year.

On 17 April the US and Mexican armies, including the San Patricios, clashed again at Cerro Gordo close to the town of Xalapa, between Mexico City and Veracruz. Thanks to the actions of an irrepressible Virginian captain named Robert E. Lee, who later led the Confederate forces during the American Civil War, the US army overran the Mexican forces. In the middle of the night Lee led a party of engineers up a treacherously steep trail to take command of an adjacent hill, allowing the American artillery to enfilade the Mexicans the following morning. Santa Anna and his men retreated, leaving behind his treasury of $20,000 in gold coins.

By 1847 the Mexican government was desperate for men, and it continued to persuade Irish immigrants to desert. John Riley called on his countrymen to side with the Mexican people against the US army, which, 'in the face of the whole world has trampled upon the holy altar of our religion' and 'set the firebrand upon a sanctuary devoted to the Blessed Virgin.'[10]

The San Patricios made their final stand at the Battle of Churubusco. On 19 August General Gabriel Valencia left Mexico City at the head of a 4,000-strong army, part of the Mexican government's last-gasp effort to cut off General Winfield Scott from his supply base on the Atlantic coast. Valencia encountered the US troops camped near the town of Contreras and prepared to attack the following morning. It was another night raid led by Lee that proved the difference. Lee and his small group of men picked their way to the rear of the Mexican army through a lava field, which Valencia had considered impassable, and charged the Mexican camp. As shells began raining down from the front, Valencia's army fled in confusion.

Santa Anna's force, which had been to the rear of Valencia's, retreated to Mexico City. The San Patricios, some 200 men, were stationed in a monastery on the Mexico City side of the River Churubusco and were ordered to protect the retreating army. It was their actions on 19 August 1847 that earned them a place in Mexican history.

The bridge over the river was protected by a 15-foot earthen embankment. The riflemen and artillerymen of the San Patricios were placed on platforms on top of the 12-foot high walls that surrounded the monastery. The US assault began at 11 a.m. The Irish defenders fought bravely against wave after wave of attacks throughout the morning and early afternoon, when they began to run out of ammunition. Retreating into the grounds of the monastery, they were forced to fight hand-to-hand with bayonet and rifle butt. According to Michael Hogan, 'the dead and wounded were now as numerous as those still fighting on the parapets. The blood stood in deep puddles and the men slipped and skidded, sometimes sliding off the balconies to crash on the rocks below.'[11] The surviving San Patricios surrendered and were taken prisoner.

The US army entered Mexico City on 14 September 1847. The war was over in all but name; however, it would take another eight months before an official treaty was signed. In the meantime the US army occupied the capital.

The Battle of Churubusco was the end of the Irish battalion's participation in the Mexican-American War, but it was not the end of the San Patricios. In June 1848, as part of the terms of the Treaty of Guadalupe Hidalgo, the San Patricios who were still in US prisons were released. They joined a new Batallón de San Patricio, which had been created by the Mexican army and was stationed north of Mexico City in the state of Querétaro. The battalion comprised discharged men and deserters from the US army, as well as the old San Patricios. They were involved in putting down a royalist revolt and were subsequently given the responsibility of policing the town of Guadalupe Hidalgo.

John Riley was promoted to lieutenant-colonel and given command of the new battalion. He had grown his whiskers to hide the brand on his cheek. However, in July 1848 the Mexican government arrested him on suspicion of being involved in a planned rebellion. The San Patricios were disbanded; one company was sent to Mexico City, the other ordered to remain in Guadalupe Hidalgo. The officers were now terrified that they too would be arrested, and the unit fell apart. The government dissolved the battalion shortly afterwards.

The existence of the Battalion of St Patrick had been short but significant. John Riley was later released, and he rejoined the Mexican army as an infantry officer. He was discharged in 1850 with the rank of major on disability pay, suffering from the effects of ill health, including a bout of yellow fever. There is no firm evidence pointing to what happened to him after his discharge.

One writer suggested in 1999 in an English-language newspaper published in Mexico City that he had died a penniless drunk in Veracruz in 1850, based on a death certificate found in the city for a 45-year-old Irishman by the name of Juan Reley.[12]

Riley and the other members of the battalion who fought in the Mexican-American War continue to be honoured in the Plaza del Jacinto in the San Ángel district of Mexico City. The Irish ambassador in Mexico unveiled a bust of Reilly in 2010 to mark the bicentenary of Mexican independence and the centenary of the Mexican Revolution. Just across the road, marking the spot where the executions of the men took place, there is a plaque, which was unveiled in 1959. It reads, in translation: *In memory of the Irish soldiers of the heroic St Patrick's Battalion, martyrs who gave their lives for the cause of Mexico during the unjust North American invasion of 1847*. There are 71 names on the plaque, though not all of these were executed. There are Irish names, including William O'Connor, Richard Hanly, Alexander McKee, Andrew Nolan, Patrick Dalton, Thomas Riley, Francis O'Connor, Peter Neil, Kerr Delaney, Harrison Kenny, John Sheehan, David McElroy, Patrick Casey, James McDonnell, Gibson McDowell, John McDonald, John Cavanagh, Thomas Cassidy, John Daly, James Kelly and John Murphy; but interspersed with these names are those of Henry Logenhamer, Henry Octker, Herman Schmidt and Parian Fritz, testifying to the fact that, though predominantly Irish, the San Patricios was a multinational battalion.

Chapter 14

THE KINGDOM OF GOD

In March 1870, in a region of wilderness known as the Cerro Corá in the north-east corner of Paraguay, a woman was digging in the earth. She was dressed in the finery of a society hostess, and not far away was the smart carriage in which she had travelled along the twisting paths that weaved their way through the thick, heavy vegetation. Around her, Brazilian soldiers shouted and screamed in jubilation; they were exultant because they had just killed the woman's lover, the Paraguayan dictator Francisco Solano López, and would be able to return home after a devastating six-year war.

The woman was 36-year-old Eliza Lynch from Charleville, County Cork. She was digging the grave of the father of her children and her 15-year-old son, a colonel in the Paraguayan army. The Brazilian soldiers had wished to bury the bodies in a shallow grave, but the proud Irishwoman had insisted that they dig a proper burial place for her men. Before the bodies of López and son were lowered into the graves, Eliza took a scissors and cut locks of bloodied hair from the heads of her lover and her son. Her final act in the face of overwhelming grief was the last in a catastrophic series of events that had brought Paraguay to the edge of oblivion. By the time López made his last stand at Cerro Corá, hundreds of thousands of Paraguayans had lost their lives.

For though Paraguay won its independence from Spain with little loss of life, it suffered more than any of the other South American republics from the devastation wrought by the War of the Triple Alliance. The story of the Irish in Paraguay is not so much about how they helped liberate the country but about the role they played in trying to protect its independence.

Paraguay is different. The small landlocked country in the heart of South America has managed to plot its own course through history, seemingly immune to the great historic currents that surged through the continent in the early 1800s. When the rest of the continent was opening up to trade, Paraguay was closing its doors, adopting a protectionist, centralised economy. While Spanish or Portuguese is predominantly spoken in the streets in the rest of South America, in Paraguay the indigenous language of Guaraní remains the vernacular. It was also in Paraguay that one of the most radical experiments in social organisation in the history of modern South America took place.

Scattered throughout the Paraguayan countryside are the beautiful remains of the Jesuit missions, symbol of a doomed attempt to synthesise European values and indigenous traditions. The Jesuits first arrived in Paraguay at the end of the sixteenth century. They were part of the Spanish monarchy's ultimately failed efforts to prevent Spanish colonists from exploiting the indigenous populations of the New World. The Spanish crown had wrestled with this problem ever since Columbus had first set foot on American soil. The early colonists, the *conquistadores* and their relatives, wanted cheap labour and cared little for the welfare of the indigenous peoples. Their representatives pleaded at court, portraying the native people as little more than animals. On the other side were the early missionaries, such as the Dominican friar Bartolomé de las Casas, who were shocked by the savage treatment meted out by the *conquistadores* and who were at the forefront of the campaign to protect the indigenous inhabitants.

Early attempts at evangelisation were little more than mass forced conversions; but gradually the missionary orders realised that only by educating them and representing the figure of Christ in terms that the indigenous people could understand within their own cosmos would they embrace Christianity. The Jesuits' willingness to adapt the customs and beliefs of the Guaraní in order to bring them closer to Christ was later to be used against them.

In the sixteenth century an Irish priest named Thomas Field (or Fehily), who had been educated at Douai, Louvain and Rome, was among the first Jesuits to arrive in Paraguay. Born in the 1540s, he worked as a missionary in Brazil and the River Plate before he was ordered to Paraguay in the 1580s. It was a solitary existence; there was just a handful of Jesuit missionaries from Europe in Paraguay in the early seventeenth century. For four decades Field worked alone among the Guaraní until his death in Asunción in 1625.[1] According to the Jesuit historian Aubrey Gwynn, Field was the first Irish priest to say mass in the New World.[2] Other Irish Jesuit missionaries followed in Field's footsteps, including Father Thomas Browne (1656–1717) from County Waterford and Father William Leny (1690–c. 1760) from County Dublin.[3]

The Jesuits created thriving communities among the Guaraní, which became self-sufficient. They grew cash crops, such as *yerba mate*, the tea-like beverage popular in the central and southern regions of South America, and raised thousands of head of livestock for export. They introduced printing presses and published books, including a dictionary of the Guaraní language. At their peak the Jesuit 'reductions' or settlements were home to 150,000 Guaraní. The reductions were built around a square, at the centre of which was the church; these were often beautifully ornate buildings with stunning baroque façades. The Jesuit fathers taught art and music to the Guaraní. Though critics would argue that the Jesuits broke up traditional ways of life, the order was also fiercely protective of the indigenous peoples, defending them from the depredations of Portuguese slave traders in an area encompassing parts of Paraguay, Brazil and Argentina.

The Jesuits' success in Paraguay created problems for the order. The Portuguese authorities resented the fact that they protected the Guaraní. There were wild rumours of the order's wealth in Paraguay and a widespread belief that the Guaraní were employed in working secret gold mines on the reductions. The Spanish and Portuguese elites, jealous of the order's economic and political power in Paraguay, conspired to curb their influence.

The award-winning film *The Mission*, which featured three Irish actors – the late Ray McAnally, Aidan Quinn and Liam Neeson, the last in the role of a Jesuit priest named Fielding – is based on the events leading up to the Guaraní War of 1756, when, under the terms of the Treaty of Madrid, Spain agreed to hand over to Portugal the missions east of the River Uruguay. The Guaraní resistance to the Spanish and Portuguese crowns is depicted in the denouement of the film.

Much of the story comes from the diary of Father Tadeo Henis, which describes the brutal suppression of the Guaraní reductions.[4] In 1766, in the notes to his translation of a letter from the seventeenth-century anti-Jesuit Spanish bishop Juan de Palafox to the Pope, Salvador Gonzalez described Henis as 'another of the Jesuit army's chiefs' in Paraguay who refused to submit to the will of the Portuguese and Spanish crowns.[5]

Father Henis's nationality is not known for certain. His surname was variously spelt 'Ennis', 'Enis', 'Hennis' and 'Henis'. He was most probably a Bohemian. The Scottish author, traveller and Liberal Member of Parliament Robert Bontine Cunninghame Graham, who wrote a history of the Jesuits in Paraguay, described him as Irish, on the dubious grounds that 'his name, Thadeus Ennis (as it is often spelt), and his love of fighting look un-Germanic.'[6]

On 27 January 1754 hundreds of Guaraní, on foot and on horseback, from the missions of San Ángel, San Miguel, San Juan, San Nicolás, San Luis and San Lorenzo – all of which now lie in the Brazilian state of Rio Grande do Sul – prepared to face the joint Spanish-Portuguese forces that were charged with ensuring the submission of the reductions.

The Jesuits were split between those who thought the missions east of the River Uruguay should be ceded to the Portuguese – mostly those in Europe who were anxious to demonstrate their fealty to the Spanish monarchy – and those, such as Father Henis, who thought the order should support the Guaraní and resist. Though there is no evidence that Father Henis participated directly in the fighting – he refused to accept a position as a medical and spiritual adviser to the Guaraní[7] – he undoubtedly supported their efforts to defend the reductions from Portuguese occupation.

The Guaraní fought with bows and arrows and with cannons made from reeds bound with leather hides, and marched into battle under banners bearing images of the saints. Though they had the advantage of knowing the terrain, they lacked military organisation and firepower. Over the course of two years they fought an unsuccessful guerrilla war against the Spanish and Portuguese. Father Henis was captured in 1756 at the taking of the San Lorenzo mission, and the war was at an end. The Jesuits' enemies at the court in Madrid took possession of Father Henis's papers and pointed to his role in resisting the transfer of the missions.

In 1767 the governor, an Irish-Spaniard named Carlos Morphy, expelled the Jesuits from Paraguay. Though Morphy was bound by royal decree to carry out the expulsion, he was personally sympathetic to the order's plight and is said to have allowed them to carry their papers and books with them into exile, against the wishes of his superiors.

In 1811 Paraguay was one of the first countries to win *de facto* independence from Spain. During the country's first 60 years as an independent state it was ruled by three dictators. José Gaspar Rodríguez de Francia came to power within two years of Paraguay declaring its independence. He was a lawyer who had once harboured ambitions of taking holy orders and had studied for a degree in theology. He was a great admirer of Enlightenment thinkers such as Rousseau. His brand of anti-clerical populism and his establishment of a much-feared political police ensured that he remained in power for 27 years.

Carlos Antonio López succeeded Francia in 1840. In 1853 he sent his son, Francisco Solano López, to Europe on a diplomatic mission, and it was in Paris that Francisco met the 19-year-old Eliza Lynch. Born in Charleville in 1833, Eliza was the daughter of John Lynch, a Catholic doctor, and his wife, Jane Elizabeth Lloyd, a member of the Church of Ireland. Eliza left Ireland for England when she was a child. At the age of 16 she married a 34-year-old French officer by the name of Xavier Quatrefages in Folkestone, Kent; but by the time she met Solano López the marriage was effectively over.

The Paraguayan officer was smitten by the young Irishwoman, and he invited her back to his homeland. In 1855 Eliza Lynch stepped off the riverboat that had brought her to Asunción and into a maelstrom of courtly intrigue. Because of her marital situation, and the unusual circumstances in which the heir to the dictatorship of Paraguay had met this exotic Irishwoman, gossip and rumour about the 20-year-old Eliza Lynch and her origins circulated throughout the capital, including claims that she was a courtesan.

Lynch was set up in her own house in Asunción, where her lover Solano López would visit her at night. The disapproval of his family meant that the couple did not live together. This did not stop her from becoming the most glamorous society hostess in Asunción. Solano López had made her a rich woman, and she set about decorating her residence with the finest European furnishings. Her arrival in Asunción, which then had a population of not much more than 20,000, prompted jealousy and admiration in equal measure.

In 1862 Solano López became dictator on the death of his father, and Eliza Lynch became his unofficial consort. She was now in a position to wreak vengeance on her rivals in Asunción society; instead she hosted one of the biggest balls Asunción had ever seen. It was her moment of triumph.

But it was not to last. Solano López was unlike his predecessors, who had sought to protect Paraguayan interests from the designs of its much larger neighbours, Brazil and Argentina, by remaining aloof from regional politics. The new dictator believed that Paraguay should not be afraid to pursue an active diplomatic and military policy, and he intervened in the long-running dispute over Uruguay and control of the River Plate. In *The Lives of Eliza Lynch: Scandal and Courage,* Michael Lillis and Ronan Fanning write:

For gigantic Brazil, little Paraguay was a nuisance and a substantial strategic inconvenience. For their part, the common people of Paraguay vividly remembered that it had been Brazilian adventurers and slave-hunters who had enslaved thousands of their ancestors in the days when the *Bandeirantes* (Brazil's equivalent of the outlaws of the American West) preyed on the Jesuits' Missions.[8]

Since the early days of the European conquest, Spain and Portugal had fought over control of the River Plate estuary. This later manifested itself in the war between Argentina and the Brazilian Empire over the Banda Oriental, which resulted in the establishment of the present-day republic of Uruguay. In 1862 Argentina and Brazil were still interfering in Uruguayan politics in order to advance their competing claims for regional hegemony of the River Plate region. The Uruguayan government called on Solano López to intervene. He responded by warning Brazil and Argentina that he would regard any attack on Uruguayan territory as an attack on Paraguay.

The War of the Triple Alliance, which began in 1864, pitted Solano López's Paraguayan army against the vastly superior forces of Brazil and Argentina. This six-year war of extermination was one of the bloodiest conflicts in the history of the continent. It is estimated that up to 70 per cent of the total population of Paraguay – as many as 300,000 people – was killed during the war.[9]

After it was over and Solano López was dead, the victors, Brazil and Argentina, blamed Eliza for manipulating him into starting the war and prosecuting it until its apocalyptic finish. Vitriolic depictions of her appeared in the pages of the Argentine press, depicting her as an avaricious courtesan who had brought Paraguay to the point of destruction. Recent scholarship has dismantled this myth, and in modern Paraguay Eliza Lynch is regarded as a national heroine who stood up to the foreign invaders who had slaughtered her lover and her son on that bleak March day in 1870.

Eliza returned to Europe after the war, dying in Paris in 1886 at the age of 52.[10] Before she died she defended herself against the vituperative claims of her critics in *Exposición y Protesta* (Declaration and Protest), a document published in Buenos Aires in 1875. It begins:

> For a long time I maintained a profound silence, though my name had for six years been attacked by determined enemies, by individuals who sought riches by writing pamphlets and books full of appalling filth, representing me as the very essence of prostitution and scandal, as though I were one of those human beasts who seek satisfaction in the extermination of society itself …
>
> I have been accused of responsibility for the actions in domestic policy of Marshal López and blamed for the war that three nations forced on Paraguay, as well as for the heroic sacrifice which immortalised this people, perishing with their leader, in more than five years of warfare unexampled in American history and which has been such a lesson to all nations, as great as that of the Spartans at Thermopylae …
>
> I was far from being involved in the Government of Marshal López or its politics, nor did I involve myself in anything during the war beyond attending to the wounded and to the families of those who followed the army and trying to reduce the suffering I found; but I do not shrink from shouldering the responsibility that any would wish me to bear for the defence that the people of Paraguay offered of their rights and their territory.[11]

This was Eliza Lynch's great contribution to Paraguay. In the nation's darkest hour she had stood resolute and proud on the battlefield. It was this last defiant act of the murderous war upon which the broken nation later began to rebuild.

PART THREE
HOME

Chapter 15

AFTER THE REVOLUTION

In November 1825 Francis Burdett O'Connor rode a mule across the Atacama Desert in present-day northern Chile. The Irish veteran of Bolívar's campaigns in Peru and Bolivia spent days crossing the cracked, parched ground. The Atacama is one of the driest regions on earth and, because it never rains, the surface has been compared to that of Mars; scientists who are interested in seeing how life might survive on the Red Planet have conducted experiments on the slopes of Licancabur, the volcano that straddles the border between Chile and Bolivia.

Though there was little on the surface to draw humans to this remote, rocky landscape, underneath the crimson sand there were rich mineral deposits: sodium nitrate and copper. Until the early twentieth century and the development of new synthetic processes, Chile exported vast quantities of sodium nitrate, also known as Chilean saltpetre, which was in global demand for the manufacture of fertilisers and high explosives.

Bolivia has maintained a territorial dispute with Chile since the end of the war against the Spanish in Upper Peru over a section of the Atacama Desert. Bolivia's borders roughly corresponded to the colonial province of Charcas, which had once been part of the Viceroyalty of Peru. The province stretched from the Amazon basin in the north almost to the present-day border with Argentina in the south. The Bolivian government claimed that the province's western boundary was more than 300 miles of the Pacific coast. In 1776 Charcas province became part of the Viceroyalty of the River Plate and fell under the jurisdiction of Buenos Aires. Under the new dispensation, exporters had to send their goods and commodities to Buenos Aires instead of to Arica, the Pacific port that was claimed by Peru after independence and is now part of Chile.

Between 1879 and 1883, during the War of the Pacific, Chile fought Peru and Bolivia over this long, dry strip of land and its valuable mineral deposits. Chile emerged victorious, and Bolivia lost its access to the sea, a national disaster that was unequalled until the Chaco War with Paraguay in the 1930s. Bolivia is still fighting for sovereign access to the Pacific, having brought its claim all the way to the International Court of Justice in the Hague in September 2015. Access to the Pacific was a priority for President Evo Morales in 2016, in the same way that it was a priority in 1825 for Simón Bolívar, after whom the country is named.

Bolívar based his claim on the boundaries of Charcas province, and he ordered O'Connor to survey the Pacific coast to determine the best site for Bolivia's main port. Setting off from Tarija in the south of Bolivia in November with a Bolivian adjutant and a Colombian servant, O'Connor passed over the Andes towards Tupiza, where verdant valleys gave way to burnt-red sierra. In a place called Santa Rosa the earth was pockmarked from gold-mining.

In early December, after days of riding across the desert with little water, O'Connor caught sight of the dark blue of the ocean, the rays of the low sun dancing like golden starbursts on the waves behind the tiny fishing port of Cobija. He rode his mule into the deserted village and found a solitary man walking on the beach. The man told him his name was Maldonado and that he and his brother were the only survivors of a smallpox epidemic that had wiped out the population of the village. He invited O'Connor to spend the night with him. When O'Connor entered the man's house, he found candles flickering in front of statues of the saints that he had taken from the church to protect against the plague.

The following day a brig appeared on the bay. It was the *Chimborazo*, under the command of Thomas Charles Wright, the Irish officer who had fought with the Venezuelan Rifles. Bolívar had given Wright, an experienced sailor who had served as a midshipman in Britain's Royal Navy, command of a flotilla in the Pacific and ordered him to help O'Connor with his survey. The Irishmen spent the night of 9 December on board the *Chimborazo*, anchored off Cobija, celebrating the first anniversary of the Battle of Ayacucho.

The next day, the Irishmen began their scouting expedition of the Pacific coast. Their mission was to find not only the best-equipped port for merchant vessels but also the one that was best connected to the silver mines of Potosí. Over the following days O'Connor made notes about each port's suitability for the development of Bolivian trade. In his final report he chose Cobija ahead of the more southerly Paposo, which was a better natural port, because there was not enough water or provisions on the route from Paposo across the Atacama Desert to the Bolivian Andes. In his memoirs O'Connor wrote:

> If I had been able to look into the future. I would have fitted out two ports, Paposo and [Cobija]; the first with warehouses for disembarking goods, and the second as a point of departure for Potosí, arranging that bundles and other cargoes were transported from one point to the other in launches, which would have hugged the coast without any danger. In this way, Chile's later unfounded claims, and its usurpation of Bolivia's richest province, would have been avoided.[1]

The Bolivian government subsequently claimed access to the sea along a corridor connecting a few hundred miles of Pacific coastline – stretching north and south from Cobija – to the state's Andean hinterland.

Once the survey was finished, Wright set sail for Arica on the *Chimborazo*, where he was to pick up Bolívar and bring him to Lima. O'Connor returned to Bolivia by way of Quillagua, which is now little more than a ghost town in the middle of the Atacama Desert. It is one of the driest places in the world. About half a millimetre of rain has fallen on the town in the last four decades. Copper mining has had a devastating effect on the town. The few inhabitants live along the banks of the contaminated River Loa. In 1825 the residents of Quillagua told O'Connor that the main street running through their town from east to west was once the boundary between Peru and Upper Peru. According to O'Connor, this was a crucial piece of evidence, backing up Bolivia's territorial claim. O'Connor regretted that his reports had gone unheeded by Sucre, his commanding officer.

> I do not know if he received the report; but he certainly made no provision regarding the information I provided him about the boundary between Lower and Upper Peru. What I can state with certainty is that if I had accompanied the commodore [Wright] to Arica, if I had met with the Liberator, who was travelling to Lima, and if I had made him aware of the information I had taken from the elders of Quillagua, the Liberator, on his arrival in Lima, would have fixed the border between Upper and Lower Peru by decree, which would have increased Bolivia's territory.[2]

The role played by O'Connor and Wright in this continuing border dispute is one example of the important ways in which Irish veterans of the wars of independence helped shape the economy, society and politics of the new republics. The experiences of the Irish who remained in Latin America after the wars of independence varied considerably. Some built successful careers in the armed forces of the post-war republics; others became politicians and diplomats. All had to negotiate the tumultuous period of violent political reorganisation that invariably bedevils infant states.

Many of the Irish officers fought in the civil wars that plagued the continent after the Spanish had been driven out. As Daniel O'Leary recognised in 1830, despite the 'work, hardships and dangers' of the campaign for independence, 'the revolution has just begun.'[3]

While separatist tensions had existed since the creation of Gran Colombia at the Congress of Angostura in 1819, Bolívar had managed to hold the state together through the force of his personality and by pleading for national unity at a time of war. The final victory over the Spanish had barely been achieved when he was forced to confront his political and military rivals. In response to the internal and external threats to the state, Bolívar attempted to impose a new, centralist constitution, much to the dismay of his political rivals in Bogotá and Venezuela, who preferred a federal system, when not advocates of outright independence from the unitary state of Gran Colombia. O'Leary was a staunch ally, and Bolívar entrusted him with the most important and delicate missions.

In 1826 Bolívar sent O'Leary to negotiate with a former ally, the Venezuelan general José Antonio Páez, to prevent him separating from Gran Colombia. Two years later O'Leary was in Lima, trying unsuccessfully to prevent war between Peru and Gran Colombia. When the Peruvians declared war, O'Leary fought in the army of Gran Colombia, with the rank of brigadier-general.

In 1828 a convention was summoned to Ocaña, close to the border with Venezuela in the north-east of the modern state of Colombia, to put to bed the various constitutional issues that had bedevilled Gran Colombia. But when Bolívar's supporters failed to win over the federalist majority, they withdrew, and Bolívar claimed dictatorial powers. The scene was now set for a bitter struggle between Bolívar loyalists, who argued that central authority was paramount at such a fragile moment in the life of the state, and those who had come to regard the Liberator's behaviour as tyrannical.

O'Leary was tough, shrewd and fiercely loyal. He worked day after day to fulfil Bolívar's dream of a unitary South American state stretching from the Pacific to the Atlantic and from the Caribbean coast to the southern Andes during the critical years between the end of the wars with Spain and Bolívar's death. These burdens were exacerbated by the absences from his family.

O'Leary was newly married, with a young daughter, and the absences from his wife, Soledad, and children caused him great pain. This can be seen from a letter to Soledad he wrote in Guayaquil in 1828, in which he expressed his desire to live in what is now Ecuador. 'I am sorry that I did not bring you here. But if our differences with Peru are concluded amicably we will come to live in the South which is, above all, the country that I love the most.'[4] In a letter written the following month he complained: 'Your letters are very short and very different from those you wrote to me when I was in Ocaña.'[5] Coupled with his love was a jealous and controlling streak, as can be seen from a letter he wrote to Soledad in March 1830.

> I see from your last letter that they have not deceived me about the visitors. You, yourself, have said it to me now. I forbid you again to allow them in under any pretext. The fewer visitors you have, the fewer enemies you will make. Neither do I like it that you are going out. It does not seem right that you do it in my absence. Every day I love you more and more ...[6]

He wrote in much the same vein a day later when he complained that, 'in the middle of chores and problems, I dedicate a great part of my week to you. And you answer me with a lot of paper, but few letters. Leisure is your world and work is mine.'[7] His baby daughter Mimi's upbringing troubled him. He ordered his wife to teach her the alphabet, and added: 'Do not let her go around with servants. She will learn shameful things and vulgarities and will turn out badly brought-up.' To emphasise his point, he added: 'Tell her from me that señoras do not sweep and that I wish her to learn to read and write.'[8]

It was in the context of the growing opposition to Bolívar within Gran Colombia that an event occurred that was to tarnish O'Leary's reputation, with some historians going so far as to brand him a murderer. In 1829 the Colombian general José María Córdova, renowned as the Hero of Ayacucho for his actions during that decisive battle, rose up in opposition to Bolívar, whom he regarded as adopting absolutist tendencies, inimical to Córdova's avowed democratic sympathies. Bolívar sent O'Leary to Antioquia, in the northern part of present-day Colombia, to put down the rebellion.

O'Leary had the reconstituted 900-strong Rifles Battalion at his command, many of them foreign volunteers, including the Irish officers Rupert Hand and Thomas Murray. Hand was a Dubliner, a wild character who had already caused trouble while serving with the foreign volunteers in the south of Venezuela. He had retired from the army in 1824 because of ill health – a bullet had lodged in his left testicle during a duel with a fellow-Irishman, William Lynch, in Achaguas in August 1820[9] – having participated in the Battle of Carabobo and the campaigns along the northern coast, and retired to live in Mérida, in the Venezuelan Andes. But he was incapable of keeping out of trouble and was arrested for robbing the local post office. After being acquitted, thanks to the testimony of former comrades in the army, he went to live in Bogotá. It was here that he was recalled to service.

On 17 October, Córdova's and O'Leary's forces faced each other at a town called El Santuario, about 40 miles east of Medellín. When O'Leary called upon Córdova to surrender and save the lives of his men, his adversary is said to have replied: 'Córdova will not surrender to a rotten, paid-for foreign mercenary.' Córdova fought bravely but was outnumbered by three to one and was forced to retreat from the battlefield because of injuries to his shoulder and chest. He was taken prisoner and given shelter in a nearby house. It was then that Hand arrived on horseback. According to witnesses, he fell off his horse and began drunkenly staggering around. Drawing his sabre, he brushed past Murray, who was in command of the guard looking after the prisoner. Upon identifying the wounded Córdova, Hand killed him in an act of unbridled savagery, repeatedly stabbing and slashing his chest and head with his sword.[10]

It is possible that O'Leary gave the order to execute Córdova; historians continue to contest his level of involvement. O'Leary himself denied having ordered the killing, but he was vilified in the opposition press by those who believed Córdova had died trying to protect the republican foundations of the revolution. In a letter to Soledad he wrote: 'The Caracas papers are using all their means to make me hateful to the Venezuelans. This would not bother me much if I was not so annoyed and tired; because the more one side attacks me, the better I look in the eyes of the other.' O'Leary was bored and disillusioned and ready to retire. 'No, I have resolved to serve no more. All desire I had to succeed is gone. All my ambitions are finished.'[11]

Part of the problem was that during the revolution, when the patriots needed manpower, foreign volunteers were welcomed with open arms; but after independence had been achieved, many viewed them as unwelcome interlopers. When Bolívar ordered O'Leary to cut loose some of the foreign officers who still held rank in the Gran Colombian army, the Irishman was unhappy, believing it was unjust to get rid of men who had proved themselves to be the most loyal, and that it was 'very late to be telling them that their services were no longer required.'[12] He again considered resigning over the issue, possessing as he did the soldier's typical mistrust of politicians.

The virtues that O'Leary held most dear are expressed in a letter in which he advised his wife how to raise their son.

> As it happens he has been born in the middle of revolutions. It is important that he knows that, in political tumults, he who is most audacious is victorious. Tell him to meditate well before uniting himself to a party, but once it is done, his choice should be constant and tenacious; that he should never be a traitor, no matter the prize for the treachery. Tell him never to be cruel nor violent, but that if the public good demands it, he should be prepared to shed blood. Nothing ennobles more the character of a man than well-intentioned generosity. My son must be affable and kind-hearted in prosperity, but remind him that disgrace lies in being proud, stubborn and inflexible.[13]

In the same letter O'Leary exhorted his son to avoid 'low company' and 'drunkenness, which reduced men to the level of beasts,' and advised him not to covet riches, to shun extravagance but to remain generous.

O'Leary was an avid reader and, as might be expected, had studied the classical campaigns. 'It is better to study men than things,' he wrote. 'I strongly recommend to my son that he prefer the character of Julius Caesar to that of Pompey, and that he looks with horror upon the crime that made a hero of Brutus.'[15] O'Leary advised his son that 'a good upbringing and fine manners' covered 'a thousand defects,' adding, 'The last piece of advice that I will give my son for now is that he worships God and that he respects the beliefs of others, no matter what they may be.'[16]

Despite Córdova's death and O'Leary's victory at El Santuario, power was trickling through the fingers of the Bolivarian loyalists. In 1828 William Owens Ferguson of County Antrim, Bolívar's loyal aide-de-camp, was shot dead in a dark alley in Bogotá in a failed assassination attempt on the Liberator. Ferguson had returned with Bolívar to Gran Colombia in 1826 and had been charged with putting down rebellion in Venezuela. He left a revealing journal of that voyage, describing the extraordinary distances and the unforgiving terrain that Bolívar and his officers covered during the period.[17] The authorities organised a public funeral, and Ferguson's remains were buried in Bogotá's cathedral.

Ferguson had been a member of the Irish-officered Rifles, Bolívar's elite unit, which had fought bravely at Bomboná, Junín and Ayacucho. The battalion was disbanded in 1830. According to Alfred Hasbrouck, rather than 'allow their colors [flags] to be sullied by ignoble hands, the officers solemnly burned them.'[18]

The other Irish officers of the Rifles also remained loyal to Bolívar in the fractious years spanning the period from the end of the war in Peru and Bolivia to the Liberator's death in Santa Marta in present-day Colombia in 1830. Arthur Sandes, who had been promoted to brigadier-general before his retirement, settled in Ecuador, serving as governor of both Guayaquil and Cuenca. The battalion's chief surgeon, Hugo Blair Brown, a Presbyterian from County Donegal, lived in the Antioquia region in the north-west of Colombia in 1824. He continued to work as a doctor and converted to Catholicism in Medellín in 1829. Seven years later he married Eduvigis Gaviria, niece of the first vice-president of Gran Colombia, Francisco Antonio Zea.

Thomas Charles Wright had served with distinction in the Rifles in Colombia, Venezuela and Ecuador. He settled in Guayaquil, where he founded the institution that became Ecuador's national naval school. In 1828 he again entered the fray as both soldier and sailor when Peru began a campaign to expel Gran Colombian forces from Bolivia. Wright was captain of the port of Guayaquil when the Peruvian *Libertad* sailed into the Gulf of Guayaquil in an attempt to blockade the city. On board the *Guayaquileña*, Wright drove off the Peruvian ship, using his knowledge of the gulf's currents. In February 1829 he rejoined the Gran Colombian army as a colonel, serving as an aide-de-camp to General Sucre. In 1835, after Ecuador had seceded from Gran Colombia, he fought in a brief civil war with the forces backing the liberal candidate, Vicente Rocafuerte – his wife's uncle, for the Ecuadorean presidency. In 1845 Wright was forced into exile, spending 15 years outside Ecuador, first in Chile, then in Peru. He returned to Ecuador in 1860 and died in Guayaquil in 1868.[19]

Growing resentment about his autocratic style caused Bolívar to resign the presidency of Gran Colombia in 1830. He died from tuberculosis on the way into exile on 17 December close to the town of Santa Marta. His tortured final days are imagined in Gabriel García Márquez's novel *The General in His Labyrinth*. The great Liberator of the continent from Spanish rule drew his last breath knowing he had failed to persuade his fellow South Americans of his vision of a unified state. Gran Colombia was abolished in 1831 and replaced by the Republics of Ecuador, Venezuela and New Granada – renamed Colombia in 1863.

Bolívar's Irish allies found themselves in an unenviable position. Hand had been promoted after the Battle of El Santuario, becoming governor of the Chocó region along the Pacific coast. In 1831 he was serving as military governor of the port of Chagres in present-day Panama when he was deposed and taken prisoner in an uprising by political prisoners. 'There were scores to be settled and revenge to be taken for past misdemeanours,' according to Matthew Brown. 'The activities of foreign Bolivarians like Rupert Hand offended the sensibilities and nascent nationalism of the New Granadan liberals who were now in power.'[20] Hand was brought to Cartagena, on the Caribbean coast, where he was tried for the murder of Córdova. He now became a victim of the political changes in New Granada and his trial a litmus test for those seeking to prove their anti-Bolivarian credentials. According to Brown, in his fascinating study of Hand's trial and escape,

> ... the tumultuous events of the late 1820s were discussed and debated, and the manner in which political groups took up positions on these historical questions played an important role in distinguishing Liberals from Bolivarians. The defeat of José María Córdova at El Santuario was one of the most contentious of these questions. Liberals defended Córdova's rebellion and attacked the foreign origin of those soldiers who had defeated him.[21]

Despite the efforts of British diplomats to secure Hand's release, in April 1833 a regional court found him guilty and sentenced the Dubliner to 10 years' imprisonment. When Hand's lawyers appealed the decision, the higher court sentenced him to death. But within minutes of being informed of the decision, Hand had escaped, walking out of the prison in disguise, boarding a French ship in the bay and fleeing to the Dutch island of Curaçao.

It is probable that his escape was effected by the combined efforts of the British, French and United States merchant and diplomatic community in Cartagena, with the local authorities turning a blind eye.[22]

Hand was one of the great Irish survivors of the revolutionary period in South America. He returned to Venezuela in the middle of the 1830s, finding work in Caracas as an English teacher – thanks to the efforts of O'Leary, his old commanding officer – and drawing an army pension.[23]

O'Leary was the most prominent Irish casualty of the anti-Bolivarian purge in Bogotá. In 1830, after Bolívar's resignation as president of Gran Colombia, O'Leary fled to Jamaica with his wife, young daughter Mimi and newborn son Simón. A second daughter, Bolivia, was born in Cartagena.

He returned to Caracas in 1833 at the invitation of his brother-in-law, Carlos Soublette, who was then the Venezuelan minister for war, and in May 1834 was sent to London to persuade the British government to recognise Venezuelan independence. It was while serving as a diplomat in Europe that O'Leary paid his first visit home to Ireland since leaving as a teenage volunteer in 1817. He spent six years in Europe working as a diplomat for the Venezuelan government, returning to Caracas in January 1840. The following year he became acting British consul in the city. After a spell as consul in the Venezuelan town of Puerto Cabello, he was appointed the British government's *chargé d'affaires* in Bogotá in 1844. In 1851 he signed a treaty on behalf of Britain which outlawed the slave trade between the two countries.[24] O'Leary spent most of the last decade of his life in the city from which he had once been exiled for his close association with the Liberator working on the great man's biography. He died in 1854 and was buried in Bogotá Cathedral.

Perhaps the saddest story is that of Bernardo O'Higgins, who left Chile with his mother and sister in February 1823. Shortly before heading into exile he had thought about travelling to England and Ireland, 'to visit the country of my education and the land of my forefathers, which retains such a deep place in my affections.'[25] In a petition to the Chilean government he wrote: 'Given that I have left behind the difficult and troublesome position of Supreme Director, I can now dedicate myself to private activities and I hope that the government will be so good as to allow me travel to Ireland for some time to reside in the bosom of my paternal family.'[26] Instead, he settled in Peru, where the government granted him the Montalván *hacienda*,

25 miles outside Lima. The war against the Spanish was far from over when O'Higgins arrived in Lima, and he offered his services to Bolívar. But though he was on the margins of Bolívar's staff at the Battle of Junín, O'Higgins played no significant part in the remainder of the Peruvian campaign.

O'Higgins spent the next two decades in Peru, cultivating sugar and greeting Chilean political exiles, who urged him to return home. Chilean politics was divided into two broad camps: conservatives, who believed Chile should have a strong, centralist government that respected traditional values, especially those of the Catholic Church, and liberals, led by Ramón Freire, who wished to see a federal, democratic government imbued with Enlightenment ideas. The *o'higginistas,* who wished to see the exiled hero of independence return to Chile, belonged to the former camp.

The liberals were in power for six years after O'Higgins's departure from Chile, until 1829, when the forces of General José Joaquín Prieto ushered in a conservative revolution after the short-lived Chilean civil war. Under Prieto, who became president, and his prime minister, Diego Portales, the government was centralised, authoritarian and conservative. In 1836, fearful of the threat to the regional balance of power, the Chilean government went to war with the newly created Confederation of Peru and Bolivia, and in 1838 a Chilean expeditionary force entered Lima.

When O'Higgins heard the news, he rushed to join the celebrating Chilean forces in the Peruvian capital. The Chilean officers are supposed to have mixed drops of O'Higgins's blood, from a finger he had deliberately cut for the purpose, with their wine. They then raised their glasses to the former supreme director, who shed tears and hugged the officers in an act of unfettered emotion.[27] His joy was replaced by profound grief a few months later when his beloved mother, Isabel, died.

The war ended in 1839 with a Chilean victory and the dissolution of the Peru-Bolivia Confederation, and O'Higgins once again made plans to return home. He had even purchased tickets on the steamship *Chile,* which made the passage from Callao to Valparaíso. But his health was failing, and after suffering a heart attack he was unable to travel. He died in his town house in Lima on 24 October 1842.[28]

Not all those who remained in Latin America were rewarded with positions in the civil administration. After the wars of independence were over, many Irishmen who had fought in the patriot armies and now found themselves down on their luck a long way from home pleaded with the new governments to give them some means of subsistence.

John Devereux was another great survivor. He arrived in South America too late to see action with his own Irish Legion. After challenging the Colombian vice-president, Antonio Nariño, to a duel over an alleged slight to the honour of James Towers English's widow, the Englishwoman Mary English, he was thrown in jail. The mutiny at Riohacha had made the Irish Legion an embarrassment, and Bolívar, who in 1820 had decided that the recruitment of foreign volunteers was more trouble than it was worth, decided to appoint Devereux as one of his government's diplomatic representatives in Europe.[29]

Devereux was never one to underestimate his own abilities. His aristocratic pretensions are evident by the fact that he changed the spelling of his name – d'Evereux and d'Evereaux being two variants – to make it look more distinguished. In a letter to Daniel O'Connell he wrote:

> This honor [sic] I did not court or seek, but, as I was for returning, the Government intimated to me in the most flattering terms, that it was their wish to confer on me some work of their distinguished favour and confidence – such ... as the Govt of the United States conferred on the illustrious Lafayette when he returned at the conclusion of the Revolutionary War of that Country – only that his was confined solely to his own Country.[30]

Devereux was arrested in Venice in 1825 over a financial transaction, and he emigrated to the United States. He died in London in 1860.[31]

John Thomond O'Brien, San Martín's former adjutant, is a good example of the type of Irish revolutionary-entrepreneur whose involvement in the independence movement was intertwined with a pursuit of commercial opportunities. Shortly after arriving in Buenos Aires in 1812, O'Brien joined the patriot army. For the next few decades of his life he dreamt of becoming a successful entrepreneur. According to the Chilean historian Benjamín Vicuña Mackenna, 'O'Brien was neither a soldier of fortune nor a mercenary, he was a "soldier and nothing more" because he fought in four republics and was born to be a soldier and fought for noble causes.'[32] O'Brien fought for the independence of four republics on the South American continent.

O'Brien had reached the rank of colonel at the end of San Martín's successful campaign in Peru and had returned to Ireland to promote a scheme for enticing Irish settlers to South America. When it failed, he joined Bolívar's army in Upper Peru as a private. After the campaign was over, Bolívar awarded a silver-mining concession to O'Brien on the outskirts of Puno in present-day Peru. The silver mines had been abandoned for a couple of decades, but there were still rich veins in the rock. Perhaps because of injury or poor health, O'Brien was unable to cope with the high altitudes of the Andes and he sold up to an English merchant by the name of John Begg.[33] He returned to Europe in the late 1820s to seek capital for investment in South America but was back on the continent in the early 1830s, tending to business interests. In 1834 he was in the Amazon, hoping to mine gold. He won the support of President Gamarra of Peru for the project, but politics intervened, and he was once again forced to return to his military career, joining the army of the Peru-Bolivia Confederation. Again he won renown as an officer. Santa Cruz promoted him to brigadier-general and awarded him the Bolivian Legion of Honour for his role in the Battle of Yanacocha in 1835.

O'Brien was on his way back to Europe and had reached Buenos Aires when he was arrested by the Argentine dictator, Rosas, who suspected him of plotting against his government. He was released, thanks to the efforts of the British foreign secretary, Lord Palmerston.

He now tried his luck at running an *estancia* in Uruguay, but his livestock was destroyed during the civil war between the liberal Colorados and the conservative Blancos, which were backed by Rosas in Argentina. The civil war lasted for 12 years. The Blancos under Rosas's ally Manuel Oribe besieged Montevideo for nine years, during which the Colorado government sent O'Brien to Britain and France to seek support. After the war, O'Brien continued to cross the Atlantic, serving as Uruguay's consul-general in London and condemning Rosas. Having decided to make his home in South America – spending his winters in Lima and his summers in Chile – in 1851 he sought financial assistance from the Peruvian government. In 1859 he returned for the last time to Ireland. In 1861, en route to South America, O'Brien fell ill in Lisbon, dying in the Portugese capital aged 74.[34]

Francis Burdett O'Connor outlived them all. In a photograph taken of him towards the end of his life, O'Connor, who was then enjoying a secluded, peaceful life in a remote part of southern Bolivia, stares at the camera with a stern gaze (see Plate 19). He is dressed in a double-breasted frock coat and check trousers. With his thinning hair and long white whiskers he resembles one of those American outlaws who survived long enough to be interviewed by reporters eager to get the story of what life was like in the Old West. In fact two of the Old West's most famous characters were to make their final stand not far from Tarija a few decades later. The notorious bank robbers Butch Cassidy and the Sundance Kid, on the run from the Pinkerton detective agency in the United States, were shot and killed in the Bolivian village of San Vicente in 1908. Looking at the photograph another way, O'Connor seems the very picture of Victorian middle-class respectability. He was a devout Catholic in his last years and a celebrated Bolivian hero, who had served as commander-in-chief of the army. It was as military governor that he first spent time in Tarija, high in the Andes of southern Bolivia.

In 1826, at the age of 35, a brush with death prompted O'Connor to consider starting a family. He was injured in a skirmish with rebels and was confined to bed for three months, allowing him time to ponder his mortality. Once recovered, he resolved to marry 17-year-old Francisca Ruyloba. The couple lost several babies in infancy but a daughter, Hercilia, survived to carry on the O'Connor name in southern Bolivia. Hercilia's son, Tomás, was born with the surname d'Arlach after his father but, unusually, adopted his mother's surname as a patronymic. The surname O'Connor d'Arlach is still common in the south of Bolivia. Eduardo Trigo O'Connor d'Arlach is a noted historian of the region and a former deputy foreign minister.[35]

O'Connor defended Bolivia from the threat of its neighbours to the west and south, Chile and Argentina. Twelve years after he mapped the borders of the new Bolivian state, he once again sought to protect the territorial integrity of the country when he fought, alongside John Thomond O'Brien, for Santa Cruz and the Peru-Bolivia Confederation, repelling the Argentine forces at the Battle of Montenegro in 1838. When he was not serving his adopted country on campaign, he worked on his farm at San Luis, outside Tarija, venturing out to attend mass or visit the Franciscan fathers in the nearby monastery. He died, aged 80, on 5 October 1871.

Chapter 16

THE 'NEW ERIN'

The Irish men and women who arrived in South America in the late eighteenth and early nineteenth century laid the basis for the large-scale migration from Ireland to the continent that followed in the middle of the nineteenth century. Coming from an impoverished country, where ownership of the land was concentrated in the hands of a privileged few, the Irish were captivated by the continent's vast, empty, fertile plains and valleys.

Francis Burdett O'Connor described arriving in the valley of Tarija in southern Bolivia for the first time as like being 'among the clouds; the tall, blue summits of the mountains were like islands surrounded by the sea.'[1] But what really caught his eye was down below on the fertile plains. 'When I arrived, the tarijeño [i.e. natives of Tarija] farmhands, so fine and unaffected, were busy collecting the maize harvest, the only crop which was cultivated on a large scale in this country which was so splendid for agriculture, in which its wealth is hidden.'[2] O'Connor tried to attract Irish farmers to Tarija, which he called New Erin.[3] The idea of fighting for liberty on a foreign shore was inextricably associated with the dream of a piece of lush, green land that could be turned into a productive agricultural enterprise.[4]

The Venezuelan-born leaders of the independence movement and the foreign recruiters who supplied the soldiers who fought in South America blatantly linked the idea of foreign service with permanent emigration in their appeals for volunteers. In an article published in the *Correo del Orinoco* in July 1819, it was argued:

> Among the different benefits that would be derived from the independence of this vast, rich and beautiful continent of South America, maybe none is greater or more interesting at the present moment than adding to our existing population by creating an agreeable home, in which those who emigrate will not only acquire ample resources for their family, but also

one day come to be of famed service to the country which gave birth to them [5]

Eric Lambert suggests that one of the reasons that service in the patriot armies was couched in terms of emigration was to avoid prosecution under the British government's Foreign Enlistment Act (1819).[6]

In the European imagination of the early 1800s South America was an unknown and exotic land, filled with fabulous creatures and native peoples with strange customs, lost jungle cities and rivers of gold. This began to change when the Prussian geographer and botanist Alexander von Humboldt visited the continent in the years 1799–1804, conducting scientific research. Yet his writings would have found a limited readership. The bulk of what was known about the distant region on the far side of the Atlantic remained within the realm of the fantastic. Most of what the Irish families who travelled to South America knew about the continent came from the recruitment propaganda that began to appear in Irish and English cities in 1817. The lure of a new life in South America, working one's own piece of land, was used to recruit the Irish volunteers who fought in the wars of independence.

John Devereux was behind a scheme to entice Irish settlers to Venezuela in September 1819. The scheme was overseen by an emigration council, comprising eminent members of Dublin society, and had the support of the Royal College of Surgeons in Ireland, which was charged with examining the suitability of potential candidates.[7]

The following example of a handbill distributed on the streets of Dublin indicates why a penniless ex-soldier or an unemployed artisan's apprentice might have been tempted to try his luck in Venezuela and shows how service with the patriot armies was linked with permanent emigration:

SOUTH AMERICA
Persons wishing to emigrate to South America have now an opportunity of having land granted to them in the following proportions, viz.:
To each single man .... 100 acres
A man and his wife .... 150 acres
Each child above 10 years of age .... 50 ditto
Each child under 10 years of age....................................... 20 ditto

They may have the choice of the above quantity, either on the banks of the Oronoko [sic], near Angostura, or in the interior of Venezuela; the whole a free gift, but on condition of residence and cultivation.

The country is chiefly clear of wood, and immediately fit for the purposes of agriculture, or feeding of cattle; it abounds with game and livestock, such as cows, horses, mules, etc., etc., and grows sugar, cocoa, cotton, indigo, delicious fruits, etc., and will produce all these articles of commerce grown in the United States, with one half the labour. The climate is salubrious, and may almost be said to possess perpetual spring.[8]

Of course, much of this was untrue, concocted by fraudsters who were interested only in pocketing the savings of poor emigrant families before they were crammed into dirty, overcrowded ships and sent off to a humid, disease-ridden jungle. But throughout the early decades of the nineteenth century there were genuine attempts to settle Irish emigrants in South America. Thomas Nowlan, Charles Herring, Richard Jaffray, William Walton and James Towers English brought a proposal for an immigration scheme before the patriot congress in Angostura in early 1819. The idea was that Irish immigrants would settle in the Guayana province of Venezuela. The province would be called New Erin and would have its own government, which would sit in the capital, New Dublin, as part of a federal Venezuela. According to its proponents, the scheme would ameliorate the circumstances of the impoverished Irish colonists, as well as bring much-needed agricultural expertise and labour to bear upon the region. It was proposed that the colonists would not have to pay a tax on the lands they were granted or on the instruments and supplies they would need for working them. The company that would be given the licence to introduce the colonists would be allowed to set up hospitals in the region. It was proposed also that the colony would be exempt from requisitioning and military service for a period of 10 years, that it would maintain its own clergy and that freedom of expression and religious tolerance would be guaranteed.[9] This scheme and others came to naught.

In the midst of his troubles in 1830, Daniel O'Leary dreamt of a rural idyll where he would be far away from 'the attacks of the intriguers and the ambitious who seek to bring about things which I detest.' In a letter to his wife he wrote: 'If I manage to get my licence and my liberty, I will go to the South or to any remote province, and there on some piece of land I will hide away from the world, content and may be happy with you, my little ones and the daily chores.' Rather sweetly, he added: 'I don't know whether you would like such a life, but I would make every effort to make it agreeable to you.'[10]

What must have impressed the Irish arrivals in the continent most was how empty South America seemed. Just like the pioneers and prospectors of the Old West, the Irish families felt they could make something of themselves there. Not only was there plenty of fertile land but it was a continent rich in all kinds of minerals, including gold, silver, tin and copper. Generations of Irish immigrants to South America had seen the agricultural potential of the continent.

In exile in Peru, Bernardo O'Higgins offered his beloved *hacienda* in Chile for the relief of the Irish poor. In 1823, in a letter to Sir John Doyle,[11] he wrote:

> Ireland gave birth to my father and Chile to my mother: I consider myself as belonging to both countries and I wish to serve both as has always been my desire. I think there are no two countries better inclined to complement each other than Chile and Ireland. The excessive population of one is the principal cause of its poverty, as its scarcity is of the other. One can predict, not only without fear of being wrong, but with absolute certainty, that the union of both will bring happiness.
>
> Only one obstacle presents itself to Irish farmers that could prevent them from establishing themselves in Chile: the distance between the bay of Cork and the port of Concepción, a four-month journey.[12]

The most successful resettlement scheme arose from one of John Thomond O'Brien's projects. After serving with San Martín in Peru, O'Brien had returned to Ireland, where he had attempted to encouraged 200 emigrants to travel to South America. Though the scheme was a failure, O'Brien did manage to persuade John Mooney, a farmer from Streamstown, County Westmeath, his sister, Mary, and her husband, Patrick Bookey, to return to Argentina with him. Both Mooney and the Bookeys were successful, farming hundreds of acres in Argentina, and they wrote home to persuade their neighbours in the midlands to join them. In their wake, thousands of emigrants from counties Westmeath, Offaly and Longford made the long journey to Argentina.[13]

These counties in the Irish midlands supplied the greatest number of emigrants to Argentina throughout the nineteenth century and up to the beginning of the First World War, but emigrants from other counties were also influential in persuading their families, friends and neighbours to start a new life at the other end of the world, most notably John and Patrick Brown, who made money in the meat-exporting business and were the catalyst for emigration from County Wexford to Argentina.[14]

By the end of the nineteenth century Irish farmers in Argentina and Uruguay were running huge *estancias* on the pampas which were exporting beef around the world, helped by new preservation techniques. Born in Ireland in 1804, Lawrence Casey arrived in Argentina in the 1830s, becoming one of the country's largest landowners and the first to pay a million pesos for a square league – about 12 square miles – of land.[15] In 1881 his son, Eduardo, bought 172 square leagues (about 2,000 square miles) of land in Santa Fe province, reselling it to Irish settlers. He bought a further 275,000 hectares (1,000 square miles) from the government of Buenos Aires, which were worked by French, Russian and Welsh immigrants. Eduardo Casey promoted horse-racing in the country. He organised races, raised thoroughbred horses and founded Argentina's Jockey Club. He also built what was at the time the largest fruit market in South America, the 47,000-square-metre (11½-acre) Mercado Central de Frutos de Avellaneda.[16]

Irish surnames, such as Casey, Dillon, Donovan, Kiernan, Lynch, Mulhall, O'Donnell and O'Gorman, became prominent not only in agriculture but in every aspect of Argentine life, including the Church, banking, sport, education, commerce, railways, industry, politics, the armed forces and the press.

The Lynch family were among the most renowned in Argentina. Patrick (Patricio) Lynch was the founder of the dynasty. Born in County Galway, he was a member of the Irish merchant family who had settled in Cádiz. He arrived in Buenos Aires in 1749, having been given a licence by the Spanish crown to trade in the American colonies.[17] His son Justo Pastor Lynch was employed by the government customs office and worked hard to crack down on smuggling. Justo Pastor's children became noted names in Argentina. Estanislao José Antonio Lynch studied law in Santiago in Chile and supplied arms and gunpowder to the patriots; he later fought with San Martín in Peru and settled in Valparaíso.[18] His brother, Benito Lynch, served in the Spanish navy before deserting and joining the patriot army in Buenos Aires in 1810.[19]

Once significant numbers of Irish families began to arrive, Irish-born priests came in their wake, playing an important role in the development of the new emigrant communities. Father Patrick Moran and Father Patrick

Gorman arrived with the first wave of emigrants that began flooding in from the midland counties in 1829 and 1830. Father Anthony Fahy from County Galway was one of the most famous Irish priests to minister to the Irish-Argentine community. He had worked in Ohio in the United States before landing in Argentina. An able administrator, he was a stern moralist, warning newly arrived Irish immigrants in Buenos Aires of the inequities of the city and enjoining them to head out to the countryside.

Father Fahy and another Irish-born priest, Father Michael Gannon, were involved in one of the most depressing episodes involving the Irish-Argentine community in nineteenth-century Buenos Aires. Adolfo O'Gorman y Périchon de Vandeuil was the son of Thomas O'Gorman and his French wife, Ana, who had played a central role in the intrigues involving the patriot leaders, the British government and the secret agent James Florence Bourke in Buenos Aires in the early 1800s. Adolfo and his wife, Joaquina, gave birth to a daughter, Camila, in 1828. The O'Gormans were a comfortable middle-class family. Camila took piano lessons, read novels, spoke French and learnt how to sew and embroider. She was chaperoned in male company but was allowed to walk alone to the city's bookshops. The O'Gormans were friendly with the local parish priest, Uladislao Gutiérrez, from Tucumán in the north of the country, who would visit them in the evenings. In this way the young priest and Camila developed a friendship that slowly developed into something more. Such a relationship would have caused scandal, but the young couple were determined, and they made the difficult decision to elope.

On 11 December 1847 Camila told her family she was going for a walk, while Father Gutiérrez told his superiors that he was travelling to nearby Quilmes. In fact the couple had arranged to meet and travel to the north of Argentina. They planned their escape carefully, travelling under assumed names up the River Paraná into Corrientes province, as far as Goya. It was in this remote town that the enamoured couple hoped to start a new life, far from the moral strictures of Buenos Aires society. They successfully founded a school for young children, and for six brief months they were happy.

But back in Buenos Aires their disappearance provoked a scandal, which began to reflect badly on the government. When Camila had not returned home, and it had been discovered that Father Gutiérrez had never arrived in Quilmes, the truth began to dawn on the O'Gormans and the church authorities. Adolfo O'Gorman denounced Father Gutiérrez as the seducer of his daughter, urged a nationwide search and called for the priest's imprisonment. The story became public, shocking Buenos Aires society. The opposition used the case as a stick with which to attack the Rosas government. Both the civil and the Church authorities were desperate to find the couple and launched a manhunt. Father Fahy condemned Camila O'Gorman's behaviour from the pulpit and demanded that the couple be severely punished. The newspapers speculated about their whereabouts, and all sorts of rumours circulated around the city.

It was Father Michael Gannon who unveiled the true identities of the young schoolteachers. After recognising them at a social function in Goya, he wasted no time in denouncing them to the authorities. The governor ordered their arrest, and news of their capture was sent to President Rosas, who in turn ordered that they be sent to the town of Santos Lugares (which translates as Sacred Places) and held incommunicado. It was during these awful days that Camila discovered that she was pregnant.

President Rosas gave the order that Camila and Uladislao be put to death. There was no trial or any type of judicial process. The authorities in Santos Lugares were shocked and argued that the sentence be commuted, citing the couple's youth and the fact that Camila was carrying a child. Rosas's sister-in-law, a friend of Camila's, also tried to intercede, but to no avail. Rosas' mind was made up, and he threatened the lives of the appointed executioners if they did not comply with his orders. On 18 August 1848 the pregnant Camila and her lover were shot by a firing squad. In a grotesque charade of sanctity, a Catholic priest, Father Castellanos, baptised Camila's unborn child moments before her death.

While the Irish did not emigrate in such large numbers to other Spanish-speaking parts of the continent as they did to Argentina and Uruguay, the fact that many Irish soldiers who took part in the wars of independence retired in Colombia, Venezuela, Ecuador, Peru and Bolivia and married local women ensured the existence of Irish surnames in those countries to this day. Because of geographical and language barriers, and the fact that they had a common religion, the descendants of the Irish settlers in Latin America were more rapidly integrated into their host culture than those in North America. But members of this Irish community remained conscious of the achievements of their illustrious ancestors and were to contribute to the historiography of the revolution.

Chapter 17

MAKING HISTORY

It took a while for the Irish contribution to the liberation of Latin America from Spanish rule to be appreciated in the new republics. The reputation of the Irish had suffered in the aftermath of the inglorious experiences of the Hibernian Regiment and the Irish Legion at Riohacha. As has been shown, however, the Irish also made up the majority of the officer corps and enlisted men who fought in the so-called British Legion and the crack Rifles Battalion. However, the names of the Hibernian Regiment and Irish Legion testified to the nationality of their officers and men, damning the Irish in the eyes of some *criollo* officers who, because of the language barrier, found it difficult to discern the difference between Irish, English, Scottish and Welsh volunteers.

The anonymous author of *Recollections of a Service of Three Years in the Republics of Venezuela and Colombia* (1828), one of several accounts written by the Irish and British officers who served in Venezuela, wrote that General Arismendi was much attached to both the English and the Irish. According to the author, Arismendi was 'extremely partial to the English, and pays them the most marked respect: every thing which he can command is at their disposal, and few circumstances can give him more pleasure or pain than their acceptance or refusal of his proferred services.' He added that Arismendi was 'very inquisitive as to their government, manners, customs, state of the army and navy, and similar matters; and delights to hear their gallant deeds in action recounted' and that Arismendi's face 'lighted up with all the enthusiasm and fire of a warrior' when listening to stories about the Duke of Wellington.[1] Despite the fact of Wellington's Irish birth and ancestry, the author related that

> ... to the Irish [Arismendi] is likewise much attached, many of whom were under his command in the war of the Revolution. He denominates them the brave blunderers; and has stored up a variety of anecdotes illustrative of that jostle between conception and utterance, the fruitful result of

which, under the name of *bull*, has been recognised as characteristic of the natives of the Emerald Isle throughout the world.²

It is not clear whether this was the Venezuelan general's honestly held view or whether the author was simply projecting his own prejudices. In either case, the English officer who wrote the book makes an implicit distinction between the Protestant Anglo-Irish officer caste (Wellington is regarded as English, not Irish) and the Catholic Irish officers and enlisted men. In fact, many of the foreign officers who reached the highest echelons in Bolívar's armies were Irish and came from different religious traditions and social backgrounds. Arthur Sandes was an Anglican from the Anglo-Irish gentry in County Kerry; William Owens Ferguson was a Presbyterian from County Antrim; Daniel Florence O'Leary was from the Catholic merchant class in County Cork; and the families of John Devereux, a Catholic from County Wexford, and Francis Burdett O'Connor, a Catholic convert from an Anglican family, had fought with the United Irishmen in 1798.

Indeed, there was an awareness of national differences, which manifested itself in a healthy spirit of rivalry between the Irish and English volunteers. On 29 April 1820, prefiguring the competitive mood between the two nations that exists today at the Cheltenham festival, a horse race was held on the banks of the Orinoco between Irish and English challengers. Major Thomas Manby of the Albion Battalion, riding a horse called Bargas, and Colonel William Middleton Power, riding a horse called Devereux, went head-to-head in the race, representing the honour of England and Ireland.³

In time, and with the maturing of the independent republics, the Irish contribution came to be recognised by historians. The great survivor of Venezuelan politics, José Antonio Páez, who served three terms as his country's president, praised the Irish contribution in his memoirs. A shared desire for liberty was emphasised, rather than the more venal motivations of some members of the foreign officer corps. Páez wrote that John Devereux – excoriated by the Venezuelan officers after the mutiny of the Irish Legion – 'had been rightly called the Lafayette of South America.'⁴

The Irish soldiers who fought in South America and their descendants, who were proud of their Irish heritage, made an important contribution to the historiography of the independence era. Two of the most important accounts of the wars of liberation in the northern part of South America were produced by Corkmen: Daniel O'Leary and Francis Burdett O'Connor.

Throughout his time campaigning with the great Venezuelan general, O'Leary had assiduously gathered together Bolívar's correspondence and documents relating to the campaigns against the Spanish. He had even travelled with his brother-in-law Carlos Soublette to La Coruña in Spain, where he met the Spanish general Pablo Morillo, his former adversary and an admirer of Bolívar, who furnished him with documents relating to the war in Venezuela.[5] The *Memorias del General O'Leary* comprised Bolívar's voluminous correspondence and O'Leary's narrative account of the war. It was both a biography of Bolívar – and a rebuttal of his detractors' accusations – and a history of the revolution in the northern part of the continent. Daniel's son, Simón Bolívar O'Leary, published this material between 1879 and 1888.

O'Connor's memoirs were posthumously published by his grandson, Tomás O'Connor d'Arlach, in 1895. They remain a valuable source for historians of the campaigns in Venezuela, Ecuador, Peru and Bolivia. They also cover O'Connor's life in Ireland before he emigrated and his postwar career.

The monumental *Memorias del General O'Leary*, running to 32 volumes, was a state-sponsored publication, and the tone is suitably elegiac. On the other hand, O'Connor's *Recuerdos de Franciso Burdett O'Connor*, which was unfinished at the time of his death, is bittersweet. He does not shy away from proclaiming the merits, including his own, of the Irishmen who fought in the war, but, reflecting his radical sentiments, he also professed himself disillusioned with what independence had achieved four decades after the events described:

> In the end, I began to suspect that we were working for the interests of English and French commerce, and I was not wrong. After more than forty years of liberty, the *patria* and the people of which it is composed are poorer than they were at the start of the war, and this lamentable state of affairs is getting worse every day.[6]

The publication of these great tomes was evidence of the decision by the nationalist regimes that emerged throughout Spanish-speaking America in the nineteenth and twentieth centuries to appropriate the Irish heroes of independence for their own purposes. One of the continent's greatest nineteenth-century historians was John Mackenna's grandson, the lawyer and politician Benjamín Vicuña Mackenna. He wrote several books about the war of independence in Chile, including two about O'Higgins, based on material that had been preserved by O'Higgins's son Demetrio. Mackenna's painstaking efforts were complicated by the fact that John Thomas, O'Higgins's secretary, would translate his correspondence into English and then lose the Spanish originals.[7]

The historiography of the revolution in Chile drew parallels between the Irish struggle against the might of the British Empire and that of the infant Latin American republics against the Spanish Empire. The noble birth and the Catholicism of the Irish volunteers were emphasised in the narrative of the revolution in Latin America constructed by the late nineteenth and early twentieth-century historians. Ironically, the Spanish authorities had previously required evidence of noble birth and Catholicism when admitting Irish immigrants to the army's officer corps and military orders or granting them trading privileges.

In his idealised biography of Bernardo O'Higgins, published in 1946, the Catholic writer Jaime Eyzaguirre depicts the Irish-Chilean general's ancestors as 'an uninterrupted chain of illustrious bards,' whose happiness was brought to an end by the depredations of the English and who were 'no longer able to keep singing while pain consumed [the family].'[8] Benjamín Vicuña Mackenna's great-grandson, Eugenio Orrego Vicuña, also published a biography of Bernardo O'Higgins in 1946. The first line of the opening chapter describes Ireland as 'the green Erin of the poets,' which 'occupies a central place among the nations that have illuminated history with its rich cultural history, noble and beautiful traditions' and in which its 'heroic adhesion to its religious faith was a symbol of its preference to the spiritual.'[9] This was written three years after Éamon de Valera's much-quoted St Patrick's Day radio broadcast in 1943 – the so-called 'comely maidens' speech – in which he spoke of an Ireland in which the people 'valued material wealth only as the basis of right living, of a people who were satisfied with frugal comfort and devoted their leisure to the things of the spirit.'[10]

This identification with a physically and spiritually pure Irish race was not confined to Chilean historians. In the first two paragraphs of his short biography of John Thomond O'Brien, the Argentine writer Mario Belgrano traces the Irish adventurer's roots back to Brian Bórú and describes his parents, Martin O'Brien and Honora O'Connor, as 'both belonging to the oldest families of the Irish nobility.'¹¹ And in his introduction to his grandfather Francis Burdett O'Connor's memoirs, the Bolivian Tomás O'Connor d'Arlach portrays his ancestors as brave Irish revolutionaries from an ancient Catholic dynasty who had suffered persecution at the hands of the English. He writes:

> My grandfather was the second son of Roger O'Connor, the last descendant of that ancient royal house of Ireland which has produced so many and such enlightened sons, who have given such undying glories to the country, in the parliamentary realm, in the law, in literature, in the diplomatic sphere and on the battlefield, and who have sacrificed their lives as martyrs on the altar of the Catholic faith and for their religious beliefs, which the family had preserved untouched through the centuries.¹²

Roger and Arthur O'Connor had in fact been United Irishmen; but Roger was also a fraudster and a highwayman. Their ancestors did not belong to an ancient Irish dynasty but were a Protestant merchant family who were recently arrived in Ireland, having bought land near Bandon, County Cork.¹³

In 1949 Alberto Eduardo Wright published a brief biography of his ancestor Thomas Charles Wright, which included the revolutionary's own memoirs. The Wright family played a central role in the political life of modern Ecuador. Thomas Charles Wright was a major figure in post-independence Ecuadorean politics. His great-grandson Alberto was born in Belgium; Alberto's father, Guillermo Hugo Wright, was serving in Antwerp as Ecuadorean consul. The family later moved to London.

Alberto was educated in Europe and was already 17 when he first set foot in Ecuador. He became a businessman and served as minister for public works and minister for finance in the Ecuadorean government in the 1940s. In 1944 a revolution brought down the government and Wright sought refuge for himself and his family in the Argentine Embassy in Quito. They fled the country in the dead of night, bound for Peru. In Alberto Wright's luggage on the ancient plane that carried the family to safety were his Irish great-grandfather's memoirs relating the deeds of the Rifles Battalion.¹⁴

Governments and revolutionary movements seek legitimacy through the organising of elaborate ceremonies in which the remains of national heroes are buried in the pantheons of the *patria*. Modern nationalist leaders have learnt that proximity to the mortal remains of the fallen leader, and their immortal memory, confer a historical continuity that can be shaped to their own ends. In the Soviet Union, Stalin developed the cult of Lenin and embalmed his body for the veneration of the masses. Franco turned the playboy fascist José Antonio Primo de Rivera, executed by the Republicans at the start of the Civil War, into 'El Ausente', the Holy Spirit in a trinity of images – the others being a crucifix and a portrait of Franco himself – that appeared on the walls of every classroom in postwar Spain.

Nor is modern Ireland a stranger to this phenomenon. It is no accident that one of the most famous events in twentieth-century Irish nationalism was Patrick Pearse's oration at the graveside of the Fenian leader Jeremiah O'Donovan Rossa, whose remains were brought home from New York in 1915 to be buried in Glasnevin Cemetery in Dublin. An obsession with martyrology runs through Irish history, from Brian Bórú to Bobby Sands by way of Tone, Emmet, Parnell and the signatories of the 1916 Proclamation.

Similarly, in nineteenth-century and twentieth-century Latin America, where questions of political legitimacy remained problematic, there was no greater means of demonstrating the regime's continuity with a glorious past than a great act of public ceremonial. The physical reinterring of the remains of the heroes of independence went hand-in-hand with the creation of a romanticised version of the deceased in state-sanctioned and subsidised histories. Throughout the nineteenth and twentieth centuries, authoritarian, nationalist governments ordered the reinterral of Irish heroes of the independence era for the purposes of regime-building.

When Daniel O'Leary died in Bogotá on 24 February 1854, arrangements were made to honour him with a grand funeral in the city's cathedral. His body, which lay before the altar, was dressed in the uniform of a Colombian general, his sword at his side. The coffin was draped in a Union Jack. Among those present were the president and vice-president of the Republic, as well as the papal representative to Colombia and the United States consul.[15] Two decades later, in 1874, the Venezuelan dictator Antonio Guzmán Blanco began planning a national pantheon and ordered that the ruined Church of the Holy Trinity in the northern districts of Caracas be redeveloped for the purpose. The National Pantheon opened the following year, and in 1876 the remains of Simón Bolívar were transferred to the building. Prefiguring President Hugo Chávez, who used the cult of Bolívar to bolster his government, Guzmán

Blanco was a populist dictator who did much to resurrect the memory of the Liberator for his own political aggrandisement. To this end he ordered the publication of Daniel O'Leary's 32-volume *Memorias*. In 1882 Guzmán Blanco also ordered the transfer of O'Leary's remains to the National Pantheon.

One of the most striking examples of the way in which a nationalist regime in South America appropriated the memory of an Irish-born figure was that of Eliza Lynch. In 1954 the dictator Alfredo Stroessner came to power in Paraguay, ruling the country for 35 years. The Irish-Paraguayan poet, journalist, historian and politician Juan O'Leary, grandson of an Irish immigrant to Buenos Aires,[16] helped Stroessner create a narrative of Paraguayan history which recalled the heroism of Francisco Solano López and his Irish lover during the War of the Triple Alliance. In this reading of Paraguayan history López had stood up to the imperial designs of the country's neighbours, Brazil, Argentina and Uruguay, at great cost to himself and his family. As part of this exercise in regime-building, Stroessner's government planned the transfer of Lynch's remains to the Paraguayan capital, Asunción. Lynch's body was exhumed in 1961 and transferred from the Père Lachaise cemetery in Paris to Paraguay. Stroessner's intention was to inter her remains beside those of López in the National Pantheon in Asunción. However, the Catholic Church objected and Lynch was instead laid to rest in a purpose-built tomb in the national cemetery, La Recoleta, in Asunción.[17]

A similar battle took place in Chile over the remains of Bernardo O'Higgins. In 1979 the dictatorship erected the Altar de la Patria in what was then the Plaza del Libertador in the centre of Santiago. It was the culmination of General Augusto Pinochet's project to take possession of the leaders of the early nineteenth-century independence movement for the military regime that had ousted President Salvador Allende's democratically elected socialist government in the bloody coup of 1973.

Both Allende and Pinochet realised the symbolic value of O'Higgins, the selfless Chilean hero of independence. The Chilean government had made efforts to repatriate O'Higgins as early as 1844, two years after his death in Lima. A law was passed by the houses of parliament approving the transfer of his remains to Santiago and the erection of a monument in his honour.[18] However, the necessary funds could not be found. It was Benjamín Vicuña Mackenna, grandson of another famous Irish independence leader, John Mackenna, who once again raised the issue in the 1860s. O'Higgins's remains were brought home to Chile in 1869 and laid to rest with due ceremony in a crypt in the city's main cemetery. Three years later an equestrian statue of O'Higgins was erected over his grave.

In 1972 the socialist government passed a law for the building of a mausoleum in which would be buried the leaders of Chilean independence.[19] The government was struggling to build a national consensus in Chile in the face of conservative opposition. It too realised that it needed to appropriate O'Higgins and the other *próceres* (illustrious figures or notable persons) in an attempt to achieve legitimacy in the eyes of the middle classes. The military coup in 1973 resulted in President Allende's death and heralded General Pinochet's 17-year dictatorship. The new regime ordered that the monument to the leaders of Chilean independence, at the centre of which was to be the figure of Bernardo O'Higgins, should go ahead. In 1978 the dictatorship made a connection between the liberation struggle in the early 1800s and what Pinochet and the generals described as the liberation of Chile from Marxism-Leninism during the celebrations to mark the bicentenary of O'Higgins's birth.[20]

Today the names of army battalions, roads, schools, towns, ships and football teams recall the contribution to national independence made by the Irish *próceres*. In Colombia a battalion was named after Coronel James Rooke. In Chile the main avenue running through central Santiago is the Avenida Libertador General Bernardo O'Higgins (popularly called the Alameda), while one of the country's 15 main administrative regions is the Región Libertador General Bernardo O'Higgins – the only one to be named after a hero of Chilean independence. In Bolivia Burdett O'Connor province is to be found in the south of the country. In Argentina, Guillermo Brown, Almirante Brown, Brown de Adrogué and Brown de Arrecife, all named after the Irish naval officer from County Mayo, are the monikers of four different football teams. In Venezuela the Plaza O'Leary is a public square in Caracas, which is adorned with a bust of the general from County Cork, and James Towers English is commemorated in the town of Juan Griego on Isla Margarita. In Uruguay one of Montevideo's main streets and a school are named after Peter Campbell. In Ecuador there is a street named after Arthur Sandes in Cuenca. In Paraguay the Avenida Elisa A. Lynch is one of the main thoroughfares running through Asunción. Finally, the San Patricios continued to be revered in their adopted country for fighting to protect Mexican independence.

Chapter 18

THE 'SPIRITUAL EMPIRE'

At the beginning of 1935 the director of the National Historical Museum in Buenos Aires, Federico Santa Coloma Brandsen, entrusted the Argentine *chargé d'affaires* in Lisbon, René Correa Luna, with an unusual mission. He asked Correa if he could find the final resting-place of one of the heroes of Argentine independence, John Thomond O'Brien.[1]

This was part of a project launched by the Argentine government to discover the whereabouts and to look after the remains of all the national heroes of the independence era. O'Brien was adjudged important enough to be included in this list, having served on campaigns with Bolívar and San Martín.

It was known that O'Brien was buried in Portugal. He had crossed the Atlantic countless times during his lifetime and, having visited his native County Wicklow for the last time in the winter of 1859, was returning to Chile when he fell ill in Lisbon. He died in his house in the Rua do Alecrim in Lisbon at 6 o'clock in the evening on 1 June 1861.

Having read Brandsen's letter that February morning, Correa began his investigations. After making a few inquiries of the Portuguese historian Antonio Ferreira de Serpa about the best manner in which to proceed, Correa looked up the old newspaper collection in the National Library. In the edition of the *Jornal do Comercio* for 3 June 1861 he came across O'Brien's funeral notice, which gave Correa the information that O'Brien was buried in the Cemitério dos Prazeres (which translates as the Cemetery of the Pleasures) in Lisbon. The Prazeres is the equivalent of La Recoleta in Buenos Aires, Glasnevin Cemetry in Dublin or Père Lachaise in Paris, being the last resting-place of some of Portugal's most eminent citizens, including poets, writers, actors and *fado* singers. Its aisles are lined with elaborate stone tombs, many of them the size of small chapels. In the registry of burials, Correa discovered that O'Brien had been buried at 11 in the morning on 3 June 1861 in tomb No. 1244. A metal badge inscribed *No. 759* was attached to the coffin.

Looking at the registry of graves, Correa found that the city council had sold the tomb to Father Patrick Bernard Russell on 11 May 1861. However, the ownership of the tomb had passed to a man by the name of José Enrique dos Santos Jones on 28 August 1893. On 8 January 1894 it passed to José da Costa.

Though he had found the place where O'Brien had been buried in 1861, Correa was now faced with a problem. There were countless families in Lisbon with the name of Costa; finding which one owned the tomb in Prazeres was going to take time. But Correa was a diligent detective and was fully conscious of the importance of the task he had been charged with by his government. After making more inquiries, he discovered that José da Costa was dead but that his son, Joaquín Faria Costa, would be able to help him.

Joaquín Faria Costa showed Correa the document confirming ownership of the tomb. It revealed that O'Brien's remains had been removed from No. 1244 on 16 August 1893 and reinterred in No. 3694. Correa returned to Prazeres cemetery to examine the registry of graves and discovered that the Irish Dominicans in Lisbon had bought tomb No. 3694 on 22 October 1890.

Correa now had a firm lead. He paid a visit to the Dominican college at Travessa do Corpo Santo. He was welcomed by the rector, a Kerryman by the name of Paul O'Sullivan. Born in Tralee in 1871, O'Sullivan had lived in Lisbon for 40 years, having arrived in 1895 for health reasons. Appalled by what he perceived as the low regard in which the Church was held in Portugal, and spurred into action by the anti-clericalism of the First Republic in 1910, O'Sullivan became an ardent Catholic propagandist. He founded a publishing company in an office in the Dominicans' premises and established Catholic magazines for distribution throughout Portugal and beyond. He wrote several of the booklets and pamphlets that were published by the company, including such titles as *The Wonders of the Holy Name, How to Be Happy – How to Be Holy, All About the Angels, The Holy Ghost: Our Greatest Friend, The Secret of Confession* and *Read Me or Rue It: How to Avoid Purgatory*.

O'Sullivan confirmed to Correa that tomb No. 3694 belonged to the Irish Dominicans, and that it contained a wooden urn with the remains of John Thomond O'Brien. He also told Correa that his predecessor, Father Patrick Russell, had spoken to him in glowing terms about O'Brien, whom he remembered well. O'Sullivan agreed to show the tomb to Correa.

On a pleasant May afternoon the two men passed through the gates of the Prazeres cemetery into the shadows of the dark-green cypress trees. They walked slowly past the doors of the faded marble mausoleums, through the windows of which one could see mouldering coffins. Lisbon is hilly, and from the elevated position of the cemetery O'Sullivan and Correa were able to look down on the River Tagus flowing through the city. Neither man was frail – indeed they were both tall and well built – but both were beginning to show signs of age. O'Sullivan was dressed in clerical black and collar; Correa wore a pin-striped suit, as befitted the dignity of his diplomatic office.

Grave No. 3694 was on the left-hand side of Rua 35. O'Sullivan took out his key and opened the metal door. Correa peered into the darkness. The tomb was clean and well looked after. On the right-hand side was an urn made of wood, in the shape of a coffin. Attached to it was a metal badge, on which was inscribed *No. 759*. Within this urn were the remains of General John Thomond O'Brien, O'Sullivan told Correa. They had been transferred to the wooden urn from the coffin in which the general had been buried, which was discovered to be completely rotten when O'Brien's original tomb was opened in 1893.

Correa had found the urn, but he needed proof that the remains within really belonged to the hero of Argentine independence. O'Sullivan did the needful: in a written declaration he certified that the urn contained O'Brien's mortal remains. The late rector, Patrick Russell, who was a friend of the general's, had often spoken of it.

Correa was pleased with his work and wrote to Brandsen, as well as to the Ministry of External Relations in Buenos Aires, reporting that he had found O'Brien's remains and that he would await further instructions. On 8 August he received a telegram from the minister for external relations in Buenos Aires instructing him to make the necessary arrangements for repatriation.

On 4 October 1935, at 11:30 in the morning, in the presence of the Argentine consul-general, the Irish Dominican fathers and other luminaries resident in the city, a commission representing the Portuguese authorities, officially handed over the remains of O'Brien to Correa in the Prazeres cemetery. The urn had already been opened to verify its contents before being resealed. Ribbons were placed at either end of the urn bearing the Portuguese and Argentine colours. The members of the Portuguese commission then signed a document verifying once again that the urn contained O'Brien's remains. The Irish Dominican fathers were obliged to carry out the same ceremony.

The urn remained in the chapel for three days, until 9 o'clock in the morning on 7 October, when it was transferred to the Church of the Corpo Santo, in the charge of the Irish Dominicans. The urn was draped in an Argentine flag and placed on a catafalque in the centre of a church; below it Correa placed a wreath on behalf of the Argentine legation.

Correa had obtained the permission of the Portuguese authorities to allow a company of a hundred sailors to disembark from the Argentine frigate and navy training vessel *Presidente Sarmiento,* which was standing by in the port ready to take O'Brien's remains to Buenos Aires. Four naval cadets stood guard around the catafalque. At 10:15 the company of Argentine sailors, including a navy band, marched up to the front door of the church. A squadron of cavalry from Portugal's National Republican Guard accompanied them. At 10:30 the Superior of the Irish Dominicans in Lisbon, Father Dominic Clarkson, assisted by other members of the order, celebrated a requiem mass. In attendance were members of the city's diplomatic corps, including representatives of Argentina, Chile, Cuba, Mexico and Uruguay. At the end of the mass the urn was carried from the church and placed on a gun carriage pulled by six horses. The bands of the National Republican Guard and the *Presidente Sarmiento* played funeral marches while the cortege made its way through the winding streets of Lisbon towards the docks. Two guards of honour, one Portuguese and one Argentine, lined up on either side as the urn was brought aboard the Argentine frigate. On board, Correa officially handed over the urn to the captain of the ship. It was placed in a specially constructed box to prevent it from being damaged during the crossing. The ceremonies in Lisbon were covered extensively in the Portuguese press.

The decree authorising the transfer of O'Brien's remains from Lisbon to Buenos Aires was signed by the president of Argentina, Agustín Pedro Justo, the minister for external relations, Carlos Saavedra Lamas, the minister for war, Manuel A. Rodríguez, and the minister for the navy, Eleazar Videla. It stated that 'General O'Brien, though born on foreign soil, identified with Argentina, joining at an early age the celebrated Regiment of Mounted Grenadiers, and taking part in a great number of battles from Chacabuco to Ayacucho.'[2]

On 28 November, O'Brien's remains were transferred from the *Presidente Sarmiento* to the gunboat *Rosario* in a ceremony on the River Plate estuary.

The following day General Tomás Martínez and Vice-Admiral Enrique G. Fliess headed a party that left the docks at Buenos Aires on board the gunboat *Paraná*, bringing with them a new urn made from an independence-era bronze cannon. On board the *Rosario*, Martínez and Fliess oversaw the transfer of the remains to the new urn. They then returned to shore with the old urn, which was deposited in the National Historical Museum. At 10 in the morning on 30 November the *Rosario* docked in Buenos Aires.

The president and the ministers for war and the navy were present to receive the remains, which were transferred to a gun carriage and escorted by a regiment of grenadiers on horseback to the Plaza de Mayo in the heart of Buenos Aires, where a minute's silence was observed in front of the cathedral. The cortege then made its way to the Church of Our Lady of the Pillar in the Recoleta district, where a solemn mass was held. After the mass the remains of O'Brien were brought to the entrance of the Recoleta cemetery. Before the urn was committed to its final resting-place, the minister of war, Manuel Rodríguez, gave an oration on behalf of the government. The ambassadors of Chile, Uruguay and Peru also spoke, as did the president of the Comisión Irlandesa-Argentina in Buenos Aires, Dr Huberto M. Ennis.

The Comisión Irlandesa-Argentina was centrally involved in the ceremonial for the repatriation of O'Brien's remains, and members of the Irish-Argentine community in Buenos Aires turned out in force for a mass in memory of the Irish general in the Church of the Holy Cross. During the speeches outside the Recoleta ceremony, Ennis said that 'those of us of Celtic blood take pleasure in thinking that [O'Brien] was able to devote all his energies to the service of the American cause, without forgetting the old traditions of his native land.'[3] According to Ennis, O'Brien's interest in Catholic Emancipation for his compatriots and his schemes for promoting Irish immigration to his adopted home showed that he belonged to the 'spiritual empire of the Emerald Isle's exiled children.' He continued:

> O'Brien was one of the innumerable children of Ireland whose ill-fated destiny was to see them abducted from her native soil and dispersed throughout the world; like those who fought in the sixteenth century on the battlefields of Spain, Italy, France, Germany and the Low Countries, and the hundreds of thousands of Irishmen who gave their lives in sacrifice in France in the eighteenth century, a countless legion which has

given the names of Brown, O'Higgins, Barry, O'Donnell, and O'Leary to other nations' histories.[4]

The spiritual empire that Ennis had in mind on that cold morning in Buenos Aires in 1935 no longer exists. It has been replaced by a global community of Irish expatriates of differing creeds and colours who share memories of home in much the same way as the hundreds of thousands of men, women and children who fled religious and political persecution and economic disadvantage in Ireland to make better lives for themselves throughout Europe and the Americas.

BIBLIOGRAPHICAL NOTE

During the course of researching this book I have turned to the work of the many scholars, past and present, who have given their attention to the Irish in Spain and Latin America during the eighteenth and nineteenth centuries. Although it is not possible to mention them all here (a select bibliography follows), I would like to acknowledge the debt I owe to a few of those scholars I have relied on most heavily.

Dr Jorge Chauca García, Dr Enrique García Hernán, Dr María del Carmen Lario de Oñate, Dr Igor Pérez Tostado, Dr Óscar Recio Morales and Dr Diego Téllez Alarcia are among the Spanish scholars who have written extensively about the Irish community in the Spanish Atlantic and whose work has contributed to this book. I would like to make special mention of Dr Téllez Alarcia's fine biography *D. Ricardo Wall: Aut Caesar aut nullus,* and Dr Recio Morales's most informative biographical essay 'Una aproximación al modelo del oficial extranjero en el ejército Borbónico', which were invaluable when it came to writing the chapters about Richard Wall and Alexander O'Reilly, respectively.

The scholarship of eminent Chilean historians, such as Jaime Eyzaguirre, Ricardo Donoso, Benjamín Vicuña Mackenna and Eugenio Orrego Vicuña, laid the basis for the chapters concerning Ambrose and Bernardo O'Higgins.

Alfred Hasbrouck's *Foreign Legionaries in the Liberation of Spanish South America* remains one of the standard works about the participation of foreign volunteers in the north of South America in the wars of independence. Eric Lambert tackles similar ground in more detail in his three-volume *Voluntarios británicos e irlandeses en la gesta bolivariana,* a work of invaluable scholarship. Dr Matthew Brown of the University of Bristol has noted the preponderance of Irish-born soldiers who served in the ranks of the patriot armies under Bolívar in his *Adventuring through Spanish Colonies,* which rigorously analyses the origins of the foreign volunteers who fought in Colombia and Venezuela and the context in which they fought.

John de Courcy Ireland drew attention to the participation of Irish sailors and soldiers in the wars of Latin American independence for an Irish readership in many articles published in the *Irish Sword,* as well as his book

The Admiral from Mayo, an English-language biography of Admiral William Brown.

Michael Hogan's *The Irish Soldiers of Mexico* provided much of the material for the chapter on the San Patricios.

Finally, I would like to mention the web site of the Society for Irish Latin American Studies, irlandeses.org, which contains a wealth of useful and fascinating information about the Irish experience in Latin America.

ABBREVIATIONS

AGI   Archivo General de Indias, Seville
AGNA   Archivo General de la Nación, Buenos Aires
AGNC   Archivo General de la Nación Colombia, Bogotá
AGS   Archivo General de Simancas, Valladolid
AHN   Archivo Histórico Nacional, Madrid
ANC   Archivo Nacional de Chile, Santiago
BLAA   Biblioteca Luis Ángel Arango, Bogotá
DIB   *Dictionary of Irish Biography*
NA   National Archives, London
NDBA   *Nuevo Diccionario Biográfico Argentino*
NLI   National Library of Ireland, Dublin
ODBN   *Oxford Dictionary of National Biography*
PRONI   Public Record Office of Northern Ireland, Belfast
RL   Russell Library, St Patrick's College, Maynooth
UCDA   UCD Archives, Dublin

SOURCES

PRIMARY

Archival records

Archivo General de Indias, Seville
Estado
Chile

Archivo General de la Nación, Buenos Aires
Despachos y Nombramientos Civiles y Eclesiásticos
Interior
Invasiones Inglesas
Reales Órdenes

Archivo General de la Nación Colombia, Bogotá
Sección Academia Colombiana de Historia, Fondo Aquileo Parra
Sección Colecciones, Fondo Enrique Ortega Ricuarte

Archivo General de Simancas, Valladolid
Estado y Guerra

Archivo Histórico Nacional, Madrid
Consejos
Estado
Órdenes Civiles
Órdenes Militares
Universidades

Archivo Nacional de Chile, Santiago
Archivo Benjamín Vicuña Mackenna
Archivo Sergio Fernández Larrain
Ministerio de Guerra

Biblioteca Luis Ángel Arango, Bogotá
Archivo Casa Moneda

Cardinal Tomás Ó Fiaich Memorial Archive and Library, Armagh
Micheline Kerney Walsh Papers

National Archives, London
Foreign Office Papers
Probate Records

Public Record Office of Northern Ireland, Belfast
Young of Culdaff Papers

Russell Library, St Patrick's College, Maynooth
Salamanca Archive

UCD Archives, Dublin
O'Connell Papers

Books

Adam, William Jackson, *Journal of Voyages to Marguaritta, Trinidad and Maturin, with the Author's Travels across the Plains of the Llaneros, to Angustura, and Subsequent Descent of the Orinoco in the Years 1819 and 1820; Comprising His Several Interviews with Bolívar, the Supreme Chief: Sketches of the Various Native and European Generals: and a Variety of Characteristic Anecdotes, Hitherto Unpublicised* (Dublin: R.M. Tims, 1824).

Anonymous [Richard Longville Vowell], *Campaigns and Cruises in Venezuela and New Grenada and in the Pacific Ocean, from 1817 to 1830, with the Narrative of a March from the River Orinoco to San Buenaventura on the Coast of Chocò*, 3 vols (London: Longman and Co., 1831).

Anonymous, *Narrative of a Voyage to the Spanish Main in the Ship 'Two Friends': The Occupation of Amelia Island by McGregor, etc. – Sketches of East Florida; and Anecdotes Illustrative of the Habits and Manners of the Seminole Indians* (London: John Miller, 1819).

Anonymous [Captain Cowley], *Recollections of a Service of Three Years during the War-of-Extermination in the Republics of Venezuela and Colombia, by an Officer of the Colombian Navy, Moving Accidents by Flood and Field*, 2 vols (London: Hunt and Clarke, 1828).

Barbé-Marbois, François de, *The History of Louisiana, Particularly of the Cession of that Colony to the United States of America; with an introductory essay on the constitution and government of the United States* (Philadelphia: Carey and Lea, 1830).

Blanco White, Joseph, *The Life of the Rev. Joseph Blanco White, Written by Himself, with Portions of his Correspondence*, ed. John Hamilton Thom, 3 vols (London: John Chapman, 1845).

— *Practical and Internal Evidence against Catholicism* (London: John Murray, 1826).

Brackenridge, Henry Marie, *Voyage to Buenos Ayres, Performed in the Years 1817 and 1818, by Order of the American Government* (London: Richard Phillips and Co., 1820).

Brown, Charles, *Narrative of the Expedition to South America, Which Sailed from England at the Close of 1817, for the Service of the Spanish Patriots* (London: John Booth, 1819).

Cloney, Thomas, *A Personal Narrative of Those Transactions in the County Wexford, in which the Author was Engaged, During the Awful Period of 1798 ...* (Dublin: James McMullen, 1832).

Courcelles, Jean-Baptiste-Pierre-Julien, *Histoire généalogique et héraldique des pairs de France des grands dignitaires de la couronne, des principales familles nobles du royaume, et des maisons princieres de l'Europe*, vol. 6 (Paris: Arthur Bertrand, 1826).

Donoso, Ricardo, and others (eds), *Archivo de Don Bernardo O'Higgins*, 39 vols, including appendixes (Santiago: Various publishers, 1946–63).

Duane, William, *A Visit to Colombia in the Years 1822 and 1823 ...* (Philadelphia: 1826).

Fox, Elizabeth (Lady Holland), *The Spanish Journal of Elizabeth Lady Holland*, ed. the Earl of Ilchester (London: Longmans, Green and Co., 1910).

Fox, Henry Richard (Lord Holland), *Foreign Reminiscences by Henry Richard Lord Holland*, ed. Henry Edward Lord Holland (London: Longmans, Brown, Green and Longmans, 1850).

Gillespie, Alexander, *Gleanings and Remarks: Collected during Many Months of Residence at Buenos Ayres, and within the Upper Country* ... (Leeds: B. Dewhirst, 1818).

Gonzalez, Salvador (trans.), *Carta del venerable Palafox y Mendoza, obispo de la puebla de Los Ángeles, al sumo pontofice Inocencio x contra los Jesuitas* (Barcelona: De Grau, 1845).

Graham, Maria, *Journal of a Residence in Chile during the year 1822 and a Voyage from Chile to Brazil in 1823* (London: Longmans and others, 1824).

Hackett, James, *Narrative of the Expedition which Sailed from England in 1817 to Join the South American Patriots* (London: John Murray, 1818).

Henis, Tadeo X., *Efemerides de la guerra de los Guaranies desde el año de 1754* (Madrid: 1755).

Hippisley, Gustavus, *A Narrative of the Expedition to the Rivers Orinoco and Apure, in South America, Which Sailed from England in 1817, and Joined the Patriotic Forces in Venezuela and Caraccas* (London: John Murray, 1819).

Howard, Edward, *Memoirs of Admiral Sir Sidney Smith*, 2 vols (London: Richard Bentley, 1839).

Johnson, Charles, *A General History of the Pyrates, from Their First Rise and Settlement in the Island of Providence, to the Present Time* ... (London: T. Warner, 1724).

Miller, John (ed.), *Memoirs of General Miller, in the Service of the Republic of Peru*, 2 vols (London: Longman and others, 1828).

Moore, Thomas (ed.), *Life, Letters and Journals of Lord Byron* (London: John Murray, 1839).

O'Connell, John (ed.), *The Life and Speeches of Daniel O'Connell* M.P., 2 vols (Dublin: James Duffy, 1846).

O'Connor, Francis Burdett, *Independencia americana: Recuerdos de Francisco Burdett O'Connor, coronel del ejército, libertador de Colombia y general de división de los del Perú y Bolivia*, ed. Tomás O'Connor d'Arlach (Madrid: Ayachucho, 1915).

O'Leary, Daniel Florence, *Bolívar y la emancipación de Sur America: Memorias del General O'Leary*, ed. Simón B. O'Leary (Madrid: Ayacucho, 1915).

— *Memorias del General O'Leary*, 32 vols, ed. Simón B. O'Leary (Caracas: 1879–88).

Power y Giralt, Ramón, *Contestación al papel publicado bajo el título De primeros sucesos deagradables en la isla de Puerto Rico* (Cádiz: 1810).
Rafter, Michael, *Memoirs of Gregor M'Gregor, Comprising a Sketch of the Revolution in New Grenada and Venezuela ...* (London: J.J. Stockdale, 1820).
Robertson, John Parish and William Parish, *Letters on South America: Comprising Travels on the Banks of the Paraná and Rio de la Plata*, 3 vols (London: John Murray, 1843).
Robinson, James H., *Journal of an Expedition 1400 miles up the Orinoco and 300 up the Arauca; With an Account of the Country, the Manners of the People, Military Operations etc.* (London: Black, Young and Young, 1822).
Sánchez, Luís Alberto (ed.), *O'Higgins pintado por sí mismo* (Santiago: Ercilla, 1941).
Swinburne, Henry, *Travels through Spain in the Years 1775 and 1776 ...*, 2 vols (London: P. Elmsly, 1787).
Ward, Bernardo, *Proyecto económico, en que se proponen varias providencias, dirigidas á promover los intereses de España, con los medios y fondos necesarios para su plantificación* (Madrid: 1779).

Newspapers
Carrick's Morning Post (Dublin)
Correo del Orinoco (Angostura)
Dublin Evening Post
El Español (London)
El Mercurio (Santiago)

Parliamentary records
Diario de sesiones de las Cortes de Cádiz Generales y Extraordinarias

SECONDARY

Articles
Belgrano, Mario, 'Biografía del General Juan O'Brien, 1786–1861, guerrero de la independencia', *Repatriación de los restos del General Juan O'Brien, guerrero de la independencia Sud Americana* (Buenos Aires: Kraft, 1938), pp. 7–47.

Bernabéu Albert, Salvador, 'Pedro Alonso de O'Crouley y O'Donnell (1740–1817) y el descubrimiento ilustrado de México', *Irlanda y el Atlántico Ibérico: Movilidad, participación e intercambio cultural (1580–1823) / Ireland and the Iberian Atlantic: Mobility, Involvement and Cross-Cultural Exchange (1580–1823)*, ed. Igor Peréz Tostado and Enrique García Hernán (Valencia: Albatros, 2010) pp. 225–41.

Brown, Matthew, 'How did Rupert Hand get out of jail? Colombia and the Atlantic Empires, 1830–1833', *History*, 95, 317 (2010), pp. 25–43.

Chauca García, Jorge, 'El grupo irlandés entre el siglo XIII y el XIX: su papel en la Ilustración e Independencia americanas', *Extranjeros en el Ejército: Militares irlandeses en la sociedad española, 1580–1818*, ed. Enrique García Hernan and Óscar Recio Morales (Madrid: Ministerio de Defensa, 2007), pp. 353–78.

— 'Irlandeses en el comercio gaditano-americano del setecientos', *Los extranjeros en la España moderna*, ed. M.B. Villar García and P. Pezzi Cristóbal, vol. 1 (Málaga: Portadilla, 2003).

Chinea, Jorge L., 'Irish Indentured Servants, Papists and Colonists in Spanish Colonial Puerto Rico, ca. 1650–1800', *Irish Migration Studies in Latin America*, 5, 3 (2007), pp. 171–81.

Donoso Anes, Rafael, 'Un análisis sucinto del Asiento de esclavos con Inglaterra (1713–1750) y el papel desempeñado por la contabilidad en su desarrollo', *Anuario de Estudios Americanos*, 64, 2 (2007), pp. 105–44.

Dunkerley, James, 'The Third Man: Francisco Burdett O'Connor and the Emancipation of the Americas' (London: Institute of Latin American Studies, 1999).

Escobar Arellano, Constanza, 'El Altar de la Patria: Una approximación estética' (Santiago: Pontificia Universidad Católica de Chile, 2009).

Fannin, Samuel, 'Alexander "Bloody" O'Reilly: "A monster of fortune"', *History Ireland*, 9, 3 (2001), pp. 26–30.

Fernández Pascua, Delfina, 'Ramón Power y Demetrio O'Daly: Diputados a Cortes por Puerto Rico', *La presencia irlandesa durante las Cortes de Cádiz en España y America, 1812 / The Irish Presence at the Cortes of Cadiz*, ed. Enrique García Hernán and Maria del Carmen Lano de Oñate (Valencia: Albatros, 2013), pp. 159–78.

González-Polo, Ignacio, 'Don Juan O'Donojú, un benemérito gobernante olvidado en la historia de México', *Boletín*, 11, 1–2 (2006), pp. 213–28.

Gwynn, Aubrey, 'The first Irish priests in the New World', *Studies: An Irish Quarterly Review,* 21, 82 (1932).

Hildner Jr, Ernest G., 'The Role of the South Sea Company in the Diplomacy Leading to the War of Jenkins' Ear, 1729–1739', *The Hispanic American Historical Review,* 18 (1938), pp. 322–41.

Lynch, John, 'British Policy and Spanish America, 1783–1808', *Journal of Latin American Studies,* 1, 1 (1969), pp. 1–30.

McGinn, Brian, 'St Patrick's Day in Peru, 1824', *Irish Migration Studies in Latin America,* 3, 2 (2005), pp. 17–24 (http://www.irlandeses.org/0503.pdf, accessed 23 November 2015).

McNerney, Robert F., Jr, 'Daniel Florence O'Leary, Soldier, Diplomat, and Historian', *The Americas,* 22, 3 (1966), pp. 292–312.

Moreno Alonso, Manuel, 'El mundo hispano-irlandés de José María Blanco White, autor de las *Letters from Spain,* y de los *Second Travels of an Irish Gentleman*', *La presencia irlandesa durante las Cortes de Cádiz en España y América, 1812 / The Irish presence at the Cortes of Cadiz,* ed. Enrique García Hernán and María del Carmen Lario de Oñate (Valencia: Albatros, 2013), pp. 231–42.

Pyne, Peter, 'A Soldier under Two Flags: Lieutenant-Colonel James Florence Burke: Officer, Adventurer and Spy', *Études irlandaises,* 23, 1 (1998), pp. 123–38.

Recio Morales, Óscar, 'Una aproximación al modelo del oficial extranjero en el ejército borbónico: La etapa de formación del teniente general Alejandro O'Reilly (1723–1794)', *Cuadernos dieciochistas,* 12 (2011), pp. 171–95.

— 'Un intento de modernización del ejército borbónico del XVIII: La Real Escuela Militar de Ávila (1774)', *Investigaciones históricas,* 32 (2012), pp. 145–72.

Rieu-Millan, Marie-Laure, 'Los diputados americanos en las Cortes de Cádiz: Elecciones y representatividad', *Quinto centenario,* 14 (1988), pp. 53–72.

Street, J., 'Lord Strangford and Río de la Plata, 1808–1815', *The Hispanic American Historical Review,* 33, 4 (1953), pp. 477–510.

Téllez Alarcia, Diego, 'Richard Wall: Light and shade of an Irish minister in Spain (1694–1777)', *Irish Studies Review,* 11, 2 (2003), pp. 123–36.

Vilaplana Montes, Manuel, 'Santiago Key Muñoz (1772–1821): Perfil biográfico de un eclesiastico del antiguo regimen', *Anuario de los estudios atlanticos,* 26 (1980), pp. 491–527.

Books

Brown, Matthew, *Adventuring through Spanish Colonies: Simón Bolívar, Foreign Mercenaries and the Birth of New Nations* (Liverpool: Liverpool University Press, 2006).

— and Martín Alonso Roa (compiladores), *Militares extranjeros en la independencia de Colombia: Nuevas perspectivas* (Bogotá: Museo Nacional de Colombia, 2005).

Carbonell, Diego, *General O'Leary, íntimo* (Caracas: Elite, 1937).

Carr, Raymond (ed.), *Spain: A History* (Oxford: Oxford University Press, 2001).

Casals Bergés, Quintí, *La representación parlamentaria en España durante el Primer Liberalismo* (Leida: Unversitat de Leida, 2014).

Chust, Manuel, *La cuestión nacional americana en las Cortes de Cádiz* (Valencia: Centro Francisco Tomás y Valiente, 1999).

Cunninghame Graham, Robert Bontine, *A Vanished Arcadia: Being Some Account of the Jesuits in Paraguay, 1607–1767* (London: Heinemann, 1901).

Cutolo, Vicente Osvaldo (ed.), *Nuevo Diccionario Biográfico Argentino (1750–1830)*, 8 vols (Buenos Aires: Elche, 1968–85).

De Courcy Ireland, John, *The Admiral from Mayo: A Life of Almirante William Brown of Foxford* (Dublin: Edmund Burke, 1995).

Díaz-Trechuelo, Lourdes, *Bolívar, Miranda, O'Higgins, San Martín: Cuatro vidas cruzadas* (Madrid: Encuentro, 1999).

Donoso, Ricardo, *El Marqués de Osorno Don Ambrosio Higgins, 1720–1801* (Santiago: Universidad de Chile, 1941).

Downey, Declan M., and Julio Crespo MacLennan (eds), *Spanish-Irish Relations through the Ages* (Dublin: Four Courts Press, 2008).

Echeverri, Aquiles, *Sangre irlandesa en Antioquia: Biografía del doctor Hugo Blair Brown, miembro de la Legión Británica y médico coronel de los ejércitos patriotas* (Medellín: Academia Antioqueña de Historia, 1972).

Eyzaguirre, Jaime, *O'Higgins*, 2 vols (Santiago: Zig-Zag, 1972).

García Hernán, Enrique, *Ireland and Spain in the Reign of Philip II* (Dublin: Four Courts Press, 2009).

García Hernán, Enrique, Miguel Ángel de Bunes, Óscar Recio Morales, and Bernardo J. García García (eds.), *Irlanda y la monarquía hispánica: Kinsale, 1601–2001: Guerra, política, exilio y religión* (Alcalá: Universidad de Alcalá, 2002).

García Hernán, Enrique, and M. Carmen Lario de Oñate (eds), *La presencia irlandesa durante las Cortes de Cádiz en España y América, 1812 / The Irish Presence at the Cortes of Cadiz* (Valencia: Albatros, 2013).

García Hernán, Enrique, and Igor Pérez Tostado, *Irlanda y el Atlántico ibérico: Movilidad, participación e intercambio cultural, 1580–1823* (Valencia: Albatros, 2010).

García Hernán, Enrique, and Óscar Recio Morales, *Extranjeros en el ejército: Militares irlandeses en la sociedad española, 1580–1818* (Madrid: Ministerio de Defensa, 2007).

Harvey, Robert, *Liberators: South America's Savage Wars of Freedom, 1810–30* (London: Robinson, 2002).

Hasbrouck, Alfred J., *Foreign Legionaries in the Liberation of Spanish South America* (New York: Columbia University Press, 1928).

Hughes, Ben, *Conquer or Die: Wellington's Veterans and the Liberation of the New World* (Oxford: Osprey, 2010).

Jacobsen, Nils, *The Peruvian Altiplano, 1780–1930* (Berkeley: University of California, 1993).

Johnson, John J., *Simón Bolívar and Spanish American Independence, 1783–1830* (New York: Van Nostrand Reinhold, 1968).

Lambert, Eric, *Voluntarios británicos e irlandeses en la gesta Bolivariana*, 3 vols (Caracas: Vol. 1, Corporación Venezolana de Guayana, 1981 / Vols 2 and 3, Ministerio de Defensa, 1993).

Lario Oñate, María del Cármen, *La colonia mercantil británica e irlandesa en Cádiz a finales del siglo XVIII* (Cádiz: Universidad de Cádiz, 2002).

Lillis, Michael, and Ronan Fanning, *The Lives of Eliza Lynch: Scandal and Courage* (Dublin: Gill & Macmillan, 2009).

Luna, Félix, *A Short History of the Argentinians* (Buenos Aires: Planeta, 2004).

Lynch, John, *The Spanish American Revolutions, 1808–1826* (New York: Norton, 1973).

Marco, Miguel Ángel de, *Corsarios Argentinos: Héroes del mar en la Independencia y en la guerra con el Brasil* (Buenos Aires: Emecé, 2002).

McGuire, James, and James Quinn (eds), *Dictionary of Irish Biography* (Cambridge: Cambridge University Press, 2009).

Moreno Alonso, Manuel, *Divina libertad: La aventura liberal de Don José María Blanco White, 1808–1824* (Seville: Alfar, 2002).

Murray, Thomas, *The Story of the Irish in Argentina* (New York: P.J. Kenedy and Sons, 1919).

O'Donnell, Hugo (co-ord.), *Presencia irlandesa en la milicia española / The Irish Presence in the Spanish Military, 16th to 20th Centuries* (Madrid: Ministerio de Defensa, 2014).

Orrego Vicuña, Eugenio, *O'Higgins: Vida y tiempo* (Buenos Aires: Losada, 1946).

Pakenham, Thomas, *The Year of Liberty: The Great Irish Rebellion of 1798* (London: Literary Guild, 1969).

Pérez Tostado, Igor, *Irish Influence at the Court of Spain in the Seventeenth Century* (Dublin: Four Courts Press, 2008).

Pyne, Peter, *The Invasions of Buenos Aires, 1806–1807: The Irish Dimension* (Liverpool: University of Liverpool, Institute of Latin American Studies, 1996).

Quinn, David B., *Ireland and America: Their Early Associations, 1500–1640* (Liverpool: Liverpool University Press, 1991).

Recio Morales, Óscar, *Ireland and the Spanish Empire, 1600–1815* (Dublin: Four Courts Press, 2010).

— (ed.), *Redes en nación y espacios de poder: La comunidad irlandesa en España y América española, 1600–1825* (Valencia: Albatros, 2012).

Roberts, Carlos, *Las invasiones inglesas del Río de la Plata (1806–1807) y la influencia inglesa en la independencia y organización de las provincias del Río de la Plata* (Buenos Aires: Peuser, 1938).

Rodríguez, Moisés Enrique, *Freedom's Mercenaries*, 2 vols (Lanham, Maryland: Hamilton, 2006).

Rodríguez O., Jaime E., *The Independence of Spanish America* (Cambridge: Cambridge University Press, 1998).

— *'We are now the true Spaniards': Sovereignty, Revolution, Independence and the Emergence of the Federal Republic of Mexico, 1808–1824* (Stanford: Stanford University Press, 2012).

Téllez Alarcia, Diego, *D. Ricardo Wall: Aut Caesar aut nullus* (Madrid: Ministerio de Defensa, 2008).

Thomas, Hugh, *Rivers of Gold: The Rise of the Spanish Empire* (London: Penguin, 2010).

Valencia Avaria, Luís, *El pensamiento de O'Higgins* (Santiago de Chile: Editorial de Pacifico, 1974).

Vicuña Mackenna, Benjamín, *El jeneral O'Brien* (Santiago: Universitario, 1902).
— *El ostracismo del general D. Bernardo O'Higgins* (Valparaíso: Mercurio, 1860).
Williamson, Edwin, *The Penguin History of Latin America* (London: Penguin, 1992).
Wright, Alberto Eduardo, *Destellos de gloria* (Caracas: Cámara Venezolano Británico de Comercio, 1983).
Zavala Cepeda, José Manuel, *Los Mapuches del siglo XVIII: Dinámica interétnicas y estrategias de resistencia* (Santiago: Universidad Bolivariana, 2008).

Electronic resources

Biblioteca Virtual Miguel de Cervantes (in Spanish): www.cervantesvirtual.com
Dictionary of Irish Biography: http://www.dib.cambridge.org/
Instituto O'Higginiano de Chile (in Spanish): www.institutoohigginiano.cl
Oxford Dictionary of National Biography: www.oxforddnb.com
Society for Irish Latin American Studies: www.irlandeses.org

NOTES

Notes to Chapter 1: Wild Geese (pp. 9–22)

1. Henry Richard Fox (Lord Holland), *Foreign Reminiscences*, ed. Henry Edward Lord Holland (London: Longman, 1850), p. 78.
2. 'Wall y Devereux, Ricardo', AHN, Órdenes Militares, Caballeros de Santiago, exp. 9020.
3. Diego Téllez Alarcia, *D. Ricardo Wall: Aut Caesar aut nullus* (Madrid: Ministerio de Defensa, 2008), p. 48.
4. Ibid., p. 60.
5. Lord Byron to Mr Hodgson, Gibraltar, 6 August 1809, in *Life, Letters and Journals of Lord Byron*, ed. Thomas Moore (London: John Murray, 1839), pp. 91–2.
6. Jorge Chauca García, 'Irlandeses en el comercio gaditano-americano del setecientos', in *Los extranjeros en la España moderna*, ed. M.B. Villar García and P. Pezzi Cristóbal, vol. 1 (Malága: Portadilla, 2003), pp. 271–5.
7. 'Diario del viaje del duque de Liria y Xérica', in *Colección de documentos inéditos para la Historia de España*, ed. José Sancho Rayón and Francisco Zabálburu, vol. 93 (Madrid: 1889), p. 125, cited in Téllez Alarcia p. 70.
8. See Téllez Alarcia, p. 71.
9. Ibid., p. 92.
10. Henry Swinburne, *Travels through Spain in the Years 1775 and 1776*, 2 vols, vol. 1 (London: P. Elmsly, 1787), p. 317.
11. Ernest G. Hildner Jr, 'The Role of the South Sea Company in the Diplomacy Leading to the War of Jenkins' Ear, 1729–1739', in *The Hispanic American Historical Review*, 18, 3 (1938), pp. 322–41 (pp. 332–3).
12. Jaime Masones de Lima to the Duke of Huéscar, 28 August 1748, AHN, Estado, 4,142, cited in Téllez Alarcia, p. 114.
13. Richard Wall to the Duke of Huéscar, 27 October 1747, AHN, Estado, 4,264-1, cited in Téllez Alarcia, p. 114.
14. Richard Wall to the Duke of Huéscar, 14 May 1748, AHN, Estado, 4,092, cited in Téllez Alarcia, p. 118.
15. Richard Wall to José de Carvajal y Lancáster, 4 December 1749, AGS, Estado, 6,914, cited in Téllez Alarcia, pp. 126–27.
16. The National Gallery of Ireland purchased the portrait in 1999.

Notes to Chapter 2: Remaking the New World (pp. 23–31)

1 Patricia M. Byrne, 'William Bowles', DIB.
2 Salvador Bernabéu Albert, 'Pedro Alonso de O'Crouley y O'Donnell (1740–1817) y el descubrimiento ilustrado de México', in *Irlanda y el Atlántico Ibérico: Movilidad, participación e intercambio cultural (1580–1823) / Ireland and the Iberian Atlantic: Mobility, Involvement and Cross-Cultural Exchange (1580–1823)* ed. Igor Peréz Tostado and Enrique García Hernán (Valencia: Albatros, 2010), pp. 225–241.
3 'Felipe Luis Ward O'More', AHN, Universidades, 672, 59, F. 23.
4 Ibid., F. 9.
5 Ibid., F. 11.
6 'Felipe Ward y otros empleos', AGS, Estado 6958, 23, F. 3v.
7 The full title translates as *An economic project in which are proposed various measures to promote the interests of Spain, with the means and funds for its development.*
8 Bernardo Ward, *Proyecto económico, en que se proponen varias providencias, dirigidas á promover los intereses de España, con los medios y fondos necesarios para su plantificación* (Madrid: 1779), pp. i–iv.
9 Ward, p. iv; see also 'Licencias y privilegios de impresión y de reimpresión de la obra de Bernardo Ward, "Proyecto económico …" solicitadas por su viuda Maria Omore', AHN, Consejos, 5539, exp. 7.
10 Ward, *Proyecto económico*, p. 27.
11 Ibid., p. 28.
12 Ibid.
13 Ibid.
14 Ibid., p. 226.
15 Ibid., p. 227.
16 Ibid., pp. 254–5.
17 Ibid., p. 245.
18 Ibid., p. 246.
19 Ibid., p. 247.

Notes to Chapter 3: A New Model Army (pp. 32–8)

1 Samuel Fannin, 'Alexander "Bloody" O'Reilly: "A monster of fortune"', in *History Ireland*, 9, 3 (2001), pp. 26–30 (p. 26).
2 'O'Reilly y Macdowell O'Reilly y Dillon, Alejandro de', AHN, Órdenes Militares, Caballeros Alcántara, exp. 1075.
3 Óscar Recio Morales, 'Una aproximación al modelo del oficial extranjero en el ejército borbónico: La etapa de formación del teniente general Alejandro

O'Reilly (1723–1794)', in *Cuadernos dieciochistas*, 12 (2011), pp. 171–95 (p. 176). See also David Murphy, 'Count Alexander O'Reilly', DIB.
4   'Una aproximación al modelo ...' p. 184.
5   Ibid., pp. 188–90.
6   Alexander O'Reilly to Jamie Masones de Lima, Prague, 18 December 1758, AHN, Estado, 6527, cited in Recio Morales, 'Una aproximación al modelo ...' p. 192.
7   'Una aproximación al modelo ...' p. 194.
8   'Manuel O'Reilly. Empleos', AGS, Estado, legajo 6844, 32, F. 3v.
9   'Count Alexander O'Reilly', DIB.
10 Recio Morales, 'Un intento de modernización del ejército borbónico del XVIII: La Real Escuela Militar de Ávila (1774)', in *Investigaciones históricas*, 32 (2012), pp. 145–72 (p. 146).
11 François de Barbé-Marbois, *The History of Louisiana: Particularly of the Cession of that Colony to the United States of America; with an introductory essay on the Constitution and Government of the United States* (Philadelphia: Carey and Lea, 1830), pp. 137–8.
12 The O'Reilly family had originally come from County Cavan.
13 Lord Holland, p. 80.
14 Ibid.
15 Fannin, p. 29.
16 Cited in Fannin, p. 29.
17 Swinburne, vol. 2, p. 10.
18 'Regimiento de Cuba. Creación', AGS, Estado, legajo 6880, 35, F. 3v.
19 Lord Holland, p. 79.
20 'Count Alexander O'Reilly', DIB.
21 'Conde de O'Reilly. Agregaciones', AGS, Estado, legajo 6875, 28.
22 'Manuel O'Reilly. Empleos', AGS, Estado, legajo 6844, 32, F. 4v.
23 Ibid., FF. 5r–5v.
24 Lord Holland, p. 80.

Notes to Chapter 4: The King of Peru (pp. 39–53)
1   He was born Ambrose Higgins but added the O' later in life. For the sake of clarity I refer to him throughout as O'Higgins.
2   Ricardo Donoso, *El Marqués de Osorno Don Ambrosio Higgins, 1720–1801* (Santiago: Universidad de Chile, 1941), pp. 46, 54.
3   For more on the complex relationship between the Spanish and the Mapuche in the eighteenth century, see José Manuel Zavala Cepeda, *Los Mapuches del siglo XVIII: Dinámica interétnicas y estrategias de resistencia* (Santiago: Universidad Bolivariana, 2008).

4   Antonio Guill y Gonzaga decree, Santiago de Chile, 1 July 1768, cited in Ricardo Donoso, *El Marqués de Osorno Don Ambrosio Higgins, 1720–1801* (Santiago: Universidad de Chile, 1941), pp. 63–4.
5   'Juan Garland. Legados', AGS, Estado, legajo 6884, 8.
6   Ambrose O'Higgins, 'Mapa del Reino de Chile', 21 February 1768, ANC; repr. as appendix in Donoso.
7   Ibid.
8   'Ambrosio O'Higgins de Vallenar, vasallo del rei de Inglaterra', ANC, Archivo Fernández Larraín, 14, 25.
9   Ibid.
10 Donoso, p. 107.
11 Jaime Eyzaguirre, *O'Higgins*, 2 vols, vol. 1 (Santiago: Zig-Zag, 1972), p. 17.
12 Ibid., p. 18.
13 'Bando de buen Gobierno expedido para la ciudad de Santiago de Chile por el presidente Gobernador Don Ambrosio O'Higgins con aprobación real en 1789', ANC, Archivo Fernández Larraín, 14, 17.
14 Chauca García, 'El grupo irlandés entre el siglo XVIII y el XIX: su papel en la Ilustración e Independencia americanas', in *Extranjeros en el Ejército: Militares irlandeses en la sociedad española, 1580–1818*, ed. Enrique García Hernán and Óscar Recio Morales (Madrid: Ministerio de Defensa, 2007), pp. 353–78 (p. 365).
15 'Bando de buen Gobierno expedido para la ciudad de Santiago de Chile …'
16 Ambrose O'Higgins to Antonio Valdés, Santiago, 24 January 1789, ANC, Archivo Vicuña Mackenna, 304-D, FF. 227–34.
17 Chauca García, 'El grupo irlandés …' pp. 369–70.
18 Ambrose O'Higgins to Manuel Negrete de la Torre, Santiago, 18 July 1793, AGI, Chile, 199, 95.
19 Ambrose O'Higgins to Manuel Negrete de la Torre, Santiago, 11 November 1794, AGI, Chile, 199, 197.
20 Testimony of Dr Juan Martínez de Rozas, Concepión, 28 April 1806, 'Antecedentes para la legitimación', repr. in *Archivo de Don Bernardo O'Higgins*, 39 vols, vol. 1, ed. Ricardo Donoso and others (Santiago: Nascimento, 1946), p. 51.
21 Testimony of Thomas Delphin, Concepción, 21 July 1806, 'Antecedentes para la legitimación', repr. in *Archivo de Don Bernardo O'Higgins*, vol. 1, p. 54.
22 Chauca García, 'El grupo irlandés …', pp. 368–9.
23 'Solicitud de O'Higgins del grado de Teniente Coronel', AGI, Estado, 75, 95.
24 Thomas O'Higgins to the Prince of Peace, Fuerte Alcudia, 6 February 1797, AGI, Estado, 85, 42.

25 'Sobre reconocimiento del archipiélago de Chiloé etc.', Marqués de Osorno, Lima, 30 May 1798, AGI, Estado, 74, 27.
26 Ibid.
27 John Mackenna to Bernardo O'Higgins, Santiago, 20 February 1811, repr. in *Archivo de Don Bernardo O'Higgins*, vol. 1, pp. 79–85.
28 Ibid., pp. 87–8.
29 Ibid.

Notes to Chapter 5: Spain under Siege (pp. 54–61)

1 Lord Holland, p. 73.
2 *Diario de sesiones de las Cortes Generales y Extraordinarias*, no. 1, 24 September 1810.
3 Ibid.
4 Delfina Fernández Pascua, 'Ramón Power y Demetrio O'Daly: Diputados a Cortes por Puerto Rico', in *La presencia irlandesa durante las Cortes de Cádiz en España y America, 1812*, ed. Enriqué García Hernán and M. Carmen Lario de Oñate (Valencia: Albatros, 2013), pp. 159–78 (pp. 161–2).
5 See Jorge L. Chinea, 'Irish indentured servants, Papists and colonists in Spanish colonial Puerto Rico, ca. 1650–1800', in *Irish Migration Studies in Latin America*, 5, 3 (2007), pp. 171–81.
6 Ibid., pp. 177–9.
7 See Manuel Vilaplana Montes, 'Santiago Key Muñoz (1772–1821): Perfil biográfico de un eclesiastico del antiguo regimen', in *Anuario de los estudios atlánticos*, no. 26 (1980), pp. 491–527.
8 Ibid., p. 513.
9 *Diario de sesiones de las Cortes de Cádiz Generales y Extraordinarias*, no. 706, 21 November 1812, cited in Vilaplana Montes, p. 513.
10 Vilaplana Montes, p. 515.
11 Marie-Laure Rieu-Millan, 'Los diputados americanos en las Cortes de Cádiz: Elecciones y representatividad', in *Quinto centenario*, 14 (1988), pp. 53–72 (p. 53).
12 Ramón Power y Giralt, *Contextación al papel publicado baxo el título De primeros sucesos deagradables en la isla de Puerto Rico* (Cádiz: 1810), p. 4.
13 *Diario de sesiones de las Cortes de Cádiz Generales y Extraordinarias*, no. 142, 15 February 1811.

Notes to Chapter 6: The Propagandist Priest (pp. 62–71)

1 Manuel Moreno Alonso, *Divina libertad: La aventura liberal de Don José María Blanco White, 1808–1824* (Seville: Alfar, 2002), p. 13.

2 Moreno Alonso, 'El mundo hispano-irlandés de José María Blanco White', in *La presencia irlandesa durante las Cortes de Cádiz en España y América, 1812*, pp. 231–42 (p. 232).
3 Joseph Blanco White, *The Life of the Rev. Joseph Blanco White, Written by Himself, with Portions of his Correspondence*, ed. J.H. Thom, 3 vols, vol. 1 (London: John Chapman, 1845), p. 3.
4 Blanco White, *Practical and Internal Evidence against Catholicism* (London: John Murray, 1826), p. 3.
5 *The Life of the Rev. Joseph Blanco White*, vol. 1, p. 173.
6 *Practical and Internal Evidence Against Catholicism*, p. 3.
7 *The Life of the Rev. Joseph Blanco White*, vol. 1, p. 4
8 Ibid., p. 5.
9 *Practical and Internal Evidence Against Catholicism*, pp. 3–4.
10 *The Life of the Rev. Joseph Blanco White,*, vol. 1, p. 111.
11 Moreno Alonso, *Divina Libertad*, p. 27.
12 *The Life of the Rev. Joseph Blanco White*, vol. 1, pp. 142–3.
13 Ibid.
14 Ibid., p. 153.
15 Ibid., p. 154.
16 Ibid., p. 159.
17 Ibid., pp. 156–7.
18 Ibid., p. 205
19 *El Español*, vol. 6, February 1813, cited in *Divina Libertad*, p. 83.
20 *The Life of the Rev. Joseph Blanco White*, vol. 1, p. 206.
21 Ibid., p. 207.
22 Ibid., p. 184.
23 Ibid., p. 188.
24 José María Blanco White to Lady Holland, Redesdale, 10 July 1832, in *The Life of the Rev. Joseph Blanco White*, vol. 1, p. 488.
25 Ibid., pp. 484–5.
26 Ibid., p. 486.
27 Richard Brent, 'Richard Whately', ODNB.
28 'Richard Whately: Ireland's strangest archbishop', in *History Ireland*, 13, 2 (2005) (http://www.historyireland.com/18th-19th-century-history/richard-whately-irelands-strangest-archbishop/, accessed 18 February 2016).
29 *The Life of the Rev. Joseph Blanco White*, vol. 1, p. 486.
30 Ibid., p. 493.
31 Ibid., pp. 494–5.

32   Ibid., p. 499.
33   *The Life of the Rev. Joseph Blanco White*, vol. 2, pp. 56–7.
34   See 'El mundo hispano-irlandés de José María Blanco White'.
35   *The Life of the Rev. Joseph Blanco White*, vol. 1, p. 496.

Notes to Chapter 7: Merchants, Sailors, Soldiers, Spies (pp. 72–87)

1   The Spanish phrase *vale un Potosí* – to be worth a Potosí – signifies someone who is worth a fortune, literally or metaphorically.
2   Félix Luna, *A Short History of the Argentinians* (Buenos Aires: Planeta, 2004), p. 30.
3   Ibid., p. 18.
4   'Padron particular de los extrangeros havitantes en las doce manzanas que comprehende el cuartel no. 14', Buenos Aires, 24 February 1807, AGNA, Interior, Sala IX, 30-08-01, legajo 50.
5   'Miguel Gorman', NDBA.
6   José Galvez to the Marquis of Loreto, San Lorenzo, 3 November 1783, AGNA, Despachos y Nombramientos Civiles y Eclesiásticos, Sala IX, 12-6-4, 123.
7   'Tómas O'Gorman, solicita carta de nativaleza', AGI, Estado, 78, 5.
8   Ibid.
9   Ibid.
10 'Sobre introducción de géneros en buques neutrales', AGI, Estado, 79, 19.
11 Entry in baptismal register. Archives Départmentales, Morbihan, Commune de Lorient, baptêmes, mariages, sépultures, 1771 (http://recherche.archives.morbihan.fr/ark:/15049/vta544881ab86113/daogrp/0/layout:table/idsearch:RECH_40d84972df1e2608e9ace4fa3a66b0ea id:1979817354, accessed 17 December 2015); tables de baptême, naissances, 1709–1820 (accessed 17 December 2015); Will of James Florence Bourke De Burgh, NA, PROB 11/1942/228.
12 Entry in marriage register. Archives Départmentales, Morbihan, Commune de Lorient, baptêmes, mariages, sépultures, 1765 (http://recherche.archives.morbihan.fr/ark:/15049/vta544881a8bd1e9/daogrp/0/layout:table/idsearch:RECH_40d84972df1e2608e9ace4fa3a66b0ea id:205160059?center=1860,-1397, accessed 17 December 2015). See also Jean-Baptiste-Pierre-Jullien Courcelles, *Histoire généalogique et héraldique de Pairs de France, des grands dignitaires de la couronne des principales familles nobles du royaume, etc.*, vol. 6 (Paris: 1826), Pairs de France, p. 81; and Will of James Florence Bourke De Burgh, NA, PROB 11/1942/228.
13 The name *Bourke* is inscribed on the Arc de Triomphe in Paris, recalling the contribution of Jean-Raymond-Charles Bourke to France's victories during the Revolutionary and Napoleonic Wars.

14 Peter Pyne, 'A soldier under two flags: Lieutenant-Colonel James Florence Burke: Officer, adventurer and spy', *Études irlandaises*, 23, 1 (1998), pp. 121–38 (p. 122).
15 Ibid., p. 124.
16 Both of Anglo-Irish stock, Canning and Castlereagh were fierce political rivals, whose enmity resulted in the latter injuring the former in a duel in 1809.
17 Peter Pyne, *The Invasions of Buenos Aires, 1806–1807: The Irish Dimension* (Liverpool: University of Liverpool, Institute of Latin American Studies, 1996), p. 3.
18 Ibid., p. 8.
19 Alexander Gillespie, *Gleanings and Remarks, Collected During Many Months of Residence at Buenos Ayres, and within the Upper Country* (Leeds: 1818), p. 80.
20 He was born Jacques but is better known in Argentine history as Santiago de Liniers.
21 'Petition of Roberto Dunn', AGNA, Invasiones Inglesas, Sala IX, 26-06-12, 120.
22 'Petition of Carlos Fitzgeld', AGNA, Invasiones Inglesas, Sala IX, 26-06-12, 127.
23 'Barrio 20. Relación de los individuos de nación estrangera que havitan en el barrio', Buenos Aires, 27 February 1807, AGNA, Interior, Sala IX, 30-08-01, 50.
24 *The Invasions of Buenos Aires,* p. 34.
25 James Florence Bourke to Lord Liverpool, London, 25 November 1809, NA, FO 72/81, F. 7r.
26 Ibid, F. 7v.
27 Ibid., F. 8r–8v.
28 Ibid., F. 12v.
29 Ibid., FF. 14v–15r.
30 Ibid.
31 See J. Street, 'Lord Strangford and Río de la Plata, 1808–1815', in *Hispanic American Historical Review,* 33, 4 (1953), pp. 477–510.
32 Street, p. 484.
33 Bourke to Liverpool, NA, FO 72/81, f. 17r.
34 Ibid., FF. 18v–19r.
35 Ibid. F. 20r
36 Ibid., F.24v–25v.

Notes to Chapter 8: The Battle for the River Plate (pp. 91–103)

1 John de Courcy Ireland, *The Admiral from Mayo: A Life of Almirante William Brown of Foxford* (Dublin: Edmund Burke, 1995), p. 21.
2 Ibid., pp. 2–5.
3 Ibid., p. 12.

4   De Courcy Ireland, pp. 27–8; Miguel Ángel de Marco, *Corsarios argentinos: Héroes del mar en la independencia y en la guerra con el Brasil* (Buenos Aires: Emecé, 2009), p. 85.
5   De Marco, p. 87.
6   De Courcy Ireland, p. 38.
7   Ibid., pp. 38–51.
8   John Parish Robertson and William Parish Robertson, *Letters on South America, Comprising Travels on the Banks of the Paraná and Rio de la Plata*, 3 vols, vol. 1 (London: John Murray, 1843), pp. 30–1.
9   Ibid., p. 31.
10 Edmundo Murray, 'Pedro Campbell', ODNB.
11 Robertson, pp. 27–30.
12 Ibid., p. 38.
13 Ibid., pp. 32–3.
14 Ibid., pp. 23–4.
15 Ibid., pp. 177–8.
16 Ibid., p. 178.
17 'Pedro Campbell', ODNB.
18 De Courcy Ireland, pp. 55–62.

Notes to Chapter 9: General O'Higgins (pp. 104–19)

1   Testimony of Thomas Delphin, Concepción, July 21 1806, 'Antecedentes para la legitimación', repr. in *Archivo de Don Bernardo O'Higgins*, vol. 1, p. 54.
2   'Baptismal record of Bernardo O'Higgins', repr. in *Archivo de Don Bernardo O'Higgins*, vol. 1, pp. 1–2.
3   Testimony of Thomas Delphin, Concepción, 21 July 1806, 'Antecedentes para la legitimación', repr. in *Archivo de Don Bernardo O'Higgins*, vol. 1, p. 54.
4   Bernardo Riqueleme to Nicolás de la Cruz, London, 19 March 1799, repr. in *Archivo de Don Bernardo O'Higgins*, vol. 1, p. 7.
5   Francisco de Miranda to Bernardo Riquelme, 'Consejos de un viejo sudamericano a un joven compatriota al regresar de Inglaterra a su país', repr. in *Archivo de Don Bernardo O'Higgins*, vol. 1, pp. 20–21.
6   Ibid., p. 20.
7   Bernardo Riquelme to Isabel Riquelme, Cádiz, 1 February 1800, repr. in *Archivo de Don Bernardo O'Higgins*, vol. 1, p. 9.
8   Bernardo Riquelme to Ambrose O'Higgins, Cádiz, 18 April 1800, repr. in *Archivo de Don Bernardo O'Higgins*, vol. 1, p. 12.
9   Bernardo Riquelme to Ambrose O'Higgins, Cádiz, 8 January 1801, repr. in *Archivo de Don Bernardo O'Higgins*, vol. 1, p. 16.

10   Eugenio Orrego Vicuña, *O'Higgins: Vida y tiempo* (Buenos Aires: Losada, 1946), p. 59.
11   Bernardo O'Higgins to John Mackenna, Las Canteras, 5 January 1811, repr. in *Archivo de Don Bernardo O'Higgins*, vol. 1, p. 64.
12   Ibid., p. 67.
13   John Mackenna to Bernardo O'Higgins, Santiago, 20 February 1811, repr. in *Archivo de Don Bernardo O'Higgins*, vol. 1, pp. 74–5.
14   Ibid., p. 84.
15   Ibid., p. 99.
16   Ibid., p. 103.
17   Bernardo O'Higgins to John Mackenna, Las Canteras, 5 January 1811, repr. in *Archivo de Don Bernardo O'Higgins*, vol. 1, p. 68.
18   Memorial to San Martín, Mendoza, repr. in *Archivo de Don Bernardo O'Higgins*, vol. 7, pp. 2–3.
19   Maria Graham, *Journal of a Residence in Chile during the Year 1822* (London: 1824), p. 208.
20   Ibid., p. 207.
21   Ibid.

Notes to Chapter 10: Bolívar's Irish Volunteers (pp. 120–40)

1   Daniel O'Leary to Soledad Soublette O'Leary, Rosario, 31 March 1830, AGNC, Colección Aquileo Parra, caja 5, carpeta 9.
2   Francis Burdett O'Connor, *Independencia americana: Recuerdos de Francisco Burdett O'Connor*, ed. Tomás O'Connor d'Arlach (Madrid: Ayacucho, 1915), p. 90.
3   John Devereux to Daniel O'Connell, London, 22 August 1824, UCDA, O'Connell Papers, P12/3/148.
4   Dr Matthew Brown estimates that 3,650 Irishmen served in the patriot armies, 54 per cent of all foreign volunteers; see Matthew Brown, *Adventuring through Spanish Colonies: Simón Bolívar, Foreign Mercenaries and the Birth of New Nations* (Liverpool: Liverpool University Press, 2006), p. 27.
5   'South America', handbill reproduced in *Carrick's Morning Post*, 8 January 1820; repr. in Matthew Brown and Martín Alonso Roa (compiladores), *Militares extranjeros en la independencia de Colombia: Nuevas perspectivas* (Bogotá: Museo Nacional de Colombia, 2005), pp. 263–4.
6   Anonymous, *The Narrative of a Voyage to the Spanish Main, in the Ship 'Two Friends'* (London: John Miller, 1819), p. 12.
7   Ibid., pp. 36–7.
8   Ibid., p. 32.

9   Ibid., p. 34.
10 Ibid., p. 15.
11 Ibid.
12 Ibid., pp. 15–16.
13 Alfred J. Hasbrouck, *Foreign Legionaries in the Liberation of Spanish South America* (New York: Columbia University Press, 1928), p. 51.
14 *Narrative of a Voyage to the Spanish Main*, p. 21.
15 Anonymous [Richard Longville Vowell], *Campaigns and Cruises in Venezuela and New Grenada and in the Pacific Ocean from 1817 to 1830* (London: Longman and Co., 1831), pp. 18–19.
16 Hasbrouck, pp. 91–3.
17 Ibid., p. 92.
18 'The following Goods, received by the Ship *George Canning* from London …' *Correo del Orinoco*, 6 March 1819.
19 Hasbrouck, pp. 92–3.
20 *Campaigns and Cruises in Venezuela and New Grenada*, p. 152.
21 Alberto Eduardo Wright, *Destellos de gloria* (Caracas: Cámara Venezolano Británico de Comercio, 1983), p. 29.
22 Gustavus Hippisley, *A Narrative of the Expedition to the Rivers Orinoco and Apure, in South America, Which Sailed from England in 1817, and Joined the Patriotic Forces in Venezuela and Caraccas* (London: John Murray, 1819), pp. v–vi.
23 *The Narrative of a Voyage to the Spanish Main*, pp. v–vi.
24 William Jackson Adam, *Journal of Voyages to Marguaritta, Trinidad and Maturin, with the Author's Travels across the Plains of the Llaneros, to Angustura, and Subsequent Descent of the Orinoco in the Years 1819–1820; Comprising His Several Interviews with Bolivar, the Supreme Chief; Sketches of the Various Native and European Generals: and a Variety of Characteristic Anecdotes, Hitherto Unpublicised* (Dublin: R.M. Tims, 1824), p. iii.
25 Daniel O'Leary, *Bolívar y la emancipación de Sur America: Memorias del General O'Leary*, ed. Simón B. O'Leary (Madrid: Ayacucho, 1915), pp. 579–81.
26 Daniel O'Leary to Soledad Soublette O'Leary, Rosario, 31 March 1830, AGNC, Colección Aquileo Parra, caja 5, carpeta 9.
27 Wilson ended up in Australia, where he became a police magistrate, tasked with reorganising the force in Sydney along the lines of the London Metropolitan Police. In 1838 he faced charges of misconduct with a female convict, which were later dropped. However, the following year it was proved that he had used members of the police force to build his house and act as liveried servants. He was suspended and removed from office. Two years later Wilson was defeated

in an election for the role of secretary-treasurer of the Australian Club, which had been founded by English settlers in the 1830s. Shortly afterwards, anonymous articles began appearing in the press casting aspersions on the club's committee. William Christie, who had defeated Wilson in the election, discovered that it was Wilson who had been behind the articles. Believing that one article had questioned his wife's honour, Christie horsewhipped Wilson. A threatened duel was prevented, and Wilson sued Christie in the Australian Supreme Court, winning £150 in damages. See Hazel King, 'Henry Croasdaile Wilson', *Australian Dictionary of Biography*, vol. 2 (1967).

28   'Coronel Wilson', *Correo del Orinoco*, 1 May 1819.
29   *Bolívar y la emancipación de Sur America*, p. 581.
30   Ibid., p. 582.
31   Ibid.
32   Moisés Enrique Rodríguez, 'James Towers English (1782–1819)', *Irish Migration Studies in Latin America* (2007) (http://www.irlandeses.org/dilab_englishjt.htm, accessed 24 June 2015).
33   See 'A Description Role with a List of Necessaries, Arms and Appointments in Possession of the British Legion', Achaguas, December 1820, Archivo Histórico de Guayas, and available on Dr Matthew Brown's *Bolivarian Times* blog (http://bolivariantimes.blogspot.ie/2014_01_01_archive.html, accessed 7 January 2016).
34   Anonymous [Captain Cowley], *Recollections of a Service of Three Years during the War of Extermination in the Republics of Venezuela and Colombia*, 2 vols, vol. 1 (London: Hunt and Clarke, 1828), p. 10.
35   Ibid., pp. 14–15.
36   Ibid., p. 16.
37   Ibid., p. 18.
38   Ibid., p. 68–9.
39   Adam, pp. 17–18.
40   Eric Lambert, *Voluntarios Británicos e Irlandeses en la gesta Bolivariana*, 3 vols, vol. 1 (Caracas: Corporación Venezolana de Guayana, 1983), pp. 128–9.
41   Hippisley, p. 470.
42   Ibid.
43   *Bolívar y la emancipación de Sur America*, p. 659.
44   The Sandes family were deeply unpopular among their Catholic tenants, so much so that in 1939, at the instigation of the parish priest, the town of Newtownsandes in north Kerry chose to rename itself Moyvane.
45   O'Connor, pp. 84, 102. See also Brian McGinn, 'St Patrick's Day in Peru, 1824', in *Irish Migration Studies in Latin America*, 3,2 (2005) (http://www.irlandeses.org/0503.pdf, accessed 27 November 2015).

46 *Memoirs of General Miller in the Service of the Republic of Peru*, ed. John Miller, 2 vols, vol. 1 (London: Longman and others, 1829), p. 405.
47 Wright, p. 31.
48 *Bolívar y la emancipación de Sur America*, p. 655.
49 Wright, pp. 31–2.
50 *Bolívar y la emancipación de Sur America*, p. 680.
51 Ibid.
52 Ibid.

Notes to Chapter 11: The Hibernian Regiment and the Irish Legion (pp. 141–61)

1   Thomas Cloney, *A Personal Narrative of Those Transactions in the County Wexford, in which the Author was Engaged, during the Awful Period of 1798* (Dublin, 1832), p. 41.
2   James Quinn, 'John Devereux', DIB.
3   'South America' (handbill), repr. in *Militares extranjeros en la independencia de Colombia*, pp. 263–4.
4   'John Devereux', DIB.
5   Arthur Sandes to Daniel O'Connell, Quito, 10 September 1822, UCDA, P12/3/112, repr. in Brown and Roa, p. 310.
6   Michael Rafter, *Memoirs of Gregor M'Gregor, Comprising a Sketch of the Revolution in New Grenada and Venezuela* (London: J.J. Stockdale, 1820), p. 128.
7   Ibid., pp. 128–9.
8   Ibid., pp. 130–32.
9   *Adventuring through Spanish Colonies*, p. 40.
10 Hasbrouck, pp. 147–52.
11 Rafter, p. 316.
12 Ibid., pp. 316–17.
13 Ibid., p. 347.
14 Ibid., p. 373.
15 Hasbrouck, p. 156.
16 Thomas Pakenham, *The Year of Liberty: The Story of the Great Irish Rebellion of 1798* (London: Literary Guild, 1969), pp. 110, 274–6.
17 C.J. Woods, 'William Aylmer', DIB.
18 James Dunkerley, 'The Third Man: Francisco Burdett O'Connor and the Emancipation of the Americas', (London: Institute of Latin American Studies, 1999), pp. 3–4.
19 Bridget Hourican, 'Francis Burdett O'Connor', DIB.
20 Ibid.
21 W.J. Fitzpatrick, rev. by Thomas Bartlett, 'Roger O'Connor', ODNB.

22 O'Connor, pp. 19–20.
23 Dunkerley, 'The Third Man', p. 8.
24 O'Connor, pp. 18–9.
25 Ibid., p. 15.
26 Ibid., p. 16.
27 Ibid.
28 Ibid., p. 9.
29 Adam, p. 9.
30 Robert James Young's journal, PRONI, D3045/6/3/2.
31 Ibid.
32 Ibid.
33 Ibid.
34 Ibid.
35 Ibid.
36 Adam, p. 11.
37 Benjamin M'Mahon, *Jamaica Plantership* (London: Effingham Wilson, 1839), pp. 11–12.
38 Young's journal.
39 Ibid.
40 *Recollections of a Service of Three Years*, vol. 1, p. 32.
41 Letter to Pedro Luis Brión signed by W. Aylmer, L. Burke, W.R. Derinzy, F. Burdett O'Connor, C. Bourne, E.H. Clinton, J. O'Lawlor, Pampatar, 5 November 1819, repr. in Lambert, vol. 2, pp. 151–2.
42 O'Connor, p. 27.
43 Letter to Brión, repr. in Lambert, vol. 2, pp. 151–2.
44 Pedro Luís Brión to William Aylmer, Juan Griego, 7 November 1819, repr. in Lambert, vol. 2, pp. 152–3.
45 Lambert, vol. 2, pp. 155–7.
46 *Correo del Orinoco*, 1 January 1820, repr. in Lambert, vol. 2, pp. 164–5.
47 *Recollections of a Service of Three Years*, vol. 1, p. 55.
48 O'Connor, p. 30.
49 Ibid., p. 33.
50 Ibid., p. 37.
51 Ibid., p. 39.
52 Ibid., pp. 40–5.
53 *Correo del Orinoco*, 5 August 1820.
54 Ibid.
55 Ibid., 30 September 1820.

56 Morgan O'Connell to Daniel O'Connell, H.Q. Margarita, 14 June 1821, repr. in *The Life and Speeches of Daniel O'Connell, M.P.*, ed. John O'Connell 2 vols, vol. 2 (Dublin: James Duffy, 1846), p. 526.
57 Ibid., p. 527.
58 Ibid., p. 528.
59 Ibid.
60 Ibid. p. 529.
61 Mathew Macnamara to Simón Bolívar, Angostura, 11 December 1820, AGNC, Collecciones, Enrique Ortega Ricaurte, caja 79, F. 25.
62 Ibid.
63 Ibid.
64 Ibid.
65 Ibid.
66 John Devereux to Daniel O'Connell, London, 22 August 1824, UCDA, O'Connell Papers, P12/3/148.

Notes to Chapter 12: Death in the Andes (pp. 162–73)
1 Wright, pp. 35–8.
2 Hasbrouck, p. 224.
3 'Juan Oughan', NDBA; see also Florencia Ibarra, 'El tratamiento moral en el período Iluminista en Argentina', in *Acta Psiquiátrica y Psicológica de América Latina*, 53, 4 (2007), pp. 190–5.
4 Mario Belgrano, 'Biografía del General Juan O'Brien, 1786–1861: Guerrero de la independencia Sud Americana', in *Repatriación de los restos del General Juan O'Brien, guerrero de la independencia Sud Americana* (Buenos Aires: Kraft, 1938), p. 12.
5 Benjamín Vicuña Mackenna, *El jeneral O'Brien* (Santiago: Universitaria, 1902), p. 13.
6 Ibid., p. 14.
7 O'Connor, p. 64.
8 O'Leary, *Memorias del General O'Leary*, 32 vols, vol. 2, ed. Simón B. O'Leary (Caracas: 1879–88), p. 137.
9 Among the fictional works inspired by the meeting is 'Guayaquil', a short story by the Argentine writer Jorge Luis Borges.
10 O'Connor, pp. 104–5.
11 Miller, vol. 2, pp. 122–3.
12 O'Connor, p. 110.
13 Ibid., p. 159.

14   Ibid., p. 164.
15   Ibid., pp. 164–5.
16   Wright, p. 56

Notes to Chapter 13: The San Patricios (pp. 174–84)
1   'Dumphi O'Donoju y O'Ryan Roothy, Bermingham, Juan', AHN, Órdenes Civiles, Estado-Carlos III, exp. 810.
2   'Sección de Guerra. Causas contra generals, oficiales, etc. para su remisión a consejos de guerra y al Tribunal de Seguridad Pública', AHN, Junta Central Suprema Gubernativa del Reino, Estado, 45, A, N.712.
3   'Real Orden de la Junta Suprema de Gobierno del Reino, comunicada a José Caro, para que se premie a las tropas del general Juan O'Donojú por la acción que sostuvieron contra el enemigo, el 20 de abril, en Algorfa (Vall de Algorfa)', AHN, Guerra, Diversos Colecciones, 91, 8.
4   'Copia de carta de O'Donojú al general don José Dávila', in *Instrucciones y memorias de los virreyes novohispanos*, vol. 2, p. 1499–1501, ed. Ernesto Torre del Villar (México: Porrúa, 1991); repr. in Ignacio González-Polo, 'Don Juan O'Donojú, un benemérito gobernante olvidado en la historia de México', in *Boletín*, vol. 11, nos. 1 and 2 (2006), p. 36.
5   George Turnbull Moore Davis, *Autobiography of the Late Geo. T.M. Davis* (New York: Jenkins and McCowan, 1891), pp. 226–7, repr. in Michael Hogan, *The Irish Soldiers of Mexico* (Guadalajara: Fondo Editorial Universitario, 2010), p. 192.
6   Hogan, pp. 193–5.
7   Ibid., p. 41.
8   Ibid., pp. 53–54.
9   Ibid., pp. 50–51.
10 Ibid., p. 69.
11 Ibid., p. 81.
12 See Robert Ryal Miller's letter in *The News* (Mexico City), 11 April 1999, p. 20; repr. in genealogyforum.com (http://www.genealogyforum.rootsweb.com/gfaol/resource/Hispanic/JohnRiley.htm, accessed 12 January 2016).

Notes to Chapter 14: The Kingdom of God (pp. 185–91)
1   Patrick M. Geoghegan, 'Thomas Field (Fehily)', DIB.
2   Aubrey Gwynn, 'The first Irish priests in the New World', in *Studies*, 21, 82 (1932), pp. 213–28 (p. 214). See also Thomas Murray, *The Story of the Irish in Argentina* (New York: P.J. Kenedy and Sons, 1919), p. 1.
3   Edmundo Murray, 'The Irish in Uruguay and Paraguay', in *Irish Migration Studies in Latin America*, 4, 1 (2006).

4   It was originally published in Latin, the English translation being *Events of the Guaraní War since the Year 1754*.
5   Salvador Gonzalez (trans.), *Carta del venerable Palafox y Mendoza, obispo de la puebla de Los Ángeles, al sumo pontofice Inocencio x contra los Jesuitas* (Barcelona: De Grau, 1845), pp. 87–8.
6   Robert Bontine Cunninghame Graham, *A Vanished Arcadia, Being Some Account of the Jesuits in Paraguay, 1607–1767* (London: Heinemann, 1901), p. 87.
7   Tadeo X. Henis, *Efemerides de la guerra de los Guaranies desde el año de 1754* (1755), p. 3.
8   Michael Lillis and Ronan Fanning, *The Lives of Eliza Lynch: Scandal and Courage* (Dublin: Gill & Macmillan, 2009), p. 97.
9   Ibid., p. 132.
10 Ibid., p. 206.
11 Eliza Lynch, *Exposición y Protesta*, Buenos Aires, 1875, repr. in *The Lives of Eliza Lynch*, pp. 208–9.

Notes to Chapter 15: After the Revolution (pp. 195–208)
1   O'Connor, p. 187.
2   Ibid., 188–9.
3   Daniel O'Leary to Soledad Soublette O'Leary, Rosario, 19 March 1830, AGNC, Colección Aquileo Parra, caja 5, carpeta 9.
4   Daniel O'Leary to Soledad Soublette O'Leary, Guayaquil, 20 September 1828, AGNC, Colección Aquileo Parra, caja 5, carpeta 9.
5   Daniel O'Leary to Soledad Soublette O'Leary, Guayaquil, 7 October 1828, AGNC, Colección Aquileo Parra, caja 5, carpeta 9.
6   Daniel O'Leary to Soledad Soublette O'Leary, Rosario, 19 March 1830, AGNC, Colección Aquileo Parra, rollo 4.
7   Ibid.
8   Ibid.
9   *Adventuring through Spanish Colonies*, p. 87.
10 Brown, 'Rupert Hand', ODNB.
11 Daniel O'Leary to Soledad Soublette O'Leary, Rosario, 19 March 1830, AGNC, Colección Aquileo Parra, caja 5, carpeta 9.
12 Ibid.
13 Daniel O'Leary to Soledad Soublette O'Leary, Rosario, 31 March 1830, AGNC, Colección Aquileo Parra, caja 5, carpeta 9.
14 Ibid.
15 Ibid.
16 Ibid.

17 See William Owens Ferguson, 'Journal from Lima to Caracas, commencing September 4th 1826', in *Irish Migration Studies in Latin America* (2006) (http://www.irlandeses.org/ferguson01.htm, accessed 25 November 2015).
18 Hasbrouck, p. 318.
19 Wright, pp. 11–12.
20 Brown, 'How did Rupert Hand get out of jail? Colombia and the Atlantic empires', in *History*, 95, 317 (2010), pp. 25–44 (pp. 28–9).
21 Ibid., p. 30.
22 Ibid., pp. 37–42.
23 Brown, 'Rupert Hand', ODNB.
24 'Tratado sobre la extinción del tráfico de esclavos entre el Reino Unido de la Gran Bretaña e Irlanda y la Nueva Granada (1851)', AGNC, Relaciones Exteriores, CO.AGN.MRE 119.35.3
25 Bernardo O'Higgins to Sir John Doyle, Lima, 16 December 1823, repr. in *Archivo de Don Bernado O'Higgins*, vol. 31, (Santiago: 1980), p. 78.
26 Orrego Vicuña, p. 331.
27 Lourdes Díaz-Trechuelo, *Bolívar, Miranda, O'Higgins, San Martín: Cuatro vidas cruzadas* (Madrid: Encuentro, 1999), p. 191.
28 Ibid., p. 194.
29 Brown, 'John Devereux', ODNB.
30 John Devereux to Daniel O'Connell, Bogotá, 16 July 1822, UCDA, O'Connell Papers, P12/3/132.
31 'John Devereux', ODNB.
32 Vicuña Mackenna, *El jeneral O'Brien*, p. 8.
33 Nils Jacobsen, *The Peruvian Altiplano, 1780–1930* (Berkeley: University of California Press, 1993), p. 62.
34 'John Thomond O'Brien', NDBA.
35 Dunkerley, p. 2.

Notes to Chapter 16: The 'New Erin' (pp. 209–15)
1 O'Connor, p. 174.
2 Ibid.
3 The name 'New Erin' was popular and was used by the proponents of several schemes for introducing Irish settlers to South America.
4 See *Adventuring through Spanish Colonies*, pp. 18–22.
5 'Emigración a la América del Sur', *Correo del Orinoco*, 31 July 1819.
6 Lambert, vol. 2, pp. 188–9.
7 Ibid., p. 188.

8   'South America', repr. in Brown and Roa, p. 263.
9   'Pendiente el proyecto de mejorar las Misiones del Caroní, se presentaron las proposiciones siguientes, y se pasaron para su exámen a la Comisión', *Correo del Orinoco*, 1 May 1819.
10 Daniel O'Leary to Soledad Soublette O'Leary, Rosario, 19 March 1830, AGNC, Colección Aquileo Parra, caja 5, carpeta 9.
11 A British army officer, born in Dublin, and a veteran of the revolutionary wars in North America and France, having raised his own regiment, the 87th Foot, in 1793. He was also at the forefront of a society of prominent figures whose aim was to grant relief to the poor of Ireland.
12 Bernardo O'Higgins to Sir John Doyle, 16 December 1823, Lima, repr. in *Archivo de Don Bernardo O'Higgins*, vol. 31 pp. 74–5.
13 Pat Nally, 'Los Irlandeses en la Argentina', *Familia: Ulster Genealogical Review*, no. 8 (1992).
14 Ibid.
15 'Lawrence Casey', NDBA.
16 'Eduardo Casey', NDBA.
17 'Patricio Lynch', NDBA.
18 'Estanislao José Antonio Lynch', NDBA.
19 'Benito Antonio Miguel Lynch', NDBA.

Notes to Chapter 17: Making History (pp. 216–23)

1   *Recollections of a Service of Three Years*, p. 37.
2   Ibid., p. 38.
3   'Desafío de caballos', Museo Bolivariano, Caracas; repr. in Brown and Roa, pp. 83–4.
4   Lambert, vol. 3, p. 452.
5   *Memorias del General O'Leary*, vol. 1 (Caracas: 1883), p. vi.
6   O'Connor, p. 59.
7   Vicuña Mackenna, *El ostracismo de jeneral D. Bernardo O'Higgins* (Valparaíso: Mercurio, 1860), p. 13.
8   Eyzaguirre, vol. 1, p. 18.
9   Orrego Vicuña, p. 29.
10 'The Ireland That We Dreamed Of', 17 March 1943, *Speeches and Statements of Éamon de Valera, 1917–1973*, ed. Maurice Moynihan (Dublin: Gill & Macmillan, 1980), p. 466.
11 'Biografía del Gral. Juan Thomond O'Brien, 1786–1861, guerrero de la independencia', p. 11.
12 O'Connor, p. 9.

13 'Roger O'Connor', ODNB.
14 Wright, p. 12.
15 Report of O'Leary's funeral in 1854 in *El Neo-Granadino*, reproduced on Dr Matthew Brown's blog *Bolivarian Times* (http://bolivariantimes.blogspot.ie/2012/02/funeral-of-daniel-oleary-bogotá-1854.html, accessed 27 January 2016).
16 Edmundo Murray, 'Juan Emiliano O'Leary (1879–1969): Poet and historian', in *Irish Migration Studies in Latin America*, vol. 4, no. 1 (2006), pp. 32–4.
17 Lillis and Fanning, p. 207.
18 Constanza Escobar Arellano, 'El Altar de la Patria: Una aproximación estética' (Santiago: Pontificia Universidad Católica de Chile, 2009), p. 24.
19 Ibid., p. 3.
20 'Encienden la llama de la libertad: Gigantesca concentración', *El Mercurio*, 12 September 1975, repr. in Escobar Arellano, p. 38.

Notes to Chapter 18: The 'Spiritual Empire' (pp. 224–9)

1 The following description is taken from *Repatriación de los restos del General Juan O'Brien, guerrero de la independencia Sud Americana* (Buenos Aires: Kraft, 1938).
2 Government decree, Buenos Aires, 23 August 1935, repr. in *Repatriación de los restos del General Juan O'Brien*, p. 93.
3 'Discurso del Doctor Huberto María Ennis, Presidente de la Comisión Irlandesa-Argentina', repr. in *Repatriación de los restos del General Juan O'Brien*, p. 139.
4 Ibid., p. 140.

INDEX

1st Division of Infantry (Venezuelan), 163
1st Lancers (Irish Legion), 153, 155
1st Rifles (Irish Legion), 150, 153
2nd Lancers (Irish Legion), 150
1st Venezuelan Hussars, 123, 129, 131
1st Venezuelan Lancers, 122, 123, 126
1st Venezuelan Rifles (Black Rifles), 123, 137
2nd Venezuelan Hussars (Red Hussars), 123, 125, 129
2nd Venezuelan Rifles, 139
3rd Division of Infantry (Venezuelan), 163
10th Lancers (Irish Legion), 148, 157–8
1798 Rising, 124, 142, 147, 148, 149, 217
1810 May Revolution, 80, 86–7, 91, 92, 97
1812 constitution, 59, 61, 67, 115, 163
1916 Rising, xxiii

Abascal, José Fernando de, 113
Acarí, 165
Achaguas, 129, 132, 200
Adam, William Jackson, 129, 135, 152
afrancesados, 55
Aix-la-Chapelle, Treaty of, 20
Alameda (Avenida Libertador General Bernardo O'Higgins), 223
Alcalde y Ribera, María, 43
alcohol, 124, 137, 146, 150–2, 153, 158, 201
Aldea, Antonio Rodríguez, 119
Alerta, 145
Algeria, 36–7, 106
Algorfa, 176
Allende, President Salvador, 222, 223
Alonso, Blas, 105
Altar de la Patria, Santiago de Chile, 222
Altar of the Kings, Mexico Cathedral, 177
Alto Magdalena Battalion, 166, 167
Alvear, Carlos María de, 115, 116
Amat, Manuel de, 47
Amelia, 145
Amelia Island, Florida, 142
American War of Independence, 106
Ampudia, General Pedro de, 181

Andes, 40–1, 46, 48, 116, 137, 138, 139, 162–73, 196–7, 207
Angostura (Ciudad Bolívar), 121, 123, 125, 126–8, 130, 131, 136, 154, 211
anti-Catholicism, 1, 10, 68, 70–1, 229
Antillón, Isidore de, 64
Antioquia, 200, 202
Anzoátegui, General José Antonio, 139
Apodaca, Juan Ruiz de, 176
Aranjuez, *motín* of, 55
Arcos, Duke of, 32, 33
Arenales, General Juan Antonio Álvarez de, 165
Argentina
  Argentine Republic, 96
  emigration to, 5
  independence, xxiii, 80
  Irish surnames, 213, 215
  Jockey Club, 213
  meat-exporting businesses, 213
  Upper Peru, 172
  War of the Triple Alliance, 189–91
  war with Uruguay, 103
Arica, 195, 197
Arismendi, General Juan Bautista, 152, 159, 216–17
Army of the Andes (Argentine), 164
Army of the East (Venezuelan), 152
Army of the North (Mexican), 181
Army of the Three Guarantees (Mexican), 175
Arriaga, Julián de, 45
Artigas, José Gervasio, 97–8, 99, 100, 101–2, 164
asiento, 18–19
Asunción, 39, 186, 189, 222, 223
Atacama Desert, 195, 196, 197
Atkinson, Major, 145–6
Auchmuty, Samuel, 80
audiencia, 46, 49, 110, 112, 166
Austrian army, 147, 149
Avenida Elisa A. Lynch, 223
Avenida Libertador General Bernardo O'Higgins (Alameda), 223

Ayacucho, 170, 171, 173, 196, 199, 202, 227
Aylmer, William, 147–8, 149, 150, 156, 157–8
Aylmer's Lancers, 150
Aymerich, General Melchor, 168
Aztecs, 29, 177

Baird, Lt-General David, 78
Balmaseda, Juan de, 45
Baltimore (U.S.), 217
Banda Oriental, 97, 101, 102, 103, 190
    see also Uruguay
Bandeirantes, 190
bandits, 99
    see also cattle-rustling
baptism, 105
Barbé-Marbois, François de, 35
Barcelona Regiment, 139
Barreiro, General José María, 139
Barreto, Colonel, 167
Batallón de San Patricio see San Patricios
Batavia Regiment (Spanish), 15
Battle of Boyacá, 140, 162
Battle of Cancha Rayada, 117, 165
Battle of Carabobo, 163, 200
Battle of Chacabuco, 165, 227
Battle of Churubusco, 182–3
Battle of El Santuario, 203
Battle of Juncal, 103
Battle of Junín, 205
Battle of Maipú, 116, 117, 165
Battle of Montenegro, 208
Battle of New Ross, 142
Battle of Rancagua, 95, 113–14, 117
Battle of San Jacinto, 178
Battle of Tacuarembó, 102
Battle of Tudela, 176
Battle of Yanacocha, 207
Bayonne, 55, 176
Beamish, Major, 133
Beauharnais, François de, 81, 82
Begg, John, 207
bejuco, 126
Belgrano, General Manuel, 91, 164
Belgrano, Mario, 219–20
Beresford, John, 78, 80, 98
Beresford, William Carr, 78
Berwick, 1st Duke of, 16, 17

Berwick, 2nd Duke of see Liria, Duke of
    (James FitzJames Stuart)
Berwick, 3rd Duke of, 18
Bioko (Fernando Pó), 164
Black Lion Club, 151–2
Black Rifles (1st Venezuelan Rifles), 123, 137
    see also rifles regiment
Blair, Hugo Brown, 170
Blake, John Ignatius, 106
Blanco White, José María
    death, 71
    early life, 62–4
    editor of *Semanario Patriótico*, 64–5
    in Ireland, 69–71
    inquisition, 64, 65–6, 67, 71
    priesthood, 63–4, 66
    propagandist in London, 66–8
    report on Cortes, 65–6
Blancos (Uruguay), 207
Blossett, Lt-General John, 134, 135
boca grande, 125
Bogotá, 5, 138, 140, 154, 162, 198, 202, 204
Bogotá Battalion (Gran Colombian), 167
Bogotá Cathedral, 5, 202, 204
Bolívar, Simón
    appearance, 130–1
    armistice with Morillo, 163
    assassination attempt, 5, 202
    audiencia of Quito, 166
    Battle of Boyacá, 140, 162
    battles fought by, 3
    Bolivian access to Pacific, 196
    conflict within Gran Colombia, 198–200
    Ecuador, 166, 167–8
    Irish volunteers, 2–4, 120–2, 123, 141, 142–4,
        147, 148, 149, 158, 206
    Liberator, 3
    meeting with John Devereux, 142
    National Pantheon, 221
    New Granadan campaign, 137–40
    Peru, 168–70
    pre-revolutionary life, 121
    propaganda, 154–5
    resignation and death, 202, 203, 204
    War to the Death, 121
Bolivia
    border dispute with Chile, 195, 197–8

Bolivia, *continued*
  Burdett O'Connor province, 223
  Charcas province, 195–7
  Francis Burdett O'Connor, 182, 195–8, 207–8, 209, 218
  Gran Colombian forces in, 202
  liberation of, 137, 171–2
  mines, 46, 72, 171, 196
  Peru-Bolivia Confederation, 205, 207
  Viceroyalty of the River Plate, 47, 73
  War of the Pacific, 195–6
  see also Upper Peru
Bolivian Legion of Honour, 207
Bomboná, 167–8, 202
Bonaparte, Joseph, 55, 56
Bonaparte, Napoleon *see* Napoleon Bonaparte
Bond, Henry, 164
Bookey, Patrick, 212
Bórú, Brian, 219, 221
Bouchard, Hippolyte, 95
Bourbon, Marie-Anne de (Duchess of Vendôme), 11
Bourbons, 9, 12, 13, 15, 23–4, 26, 91
Bourke, James Florence, 4, 77–8, 81–6, 214
Bourke, Jean-Raymond-Charles, 77
Bourke, Richard, 77
Bowles, William, 24–5
Boyacá, 140, 162
branding, 179
Brandsen, Federico Santa Coloma, 224, 226
Brazil
  audiencia of Quito, 166
  Banda Oriental, 102
  Brazilian Empire, 102
  economic blockade, 102–3
  Federal League, 101
  Paraguay, 185, 189–90, 222
  War of the Triple Alliance, 189–91
Bridgetown (Barbados), 96
Brión, Pedro Luis, 154, 155
Britannia, 123
British Legion, 3, 131–5, 138, 139, 153, 163, 216
Brown, Dr Matthew, 203, 230
Brown, Hugo Blair, 202
Brown, John, 213
Brown, Michael, 95, 96

Brown, Patrick, 213
Brown, William
  biography, 231
  Brazilian economic blockade, 102–3
  capture by British, 96
  capture of Montevideo, 94
  character, 92
  childhood, 92
  court martial, 97
  fame in Ireland, 1
  football teams named after, 4, 223
  illnesses and suicide attempt, 96–7
  merchant mariner, 87, 92–3
  physical demeanour, 93
  as privateer, 95–6
Browne, Father Thomas, 186
Buena Vista (Mexico), 181–2
Buenos Aires
  1810 May Revolution, 80, 86–7, 91, 92, 97
  Brazilian economic blockade, 102–3
  British invasions, 78–81
  Carlota Joaquina, 83
  Church of Our Lady of the Pillar, 228
  Church of the Holy Cross, 228
  commercial trade, 76
  criollos, 76, 81
  importance to Spanish monarchs, 72
  John Dillon, 86
  La Recoleta, 224, 228
  Ministry of External Relations, 226
  National Historical Museum, 224, 228
  Plaza de Mayo, 228
  Spanish blockade, 87, 93
  see also Viceroyalty of the River Plate
Bulfin, Éamon, xxiii
Burdett, Sir Francis, 148, 149
Burdett O'Connor province, 223
Burke, Honora, 16
Burke, James Florence *see* Bourke, James Florence
Burke, Luke, 153
Butler, Sir Edward, 80
Butler family, 15, 39
Byrne, James, 172
Byron, Lord, 14

cabildos, 60, 81

caciques, 42, 44, 52, 105, 118
Cádiz, 13–15, 19, 25, 29, 39, 51, 57, 67, 104, 106, 136, 163, 176
Cádiz Constitution (1812), 59, 61, 67, 115, 163
Cádiz Cortes, 2, 56–7, 59–62, 65, 67–8, 115
Cahill, Thomas, 63
Callao, 26, 46, 52, 95, 172, 205
Campbell, Peter
  appearance, 99
  British army, 98, 101
  character and reputation, 98, 99, 101
  employment by John Parish Robertson, 99–101
  exile, 102
  gaucho, 98–9
  guerilla fighter, 101–2
  Montevideo school, 223
  naval career, 101–2
Campbell, Peter, 123, 126
Campomanes, Pedro Rodríguez de, 28
Cancha Rayada, 117, 165
Canning, George, 4, 78
Canterac, José de, 170–1
Cape Horn, 95, 96
Carabobo, 163, 200
Caracas, 46, 60–1, 67, 106, 121, 163, 200, 204, 221, 223
Carmen, 94
Carrasco, Francisco Antonio García, 110
Carreño, José María, 166
Carrera, Don Pedro Pablo de la, 105
Carrera, José Miguel, 112–13, 114–15, 117, 164
Carrera, Juan José, 112, 115, 117, 164
Carrera, Luis, 112, 115, 117, 164
Cartagena (Colombia), 203, 204
Carvajal y Lancáster, José, 17, 18, 19, 20, 21
Casa Amarilla, 93
Casas, Bartolomé de las, 186
Casas, Luis de las, 33–4, 38
Casey, Eduardo, 213
Casey, Lawrence, 213
Cassidy, Butch, 208
Castellanos, Father, 215
Castle of San Carlos, 176
Castlereagh, Lord, 4, 78
Castro, Ramón de, 58
casuchos, 46

Catherine the Great, 107
Catholic Emancipation, 68, 148, 228
Catholicism
  anti-Catholicism, 1, 10, 68, 70–1, 229
  Catholic Emancipation, 68, 148, 228
  education in Ireland, 69–70
  nativist movement, 180, 181
  religious persecution, 15, 27, 71, 74, 220, 229
  role in Spanish colonialism, 9
  Spanish liberal criticism of, 71
  Treaty of Limerick, 10
cattle hides, 100, 101, 128
cattle-rustling, 99
Cavan, Viscount of (Alexander O'Reilly), 35
  see also O'Reilly, Alexander
Céfiro, 93
Cemitério dos Prazeres, 224–7
Cerro Corá, 185
Cerro de Pasco, 165, 169, 170
Cerro Gordo, 182
cerro rico, 72, 171
Cevallos, Pedro Antonio de, 74
Chacabuco, 116, 165, 227
Chaco War, 195–6
Chagres, 203
Chapultepec, 179
Charcas province, 195–7
Charles II, 12
Charles III, 16, 21–4, 26, 27, 31, 34, 37, 54–5
Charles IV, 26, 54–5, 81, 83
Charlotte Gambier, 150
chasquis, 30
Château de Saint-Germain-en-Laye, 11
Chávez, President Hugo, 221
chicha, 139
Chile
  Ambrose O'Higgins expeditions, 39–46
  Bernardo O'Higgins *see* O'Higgins, Bernardo
  Charcas province, 195
  Chilean National Congress, 112, 113
  Chilean-Argentine expedition, 164
  coastline, 163
  criollos, 112–13, 117
  Disaster of Rancagua, 113–14
  José Miguel Carrera, 112–13
  navy, 118

Chile, *continued*
  precious metals, 26, 44
  Santiago, 41, 43, 46, 48–50, 110, 112, 116, 117, 118, 213, 222–3
  silver mines, 26
  War of the Pacific, 195–6
  war with Confederation of Peru and Bolivia, 205
Chile (ship), 205
Chilean saltpetre, 195
Chilean-Argentine expedition, 164
Chillán, 105
Chiloé, 44, 51
Chimborazo, 196, 197
Chitty, William, 95
Chocó region, 203
cholera, 69
Church, Charles, 173
Church of Ireland, 70–1, 189
Church of Our Lady of the Pillar, 228
Church of the Corpo Santo, 227
Church of the Holy Cross, 228
Church of the Holy Trinity, 221
Churubusco, 182–3
Ciénaga de Santa Marta, 163
cimarrones, 100
Cisneros, Baltasar Hidalgo de, 86–7
Ciudad Bolívar (Angostura), 121, 123, 125, 126–8, 130, 131, 136, 154, 211
Clarkson, Father Dominic, 227
Cloney, Thomas, 142
Cobija, 196–7
Cochrane, Thomas, 118, 163–4
Colegio de Naturales, 105
Colombia
  audiencia of Quito, 166
  Colonel James Rooke, 223
  Daniel O'Leary, 221
  establishment of Republic, 203
  Foundation of Gran Colombia, 140
  John Devereux, 206
  see also Gran Colombia; New Granada; Viceroyalty of New Granada
colonialism, xxiii, 4
Colorados (Uruguay), 207
Columbus, 13, 186
Comisión Irlandesa-Argentina, 228

Concepción, 43, 48, 112, 113, 212
Confederation of Peru and Bolivia, 205, 207, 208
Confianza, 108
Congreso, 103
Congress of Angostura, 198
Congress of Tucumán, xxiii
Connelly, Thomas, 26
Conner family, 148
conquistadores, 41, 171
Consecuencia, 95
constitution (1812), 59, 61, 67, 115, 163
Contreras, 182
copper, 195, 197, 212
cordillera, 40, 41, 46
Córdoba, Treaty of, 176–7
Córdova, José María, 199–200, 203
Cornbury Park, 135
Corrales de Bonza, 140
Correa Luna, René, 224–7
Correo del Orinoco, 127, 130, 154–5, 158, 209–10
Corrientes (city), 102
Corrientes (province), 98, 99, 101, 214
Cortés, Hernán, 177
Costa, Joaquín Faria, 225
Costa, José da, 225
Costa Rica, 177
cotton, 50, 58, 75, 79, 132–3, 211
Counter-Reformation, 11, 15
Cowley, Captain, 133, 134
criollos
  Buenos Aires, 76, 81
  Chilean, 112–13, 117
  definition, 2
  Lima, 46, 47
  Mexican, 175
  New Granadan, 146–7
  political rights, 60, 79
  Puerto Rican, 58
  Quito, 166
  Venezuelan, 106, 121, 129, 158
Cruz, Nicolás de la, 104, 106, 108–9
Cuba, 34, 38
Cuenca (Ecuador), 202, 223
Cumaná, 134, 153
Cundinamarca Battalion (Gran Colombian), 153, 155

Curaçao, 155, 203
Cuzco, 169, 170, 171

Dalton, Patrick, 179
Dangan Castle, 148, 149
de Courcy, Michael, 84
de Courcy Ireland, John, 92, 230–1
de Valera, Éamon, 219
Declaration of Independence (Argentina), xxiii, 80
Delphin, Thomas, 51, 105
Derinzy, William Richard, 153, 155
Descripción del Reyno de Chile, 44
A Description of the Kingdom of New Spain, 25
desertion, 34, 77, 80, 120, 126, 129, 138, 141, 179, 180–1, 182, 183, 213
Devereux, John, 3, 120, 141, 142–4, 147, 149, 154, 155, 158–9, 160–1, 206, 210, 217
Diccionario nuevo y completo de las lenguas española é inglesa, 26
dictionaries, 26
Diderot, Denis, 65–6
Dillon, John, 86
Dillon's Regiment (French), 77
Disaster of Rancagua, 113–14, 115, 118
diseases, 120, 125, 127–8, 139, 145–6, 153
    see also cholera; smallpox; yellow fever
Dolores, 174
Dominican College, Lisbon, 225
Dominican College, Seville, 63
Dowson, 123
Doyle, Sir John, 212
Dragoons Regiment (Spanish), 24, 50–1
drinking, 124, 137, 146, 150–2, 153, 158, 201
Dublin Society, 28
duelling, 115, 124, 125, 143, 152, 153, 165, 200, 206
Duke of San Carlos, 160
Dunne, Robert, 80

earthquakes, 48
Easter Rising (1916), xxiii
Ecuador
    Arthur Sandes, 202, 223
    audiencia of Quito, 166
    establishment of Republic, 203
    Gran Colombia, 168, 202
    Guayaquil junta, 166
    naval school, 202
    Quito, 4, 138, 143, 166–8, 220
    Simón Bolívar, 166, 167–8
    Thomas Charles Wright, 220
    see also Viceroyalty of New Granada
Eels, Mr, 106
Egan, James, 74
El Álamo, 178
El Ausente, 221
El Español, 66, 67, 68
El Salvador, 177
El Santuario, 200, 203
Elío, Francisco Javier de, 97
Emerald, 123
emigration
    to Argentina, 5
    emigration council, 210
    Irish counties with high levels of, 212
    linkage to foreign service, 143, 209–10
    mid-nineteenth century, 209
    to Paraguay, 75
    post-independence, 5
    priests, 213–14
    San Patricios, 180
    schemes, 209, 210, 211–12
    to Spain, xxi, xxii–xxiii, 1, 9–11
    to Uruguay, 5, 215
    to Venezuela, 131–3, 142–7, 210–11
    Wild Geese, xxi, 10, 11, 22
    see also recruitment, Irish volunteers
Emperor Augustine I, 177
    see also Iturbide, Agustín de
encomienda, xxii, 49
England see Great Britain
English, James Towers, 131, 134–5, 153, 206, 211, 223
English, Mary, 206
English Protestantism, 64
Enlightenment, xxii, 9, 17, 24, 25, 28, 59, 112, 121, 148, 174, 188, 205
Ennis, Dr Huberto M., 228
Ensenada, Marquis of, 17, 21
Escorial, 12, 81
espionage, 4, 14, 19, 36, 76–8, 81–6, 116, 117, 130, 160
estancias, 73, 86, 97, 100, 109–10
Explicación de los metales de Huantajaya, 26

Exposición y Protesta (Declaration and Protest), 190–1
Eyre, Richard, 141
Eyre, Thomas, 141, 142–4, 145, 146–7
Eyzaguirre, Jaime, 219

Fahy, Father Anthony, 214, 215
Fallon, Captain, 172
Fanning, Ronan, 189
Farnese, Elisabeth, 17, 24, 26
Federal League, 101, 102
Federal Republic of Central America, 177–8
  see also Iturbide, Agustín de
Ferdinand VI, 17, 21, 83, 87
Ferdinand VII, 55, 56, 57, 82–3, 110, 115, 121, 163, 166, 168, 176, 177
Ferguson, William Owens, 5, 137, 170, 201–2, 217
Fernando Pó (Bioko), 164
Ferriar, Thomas, 163
Field, Father Thomas, 186
Fielding, Father, 187
Figueroa, Tomás de, 112
Fitzgeld, Carlos, 80
flecheras, 125
Fliess, Vice-Admiral Enrique G., 228
Foley, Thomas, 139
football teams, 4, 223
Foreign Enlistment Act (1819), 210
Foreign Legionaries in the Liberation of Spanish South America, 127, 230
Foreign Reminiscences, 36, 54
Fortuna, 94
foundation of Gran Colombia, 140
France
  French Revolution, 66, 74, 84, 107, 121, 135, 148
  invasion of Portugal, 83
  invasion of Spain, 81, 82, 176
  Terror, 107
  see also Napoleon Bonaparte
Francia, José Gaspar Rodríguez de, 91, 102, 188–9
Franciscans, 105
Franco, Francisco, 221
Frederick II, 33
Frederick William I, 16

freemasons, 175, 176, 177
Freire, Ramón, 119, 205
French, Domingo, 80
French Revolution, 66, 74, 84, 107, 121, 135, 148

gaditanos, 13, 14
Galeras volcano, 167
Gálvez, José de, 74
Gamarra, President Agustín, 207
gambling, 135–6, 137–8, 152
Gameza, 139
Gannon, Father Michael, 214, 215
García, Colonel Basilio, 167
Garland, John, 9, 40–1, 42–4
gauchos, 73, 97, 98–101
Gaviria, Eduvigis, 202
The General in his Labyrinth, 203
George Canning, 127
Geraldino, Tomás (Fitzgerald), 19
Gilbert, James, 132
Gillmore, Joseph Albert, 122, 123, 126
Glasnevin Cemetry, 221, 224
Godoy, Manuel, 52, 54, 55, 81–2
gold, 104, 124, 155, 171, 182, 187, 196, 207
Gómez, Bartola, 80
Gómez, Francisco, 159
Gonzalez, Salvador, 187
Gorman, Father Patrick, 213–14
Gorman, Michael, 74
governor of Osorno, 4, 52
Goya (painter), Francisco José de, 23, 55
Goya (town), 101, 214, 215
Graham, Maria, 118–19
Graham, Robert Bontine Cunninghame, 187–8
Gran Colombia, 140, 166, 168, 198–200, 201–4
  see also Colombia; Venezuela
Great Britain
  1797 invasion of Puerto Rico, 58
  1806 invasion of Buenos Aires, 79–80
  1807 invasion of Buenos Aires, 81
  1808 invasion of Portugal, 56
  alliance with Spain, 4
  blockade of French controlled ports in Spain, 57
  slave trade, 204
Great Famine, 103

Grito de Dolores, 174–5
Guadalupe Hidalgo, Treaty of, 183
Guajiro, 156, 162
Guaraní, 101, 186–8
Guayana province, 211
Guayaquil, 95, 166, 167, 168, 202
Guayaquileña, 202
Guerrero, Vicente, 175
Guill y Gonzaga, Antonio, 41, 42, 43
Gutiérrez, Father Uladislao, 214–15
Guzmán Blanco, Antonio, 221–2
Gwynn, Aubrey, 186

Habsburgs, 11–12, 23, 29
Haiti, 144–5
Hand, Rupert, 200, 203–4
Hannah, 150, 152
Harney, Colonel William, 179
Hasbrouck, Alfred, 124, 127, 202, 230
Henis, Father Tadeo, 187–8
Hércules, 93–6
Herring, Charles, 211
Hibernia Regiment (Spanish), 15, 32–3, 40, 50, 52, 74
Hibernian Regiment (Gran Colombian), 3, 142, 143–4, 145–7, 150, 156, 216
Hidalgo, Miguel de, 174–5
Higgins, Thomas, 128
Hildner Jr, Ernest G., 19
Hippisley, Gustavus, 123, 124, 126, 128, 129, 131, 141
Hogan, Michael, 181, 183, 231
Holland, Lord, 10, 36, 38, 54, 68
Honduras, 177
Hopkins, Martin, 132
Hore, Alexander, 144
horse-racing, 138, 213, 217
Huamachuco, 137, 168
Huara, 165
Huéscar, Duke of, 17–18, 19, 20, 21
Humboldt, Alexander von, 24, 210
hunting, 149
Hussars of Death, 117

Inca of New Granada, 146
Incas, 29, 30, 170
Indian, 123

índios, 47
ingleses, 3
Inquisition, 23, 51, 59, 65–6, 67, 71, 107, 175
intendencies, 23
Introducción a la historia natural y á la geografía física de España, 25
Ireland
  1798 Rising, 124, 142, 147, 148, 149, 217
  1916 Rising, xxiii
  Anglican hierarchy, 70
  anti-Catholicism, 1, 10, 68, 70–1, 229
  counties with high emigration, 212
  education, 69–70
  emigration *see* emigration
  Great Famine, 103
  recruitment for British army, 142
  recruitment for Latin America, 142–4, 153
    see also recruitment, Irish volunteers
  relationship with Britain (late 18th century), xxiii
  romanticised views of, 219
  Wild Geese, xxi–xxii, 10
Irish Colleges, 15
Irish Dominicans, 225–7
Irish Legion, 3, 120, 142–4, 147, 150–61, 162, 163, 206, 216, 217
The Irish Soldiers of Mexico, 182
Irlanda Regiment (Spanish), 15, 27, 50, 52
Isla de la Laja, 42, 109
Isla de León, 56, 57
Isla Margarita, 124–5, 134, 135, 137, 147, 152–3, 154–5, 158–9, 223
Island, Patrick, 80
Iturbide, Agustín de, 174, 175, 176, 177

Jacobites, 1, 10, 11, 16, 18, 19, 21, 44, 77
Jaffray, Richard, 211
Jamaica, 153, 157, 158, 204
James, John, 132
James II, 10, 11, 16, 32
jefe político superior, 174, 176
Jesuits, 44, 105, 186–8, 190
Joaquina, Carlota, 82, 83, 84–5, 86
Jockey Club (Argentina), 213
John VI, 82, 102
Johnston, John, 123, 139
Jornal do Comercio, 224

Jovellanos, Gaspar Melchor de, 65
Juan Griego, 135, 153, 223
Juliet, 94
Juncal, 103
Junín, 170, 202, 205
Junín Cavalry Regiment (Peruvian), 171
Justo, President Agustín Pedro, 227, 228

Kearney, James, 103
Keene, Benjamin, 20, 21
Keogh, Timothy, 173
Key Muñoz, Santiago, 59
King, John, 103
King's 1st Regiment (Spanish), 139

La Lava, 169
La Paz, 169, 171
La Perichona, 85
La Recoleta, 222, 224, 228
Laforey, 150–2
Lake Maracaibo, 166, 173
Lamas, Carlos Saavedra, 227
Lambert, Eric, 154, 210, 230
Lancers (Irish Legion), 163
Lara, General, 170
Lautaro Lodge, 114, 116
Lavalle, Juan, 165
Lee, Robert E., 182
Lenin, Vladimir, 221
Leny, Father William, 186
ley Power (Power's Law), 60
liberalism, 62, 64–5, 71
Liberating Army of Peru, 165
Libertad, 202
Lillis, Michael, 189
Lima, 41, 43, 46–7, 72–3, 92, 110, 114, 165–6, 170, 174, 205
limeños, 46, 47
Limerick, Treaty of, 10
limpieza de sangre, 12
Liniers, Santiago de, 79, 80, 81, 85, 86, 91
Liria, Duke of (James FitzJames Stuart), 16
Lisbon, 78, 84, 207, 224–7
The Lives of Eliza Lynch: Scandal and Courage, 189–90
llaneros, 120, 129
llanos, 135, 137

Lloyd, Jane Elizabeth, 189
looting, 144, 146, 156, 158, 160
López, Carlos Antonio, 189
López, Franscisco Solano, 185, 222
Lord Wellington (Arthur Wellesley), 56, 67, 83, 148, 176, 216, 217
Louis XIV, 11, 12, 13
Louis XV, 13
Louisiana, 34–5
Lovely Ann, 145
Low, Colonel, 159
Luna, Félix, 73
Lynch, Benito, 213
Lynch, Eliza, 185, 189–91, 222
Lynch, Estanislao José Antonio, 213
Lynch, Francisco, 103
Lynch, John, 189
Lynch, Justo Pastor, 213
Lynch, Patrick, 213
Lynch, William, 200

MacDonald, Donald, 122, 123, 124, 126
MacGregor, Gregor, 141–2, 144–7
Mackenna, John, 4, 9, 52–3, 110, 111–12, 113, 115, 218, 222
Macnamara, Matthew, 159–61
Madrid, Treaty of, 187
Maipú, 116, 117, 165
Maldonado, 196–7
Manby, Thomas, 217
Mapuche, 41–2, 43, 44, 45, 46, 47, 49, 51, 52, 109, 112
Marcano y Arismendi, Francisco Josef, 74
Marco, Miguel Ángel de, 94
María Luisa, 54, 55, 81–2
Márquez, Gabriel García, 203
Martín García, 93–4
Martínez, General Tomás, 228
martyrology, 221
Masones de Lima, Jaime, 19
matanzas, 128
Matará, 170
Maturín, 134, 153
Mauritius, 75
mausoleums, 220, 221, 223
May Revolution (1810), 80, 86–7, 91, 92, 97
McAnally, Ray, 187

McMahon, Benjamin, 152
Meade, Robert, 150
meat, 73, 75, 100, 138, 213
Memorias de General O'Leary, 218, 222
Méndez, Luis López, 121, 122, 142
Mendoza, 114, 165
Mercado Central de Frutos de Avellaneda, 213
Mérida, 200
mestizos, 44, 47, 128
Mexican-American War (1846–1848), 178–84
Mexico
    independence, 174, 177
    Mexican-American War (1846–1848), 178–84
    Mexico City, 174–5, 177, 178, 182–4
    precious metals, 12
    see also New Spain
Middleton, John, 132
Miller, William, 137–8, 169
mines, 12, 24–5, 26, 29, 44, 46, 72, 187, 196, 207
Ministry of External Relations, Buenos Aires, 226
Miranda, Franscisco de, 78, 106–8, 109, 121
The Mission, 187
missionaries, 30, 42, 74, 104, 162
Mixcoac, 179–80
monkeys, 126
Montalván *hacienda*, 204–5
Montenegro, 208
Monterrey, 181
Montesquieu, 121
Montevideo, 46, 80–1, 87, 91–4, 97–8, 101–2, 164, 207, 223
Montilla, Mariano, 155, 156, 157–8
Mooney, John, 212
Mooney, Mary, 212
Morales, Francisco Javier, 46, 47
Morales, President Evo, 196
Moran, Father Patrick, 213–14
Morelos, José María, 175
Moreno (town), 156
Moreno Alonso, Manuel, 62, 64
Morillo, General Pablo, 144, 163, 218
Morphy, Carlos, 188
motín of Aranjuez, 55
Mount Pichincha, 168
Murray, James, 132
Murray, Thomas, 200

mutiny, 133–4, 146, 150–1, 156–8, 163, 172, 206, 217

Nancy, 93
Nantes, 10
Naples, 24
Napoleon Bonaparte
    Battle of Tudela, 176
    British and Spanish alliance against, 4
    continental blockade, 54, 68, 78
    defeat, 121
    escape from Elba, 149
    invasion of Portugal, 54
    invasion of Spain, 2, 54–6, 65, 82
Napoleonic Wars, 120, 132, 137
Nariño, Antonio, 206
National Congress (Chile), 112, 113
National Historical Museum, Buenos Aires, 224, 228
National Pantheon, Asunción, 222
National Pantheon, Caracas, 221, 222
National Republican Guard (Portugal), 227
nativist movement, 180, 181
Navarre, 176
Nazca, 165
Neeson, Liam, 187
Neil, Edward, 80
New Dublin, 211
New Erin, 209, 211
New Granada, 34, 46, 138, 146–7, 203
    see also Colombia
New Orleans, 35
New Ross, 147
New Spain, 25, 174
    see also Mexico
Nicaragua, 177
Noble, John, 132
Norcott, Lieutenant-Colonel, 145–6
Novella, Pedro Francisco, 176, 177
Nowlan, Thomas, 211

O'Brien, Antonio, 25–6
O'Brien, John Thomond, 5, 164–5, 206–7, 208, 212, 219–20, 224–9
O'Brien, Martin, 219–20
Ocaña, 198
O'Connell, Daniel, 3, 14, 125, 143, 158, 159, 160

O'Connell, Maurice, 143, 159, 173
O'Connell, Morgan, 3, 143, 159
O'Connor, Anne, 148
O'Connor, Arthur, 148, 220
O'Connor, Feargus, 148
O'Connor, Francis, 179, 184
O'Connor, Francis Burdett
  1st Lancers, 153, 155
  Antonio José de Sucre, 170–2
  Aylmer's Lancers, 149–50
  Battle of Ayacucho, 170
  Bolivia, 209, 218, 298
  drinking, 137, 153
  encounters with Simón Bolívar, 168–70
  family, 148, 208
  later life, 207–8
  liberation fighter, 2
  memoirs, 3, 120, 217–18, 220
  Panama, 166
  recruitment of Irish farmers, 5, 209
  San Juan, 156–7
  survey of Pacific coast, 196
O'Connor, Hercilia, 208
O'Connor, Honora, 219–20
O'Connor, Roger, 148, 149, 220
O'Connor d'Arlach, Eduardo Trigo, 208
O'Connor d'Arlach, Tomás, 150, 218, 220
O'Crouley, Pedro Alonso, 25
O'Daly, Thomas, 58
O'Donoghue, Richard Dunphy, 175
O'Donojú, Juan, 174, 175–7
O'Donovan Rossa, Jeremiah, 221
O'Farrell family, 38
O'Gavan, Juan Bernardo, 59
O'Gorman, Ana (Marie-Anne Périchon de Vandeuil), 75, 76–7, 79, 85, 214
O'Gorman, Thomas, 4, 74–7, 79, 214
O'Gorman, Adolfo, 214–15
O'Gorman, Camila, 214–15
O'Gorman, Joaquina, 214
o'higginistas, 205
O'Higgins, Ambrose
  appearance, 48
  Chilean expeditions, 39–46
  early life, 39
  as father, 104–5, 106, 109
  first expedition to Chile, 39–40
  governor of Chile, 48
  Isabel Riquelme, 48
  military career, 45
  return to Europe, 44–5
  valediction by John MacKenna, 53
  viceregal palace, 174
  viceroy of Peru, xxii, 1–2, 51, 109
O'Higgins, Bernardo (Bernardo Riquelme)
  adopted children, 118
  appearance, 110, 118
  Battle of Rancagua, 113–14
  as Bernardo Riquelme, 104–5, 107–9
  biographies, 219
  cavalry officer, 110–11
  campaign in Peru, 163–4
  Carrera junta, 112–13
  childhood and youth, 104–6
  Chilean National Congress, 112, 113
  domestic life, 118–19
  encouragement of Irish settlers, 5
  exile, 115–16, 119, 204–5, 212
  fame in Ireland, 1
  independence fighter, xxii, 2, 4
  inheritance, 109
  move to Europe, 51
  reinterral of remains, 222–3
  relations with José Miguel Carrera, 114–15
  Supreme Director of Chile, 116–18, 205
O'Higgins, Charles, 50
O'Higgins, Demetrio, 118, 119, 219
O'Higgins, Peter, 50
O'Higgins, Thomas, 50, 51–2, 108
O'Higgins, William, 39
Olañeta, Casimiro, 172
Olañeta, General Pedro Antonio de, 168, 169, 171–2
O'Lawlor, John, 153, 155
O'Leary, Bolivia, 204
O'Leary, Daniel Florence
  Alto Magdalena Battalion, 166–7
  anti-Bolivarian purge, 211–12
  Colombia, 221
  diplomat, 204
  funeral, 221
  glory, 120
  Gran Colombia, 198, 201
  James Rooke, 136–7

meeting with Simón Bolívar, 129–31
memoirs, 3, 217–18, 222
murder of Córdova, 199–200
New Granada, 140
Red Hussars, 125
relationship with wife, 199
O'Leary, Jeremiah, 125
O'Leary, Juan, 222
O'Leary, Mimi, 199, 204
O'Leary, Simón Bolívar, 204, 218
O'Leary, Soledad, 198, 199, 200, 204, 211–12
O'More, Maria, 26
O'Neill, James, 132
Order of Alcántara, 34
Order of Santiago, 16–17
O'Reilly, Alexander
  Algerian expedition, 36–7, 106
  character, 35–6, 37, 38
  death, 37
  governor of Cádiz, 37
  Hibernia Regiment, 32–3
  military adviser, 33–4
  re-establishing control of Lousiana, 34–5
  Viscount of Cavan, 35
O'Reilly, Diego, 4, 165
O'Reilly, John, 32
O'Reilly, Manuel, 38
O'Reilly, Pedro, 38
O'Reilly, Thomas, 32
Oribe, Manuel, 207
Orrego Vicuña, Eugenio, 110, 219, 230
O'Ryan, Edmundo, 26–7
O'Shea, Patrick, 27
Osorio, Mariano, 113
Osorno, 51, 52
O'Sullivan, Father Paul, 225–6
Oughan, John, 164
Ourense, Bishop of (Pedro de Quevedo y Quintano), 56

Pack, Denis, 79
Páez, José Antonio, 129, 130, 131, 135, 198, 217
paisanos, 2
Palafox, Juan de, 187
Palmerston, Lord, 207
Pampatar, 153
Pamplona (Colombia), 162

Panama
  Alexander O'Reilly, 34
  Alto Magdalena Battalion, 166
  Gran Colombia, 166
  Panama City, 72, 166
  Portobello, 44, 72, 144, 145
  see also Viceroyalty of New Granada
Pantano de Vargas (Vargas Swamp), 139, 140
pantheons, 220, 221, 222, 223
Paposo, 197
Paraguay
  Brazil, 185, 189–90, 222
  Chaco War, 196
  demise of Francisco Solano López, 185
  dictators, 188–90
  Eliza Lynch, 222
  independence, 91, 188
  José Gaspar Rodríguez de Francia, 102
  National Pantheon, Asunción, 222
  River Paraguay, 102
  Thomas Gorman, 75
  War of the Triple Alliance, 185
Páramo de Pisba, 138, 139
Paraná, 228
Parish, Woodbine, 164
parlamentos, 42, 44
Parsons, Robert, 155
Pasto, 168
Patiño, José, 13, 15
Peacock, William, 163, 173
Pearse, Patrick, 221
Pedro Campbell, 4
Pedro I, 102
Pelham, Henry, 20
Peninsular War, 114, 115, 121, 141
peninsulares, 47
Père Lachaise cemetery, 222, 224
Pereira, Juan Albano, 105
Périchon de Vandeuil, Marie-Anne (Ana O'Gorman), 75, 76–7, 79, 85, 214
Perkins, John, 106
Pernambuco, 96
persecution, religious, 15, 27, 71, 74, 220, 229
Peru
  Ambrose O'Higgins, 1, 46
  Antonio O'Brien, 25–6
  Bolívar campaign, 120, 168–70

Peru, *continued*
  border dispute with Bolivia, 197–8
  Diego O'Reilly, 4
  Lima, 41, 43, 46–7, 72–3, 92, 110, 114, 165–6, 170, 174, 205
  precious metals, 12
  proclamation of independence, 165–6
  viceroy, xxii, 1–2, 26, 41, 46, 47, 48, 51, 53, 104, 109, 113, 114, 165
  Viceroyalty of Peru, 72, 73, 165, 172, 195
  War of the Pacific, 195–6
  war with Gran Colombia, 198
  see also Upper Peru
Peru Division, 171
Peru-Bolivia Confederation, 205, 207
Pezuela, Joaquín de la, 165
Phelan, James, 163, 173
Philip II, 12, 81, 111
Philip V, 12–13, 15, 17
Pichincha, Mount, 168
Piggott, Richard, 126, 128
Pinochet, General Augusto, 222, 223
piracy, 36, 38, 96
Pisco, 165
Plan of Iguala (Plan of the Three Guarantees), 175, 176
Plate, River *see* River Plate
Plaza de Armas, 112, 118
Plaza de Mayo, 228
Plaza del Jacinto, Mexico City, 184
Plaza O'Leary, 223
Plunkett, Michael, 128
Poole, Edward, 172
Popham, Rear Admiral Home Riggs, 78
Portales, Diego, 205
porteños, 73, 75, 76, 79, 80, 99, 101, 164
Portobello, Panama, 44, 72, 144, 145
Portugal
  annexation of Banda Oriental, 102
  capture of Montevideo, 101
  Cemitério dos Prazeres, 224
  colonial ambitions in South America, 84
  Guaraní War, 188
  invasion by France, 83
  invasion by Great Britain, 56
  invasion by Napoleon Bonaparte, 54
  National Republican Guard, 227

War of the Triple Alliance, 189–91
Potosí, 72, 168, 169, 171, 172, 196–7
Power, Joaquín Ramón, 58
Power, William Middleton, 217
Power y Giralt, Ramón, 2, 57–9, 60–1
Power's Law (*ley Power*), 60
Poyais, 147
precious metals, 11, 12, 26, 29, 44, 91, 104
Presidente Sarmiento, 227
priests, 213–14
Prieto, General José Joaquín, 205
Primo de Rivera, José Antonio, 221
Prince, 123, 125
Prince of Orange, 136
próceres, 223
propaganda, 68, 130, 154, 180, 181, 210
Proyecto económico, 27–31
Prussian army, 33
Puerta, María Francisca Calvo de la, 38
Puerto Cabello, 204
Puerto Rico
  criollos, 58
  governor Alexander O'Reilly, 34
  invasion by Great Britain, 58
  Irish planter community, 58, 60
  ley Power, 60
Pueyrredón, Juan Martín de, 81, 116
pulperias, 101
Puno, 171, 207

Quatrefages, Xavier, 189
Quevedo y Quintano, Pedro de (Bishop of Ourense), 56
Quillagua, 197
Quinn, Aidan, 187
Quintana, Manuel José, 64, 65
Quito, 4, 138, 143, 166–8, 220

Rafter, Michael, 143–4, 145, 147
Ramírez, Captain, 167
Ramírez, Francisco Javier, 105
Rancagua, 95, 113–14, 115, 117, 118
Real, José María del, 142
Recollections of a Service of Three Years during the War-of-Extermination in the Republics of Venezuela and Colombia, 133, 216–17

recruitment, Irish volunteers
  for Bolívar's armies, 3, 121, 122, 123, 141,
    142–4, 147, 148, 149, 158, 206
  Cundinamarca, 153
  James Towers English, 131
  John Devereux, 141, 142, 143, 148, 210
  John Thomond O'Brien, 206–7
  linkage to emigration, 209–10
  Thomas Eyre, 141, 142, 143
  see also emigration
Recuerdos de Francisco Burdett O'Connor, 218, 220
Red Hussars (2nd Venezuelan Hussars), 123, 125, 129
Redesdale House, 69
reductions (Jesuit), 187–8
Regiment of Mounted Grenadiers (Argentine), 227
Región Libertador General Bernardo O'Higgins, 223
religious persecution, 1, 15, 27, 71, 74, 220, 229
Rhodes, James, 132
Riego, Rafael de, 163, 175
Rieu-Millan, Marie-Laure, 60
rifles regiment, 123, 126, 162–3, 167, 170, 172–3, 196, 200, 202, 216, 220
Rigge, Mary, 135
Riley, John, 180, 182, 183–4
Río, Pedro Nolasco del, 109
Rio Grande do Sul, 188
Riohacha, 145–7, 156–8, 163, 206, 216
Riquelme, Bernardo (Bernardo O'Higgins) see O'Higgins, Bernardo
Riquelme, Isabel, 48, 51, 104, 110, 114, 118–19, 205
Riquelme, Simón, 48
Rising (1916), xxiii
River Apurimac, 170
River Biobío, 42
River Guáitara, 167
River Loa, 197
River Magdalena, 162
River Orinoco, 121, 123, 125, 137, 211, 217
River Paraguay, 102
River Paraná, 101, 102, 214
River Plate, 73, 77, 78–9, 80–1, 83, 84, 85, 102–3, 186, 189, 190

Robertson, John Parish, 98, 99–101
Rocafuerte, Vicente, 202
Rodríguez, Manuel, 117
Rodríguez, Manuel A., 227, 228
Rodríguez y Riquelme, Rosa, 110, 114, 118, 119
Romerate, Jacinto de, 93, 94
Rooke, Anna, 136
Rooke, James, 135–7, 138, 139–40, 223
Rosario, 227–8
Rosas, President Juan Manuel d, 207, 215
Rousseau, Jean-Jacques, 121, 189
Royal College of Surgeons in Ireland, 210
Rozas, Juan Martínez de, 51, 110, 111–12, 113
Rudd, Charles, 173
Russell, Father Patrick Bernard, 225, 226
Ruyloba, Francisca, 208
Ryan, Alice, 176
Ryan, John, 132
Ryan, Thomas, 132
Ryswick, Treaty of, 11, 12

Sagrario, 175
Saint Christopher Island (Saint Kitts), 136
Saint Thomas, 123
salmagundi (Solomongrundy), 151
Salom, General Bartolomé, 167
saltpetre, Chilean, 195
Sámano, Juan José de, 140
San Ambrosio de Ballenary (Vallenar), 39
San Ángel, 178–9, 184, 188
San Bartolomé de Chillán, 48, 104–5
San Carlos, Duke of, 160
San Fernando, 129
San Jacinto, 178
San Juan, 156–7, 188
San Juan de las Siete Corrientes, 102
San Lorenzo, 188
San Luis, 188, 208
San Luis (ship), 94
San Martín, General José de, 114–15, 116, 117, 118, 163, 164, 165–6, 168, 206–7
San Miguel, 188
San Nicolás, 188
San Patricios, xxiii, 178–84
Sánchez, María Josefa, 177
Sandes, Arthur, 137, 138, 139–40, 163, 167, 170, 173, 202, 217, 223

Sands, Bobby, 221
Sanlúcar de Barrameda, 104
San Jose de las Canteras, 42, 109–10
Santa Ana de Trujillo, 163
Santa Anna, General Antonio López de, 178, 181–2
Santa Cruz, 171, 207
Santa Marta, 202, 203
Santa Rosa, 196
Santander, Francisco Paula de, 138, 139
Santiago, Chile, 16, 41, 43, 46, 48–50, 110, 112, 116, 117, 118, 213, 222–3
Santiago, Cuba, 159
Santos Jones, José Enrique dos, 225
Santos Lugares, 215
Sarsfield, Patrick, 16
Scott, General Winfield, 182
Semanario Patriótico (Patriotic Weekly), 63
Senlis, 25
Serna, José de la, 168
Serpa, Antonio Ferreira de, 224
Seven Years' War, 21, 32, 34, 38, 41
Seville, xi, 11, 12, 13, 63, 64, 65, 104
Seymour, John, 172
Sicily, 24
Siege of Derry, 32
Sierra, Miguel de la, 94
Sierra, Nicolás María de, 56–7
siglo de oro, 12
silver, 12, 26, 29, 46, 72, 104, 165, 171, 196, 207
Skeen, Robert, 123
slaves, 10, 18, 72, 75, 187, 204
smallpox, 196–7
Smith, Rear-Admiral Sidney, 84, 85
smuggling, 14, 18–19, 73, 75, 97, 213
Smythe, Percy Clinton Sydney (Lord Strangford), 4, 83–4, 85
Sobremonte, Rafael de, 76–7, 79, 80
Socha, 139
sociedades económicas de amigos del país, 28
Society for Irish Latin American Studies, 231
sodium nitrate, 195
Solano López, Francisco, 189–90, 191
Soler, General Miguel Estanislao, 164
Solomongrundy (salmagundi), 151
Soublette, Carlos, 204, 218

Spain
  acquisition of Louisiana, 34–5
  alliance with Great Britain, 4
  criollos, 175
  economic development, 27–8
  Guaraní War, 188
  Habsburgs, 11–12
  immigration from Ireland, 9–11
  Inquisition, 23, 51, 59, 65, 66, 67, 71, 107, 175
  invasion by France, 2, 54–6, 65, 81, 82, 176
  liberal criticism of Catholicism, 71
  modernisation of armed forces, 32–8
  refuge for Catholics, 15
  War of the Triple Alliance, 189–91
Spencer, Emanuel, 106
spies *see* espionage
St Patrick's Battalion (Batallón de San Patricio) *see* San Patricios
Stalin, Joseph, 221
Stopford, Edward, 155
Strangford, Lord (Smythe, Percy Clinton Sydney), 4, 83–4, 85
Street, John, 84
Stroessner, Alfredo, 222
Stuart, James FitzJames (Duke of Liria), 16
sub conditione (baptism), 105
Sucre, Antonio José de, 138, 167, 168, 170–2, 197, 202
Sundance Kid, 208
Supreme Central Junta, 56, 64, 65, 67, 176
Swinburne, Henry, 18, 37
syphilis, 18

Tabuérniga, Marquis of, 19, 20
Tacuarembó, 102
Tagle, Francisco Ruiz, 116
Talca, 105
Tarija, 196, 208, 209
Taylor, General Zachary, 181–2
Teatro Cómico, 57
Tenerife, 59
Tercio de Andaluces, 80
Terror (French Revolution), 107
Texas, 178
Thomas, John, 219
Three Guarantees, Plan of (Plan of Iguala), 175, 176

Tierra del Fuego, 95
tin, 212
Torre, General Miguel de la, 163
Torres, General Pedro, 167
Townshend, George, 135
Travessa do Corpo Santo, 225
Treaty of Aix-la-Chapelle, 20
Treaty of Córdoba, 176–7
Treaty of Guadalupe Hidalgo, 183
Treaty of Limerick, 10
Treaty of Madrid, 187
Treaty of Ryswick, 11, 12
Treaty of Tucumán, xxiii
Treaty of Utrecht, 18
Trinidad, 95
Tropic of Cancer, 122
Tucumán, xxiii, 164, 214
Tudela, 176
Tumusla, 172
Tupiza, 196
Two Friends, 122–5, 128
Two Spains, 60
typhus, 44
Tyrry, Pedro (Terry), 19

Ultonia Regiment (Spanish), 15, 25, 52, 58, 176
uniforms, 123–4, 129, 141, 143–4, 155
United Irishmen, 148, 217, 220
United Provinces of the River Plate, 96, 103, 172
  see also Argentina
United States, xi–xii, 72, 91, 106, 142, 174, 178–83, 211
Upper Peru, 77, 91–2, 164, 166, 168, 171, 172, 195, 197, 207
  see also Bolivia
Urdaneta, Rafael, 134, 156
Uruguay
  Banda Oriental, 97
  civil war, 207
  emigration to, 5, 215
  independence, 103, 190
  meat-exporting businesses, 213
  Montevideo *see* Montevideo
  navy, 4, 98, 102
  Peter Campbell, 98
  River Uruguay, 94, 97, 99, 102, 187, 188

Viceroyalty of the River Plate, 47, 73
War of the Triple Alliance, 189–91
war with Argentina, 103
Uspallata, 114
Utrecht, Treaty of, 18

Valdeparaíso, Count of, 21
Valdés, General Jerónimo, 167, 168, 169, 170
Valdivia, 42–4, 51, 52
Valencia, General Gabriel, 182
Valledupar, 156, 157
Vallenar (San Ambrosio de Ballenary), 39
Valparaíso, 52, 53, 105, 109, 164, 205, 213
van Loo, Louis Michel, 20
Vargas Battalion (Gran Colombian), 167
Vargas Swamp (Pantano de Vargas), 139, 140
Velasco, Bernardo de, 91
Velázquez, Diego, 16–17
Vendôme, Duchess of (Marie-Anne de Bourbon), 11
Venezuela
  criollos, 106, 121, 129, 158
  establishment of Republic, 203
  foundation of Gran Colombia, 140
  Francisco de Miranda, 78, 106–8, 121
  immigration from Ireland, 210–11
  National Pantheon, Caracas, 221, 222
  see also Bolívar, Simón; Gran Colombia; Viceroyalty of New Granada
Veracruz, 174, 176, 177, 182, 184
Vértiz, Juan José de, 74
viceroy of Peru, xxii, 1–2, 26, 41, 46, 47, 48, 51, 53, 104, 109, 113, 114, 165
Viceroyalty of New Granada, 34, 46, 138, 140, 203
  see also Colombia; Ecuador; Panama; Venezuela
Viceroyalty of New Spain, 72, 174, 176
Viceroyalty of Peru, 72, 73, 165, 172, 195
Viceroyalty of the River Plate, 46–7, 73–4, 87, 91, 114, 172, 195
  see also Argentina; Buenos Aires
Victoria, Guadalupe, 175
Vicuña Mackenna, Benjamín, 206, 219, 222, 230
Videla, Eleazar, 227, 228
Villegas, Micaela, 47

Virgin of Guadalupe, 175
Voltaire, 121
von Humboldt, Alexander, 24
Vowell, Richard Longville, 126, 128

Wall, Matthew, 11, 16
Wall, Ricardo *see* Wall, Richard
Wall, Richard
   childhood, 10, 11
   diplomat, 18–21, 32
   military career, 13, 15–16, 17
   prime minister of Spain, xxii–xxiii, 1, 2, 9
   relationship with Ambrose O'Higgins, 44–5
   relationship with Charles III, 24, 31
Walsh's Regiment (French), 74, 77
Walton, William, 122, 211
War of the Austrian Succession, 32
War of Jenkins' Ear, 19
War of the Pacific, 195–6
War of the Spanish Succession, 13, 17, 18
War of the Triple Alliance, 185, 189–91, 222
War to the Death, 121
Ward, Bernard, 9, 26, 27–31
Ward, Felipe, 26, 27
Waterloo, Battle of, 136, 142, 148, 153

welfare systems, 27
Wellesley, Arthur (Lord Wellington), 56, 67, 83, 148, 176, 216, 217
Wellesley, Henry, 67
Whately, Richard, 69–70
Whiteboys, 148
Whitelocke, John, 77, 81, 98
Wild Geese, xxi, 10, 11, 22
Wilson, Henry Croasdaile, 122, 123, 125, 126, 129–30, 141
Wright, Alberto Eduardo, 220
Wright, Guillermo Hugo, 220
Wright, Thomas Charles, 162, 167, 170, 172, 196, 197, 198, 202, 220

Xalapa, 182

Yanacocha, 207
yellow fever, 14, 104, 108, 120, 127–8, 152, 172, 173, 183
yerba mate, 187
Young, Robert James, 150–2, 153

Zambrano, Mateo de Toro, 110
Zea, Francisco Antonio, 131, 202